ELECTRIFYING EDEN

PLEDGE

ELECTRIFYING EDEN

Portland General Electric 1889-1965

CRAIG WOLLNER

Oregon Historical Society Press

To My Teachers

MICHAEL F. REARDON

W. WARREN WAGAR

GORDON B. DODDS

CONTENTS

ACKNOWLEDGMENTS

I AM DEEPLY OBLIGED to all those who have helped in the preparation of what will be a two-volume work. Here, I would like to thank specifically those who have contributed directly to the preparation of Volume 1.

Robert Short, retired chairman and CEO of Portland General Corporation, was the originator of the entire project. His belief in, and insistence on, an objective, scholarly history of the company's development was crucial to this work. His willingness to share his time and his recollections, to advise and encourage was a great gift to the sometimes weary historian. His administrative assistant, Margaret Smith, unfailingly aided me whenever circumstances dictated. I owe a large debt to Dick Reiten, a successor to Bob Short as president, for his readiness in seeing the project through to its conclusion.

Thomas Vaughan and Elizabeth Crownhart-Vaughan of the Oregon Historical Society must be recognized for supporting the book from concept to creation. Their commitment to the uncovering and preservation of the state's history was the driving force behind the publication of this work.

At PGE many other people gave me a wealth of invaluable aid. In particular, Janet Holtzman's assistance, her knowledge of the company and its employees, and her optimistic attitude were indispensable assets. The staff in library services and in records management gave extraordinary amounts of time and energy in response to my many and frequent requests for help. I would also like to recognize the yeoman's service performed by members of the typing pool. Jack Phillips, Bob Lee, and all the other PGE employees both past and present who shared their memories and photographs with me endowed the sometimes sterile facts with a touch of humanity. Don Kielblock, Sam Christensen, and my friend Bob James checked the manuscript for technical and factual accuracy. A less apt student of electrical engineering than the author could not be found, but Bob James undertook my education in its rudiments with patience and humor. Others too numerous to name were helpful in a thousand ways. I am humbled by the knowledge that this book would be far poorer had they not been so forthcoming.

Susan Jackson, PacifiCorp librarian, put the extensive resources of that utility at my disposal, as did the staff of the Bonneville Power Administration library. Irma Lady, now retired from the Oregon State Library, was similarly gracious with the materials in her care. I am also indebted to the staff of the Edison Electrical Institute at Palo Alto for the use of its holdings. Mrs. Clarence Phillips, widow of PGE employee Clarence Phillips, was extremely generous with her time and her husband's scrapbooks.

At Portland State University, I was aided, as usual, by the library staff with efficiency and willingness. Students who added their skills and energy to the cause, greatly to its enhancement included Ruth Dodds, Michelle MacArthur, Scott Satterlee, and Catherine Carter. Among my colleagues, advice, expertise, and commiseration were offered by Bernard Burke and Frederick Nunn. Lew Goslin and Janet Hamilton, of the business school and Giles Burgess, of the economics department, provided skilled knowledge of management, utility finance, and economics. I was also fortunate in having three historians of the highest professional standing to criticize the manuscript at every turn. Gordon Dodds and Jim Heath of the history department are both friends and mentors, so that my many impositions on their goodwill were met with stoicism if not pleasure. Similarly, Harold Vatter, professor emeritus in economics, offered me his knowledge of economic history and the wisdom of his experience. Thanks are poor payment for the care taken in making this book as strong as I wished it to be, but I give them with utter sincerity nevertheless. In this connection, too, I wish to acknowledge my friend Ralph Wiser, who offered insight into the various legal issues that from time to time cropped up in the work.

I would be remiss if I did not thank the director of publications at the Oregon Historical Society Press, Bruce Taylor Hamilton, for his advice and support throughout what became a protracted struggle against time and circumstance. Adair Law, my editor, was also critical to making this a presentable work of scholarship. Her tireless work and patience are deeply appreciated, as are those of the book's designer, George Resch. Sandy Meadows, an intern with the Press, gathered and researched the materials for the sidebars throughout the book, while Tessa Hinrichs logged many hours in checking facts. Philippa Brunsman did her usual careful copy-editing. I thank them all for their fine work.

The person to whom this publication owes its existence is Judy Hartman, without whose dedicated, selfless, intelligent, and good-humored research this book would never have reached completion. Whenever I felt tired or defeated by the material, I had only to think of her unflagging commitment, her iron will, and her curiosity to recoup my energy. In that sense, *Electrifying Eden* is Judy's book as much as mine.

Finally, let it be said that errors of fact and interpretation are ultimately and only my responsibility. Those named herein offered their knowledge and insights, but I as the author shaped them, and the documents that constituted the raw history of PGE, to my own ends. I hope that readers will not think their magnanimity has been in vain.

ELECTRIFYING EDEN

INTRODUCTION

F EW STORIES IN THE HISTORY of American business are as obscure and yet as quintessential- ly American as that of the private electrical utility industry. It is a story driven by funda- mental American urges, values, ideals, and imperatives. It is a story about commercial enterprise—the animating principle of the initial settlements along the James River in Virginia and Massachusetts Bay—and about a continuing struggle with nature to wrest from it the materi- als of the good life. In his second *Treatise on Government*, the Puritan apologist John Locke wrote, "God commanded man to subdue the earth," and accordingly, like-minded New Eng- landers and their descendants sought to force the environment to yield its bounty as by divine right.

The history of electrical utilities flows from yet another American preoccupation—that of technology. The romance of technological advancement has always exerted a powerful fascina- tion over the American mind, to such an extent that men like Thomas Edison and Henry Ford are among our greatest heroes because of their inventions, despite having had quite unattractive personalities.

The production and marketing of electrical current sprang from the increasing American interest in commercial enterprise and technology. Edison, the father of the American utility industry, understood and exemplified this preoccupation. He wanted to unlock the secrets of nature, harness them through technological innovation, and enrich himself. He saw nature as a realm to be bent to his will. The industry he sired never flagged in pursuing his initial aims.

No less than Edison, the men who in 1889 founded Willamette Falls Electric Company in Oregon City, the company that eventually became Portland General Electric, saw in the falls a source of easeful living for the masses while they themselves would be enriched. They would exploit this aspect of nature, build the local economy, and profit from it.

The founders of Willamette Falls Electric, Parker F. Morey and Edward Eastham, built a company that was taken over by eastern capital until, through the inexorable expansion of the late nineteenth and early twentieth centuries, it turned into Portland's first bona fide monopoly in 1906. As Portland Railway Light and Power Company, it provided power and transport. But the American people, since the earliest days of the republic, had always despised monopolies and the company was not well loved. Gradually, with the appearance of regulation and Progressivism, and because of competition in both transit and electricity, Portland Railway Light and Power lost its stranglehold on the generation of the city's electrical current. The first phase of the company's history was over by 1913.

Its real significance in the local and regional economy and culture began to emerge in its next phase, partly because of the vision and foresight of Franklin T. Griffith, the company president. A lawyer and a self-made man, Griffith recognized that Portland Railway Light and Power's best bet was to emerge as a public-service company to boost Portland, because he saw the company's fate as being intimately linked with the economy of the region. Oregon had traditionally been seen by its boosters as a new Eden—a garden, as Hall J. Kelley, an early promoter, had called it. The company merely echoed this rhetoric and embraced city, state, and regional goals for economic development as its own. This is most clearly seen much later, in the company's relationship with the Bonneville Power Administration (BPA). Griffith was one of the few Northwest utility executives who recognized from the first the meaning and importance of the New Deal's hydro-development policy, as embodied in the creation of the federal BPA, to the private utilities. He embraced the concept entirely, seeing in the government agency the key to low rates for his customers and thus a competitive advantage in the struggle for survival against takeover by public bodies. For years, Portland General Electric prided itself on being the region's biggest distributor of BPA energy.

As the postwar era progressed, the company was involved in critical issues of regional development, the most significant of which was that of hydroelectric development on the Columbia River. The debate in the fifties was over whether this should be a wholly public or partially private responsibility. Besides building its own dams on secondary streams, Portland General Electric attempted to lead the private development on the Columbia. Although this policy was ultimately unsuccessful, it was a measure of the company's commitment that it persisted until the final death knell of the so-called "partnership" policy.

By the time the third phase of the company's life drew to a close, with the retirement of Thomas Delzell from the chairmanship in 1964, Portland General Electric had lived out the first seventy-five years of a history that was marked in 1989 with a centennial observance. This book, which marks that occasion, encompasses that period—from 1889 to 1965. A second volume,

Power and Responsibility, will deal with the years from 1965 to 1989 and look beyond into the nineties. It will consider how the utility has wrestled with the unforeseen consequences of its own growth, has handled the startling new imperatives of technology, and has dealt with the demands of an increasingly fragile environment. It will look at the strains put on local and national economies confronted with the problems brought on by scarcity rather than abundance.

This, then, is the first installment of the history of a company that was originally the product of Gilded Age business practice and values. The utility's survival and growth eventually came to hinge on its management's perception that Portland was a garden, an Eden, and that the company's fate was intimately entwined with that Eden. It came to see that the prosperity of the Pacific Northwest and of Portland in particular was the basis of Portland General Electric's health. Thus, over the period under discussion, the company attempted to achieve a harmony with Oregon's social, political, and economic values. Its successes and failures in that regard over more than a century are the focus of this two-volume history.

The Westinghouse alternating current dynamo and exciter. The dynamo, illustrated here, includes a field excited by a small direct current generator, shown in the background upon a pedestal. The field contains an even number of cores, placed radially as shown, so wound that the cores terminate alternately in north and in south poles. (Scientific American, *February 1890)*

1 CONTEXT AND COMMENCEMENT

ENRY VILLARD WAS A NATURALIZED AMERICAN of unnatural talents and almost supernatural enthusiasm. When Thomas Edison's perfection of the incandescent light was announced in 1879, Villard, a budding entrepreneur and transportation magnate, the hub of whose growing business empire was the frontier city of Portland, Oregon, immediately made a pilgrimage to Menlo Park, New Jersey, to see the technology in operation. He had recently purchased the Oregon Railway and Navigation Company, and his enthusiasm for the commercial and industrial possibilities of Edison's system was such that he immediately installed dynamos and incandescent lamps on his new steamer, the *Columbia*, then under construction at Philadelphia.[1] "The enterprise of a western railroad in 1880," the *Oregonian* later gloated with boosterish enthusiasm and pride, "gave Edison's greatest invention, the electric light, its first practical use while the conservative east was still trying to laugh it off as a ridiculous joke."[2]

The *Oregonian* also described the first docking of the *Columbia* at the Portland seawall on 21 July 1880, when, its reporter noted, wires from the vessel were run to the porch of the Clarendon Hotel (at the corner of what are now Northwest First and Flanders streets) with the lights from the rigging suspended over First Street. "The powerful ray," said the story, "lighted up the whole neighborhood to the brightness of day." The public was mesmerized: "Thousands visited the light and the vessel."[3]

1

In his memoirs published in 1904, Villard wrote of himself, "Mr. Villard took a strong interest in electricity from its earliest stages."[4] Always in need of capital for new ventures or souring old ones, he was so enamored of the incandescent light that he could admit that "his faith in the incalculable value of the invention was . . . so great that he did not dispose of his holdings [in the Edison Light Company] even when the shares on the par value of one hundred dollars . . . rose to four thousand."[5]

This was a species of high finance so remarkable that it seems only just that Villard should have made and lost a couple of fortunes. But the reality behind the statement was different. For Villard had placed his faith, with customary intensity and prescience, in nothing less than the pivotal technology of his time. He well understood its significance. He saw electricity as the basis of a great generating and appliance manufacturing empire, as the motive power of interurban and transcontinental railways.

Over the course of a century, his vision proved to be of greater, or at least more lasting, significance to the Pacific Northwest than it was to himself. He was the catalyst of a process that eventually produced Portland General Electric, a company with which he had little to do, but which became a principal factor in the economic and social development of the state of Oregon, and the city of Portland, as well as the entire region.

In early 1874, Villard, a thirty-eight-year-old Bavarian in the employ of some German financiers, had arrived in the United States to investigate and resolve for them the fate of the Oregon and California Railroad bonds that they held. The American financial panic of the previous year had led to a full-scale depression, which had adversely affected the fate of the railroad. Its owner, Ben Holladay, was unable to secure additional capital to operate the line.

Villard, the former Washington correspondent of the New York *Tribune* in the years of the Civil War, was bright, creative, persuasive, and opportunistic. After negotiations with Holladay, he successfully salvaged his employers' investments in the Oregon and California Railroad by gaining control of it in settlement of Holladay's debt. In addition, he came away with Holladay's other major holdings, the Oregon Real Estate and Portland Dock and Warehouse companies. The delighted bondholders promptly put him in charge of their new Northwest business empire. By late 1876, Villard had begun the process of transforming himself from their employee into an independent railroad magnate and entrepreneur.

Villard was only one of those businessmen whom the journalist and historian Matthew Josephson labeled "robber barons." In the post-Civil War business world, they amassed power and wealth while spurring the nation's belated industrial revolution in the decades immediately following its greatest catastrophe. In retrospect, their motivation might seem to have stemmed merely from greed. Yet, as more than one historian has pointed out, such a view does not begin to describe their activities. Allan Nevins has written:

> What these figures were really interested in was competitive achievement, self-
> expression, and the imposition of their wills on a given environment. All these were
> precisely the motives which actuated Carnegie, Westinghouse, and Rockefeller . . . the

men who built the really towering economic structures were not thinking primarily of dollars, or they could have halted at the first story.[6]

They were men of the Gilded Age. Mark Twain and Charles Dudley Warner had given that name to their novel of 1878, an indictment of an epoch that historians have come to believe ran from about the end of the Civil War to 1895. They depicted it as a time in which a dazzling surface covered base metal. Yet, if superficiality prevailed, the period has also been referred to as the "Age of Energy."[7] Crosscurrents of the greatest material extravagance fought for primacy with intellectual, political, and technological initiative as the rich, the ambitious, and the brilliant expressed themselves in a newly industrialized and urbanized America. The era was propelled by many forces, the most prominent among which were an optimism manifested in an unshakable belief in progress and the view that Americans had a birthright of prosperity. The West and its natural riches lay before the nation like a repast at what the historian Vernon Parrington characterized as "a great barbecue."

> All the important persons, leading bankers and promoters and businessmen received invitations. There wasn't room for everybody and these were presumed to represent the whole. . . . If the waiters saw to it that the choicest portions were served to favored guests, they were not unmindful of their numerous homespun constituency and they loudly proclaimed the fine democratic principle that what belongs to the people should be enjoyed by the people—not with petty bureaucratic restrictions, not as a social body, but as individuals, each free citizen using what came to his hand for his own private ends, with no questions asked.
>
> It was sound Gilded Age doctrine. . . . Let all come and help themselves. As a result the feast was gargantuan in its rough plenty. . . . more food, to be sure, was spoiled than eaten and the revelry was a bit unseemly but it was a fine spree in the name of the people.[8]

The egalitarian Parrington was offended by the giveaway of the public domain primarily to big business by weak administrations of the period, and his image of a brawling, ill-mannered barbecue perfectly captures the tenor of the times. It was business and not government that drove the Gilded Age forward. It was the businessmen—from larger-than-life railroad barons like Collis Huntington, Jay Gould, and Cornelius Vanderbilt, financiers such as J.P. Morgan, and captains of industry like Andrew Carnegie and John D. Rockefeller, to local and regional entrepreneurs like Ben Holladay—who shaped the economy and society. Using whatever resources—human or natural—were at hand, they created commercial and industrial empires. Capitalizing on innovations such as Bessemer-process steel, petroleum derivatives, and the combine, men of business built private empires and a mature industrial economy. "Within the next half century," Parrington observed, "America with its heritage of crude energy . . . was transformed into a vast uniform middle-class land, dedicated to capitalism and creating the greatest machine order known to history."[9]

3

The favored medium of business for the entrepreneur of the Gilded Age was the corporation. As the nineteenth century began, there were few incorporated businesses. Those that existed were mostly banks and turnpike and canal companies. Most business was conducted by proprietorships or partnerships. The nation's economy was primarily agrarian, with only small-scale industry. Textiles was the largest of the small-scale industries and required no complex formation. The state of its technology before the Civil War made a small mill as productive as a large one. The same could be said of the lesser shoe or glass industries. The vogue of the corporation had to await the postwar transportation and communications revolution. Together with the new technology in steel, improved communications made marketing on a mass basis feasible, production on a mass scale profitable, and the corporation therefore the desirable business format.[10]

For the individual investor, the advantages of corporate enterprise were clear. Mass production meant large factories and expensive machines. This usually required more capital than one person alone could accumulate. Through stock issues, the corporate vehicle allowed thousands of investors to come together to finance such an enterprise. The obverse of shared capitalization was shared risk, another attractive feature of the corporate scheme. Risk was further minimized by making stock transferable so that an individual's investment was not "sunk" into the venture. Limited-liability laws also protected investors from losses incurred by the corporation, which was regarded as a legal entity before the law. The evolution of legal protections for corporations in the Gilded Age is traceable to the Fourteenth Amendment to the Constitution. Added to the Constitution in 1868, the amendment (intended as a protection for freed slaves) barred states from passing laws "which shall abridge the privileges or immunities of citizens of the United States," depriving "any person of life, liberty, or property without due process of law," and from denying "to any person . . . the equal protection of the laws." When, in time, the federal courts, staffed by social and economic conservatives appointed by conservative presidents, began to interpret the word "person" to include corporations, the allure of the form for the business-minded was complete.[11]

Opportunity and circumstances seem, then, to have been in perfect conjunction for those who dreamed most creatively in the Gilded Age. The emerging mass American market became ever easier to penetrate as the nation became predominantly urban rather than rural by the end of the eighties. As the historian Frederick Jackson Turner pointed out shortly after the publication of the census of 1890, the frontier had ended. The concentration of the American population in urban centers facilitated the rise of national sales efforts. In short, the emergence of these self- and mutually reinforcing factors in the new American social and economic order made enterprise particularly attractive.

For the entrepreneur, a key to success in business traced back to technology—a traditionally powerful stimulus of the national psyche. The American fixation on "practical science" was well established: in 1835, the French traveler Alexis de Tocqueville had remarked on the dwindling advantages of inherited wealth in the United States. Social mobility was afforded not by birth, but by making money. The emphasis on moneymaking demanded not just ambition, but cognizance of the shortest paths to riches. "To minds thus disposed," wrote Tocqueville, "every new method that leads by a shorter road to wealth, every machine that spares labor, every instrument that diminishes the cost of production, every discovery that facilitates pleasures or augments them, seems to be the grandest effort of the human intellect."[12]

Technological innovation seemed to occur almost daily and was a focus for the efforts of the venturesome. Besides steel, there were significant developments in petroleum refinement; and there were the inventions of cement, machine refrigeration, oleomargarine, the steam tractor, the Draper-Northrup automatic bobbin-changing loom, and an automatic bottle-blowing machine.[13]

Among the most important innovations for business were those that made use of Villard's fixation, electricity. It became central to the new economic order that emerged in the United States after the Civil War. In the last third of the nineteenth century, electricity became what economists call a "backward and forward linkage," a discovery or invention that is a pivotal piece of the economic equation because it weds old and new technologies, fosters others, and thereby enhances the economic life of a society. Taken together, the developments attributable to such linkages may revolutionize and accelerate economic development.[14]

Science had been, as it were, pregnant with electricity for a long time before its arrival as a full-fledged technology.[15] In 1780, the laboratory assistant of Luigi Galvani, an Italian anatomist, accidentally sent an electric charge through the leg of a dissected frog by lightly scraping a metal scalpel across it. The fascinated Galvani discovered that by linking the frog's spinal cord to its leg muscle with a connector composed of two dissimilar metals, the lifeless leg would convulse. He called this "animal electricity," but what he had really stumbled upon was an electric current. The word "galvanism," at any rate, soon entered the lexicon of science to denote a continuous flow of electricity.

Another Italian, Alessandro Volta, reproduced Galvani's results on a live frog, joining its leg and back with dissimilar metals, thus causing a current to flow. He had made a battery: two metals separated by a moist conductor—the frog. He then tried to make a more practical battery by building up layer upon alternating layer of silver discs, moist cardboard (to replace the frog), and discs of zinc. Such stacks, which came to be called voltaic piles, generated greater and greater force, depending on their height. The chemical reaction between the metals and a fluid, or electrolyte, produced the same result as in the previous frog experiments.

Volta described continuous current, the effect he had achieved with his battery, in a letter of 1800 to the Royal Society in London, the preeminent scientific body. In 1807, one of its members, the chemist Sir Humphry Davy, stimulated by Volta's work, passed a current through two familiar compounds, potash and soda. The process, now called electrolysis, isolated two new elements, potassium and sodium. Davy also added magnesium, calcium, strontium, barium, boron, and silicon to the periodic table of chemistry by this method.

By creating a 2,000-cell battery at the Royal Society, one of the foremost effects Davy produced with the great volume of current was an electrical arc. Connecting the battery's terminals by a wire caused the wire to become hot and then to glow. When he inserted two pieces of charcoal into the wire circuit and then pulled them slowly apart, a spark leaped across the gap. If he held the charcoal close together, a continuous spark or arc resulted. Davy thus anticipated both incandescent and arc lighting.

5

In 1820, a Danish scientist named Hans Christian Ørsted discovered the relationship between electricity and magnetism. In a classroom demonstration of continuous current at the University of Copenhagen, he showed a magnetic field surrounding the wire as he sent electricity through it from a battery. Other Europeans, including the Frenchman André Marie Ampère and the German Georg Simon Ohm, picked up Ørsted's work on electromagnetism, as did Joseph Henry in the United States. Henry made large magnets by sending powerful currents through insulated wire wrapped around iron bars.

Michael Faraday, who began his career as Davy's laboratory assistant, eventually became known as the father of electricity, a decade after Ørsted's work came to light. Faraday's experiments focused on electromagnetic induction. He wrapped copper wire around a paper tube and connected the wire ends to a galvanometer (an instrument indicating the flow of electricity). By moving a bar magnet back and forth within the tube, the galvanometer needle mimicked the magnet's movement. The electric current was a magnetic effect. Using the principle of electromagnetic induction, he built a machine that held a copper disc between the poles of a horseshoe magnet. As the disc turned, a continuous current ran through it. Faraday had created the first electric generator. The stage was set for the development of power generation, dynamos, electric motors, transformers, and electromagnets—the machines that would do the work of the modern world.

Meanwhile, Henry was producing interesting results from his experiments with electromagnetism. He made a large magnet, whose power was greatly increased when the current was turned on. By itself it could pick up about seven pounds of metal; with electricity it could lift seven hundred fifty. An ironworks in New York used his electromagnets to separate iron ore from rock, one of the earliest uses of the new electrical technology in industry. Henry also created the first telegraph by separating a battery from an electromagnet with a mile of wire. When a switch closed the circuit, the current activated the electromagnet over the 5,280 feet of wire. One pole of the electromagnet repelled the similar pole of a second, free-swinging magnet that struck a bell, proving that electric current could stimulate an instantaneous mechanical action from a distance.

It is hardly possible to overstate the significance of Samuel F.B. Morse and the telegraph, or Alexander Graham Bell and the telephone. As the most critical scientific discoveries and their implications surrounding electricity had already been made when Morse perfected the telegraph in 1837 and Bell the telephone in 1876, their contributions, which rested on Henry's experiments, brought attention to the enormous economic and, more specifically, commercial potential of electricity. They were thus responsible for the transformation of electricity from science into technology.

The telegraph made an instant worldwide impact. In 1847, the financial markets changed forever when stock quotations were sent over the wire from London to Manchester on 14 November. Two years later, Reuters wire service was born and the press was launched on its way to becoming a globally linked institution. The military made use of the telegraph for the first time during the Crimean War in 1855, the year in which the telegraph was refined so as to print out words. By 1861, Western Union lines stretched from the Atlantic to the Pacific, almost a decade before the completion of the first transcontinental rail line, and by 1865 they covered two hundred thousand miles of the United States. In 1866, a transatlantic telegraph cable was laid.

The telephone had a similar success. In June 1876, at the Philadelphia Centennial Exposition, Bell demonstrated the telephone to scientists and other important persons by reading soliloquies from *Hamlet* over the wire and into their ears. Within four years of his dramatic readings, some forty-eight thousand telephones had been installed in America.

The modest electrical needs of telegraph and telephone could be satisfied by cell or batteries of cells. Other processes, devices, and machines that might make use of electricity were to require gross amounts of energy for commercial or industrial use. Providing electricity in great quantity without nearby waterpower, subdividing it, and leading it into machines and appliances at long distances was, to the minds of most experts, an insurmountable task.

To Thomas Edison, however, the task was not insurmountable. True to Tocqueville's rendition of the American character, Edison made himself "America's Most Useful Citizen," with more than a thousand patents to his credit by his death in 1931. These included an electric typewriter, the electric locomotive, the phonograph, the fluoroscope, a mimeograph, waxed paper, a synthetic rubber, and the guided torpedo. But his greatest triumph was his electric-lighting system, of which the incandescent bulb was the essential component. The system addressed and surmounted nearly all of the problems the experts had posed.

With the light bulb as its centerpiece, the system was a magnet for other entrepreneurs, an archetype of practical science. Edison himself cared nothing for the advancement of scientific knowledge. He was contemptuous of "bulged-headed theorists," as he called scientists. He wanted to make marketable products, not abstractions. As Thomas P. Hughes comments in his brilliant book *Networks of Power*, Edison's historical peers were Morse, Robert Fulton, and Cyrus McCormick, men who created useful products and then built companies around them.[16] It was to make money that Edison worked in his laboratory through the night and drove his colleagues to do likewise. But the effect was to create a system for the transmission and distribution of electrical energy that was entirely replicable in other places and that had at its terminus, with a kind of poetic symmetry, a glowing symbol of its efficiency.

This system perfectly answered the needs of the increasingly settled, and status- and comfort-seeking existence of post-frontier, industrial, urban America. The new society was marked by machines that replaced animals and human muscles. Moreover, in city life, each day was fractured into compartmentalized time. The hours of work were segregated from those of leisure in a way that was alien to rural and frontier Americans, with their dawn-to-dusk workdays. The so-called "Eight-Hour Leagues" of organized labor, for instance, chanted in the streets "Eight hours for work, eight hours for sleep, eight hours for what we will."[17] The hours of privacy in the home for the lower class and the expanding bourgeoisie thus grew. There was a demand too for rooms that were safely and cheaply illuminated as Americans struggled in comfortable parlors and squalid tenements to entertain and enlighten themselves. Edison and his subsequent imitators saw this need as a market, not as a problem of science.

Edison's contributions to the technology of electricity came from his interest in lighting, not in communications. As we have noted, Davy had experimented with arc lighting at the outset of 7

MAGNETISM AND ELECTRICITY: these two forces are linked, rather like Siamese twins. Generation of electricity takes advantage of this connection.

A simple bar magnet radiates a field of force from its poles—traditionally named north and south. While a portion of this field circles back toward its opposite pole, most is dissipated. If the magnet is broken, each piece has its two poles. And while each magnetic piece is weaker, since each is half the original bulk, the magnetic field is relatively stronger due to proximity and alignment. Another way to strengthen a magnetic field is to bend a bar magnet into a U shape. When the polar ends are bent once more to face each other, the field is made still more effective. If, then, a copper wire is moved through the gap and through the magnetic field, a small amount of electricity is generated in the wire. Electrical generators are designed to amplify this effect.

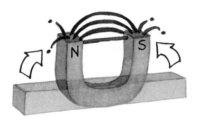

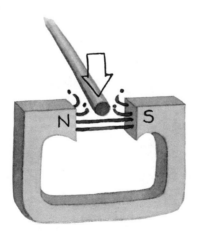

JAMES CLERK MAXWELL (1831-1879), a Scots physicist, formally described the linkage between electricity and magnetism in a series of synthesizing equations published in 1873. These formal statements, which also extend to the whole electromagnetic spectrum (the range of radiation that includes visible light, radio and television waves, radar, microwaves, infra-red and ultra-violet light, and x-rays), are still valid today, except in the relativistic domains revealed early in the twentieth century by Albert Einstein.

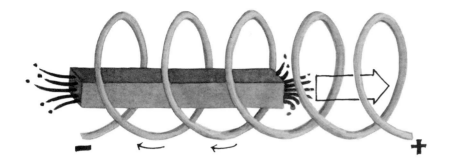

MICHAEL FARADAY, by shaping a copper wire into a coil, was able to increase the electricity generated when he moved a bar magnet into the coil. He also showed that electricity was produced whether the copper conductor moved through the magnetic field, or if the field moved past the conductor.

CONDUCTORS in electrical circuits have magnetic fields surrounding them. In a simple, single-wire arrangement, the field circles the wire like a continuous sheath. (This field can be readily detected—just as Ørsted did early in the nineteenth century—with a simple compass. Brought near any electrical cord, the compass needle will swing to align with the magnetic field; moved to the opposite side of the cord, it will swing 180° to realign with the field.) If the wire conductor is shaped into a coil, the magnetic field is compressed and strengthened into an elongated shape rather like a bar magnet. Powerful electromagnets are designed to take advantage of this effect.

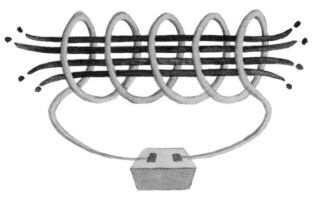

9

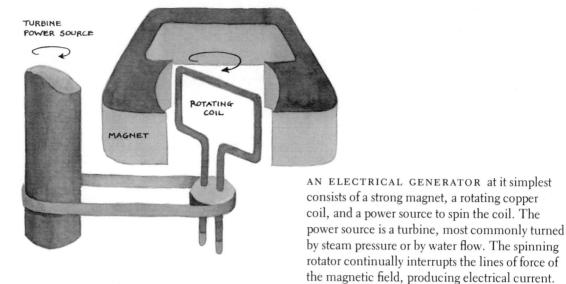

TURBINE
POWER SOURCE

ROTATING
COIL

MAGNET

AN ELECTRICAL GENERATOR at it simplest consists of a strong magnet, a rotating copper coil, and a power source to spin the coil. The power source is a turbine, most commonly turned by steam pressure or by water flow. The spinning rotator continually interrupts the lines of force of the magnetic field, producing electrical current.

A DC GENERATOR produces its one-way current flow by means of a commutator—a split metal cylinder with each half attached to one leg of the rotating coil. Stationary contacts, called brushes, on either side of the commutator, pick up the current and send it off into the electrical circuit. As the side of the coil near the magnet's north pole passes, a clockwise flow is generated.

Once that side is beyond north's field, the gaps in the commutator reach the brushes and the current briefly stops. Rotation continues, and again the commutator is in contact with the brushes. Now the opposite side of the rotating coil approaches the field of the north magnetic field. Current is generated, still flowing in a clockwise direction.

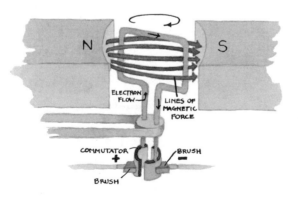

N   S

ELECTRON
FLOW
LINES OF
MAGNETIC
FORCE

COMMUTATOR   BRUSH
+   −
BRUSH

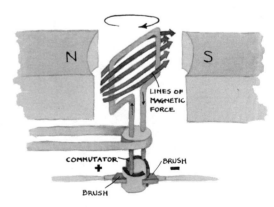

N   S

LINES OF
MAGNETIC
FORCE

COMMUTATOR   BRUSH
+   −
BRUSH

AN AC GENERATOR produces current that flows briefly first in one direction and then briefly in the opposite direction, in synchronization with the rotating coil. Each leg of the coil is attached to a slip ring. The upper slip ring is larger to allow the leg attached to the lower ring to pass through freely. Brushes contact both rings. While one side of the rotating coil passes the magnet's north pole, the generated current flows clockwise. As the coil continues to turn, its opposite side approaches the north pole and the current, formerly flowing down its leg, reverses its direction. For half a revolution (or cycle) of the coil, then, current flows from the slip rings in one direction; and for the second half, in the opposite direction. The positive/negative polarities at the brushes flip-flop with each complete rotation. Early AC generators were often run at 125 cycles per second; today's North American standard is 60 cycles, although many parts of the world generate 50-cycle AC.

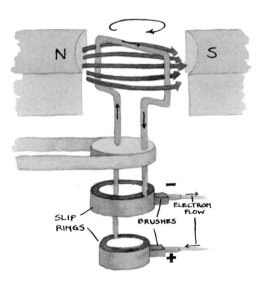

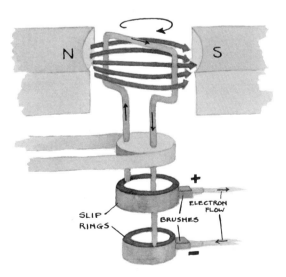

11

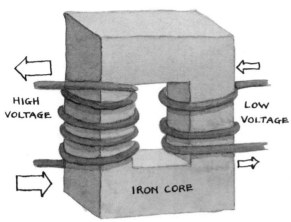

HIGH
VOLTAGE

LOW
VOLTAGE

IRON CORE

A TRANSFORMER changes the voltage of alternating current. It is an essential link in transmitting electrical power. Incoming current flows into a primary coil of wire wrapped around an iron core. The AC current produces a magnetic field that continually switches on and off. The core transfers this field to a secondary coil, where it induces the output current. The amount of change in voltage depends on the ratio of turns in the two coils. The transformer shown here *steps up* current two times (if the primary coil is on the right side) or *steps down* current by one half (if the primary coil is on the left).

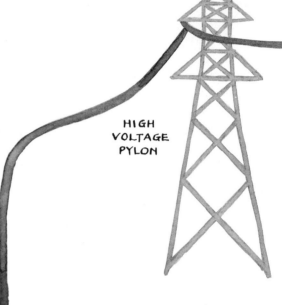

HIGH
VOLTAGE
PYLON

TRANSMITTING ELECTRICITY: A power plant produces power of several thousand volts. To minimize energy loss that occurs over the long distances it must travel, this current is stepped up a hundred-fold by a transmission transformer and then fed into high voltage power lines suspended from a parade of tall, carefully insulated pylons. Once the power network nears the locations of its users, current is stepped down to several thousand volts by a distribution transformer. Some current at this voltage may go

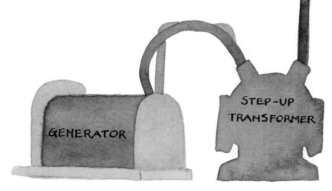

GENERATOR

STEP-UP
TRANSFORMER

WHEN AN ELECTRIC LIGHT is turned on, the power to illuminate that light is generated, delivered, and received in practically the same instant. The electricity is not stored somewhere, but is continually generated and distributed through the wiring attached to the switch. Only when an appliance is switched on does the current flow into it.

STEP-DOWN TRANSFORMER

directly to industrial users. The remainder travels into neighborhood power grids where it is stepped down once more to 220 or, more commonly, 110 volts, by home supply transformers—those large, gray, squarish cylinders commonly seen hanging from residential power poles. The electricity arrives at a particular house, passes through an electric meter that measures its flow, and then inside to provide power, as needed, to lights, appliances, outlets, and the like.

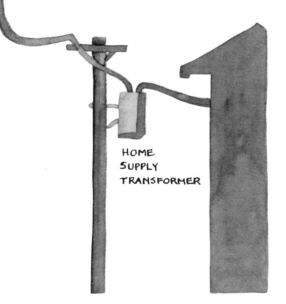

HOME SUPPLY TRANSFORMER

13

THE LANGUAGE OF ELECTRICITY

AMP   a measure of the amount of current flow (electrons per second) moving past a point.

CURRENT   the flow of charged particles (electrons) through a conductive material.

LOAD   the amount of electric power delivered or required by all a utility company's customers' demand.

VOLT   the unit of electromotive force or electric pressure analogous to water pressure in pounds per square inch. It is the electromotive force which, if steadily applied to a circuit having a resistance of one ohm, will produce a current of one ampere.

ALTERNATING CURRENT (AC)   an electric current that reverses its direction of flow periodically (usually several times per second), as contrasted to direct current. It is the type generally produced and consumed in the United States.

DIRECT CURRENT (DC)   electricity that flows continuously in one direction.

DYNAMO   a machine which converts either mechanical energy into electric energy or electric energy into mechanical energy by utilizing the principles of electromagnetic induction and electromagnetism. A dynamo is called a generator when mechanical energy supplied in the form of rotation is converted into electric energy; it is called a motor when the energy conversion takes place in the reverse order, that is, from electrical to mechanical.

GENERATION   refers to the act or process of transforming other forms of energy into electric energy, or to the amount of electric energy so produced, expressed in kilowatts.

GENERATOR   a device for converting mechanical energy into electric energy.

KILOWATT (kw)   1,000 watts. A unit used to measure the production capacity or capability of electric generators and also the power or requirement of electrical appliances and equipment.

KILOWATTHOUR (kwh)   the energy that will be expended by using 1000 watts of electricity for one hour.

SUBSTATION   an assemblage of equipment for the purpose of switching and/or changing or regulating the voltage of electricity.
Step-up substation changes electricity from lower to higher voltage.
Step-down substation changes electricity from higher to lower voltage.

WATT   the rate of energy flow per second. Amps × volts = watts.

AFTER 1882 (when electric power was first distributed commercially in the United States), as more and more homes were wired for electricity, inventors and entrepreneurs began to develop a range of electrically powered machines. Electric appliances began to appear immediately after the light bulb, although it took some time for some of the devices to catch on commercially—electricity rates were still high, the appliances still were not notably efficient, and, perhaps most importantly, in most service areas, even as late as 1905, electricity was supplied only at night, since the primary use for power at the time was for lighting. However, in 1905, one Earl Richardson, a meter reader for a power company in Ontario, California, began to distribute electric irons of his own design and found that many homemakers would agree to use them in place of their old stove-heated irons if they could use them during daylight hours. Richardson convinced his company to experiment by providing twenty-four hour service on Tuesdays which he had learned was the day of the week that most local homemakers did their ironing. The company was satisfied with the rate of consumption during the trial, and gradually extended their hours of service throughout the week. As electricity began to be supplied at more convenient times for doing chores, electric appliances became more widely used. The two most affordable electric appliances, excepting light, were the iron and the vacuum cleaner. By 1927, three-quarters of electrified American households had an iron, and one-half had a vacuum. A term was coined to describe the new devices: "labor-saving appliances." No longer did irons weigh twelve pounds, no longer were carpets dragged outside and beaten dust-free, no more were clothes scrubbed and rinsed and wrung by hand. Housework had become a little less time-consuming and less exhausting.

BY THE 1880s, electrically powered trolleys were operating regularly along Brooklyn's crowded streets. The speed of the new trolleys alarmed passengers and pedestrians alike, and residents poked fun at their predicament by calling themselves the "Trolley Dodgers." When Brooklyn later hosted its own major-league baseball team, the owners revived the old appellation and called it the "Brooklyn Dodgers."

THOMAS ALVA EDISON (1847-1931). After Edison had been at school three months, his mother decided to educate him herself when his teacher told her that he was "addled." As a young boy, he was intensely curious and devised all kinds of experiments which he carried out at home.

By the age of twelve, he was working on a train, selling newspapers and candy and spending layover time in public libraries, studying. At sixteen, Edison became a telegrapher, while continuing to study and invent. In 1870, when he was twenty-three, he was paid for the first time for an invention: forty thousand dollars for his stock ticker, a device that printed stock quotations for brokers to use in trading. Two years later he went to work for the Western Union Telegraph Company, manufacturing telegraphic instruments. Edison continued to develop his own inventions and opened the world's first laboratory for conducting organized industrial research in Menlo Park, New Jersey, in 1876. On 21 October 1879, he came up with his most notable invention, the incandescent lamp.

the nineteenth century, although nothing resulted from his efforts until the 1840s, when the first patents were issued on the technique in Great Britain. By the next decade, arc lights were used as flood lamps and streetlights, though not for home illumination because of their brilliance. In the 1860s, Joseph Swan, an English chemist, produced incandescence by passing a current through carbonized paper and cardboard until they glowed. In 1878, he patented a carbon rod lamp, but it never proved commercially appealing. The stumbling blocks were two: the familiar one of battery power, which was too expensive to render attractive an idea for which various alternatives existed, and the fragility of elements that oxidized or melted rather quickly. Dynamos were gradually introduced to replace batteries by converting mechanical energy into electric power. The development of the mercury pump promised to seal off electrical elements in a globe or bulb within a vacuum, thus protecting them from oxidation. Still, commercialized incandescent illumination on a mass basis remained a distant dream. By trial and error, Edison eventually arrived at a long-lasting element that burned for a hundred seventy hours. The element was carbonized bamboo from a hand-held fan that happened to be in his Menlo Park office.

Although Edison regarded the electric light in itself as merely a technological curiosity, he recognized its possibilities. Connected to power stations with dynamos, and to lines from the stations to homes, offices, stores, factories, meters, light switches—all the trappings of a generation, transmission, and distribution system—the incandescent light could be the seed of a great commercial organism. Edison had worked out the circuitry of the system he envisioned for sending power to his light as he developed the light itself.

On Pearl Street, in the Wall Street financial district of New York, he established the first commercial power station, solely to attract financial backing. On 4 September 1882, he switched on the power to eighty-five recipients of his new service.

Yet another obstacle to the perfection of central-station electrification was overcome. Edison at once began to refine his distribution system, and others worked on its various aspects. Dynamos were improved, and the electric motor was applied to a number of new ideas such as elevators and sewing machines. But Edison's system, because it was founded on simple direct current, was wedded to this type of power. The problem was that direct current was soon confronted by a rival system—alternating current.

The two systems competed with one another as Edison shamelessly and sometimes unscrupulously attempted to block the acceptance of alternating current, despite its apparent advantages over its rival. The "Battle of the Currents," as the debate was known, focused on the liabilities of direct current, despite Edison's efforts. Alternating current, in which the transmission of electricity reverses itself every 1/120 of a second, was said by its proponents to be safer and less costly to transmit than direct current. It could be sent out over a smaller wire than direct current and was less hazardous to install. Most important, according to its partisans, because of its cyclical nature, alternating current could be more efficiently transmitted over long distances than direct current. The intensity of direct current could burn up the lines over long distances. Even if that did not occur, much of the load would be shed in the course of transmission. Another drawback of direct current was that, although the DC motor was employed industrially during the 1880s, its general use was still restricted, since it required the right combination of plant site and waterpower. As

NIKOLA TESLA (1856-1943). Tesla's genius for invention and scientific innovation first became apparent when he was a child in Croatia. Possessed of a photographic memory, he excelled in mathematics and developed a great interest in engineering, with which he experimented by inventing various useful machines such as a bladeless waterwheel. He attended the Austrian Polytechnic School in Graz until 1876, when he was forced by lack of funds to leave.

In his last months at the polytechnic, he had begun to consider the idea of an alternative to direct-current electrical machinery. Tesla wrestled with the idea for several years, until in 1882, he built the first practicable alternating-current motor. Until that time, alternating current was not suitable for powering motors, as with each reversal the current passed through zero in phase, interrupting the motor's action. Tesla had discovered that an efficient motor could be designed by displacing the reversals of two or more currents by ninety degrees in phase. The out-of-phase currents produce a rotating magnetic field, which remains practically constant, since when one current is at zero degrees in phase, the other is at ninety degrees. This allows the motor to run smoothly. Tesla's invention was known as the polyphase system. The significance of the discovery was that alternating current could then be used for long-distance transmission.

Tesla left for the United States in 1884 and went to work for Thomas Edison. Within a year, he had left Edison's employ, over a combination of personality differences and a serious dispute about the potential and merits of direct and alternating currents. He opened the Tesla Electric Company and began to refine his AC inventions, many of which he patented, later selling the patents to George Westinghouse. The latter also hired Tesla as a consultant to develop further his AC system. The collaboration of Tesla and Westinghouse in promoting alternating current systems enraged Edison, who began an all-out attack on the new technology. Tesla and Edison continued for years to be rivals and even enemies.

GEORGE WESTINGHOUSE (1846-1914). Most famous for his invention of the railroad air brake in 1869, Westinghouse never finished college and had no scientific background. Nevertheless, he was able to devise a revolutionary braking system for railroad cars that allowed them to stop quickly and safely. Before that, crews had had to begin braking a train half a mile before an expected stop and were often quite unable to stop in an emergency.

Westinghouse later founded the Westinghouse Electric and Manufacturing Company and became the primary promoter of AC systems in the United States. He was the first to see that the key to inexpensive, long-distance transmission of electrical power was high-voltage generation and distribution. Along with Nikola Tesla, who at that time worked as the head of Westinghouse's research department, George Westinghouse did eventually establish alternating-current systems as the principal form of power supply in the United States.

17

this had been a typical problem before the coming of electricity, the industrialist who employed it was little better off than previously.

Edison and his followers propagandized the public relentlessly about the hazards of alternating current, which they characterized as lethal. One piece they published listed the names of those allegedly killed by alternating current. New York State adopted electrocution as its method of capital punishment and bought an AC generator for the purpose. Edison's publicists labeled it "the executioner's current."[18]

However, men as determined as Edison were arrayed against him. The two most important of them were the Pittsburgh industrialist George Westinghouse and an émigré Serbian engineer named Nikola Tesla. Critical to their cause was that in the 1880s the rapidly industrializing United States was still three-quarters rural. Electricity would have to traverse great distances to get to much of the population. Of the two electric currents, alternating current would address that requirement better.

Tesla, a brilliant engineer, had arrived in the United States in 1884. He worked briefly with Edison, but left Menlo Park after a disagreement. Westinghouse bought the rights to the forty patents on AC devices that Tesla had invented, including the AC induction polyphase electric motor, the key to the eventual adaptation of alternating current's universal use. A charming, if odd, figure, Tesla had on his own waged a flamboyant campaign for alternating current in the press. Countering Edison's claims about the danger of the current, in the presence of reporters he would hold and light lamps without wires, allowing the high-frequency current to course through his own body. Working with Westinghouse, he gradually convinced the scientific community, investors, and the public of the superiority of alternating current.

The turning point in the current's acceptance was the Chicago World's Fair of 1892, where Westinghouse, who had won the fair's lighting contract from Edison, staged a brilliant display of the properties of alternating current. With dynamos, as well as transformers and converters, he powered a variety of DC and AC equipment, both large machines and small appliances. He demonstrated what Edison had originally recognized: that one electrical generating plant could send power to any number of different users. The implication was that, through alternating current, industry would be unfettered and more cost-efficient. Finally able to receive large and reliable loads of power from a distant source and thus no longer confined to areas with usable waterpower, companies could move closer to labor pools, to the sources of raw materials, and to important markets. At the same time, a trolley running on 500 V DC could be supplied with the mediation of a converter, while a fan requiring 110 V AC could also be accommodated. In the factory, on the streets, and in the parlor, electricity was poised to transform society. Henry Adams, the great nineteenth-century historian and a visitor to the Chicago fair, put his finger on it when, after standing before the great dynamos, he wrote that "they gave to history a new phase."[19] He was right. Between 1889 and 1899, the percentage of American manufacturing establishments using power equipment grew from 48.1 to 64 and, by 1914, reached 74.2.[20] In 1902 alone, 1.5 billion kilowatt-hours of electrical energy were used by industry.[21] The adoption of alternating current in this century made electrification the most sweeping technological change of the nineteenth century.

18

PORTLAND'S ELECTRIC PIONEERS

Despite Henry Villard's early demonstration of electricity on the *Columbia* in the Pacific Northwest, in 1889 the state of Oregon, and the city of Portland, had only just begun to participate in these developments. In that year the region's economy was fundamentally colonial.[22] Economic life was based largely on the extraction of resources such as timber for shipment elsewhere, thence to return as finished, value-added products for retail consumption. Alternatively, local industrial plants were owned outside the Northwest. The coming of a transcontinental rail line in 1883 had been the first step in integrating the region efficiently with the great national markets.[23] In short, in 1889 the Northwest was still an economic backwater.

Founded in 1851, Portland was, as its historian E. Kimbark MacColl has labeled it, a "cumulative growth city."[24] Expansion was by accretion, not planning. In keeping with the tenor of the age, speculators and entrepreneurs "designed" the city through the acquisition and development of land—in other words, on the basis of commercial rather than social considerations—in what today is the downtown area. In 1889, some forty-four thousand people were living in Portland.[25]

Despite its remoteness from the nation's centers of power and money, the city was a busy, affluent commercial center. If much of Portland's wealth was controlled elsewhere, there was nevertheless an aggressive, daring class of businessmen and investors who eagerly expanded the number of commercial and industrial enterprises in the city. Like Villard and the better known captains of industry who bestrode the national scene, they were shrewd and opportunistic, but also endowed with the characteristic faith of the Gilded Age in progress, especially progress that derived from technological innovation. They included Henry Corbett and William S. Ladd in banking, Captain John C. Ainsworth in transportation, Simeon Reed in lumber, and Charles F. Swigert in construction.

As a new and potentially lucrative technology, electricity interested men of this type from the first word of Edison's incandescent light in 1879. They recognized its possibilities in manufacturing as well as in domestic life. In the earliest years of white settlement, the falls of the Willamette had been the most obvious (if not the only feasible) source of energy for industry in the territory's settled regions. In 1832, Dr. John McLoughlin, chief factor of the Hudson's Bay Company, had started a small community near the falls at Oregon City and, at the same time, the first water-powered sawmill and flour mill in the Oregon Territory. Both the first furniture factory and the first paper mill in the Pacific Northwest were also begun in the town.[26]

Inevitably, despite the falls, Portland's location proved better than Oregon City's. Situated as it was between two rich agricultural valleys, the Willamette and the Tualatin, at the confluence of the Columbia and Willamette rivers, and fifteen miles nearer the sea than Oregon City, Portland was the natural commercial center of northwest Oregon. This explains its rise to urban preeminence.

Yet if Portland was commercially expansive, industrially it was retarded by lack of the requisite cheap source of abundant energy. When the *Columbia* arrived in town in 1880, its wonderful display of electrical illumination and power lured the entrepreneurial in spirit with its economic possibilities and spurred the imaginative, especially the young, firing their dreams with its glow of

19

AS NIKOLA TESLA'S AC SYSTEM gained widespread approval from other engineers, Thomas Edison embarked upon an extraordinary campaign to debunk its safety and usefulness, much as he had years ago promoted his DC system by assailing gas flame. He and his associates paid local boys twenty-five cents for each dog and cat they could bring to their laboratories. Neighborhood pets began to disappear as Edison set up purposefully crude experiments with alternating current and proceeded to electrocute the animals. The inventor then distributed leaflets warning consumers that they should be aware that they, too, might be "Westinghoused" by alternating current. Eventually Edison and his associates electrocuted animals in public and openly displayed the dead bodies.

In an effort to cast alternating current in a horrific light, one of Edison's assistants paid a visit to New York's Sing Sing prison. Soon afterward, prison authorities announced that henceforth condemned criminals would be put to death not by hanging (the usual method at the time) but by the more "humane" means of electrocution. Such humanity was not evident during the first execution. The current administered was too weak, and since the first jolt was insufficient to kill the condemned man, another had to be given.

CANADIAN-BORN JOHN McLOUGHLIN (1784-1857) first arrived in the Oregon Territory in 1824, as chief factor of the Hudson's Bay Company. Oregon was at that time under joint British and American control, although no Americans had yet settled there. McLoughlin had been sent to the area to monopolize the fur trade, and he proceeded to build a huge establishment—farms, mills, a shipyard—Fort Vancouver, Washington. During the 1830s, French Canadians and Americans stayed in the Oregon Territory to farm. McLoughlin extended them credit for supplies at Hudson's Bay Company stores until their first harvests came in. Many of them were never able to repay the loans, and the Hudson's Bay Company reprimanded McLoughlin for continuing to offer credit. But he carried on, and through his generosity many farmers were able to establish themselves. McLoughlin also gave aid to missionaries and other newcomers to the area and it was the missionaries' glowing reports that were to some extent responsible for the massive migration to the territory that followed.

McLoughlin's settlement paved the way for much of the development of the state of Oregon. When he left the Hudson's Bay Company in 1846, he retired to the site of what is now Oregon City, the town he had founded years earlier. His home there was at the falls of the Willamette— the same falls that were the first to provide electrical power to the Northwest.

lights. Orin B. Coldwell, who later became a vice president of Portland General Electric, recalled his own fascination and that of other Portland residents, including Philip Malcolm, with the event and how it urged on their own electrical investigations. Malcolm, who had a long-standing interest in electricity, built a bichromate-and-potash battery and used it to power lights in the display window of his father-in-law's store. It was the first use of electric lights for commercial purposes in the city's history.[27] The batteries lasted five hours before they needed to be recharged.

In September 1880, George Weidler installed a dynamo that powered arc lamps at his sawmill on the Willamette. Three more arc lamps were put in at the nearby dock of John Ainsworth. Yet another was placed by the Clarendon Hotel at the intersection of First and Front streets. They were also powered by Weidler's dynamo.[28]

The success of this and other such experiments (at the Portland Mechanics' Fair in 1881, visitors were impressed by the ten arc lights used to illuminate the exhibits) proved fortunate for George Weidler. As agent for the Weston Company, maker of the lamps, he took orders from a number of First Street merchants, who, impressed by the various displays, wanted lights of their own. The *Oregonian* reported that ten lamps and one mile of wire were shipped from New York to supply them. Weidler furnished their power from the dynamo at his mill.[29]

In June 1882, an essay by Will Meeker, a recent Portland high-school graduate, projected the imminent generation of electricity from the Willamette Falls to Portland for general consumption. The *Oregonian* somewhat patronizingly called the prediction "unimaginatively portrayed." But Meeker was not merely a dreamer. He and a friend, George Low, a Wells Fargo mail clerk, later ran a telegraph line from an electric plant owned by Villard's Oregon Railway and Navigation Company at the Ainsworth dock to Low's room at Front and Salmon streets. There it lit a globe. This was probably the first residential use of electricity in Portland.[30] In the meantime, Villard, in his enthusiasm for electricity, commissioned a report by a well-known Swiss engineer, P. Meischer, who was to study the possible use of Willamette Falls for industrial power.

It was Meischer's opinion that electricity was only the fourth most practical form of energy transmission from the falls. He much preferred another method. "The cheapest and most effective transmission of large powers," he wrote, "is made by means of endless wire ropes running with great speed over large pulleys. It will prove a great success if properly built and managed."[31] Meischer's cheerfully obtuse certitude and breathtaking lack of foresight notwithstanding, his report was an exhaustive study of the falls' energy. Although Villard went bankrupt in 1884 and was unable to implement its recommendations, in the same year, United States Electric Lighting and Power Company (u.s. Electric) was formed by Parker Morey, George Weidler, and Fred Holman, who, noting the report, planned to make use of the falls' potential.

Morey had arrived in Portland in 1879 from San Francisco as "a competent mechanical and electrical engineer," according to the *Oregonian*, which added that he had "a strong turn toward invention." Coming to Portland as the result of a contract to install the city's first hydraulic ram elevator, he had found the city to his liking, left his employer, and organized his own firm, the Portland Hydraulic Elevator Company.[32] Although this was apparently a successful enterprise, he was eager to branch out into electrical generation, which he saw as being commercially viable. 21

A co-founder and president of Willamette Falls
Electric Company (1891-1892) and an incorpora-
tor and president of Portland General Electric
Company (1891-1902), Parker F. Morey came to
Portland in 1880 to operate the Portland Hydraulic Elevator Works, just after the city had seen the
wonders of electricity through the docking of the
steamship S.S. California. Intrigued by the new
technology, Morey installed dynamos at his elevator company. In 1884, he and two partners formed
the United States Electric Light and Power Company and began powering city streetlights the following year. In 1888, he joined forces with Edward
Eastham and formed Willamette Falls Electric
Company, PGE's predecessor. In 1889, their company made history in producing the nation's first
long-distance transmission of electricity. It traveled fourteen miles from Station A above Willamette Falls to the streetlights of downtown Portland.
(PGE collections)

Frederick Van Voorhies Holman was one of the
original founders of United States Electric Light
and Power, a company that eventually became
Portland General Electric. One of the city's most
prestigious lawyers, he was born on 29 August
1852 in Pacific County, Washington which was at
that time part of Oregon Territory. He was admitted to the bar in 1874. He served as general counsel
and as director. At the time of his death, he was
honorary president of PEPCO's Twenty Year Club
because of his forty-one-year connection with the
company. An avid rose gardener, he was the originator of Portland's appellation "The Rose City."
(PGE collections)

His partnership with Weidler came about from an obvious community of interest. Weidler had a meager customer base and dynamos, while Morey had a large boiler at his elevator plant that could drive the dynamos. With Holman, the other investor and a leading Portland lawyer, they formed U.S. Electric in March. The company expanded its operations apace, gaining the franchise for streetlighting from the Portland City Council and even moving into incandescent lighting for offices and residences. (Usually, this service took the form of a five-light chandelier hung in the customer's parlor or office.)[33]

U.S. Electric quickly became a sort of community institution in Portland. As more home-owners and businessmen became acquainted with electricity and its benefits, particularly light-ing, the company's load expanded. To make certain that its fame spread, the company conducted tours of its works at the foot of Oak Street. The *Oregonian* recorded one such event, following a field trip to U.S. Electric by a high-school class in March 1885. This excerpt of the remarks of a student who visited the paper's newsroom with a friend after the tour catches the wonder a good many Portlanders must have felt about the exciting, but invisible, new force.

"I called, that is we called," blushingly the young lady said, looking timidly yet trustfully in the face of her escort who blushed also, "to have you thank Mr. Hawkins [L. L. Hawkins, then president of the company] who is a dear, nice man and learned. He knows so much about electricity. He explained all about the dynamos and things and showed us how much electricity was created by the belt. And I just thought it was a pity that it couldn't be run into bottles or barrels and saved. And—oh my!—you should have seen how funny Charley—oh, I mean Mr. Blank—how funny he looked when he put his head toward the belt. Why his hair stood out like a brand new dude—straight you know," she explained, "like a Russian or a caviar or something, and we were so surprised because I—that is—we never knew Charley had so much life or electricity in him. But it seemed to run out of him as though he was made of it. I felt kind of scared. You are all right now, Charley, aren't you?" This with solicitude. "And then it made some powder on some of the girls' faces show up so plain. And the man said it would ruin a watch to hold it near the dynamo. But it didn't hurt Charley's because the works are all brass." Here she stopped, but added, "Please, Mr. Editor, say that we are awfully obliged to Mr. Hawkins and all that sort of thing, and we will be so awfully obliged."[34]

While Morey and his colleagues worked zealously to succeed with U.S. Electric (it was said that Morey, who, despite the *Oregonian*'s claims, was not really an electrical engineer, often slept on a cot in the plant in case of trouble), in Oregon City, Edward L. Eastham, a leading citizen and booster, was making great efforts to attract industry to the town. Naturally, he hoped to rest his case for the city on the abundant energy of the falls.

As early as 1883, Eastham, a lawyer, bank president, state legislator, and entrepreneur, had formulated a plan to buy the Willamette Transportation and Locks Company, which had a virtual monopoly on the falls.[35] At the same time, he purchased water rights in the area of the falls, as well as most of the adjacent land.[36] By 1887, he had practical control over Willamette

Falls in all its aspects. He then sent an associate, Thomas L. Charman, to investigate the electrical industry in San Francisco. Charman's report must have been favorable because, on his return, Eastham incorporated the Oregon City Electric Company. On or about 1 November 1888, the company began generating electricity from the falls to the town for purposes of residential, commercial, and public lighting.[37] The company's first generator was a 450-light Edison dynamo that was belted to the waterwheel at the Excelsior and Shoddy Lumber Mill. Eastham felt he, his hometown and his associates, and their enterprises would now prosper as they supplied both land and electricity to new business and old residents.

Cognizant of the developments at the falls, the aggressive Morey, ever alert to business opportunities, came to see Oregon City Electric's generating capacity at the falls as a key to expanding U.S. Electric's already growing customer base. Although Meischer's report to Villard had been mute about power transmission to Portland (it had regarded Canemah, a little river town just below Oregon City, long since abandoned, as the farthest feasible industrial site from the power source), it was detailed and explicit about the falls' enormous energy potential. Morey was certainly aware of the report. Even the growing possibility of long-distance transmission of electricity, thanks to the advances in AC technology by Westinghouse, and the publicity surrounding the war of the currents, promised that its time was not far off.

For his part, Eastham had always believed that Portland represented a primary market for Willamette Falls electricity. Inevitably, the two businessmen were drawn together to form a new company that would harness the power of the falls in the service not only of Oregon City, but of Portland. On 8 November 1888, they incorporated the Willamette Falls Electric Company.[38] Based on Oregon City Electric, the new company took over the assets of U.S. Electric. Eastham became president of the new company and Morey vice president and superintendent. Other stockholders were David P. Thompson, R.H. Thompson, Lester Leander Hawkins, and William K. Smith. The company was capitalized at a million dollars.[39] It was also about to make history.

The new company began to take shape immediately. Construction started on a dynamo house with rock-filled wooden bulkheads on the east side of the river, the same side as the transmission line to Portland. By the end of March 1889, all but four miles of the line were complete. New equipment, including four Brush arc-light dynamos manufactured by the California Electric Light Company, was purchased.[40]

Morey hired a consulting engineer, W.C. Cheney, to supervise the project. An electrical engineer who had overseen the construction of generating plants throughout the western hemisphere, Cheney was a recognized expert in hydroelectric transmission and an early advocate of the use of alternating, rather than direct, current.[41] Although induction motors were in use by 1887, Tesla's three-phase motor would not be ready for general use until about 1890. The advocacy of alternating current at this stage thus made Cheney something of a visionary, although, in the electrical industry at large, the debate fostered by competing interests over its feasibility had been raging for several years.

Cheney and Morey decided on 125-cycle, 4,000-V AC dynamos, a voltage higher than anything then manufactured. No doubt they thought that the fourteen miles to Portland was light-years away in terms of the transmissions commonly made in 1888. It would require a great deal of

Born in Oregon City in 1848, Edward L. Eastham grew up as a farm boy and later attended Willamette University. He studied law while working as a school teacher in Oregon City, was admitted to the bar in 1876 and started a law practice in town. In 1881, he organized the Bank of Oregon City. In 1888 he retired from his law practice and put all his energies into the development of Willamette Falls and the surrounding area. He was able to secure practically all water rights at the falls and acquired one thousand acres of the surrounding land. With Parker F. Morey, he incorporated Willamette Falls Electric Company. Eastham was president of the company until his death in 1891. (PGE collections)

voltage for electricity to arrive in Portland with anything like the load needed to service the city. The engineers expected much of the current simply to dissipate from the transmission line along the way.

Although several manufacturers of AC dynamos were skeptical that they could build reliable equipment of that capacity, Cheney was insistent, and even enlisted a prestigious engineer, Henry M. Byellsby, to persuade the Westinghouse Company to undertake the job. Orin B. Coldwell reported that Byellsby told George Westinghouse: "If Cheney wants those machines, build them for him. If any man can make them go, he can."[42] Eventually, Westinghouse contracted to build six 80-kw (1600-light), No. 2, 4,000-V single-phase, 125-cycle alternators, but only with the stipulation that the company did not have to guarantee the machines.[43] The first alternator arrived on 30 April 1890.

If Cheney and Morey were determined to gamble on alternating current, it was a well-calculated risk, based not only on the current state and anticipated advancement of technology, but on the success of generating direct current from the falls. The demand for electricity in Portland had been so acute that transmission to the metropolis from the Brush DC dynamos at the falls had been undertaken despite the anticipated load loss in 1889, almost a year before the arrival of the AC equipment.

"Works like a charm," the *Oregonian* headlined on 4 June 1889, when the first switch was thrown for direct-current generation from the falls to Portland.

> The Willamette Falls Electric Company started up one of their Brush arc dynamos last evening, and the electricity was sent from Oregon City for lighting one of their 10 o'clock circuits in this city. It worked magnificently and conclusively demonstrated the fact that our city can be lighted successfully from the Falls. The result was a pleasing surprise to the company, the percentage of loss of electricity by transmission being much less than their most sanguine expectations. The work of removing the machinery from the station here to the falls will be carried on as expeditiously as possible. Another large dynamo will be moved up today.[44]

The *Oregonian*'s matter-of-fact tone belied the occurrence of a momentous event in the history of American technology. The third of June 1889 was the first instance of long-distance transmission of electricity in the nation's history. In fact, Willamette Falls Electric could claim two distinctions, in that it was first to transmit both direct and alternating current long distance, although the exact date of the AC transmission is lost. It appears to have occurred in September of 1890.[45]

A practiced entrepreneur like Morey was following well-honed instincts in taking such a gamble. He perceived the rapidly growing market for his product in Portland, which was exploding both economically and physically. In 1889, the city was in a cycle of economic boom, having recovered from the doldrums brought on by the mild depression of 1886. In 1889 alone, more than $54 million worth of commercial and residential construction was undertaken.[46] Between 1885 and 1891, new banks and insurance companies were formed, and the Morrison Street (then

*Pictured here in his laboratory, William C. Che-
ney was a recognized expert in hydroelectric transmission and an early advocate of alternating current. Hired by P.F. Morey to work for the newly
incorporated Willamette Falls Electric Co., Cheney and Morey decided on 125-cycle, 4,000-V AC
dynamos, which were a higher voltage than anything currently being built. In pleading with the
Westinghouse Company to take on the project,
Henry M. Byellsby reportedly told George Westinghouse, "If Cheney wants those machines, build
them. If any man can make them go, he can."
(PGE collections)*

This power line carried the first long-distance transmission of electricity in the United States. The line ran from Willamette Falls in Oregon City (Station A) to downtown Portland, a total distance of 14 miles. (PGE collections)

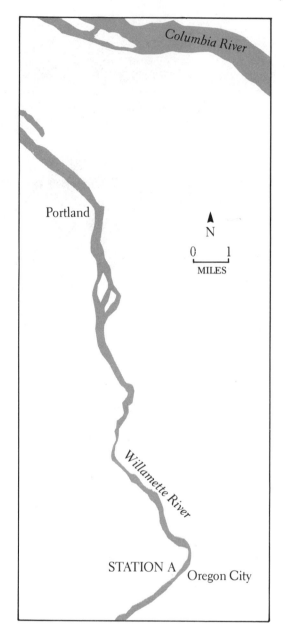

the largest west of the Mississippi), the Railroad (later the Steel), and the Madison Street (renamed the Hawthorne) bridges were built to connect the growing east-side hinterland with the city proper. The Portland Hotel, the city's foremost, was built at the time, and the city's water system was enlarged. Finally, by 1889, the electrification of Portland's horsecar lines had begun. During these years, the city's ten streetcar companies were granted twenty-four new franchises by its council.[47] Although the companies had their own generating plants, the demand for electricity was bound to grow beyond the line's own generating capacity. This was certainly clear to Morey, as it was to the local investors of the day.

When generation from the falls began, the dynamo house that had been built there became known as Station A. The company also erected a substation in Portland at the foot of Southwest Montgomery Street, on land purchased for that purpose and for a general office. In September 1891, the company's directors held a board meeting at the site. Later, an office and substation were built on the east bank of the river at Union Avenue, close to Morrison Street. It received 4,000 v and stepped the load down to 2,000 v for distribution to the east side. The west-side office received the same load and stepped it down to 1,100 v for that part of the city.[48]

The early growth of Willamette Falls Electric was not achieved without competition. In 1888, another streetlighting plan for the west side was attempted by a company operating a small generator at the Smith and Watson Iron Works. The enterprise failed. In 1891, John F. Cordray, the owner of a string of amusement houses in the downtown area, generated electricity from a steam plant at Southwest Third and Yamhill streets, largely to illuminate his own properties. Though a few other businesses along Third Street eventually hooked up to his system, it soon proved unsuccessful and was dismantled.[49]

Nevertheless, the business of generating electrical energy in Portland, at least for Willamette Falls Electric, kept pace with the expansion of the city's population and economy. After 18 January 1891, when Eastham died, Morey was elected president of the company and plunged into a building program to match the city's growth. However, this required a huge infusion of capital. For reasons not entirely clear (but probably because of a desire to remind customers of the recently formed General Electric of Thomas Edison), he sought new funds under the aegis of a reorganized company with a new name. The new company, Portland General Electric, displayed a glittering array of the city's leading business lights who had been enticed into making major investments. They included William S. and William M. Ladd, Charles Swigert, John C. Ainsworth, Henry Failing, Henry Goode, Tyler Woodward, and Fred Holman.

These were men to match both the times and the original company's founders. William S. Ladd, for example, has been said to "fit the prototype of the successful 'self-made man in America' image."[50] Born to a family of modest means in Vermont, he left for California's gold fields at the age of nineteen but after a short time wandered to Portland, where he entered the liquor and saloon business. He did well, amassing enough money to loan some out. Eventually, with a silent partner in San Francisco named Charles E. Tilton, he opened a private bank, which by 1875 was worth more than a million dollars each to Ladd, Tilton, and a third partner.[51] Ladd invested heavily in real estate and gathered in more through seizures of property in cases of defaulted mortgages and bad loans. He was also active in Portland politics. At the age of twenty-eight, he was elected mayor.

Station A exterior, Willamette Falls at Oregon City, 22 February 1890. On 3 June 1889, PGE's predecessor, Willamette Falls Electric, made the first long-distance transmission of electricity in the United States from this site. (PGE collections)

Station A's interior shows the turbine deck of the company's first power plant at Willamette Falls in Oregon City. The first uses of electricity from Station A were for street lighting and operation of electric trolleys. (PGE collections)

An early Portland General Electric line crew circa 1890 in the vicinity of NW 23rd and Johnson streets. (PGE collections)

An 1890 electric bill from Portland General Electric. The cost per 1,000 kilowatt-hours was twenty cents. (PGE collections)

Portland, Oregon,

W. B. Shively,

To Portland General Electric Co., Dr.

Amount Forward,

Incandescent Lighting as per meter

Present state of meter, — 10812 00 watt-hours.

Last state of meter, — 10375 00 "

Constant, X — "

Current Consumed, — 437 00 " @ 20 per M. 8 75

Discount — 1 30

Rental of meter for month — — —

Received payment,

For the Company. 7 45

Charles Swigert was in his early thirties when he invested in the utility. Although not formally trained, he was what today would be called a civil engineer. Before he reached middle age, Swigert, who had arrived in the city from San Francisco to manage an uncle's elevator company, would design and build the first bridge across the Willamette in Portland, construct the city's first electrified street railway, and become the president of both the Chamber of Commerce and the Port Commission. An inveterate builder and entrepreneur, especially where businesses dependent on technologies were concerned, he was instrumental in the city's physical development.

Henry Failing arrived in Portland from New York in 1851 at the age of seventeen. He entered his father's hardware business, but moved rapidly into greater commercial and financial fields. Marrying into Portland's powerful and influential Corbett family, he allied himself with his brother-in-law, Henry Corbett. They obtained control of the city's First National Bank even as they merged their families' respective merchant operations. Failing served two nonconsecutive terms as Portland's mayor and remained an economic and political force in the city throughout his life through his influence with Corbett, a u.s. senator, and their joint ownership of key businesses besides the bank.

John C. Ainsworth was a banker, scion of the fortune of the pioneering Captain John C. Ainsworth, founder and owner of the Ainsworth National Bank and president of the Oregon Steam Navigation Company (forerunner of the Oregon Railway and Navigation Company). The younger Ainsworth improved the family fortune significantly, particularly with his utility investments. Tyler Woodward was an active entrepreneur in the street-railway business.[52]

In short, these were men of substance and energy. The prestige and collective net worth of the major stockholders and the basic fiscal strength of Willamette Falls Electric ensured that the new company would be able to secure a massive infusion of new capital. The funds, which brought capitalization to about $4.25 million, eventually came from a staid eastern investment bank, The Old Colony Trust Company of Boston, then the nation's main financial center for utility investments.[53]

Working with his considerably enhanced treasury, Morey moved with typical vigor to expand. In October 1892, he purchased the Albina Light and Power Company, a small three-year-old firm founded by Swigert, which was providing power to a few customers in the city's near northeast section. Early in the next year, Morey began negotiations with the city council to purchase "machinery, material, and pole line now in use in connection with the city east side electric light plant" at Powell and Milwaukie streets. Part of this agreement was a commitment by Portland General Electric to power all arc lights on the city's line from that station for no more than $9.72 per month each for any arc lamps that might be required.[54]

By 4 March 1895, construction of a new powerhouse, begun in 1893 on the west side of the Willamette at the falls, was completed. With a number of other new facilities that Portland General Electric built before the turn of the century, it was part of a specific response to electric-load growth on Portland's west side. This growth was stimulated largely by the success of the local and interurban electric railroads in the city. The rise of the electric railway had proved economically and socially beneficial in the larger eastern and midwestern cities after the Civil War and was subsequently embraced with enthusiasm in the West. They were clean, nonpolluting (as opposed

THE PORTLAND GENERAL ELECTRIC
COMPANY, in all its early incarnations, had a
tremendous impact on the physical development
of the entire Portland area. Since most Portlanders did not own horses, and since it was impractical to walk long, muddy distances to and from
work every day, few ventured far from the business district until the first streetcars had been
installed. Before construction could start in an
area, streetcar lines had to be established so that
new residents could get to work. The first horsecars were in use in Portland by 1871; in the years
to follow, investors wishing to develop the suburbs of Portland put their money into new lines
serving Albina, East Portland, the West Hills,
Multnomah, Hillsdale, Portland Heights, and
Hillsboro.

In 1887, the Willamette Iron Bridge Company
built the Morrison Street Bridge, the first to connect West and East Portland. Like others that
followed, the Morrison Street Bridge was open to
general traffic, but the developers reserved the
right to operate a streetcar line across it. The next
to be built was the Steel Bridge, which opened in
1889. It carried railroad trains on its lower deck
and local traffic and streetcars on its upper one.
Two months later, the Fifth Street Bridge connected Albina and East Portland. In the next
year, work began on the Madison Street Bridge.
These bridges integrated Albina, Portland, and
East Portland, so that in 1891 the three communities consolidated into one city—Portland; the
metropolis by then embraced a population of
88,200 and forty miles of streetcar track.

By 1892 four kinds of streetcars were running
in the Portland area: electric cars throughout the
city, cable cars up the hills, steam cars to the
suburbs, and a few horsecars on First Street. The
next year, the East Side Railway Company began
regular service to Oregon City, establishing what
was probably the first long-distance interurban
service in the country. After witnessing the first
long-distance transmission of electricity in 1889,
Portland had racked up yet another technological
"first."

AS ELECTRIC APPLIANCES were developed
and patented, Portland Railway Light and Power
quickly began to promote the purchase and use of
electric machinery. The company called this
sales drive "load building." As early as 1905, it
advertised electric irons and teakettles, with electric chafing dishes, lamps, radiators, grills, refrigerators and curling irons appearing in the next
few years. Company bulletins even advertised
such items as electric baby-bottle warmers, cigar
lighters, foot warmers, and personalized waffle
irons.

Early advertisements place ecstatic faith in the
abilities of electric appliances. A 1906 ad for
irons promised that their use would "save one's
complexion, clothes, temper, money, health
[and] time." Another page cautioned in all seri-
ousness that "an office without Electric Fans
during the heated term means the inevitable
illness and absence of some of the employes,
work delayed and general disorganization."

Company publications made it clear that electricity was quickly becoming an indispensable
part of everyday life and printed many items on
its use, including a recipe for "Frog Legs a la
electric." In the twenties and thirties "building
the load" became a responsibility of the whole
PEPCO "family." Lists of the numbers of shares of
company stock sold by employees were constantly
published. Marketing drives exhorted employees
to turn in names of friends interested in buying
an electric appliance. If a salesperson made a
sale, the referring employee would receive a
commission of a few dollars.

Horse trolley at SE Grand and Morrison in 1884.
(PGE collections)

Cable line to Portland Heights, Chapman Street
above Mill Street. (PGE collections)

34

to horsecars, which left mountains of manure in their wake), safe, and carried large numbers of passengers relatively quickly, quietly, and cheaply from place to place. This delighted city officials as well as business and social leaders, because it meant that the working class need not congregate in the unsightly, overcrowded, and depressing tenement housing characteristic of nineteenth-century central cities. The tenements had been built in core areas because they were close to the large industrial concerns, which themselves were sources of urban ugliness, noise, and filth. The convenient electric trolleys eventually carried both the working class and the factories away from the central districts of American cities, leaving them to the well-to-do and their residences and to commercial interests. In so doing, they helped to create new residential and industrial areas that also required electricity.[55]

Portland General Electric met this trend in the context of Morey's expansion plan with the installation of equipment at the Montgomery Street substation, which gave it a capacity of 10,000 v, and the addition of Station B in 1895, on the west bank of the Willamette between the river and the ship channel in Oregon City. Three 6,000-v revolving armature AC generators and two 500-v DC generators powered by two waterwheels were housed at Station B. They were specifically designed to transmit electricity to the trolleys.[56]

CIRCUIT FOR SUCCESS

In retrospect, the rise of a successful, privately owned electric utility in Portland seems inevitable. If ever there were an idea whose time had come, in the last third of the nineteenth century, it was that of electricity. Everything in the American economy and society pointed to it: the rapid industrialization, the shifting of the population from the frontier to the city, the introduction of energy-dependent technologies such as the telephone and the trolley, and the rise of national markets. Largely gone were the self-sufficient farmer and the independent craftsman who used their own muscle, animals, nearby waterpower, or naturally occurring fuels to address modest needs. In their place was the factory worker and urban dweller who required energy from a central source of supply—energy that was cheap, reliable, and efficient. All these developments demanded electricity's appearance and widespread use.

In the case of Portland, add to these conditions the alertness and competitiveness exhibited by men like Morey and Eastham. Animated by Eastham's classic western small-town boosterism, which saw in Willamette Falls an unsurpassable chance to lift his own fortunes as well as those of his city, and the boundless, ever-optimistic enterprise of Morey, the archetype of the Gilded Age businessman, and the rise of the first Portland General Electric Company was bound to be swift and sure.

Such men were doing much the same thing throughout the nation and succeeding in much the same way. In 1860, no central electrical stations existed anywhere in the United States. Forty-two years later, in 1902, the issued capitalization and funded debt of commercial electric stations was $627.5 million. Other urban services also showed phenomenal growth. In 1902, street railways were capitalized and owed funded debt of more than two billion dollars, while waterworks were funded at a sum somewhat greater than a billion dollars.[57]

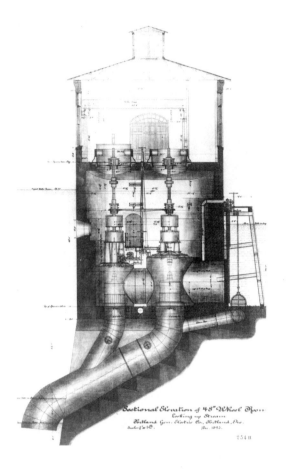

Cut-away schematic drawing of one section of a generating unit for Station B (later named the Sullivan Plant) in Oregon City. (PGE collections)

Various companies' bases for incandescent lamps before their design was standardized by the electrical industry. (PGE collections)

Bases for Incandescent Lamps.

Edison.

Thomson-Houston.

United States.

Westinghouse or Sawyer-Man.

Schaefer or National.

Perkins or Mather.

Hawkeye.

Brush-Swan.

Typical alternating current switchboard as used in central stations during the 1890s. This is a Thomson-Houston switchboard. Alternators and exciter rheostats are on the bottom row of the wooden frame. Above them are two rows of 12 current indicators and four knife switches. On the second row from the top are lightning arrestors, and on uppermost row, potential transformers. High voltage current (1,100 or 2,200 volts at 125 cycles per second—in contrast to today's 60-cycle standard) flows directly from overhead to the current indicators and switches. (PGE collections)

In 1900, gasworks, their plants, and distribution systems were at half a billion dollars, approximately twenty times the 1860 figure.[58] In other words, businessmen were eager to involve themselves in urban services.

Electrical generation was among the most attractive kind of urban service in which the business-minded could engage. There was a dual market for it in homes and businesses; it was safer than gas; much less social risk was involved in electricity than the water and sewage businesses, with their considerations of public health; it was, by nature, oligopolistic in its conduct; and local politicians disliked increasing the municipal debt to fund utility services, an activity that was costly and essentially at the mercy of the law of supply and demand.[59]

The founders of Willamette Falls Electric and Portland General Electric had, thus, acquired for themselves a remarkable but prudent opportunity for investment. It seems clear that they could hardly fail. Moreover, they all but locked themselves into success when they secured the participation of eight members of Portland's business elite. Fred Holman was one of the city's most prestigious lawyers. Between 1885 and 1905, the Ladds held investments in twenty-two Portland firms, including the city's leading bank. Henry Failing had financial positions in nine ventures besides Portland General Electric. John Ainsworth was in six businesses, including the Ainsworth National Bank. Charles Swigert had investments in nine firms.[60]

They were also men of prominence and wealth. In 1903, Morey, Ainsworth, Henry Goode, and William M. Ladd were said to have personal worth in excess of three hundred thousand dollars each.[61] In short, it is not imprudent to say that if these men could not guarantee the success of a business venture in Portland, nobody could.

Yet it is ultimately unsatisfying merely to state that shrewd and ambitious men found for themselves a tame goose capable of laying golden eggs. The prime movers, Morey and Eastham, were visionaries, even in the context of their day, which seems to us rife with men of foresight. Undertaking long-distance transmission of electricity probably seemed eccentric to many in 1889. Others laughed, as we have noted, at the faith Morey and Cheney showed in alternating current. Morey, an engineer, understood technological potential, but it was Eastham, a lawyer, who, when he looked at Willamette Falls, saw an enormous engine of economic growth. If theirs was not a heroic gamble, it was nonetheless one requiring courage, commitment, and creativity. Men steeped in the characteristic enthusiasm and values of the middle class of the late-nineteenth century, they led a city into the twentieth.

2 THE MAKING OF A MONOPOLY

PHOENIXLIKE, A NEW COMPANY arose from the ashes of the various small utilities consolidat-ed under Portland General Electric. The new entity immediately experienced a period of growth. From 1895 to 1920, the company quickly became a Portland institution, but a protean one that presented a variety of faces and a different name to the community. A large and growing electrical utility, the city's major trolley company, a major force in the Lewis and Clark Exposition (Portland's tribute to its first half century), an impersonal monopoly, a social and political force in the life of Portland—these were all facets of Portland General Electric. The nature and extent of the company's activities seemed inevitably to thrust the company's principals further into roles of leadership in the city's highest councils. In the middle years of this period, the same activities also brought them into frequent conflict with reform-minded politicians and citizens.

From 1895 to 1902, Parker Morey made great strides in Portland General Electric's generat-ing capacity. This was in part a result of the public's acceptance of electricity as a safe, depend-able, and altogether necessary source of energy. Nationwide, utilities and manufacturers of electrical appliances, lights, and industrial machines took every opportunity to trumpet the efficiency and cost-saving features of their products. The *Bulletin of the Portland General Electric Company*, which went out to the company's customers, was full of photographs of the most modern local homes and radiantly lighted office buildings. "Effective Use of Incandescent Lights Outlining Meier & Frank Company's Department Store Building and Interior Electric Illumination" was the caption to one of them illustrating a brief essay in the *Bulletin* entitled "Store Lighting That Pays." The essay admonished retailers that "proper illumination of the store is a question which the enterprising man of business considers of vital interest."[1] In the same issue, manufacturers were awakened to the horrors of "The Wasteful Steam Plant." Naturally, the remedy was electric power: "you use what you need, when you need it, and where you need it. There is neither waste of power nor of money."[2] This held an undeniable allure for a generation of businessmen nurtured on the "gospel of efficiency," a label historians have used to describe those aspects of Progressivism dedicated to scientific management. It was made even more potent by the rise of the engineering profession. The engineering ethic loathed waste, and businessmen avidly sought the advice of engineers, one more species of experts to which the age was attracted.[3]

When the public expressed fears about electrical energy's possible harms, the company and local newspapers allayed those concerns with exhaustive and sympathetic reportage of disquieting incidents. The *Oregonian* detailed the electrocution of Edgar Mayer, a youthful employee of Portland General Electric, in 1895. "Death in a Live Wire," the paper called it.[4] Describing the events leading up to the incident, the story explained that Mayer had inexplicably picked up a live wire. Had the boy not been an asthmatic with a weak heart, the 1,000-v shock might not have been lethal, the story claimed.

Against this steady drumbeat of effective publicity, Morey kept the company moving and expanding. He turned his attention to capital improvement and expansion, taking advantage not only of electricity's acceptance but of the city's surging growth. Electricity's marketability took on real meaning in this context. From the nineties, when according to the *City Directory* Portland's population began at about 50,560, to when it reached about 93,000 in 1902, Morey committed Portland General Electric's resources to expansion of capacity and improvement of existing generating facilities. Station B, or the Sullivan Plant, as it came to be called in honor of its designer, Thomas Sullivan, had been the first such step. Its capacity was expanded in January 1896 with the addition of a third generator and soon afterward a fourth unit to supply power for interurban rail lines and to excite the plant's AC generators. In 1897, four 750-kw generating units and alternators from Station A were added, only to be replaced in 1899 with 500-kw revolving field generators, with a similar machine added to the No. 5 section of the plant. In 1899, Morey began a further expansion of Station B with two additional generation sections, nos. 12 and 13, which were completed in 1903. In all, seven additional sections were added to Station B. In 1897, Station A, by that time obsolete and redundant, was shut down.[5]

Station B's increased capacity led to the construction of a new building at the Alder Street substation, which was topped by what became known as "The Tower," where all lines to and from the substations converged.[6] The substations at Montgomery and Water and at east Morrison and Union streets were abandoned when the new substation came on-line.

Impatient with the old, and fascinated by new technology as he was, Morey constantly planned for better as well as greater generating capacity. With electricity an established fact in Portland's daily life, he reassessed the company's commitment to the falls as its sole power source.

*An advertisement from the 19 August 1905 Port-
land Evening Telegram. (OHS neg. OrHi 08730)*

*An evening photo of an electrically lit store window
showing the latest fashions for the seashore. The
photo was in the August 1906 Bulletin of the Portland General Electric Company. (PGE collections)*

A *portion of the pressroom of the Irwin Hodson Company, a Portland printing company still in existence today, where electric power was used in printing, lithographing, bookbinding and embossing.* Bulletin of the Portland Railway Light and Power Company, *January 1908. (PGE collections)*

"Remarkably effective photograph of a section of Portland's decorative street illumination showing complete detail of buildings for several blocks. Picture taken at Second and Washington streets at 10:30 P.M. looking up (west) Washington Street. Four minute exposure. Photo by George F. Holman." Original caption from January 1906 Bulletin of the Portland General Electric Company. *(PGE collections)*

Downtown Portland at the corner of Fifth and Morrison in 1905. Pioneer Courthouse is to the left and in the background stands the proud Portland Hotel. Notice the electric lights festooned between the utility poles. (OHS neg. OrHi 13134)

ELECTRIC FLAT IRONS

THE "STAY-HOT" KIND

ON 30 DAYS' TRIAL—FREE

Saves your complexion.
Saves your clothes.
Saves your temper.
Saves your money.
Saves weary steps.
Saves your health.
Saves your time.

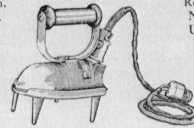

Requires no changing.
No scorching, no dirt.
Uniform temperature.
Is never too cold.
Is never too hot.
Is always ready.
No reheating.

All equipment is delivered with each iron, which may be attached
to any electric lamp socket in any room.

An Opportunity to Test One of the Greatest of All Household Conveniences Before Buying

SELECT THE STYLE YOU DESIRE

STYLE No. 1—Regular household, 6-lb. Flat Iron.

STYLE No. 2—Nickel-Plated, 3-lb. Smoothing Iron, for Shirtwaists, Etc.

Fill in coupon—Specifying style of iron you prefer, and mail to us. The iron will be delivered promptly, free of charge.

CUT OUT COUPON.

- -

PORTLAND GENERAL ELECTRIC COMPANY,
First and Alder Streets, Portland, Oregon.

Gentlemen—You may deliver to me one Electric Flat Iron, No._____
which I agree to try, and if unsatisfactory, to return to you within 30 days
from date of delivery. If I do not return it at that time you may charge
same to my account. It is understood that no charge will be made for the iron
if I return it within 30 days.

Name_____ Address_____

DEPARTMENT B

Flat iron advertisement on the back of the Bulletin of the Portland General Electric Company, *October 1906. (PGE collections)*

Electric coffee maker advertised in the Bulletin of the Portland General Electric Company, *January 1906. (PGE collections)*

COFFEE MAKING BY ELECTRICITY

ELECTRIC APPLIANCES began to appear immediately after the light bulb:

1882   Iron

1889   Sewing machine

1899   First refrigerator patented

1890   Range

1891   Fan

1892   Heater

1901   Vacuum cleaner

1910   Toaster

1915   Clothes washer

1918   Dishwasher

1926   Pop-up toaster

This illustration shows "economy in the dining room" through the use of an "economical turn-down lamp." This can effect savings because "servants leave the light burning with the result that bills often seem exorbitant." The turn-down lamp "can go from bright to dim." It is also versatile because "in homes where there are no servants the saving is the same." Bulletin of Portland Railway Light and Power Company, January 1908. (PGE collections)

FOR PEOPLE WHO DON'T USE ELECTRICITY

Don't expect ironing to be a pleasure.

Don't knock the kerosene lamp over.

Don't imagine your home looks modern.

Don't chafe at the alcohol chafing dish.

Don't answer the door bell carelessly at night without a porch light.

Don't storm because your lace curtains caught fire.

Don't kick because your business is "bad."

Don't blame the engineer because you can't get power all night.

Don't scold your workers because you can't increase your production.

Don't forget that 50 percent of your steam power goes to drive shafting and belting.

Don't neglect to read the Bulletin, it will make you Electric-Light-Wise.

Don't forget our telephone is private exchange 13.

From the Bulletin of the Portland General Electric Company, January 1906.

Electric irons and electric lights in use in a Portland laundry. (Bulletin of the Portland Railway Light and Power Company, *March 1907. PGE collections*)

*Looking from Substation A east on Alder during a
1907 ice storm. The substation remained in the
Electric Building until 1942. (PGE collections)*

Power outages at Station B caused by storms illustrated that it was unrealistic to depend on one plant in Oregon City to service the ever-growing Portland market. Consequently, in 1901, Portland General Electric constructed a steam plant, Station C, at Front and Nicolai streets in what today is the northwest quadrant of Portland.[7] The plant was close to the Eastern and Western Lumber Company, which supplied it with cheap hog fuel (wood waste that was easily burned). Originally, Station C was equipped with generators from Station A. By 1905, it had a rated capacity of 2,150 kw, produced by an 800-kw, 550-v railway service generator, rope driven by a 1,600-HP steam engine. It also contained one 750-kw, 10,000-v, 33-cycle generator, rope driven by a 1,000-HP cross-compound condensing steam engine and two marine-type, compound steam engines direct-connected to a 400-kw and 200-kw, 550-v railway generator. By 1905, it had generated a total of 3,851,892 kwh.[8]

Morey died on 7 July 1904, a wealthy, much honored citizen. He had secured his status, if riches were not enough, by marrying Edward Eastham's widow, Clara Caulfield Eastham.[9] His death, like those of other local entrepreneurs of his age—Henry Failing and Henry Corbett—marked the passing of the old-style nineteenth-century business leader. The Oregonian's obituary of him aptly characterized his life. "He had deep foresight," the paper said, "and everything he attempted turned out as he anticipated. It is through the work of men of his stamp that the large enterprises of the country are built up and the progress of the world is carried on. Mr. Morey was a man with nothing little in his nature."[10]

By 1895, Morey had begun to remove himself from the day-to-day operations of the company. He could do this confidently because the company was attracting a new generation of talented and aggressive managers and consultants, drawn by the allure of the new and glamorous field of electrical generation. Two of these young men were of particular importance to the company's history. The first to become associated with the company was a young lawyer named Franklin T. Griffith, who was retained by Portland General Electric in 1894 to handle its legal affairs. He was not to become a full-time employee of the firm for some years, but his impact on it would be great.

If Griffith's influence came later, Henry W. Goode made an immediate and significant impression. Largely self-educated, Goode had arrived in Portland in 1890 at the age of twenty-eight from St. Paul, Minnesota, as manager of the Northwest Thomson-Houston Company, which in 1892 was merged with Edison Electric to form General Electric.[11] The merger occurred mainly because of the complementary nature of the two firms' patents. Thomson-Houston was a force in arc lighting and alternating currents, while Edison was a leader in DC generation and transmission as well as street railways. The combination, as Thomas P. Hughes has pointed out, was a significant step toward General Electric's early dominance of the utility industry.[12] Morey, who was trying to capitalize on the reflected glory of Edison's company in naming his own Portland General Electric Company, hired Goode away in 1892 and made him vice president and general manager of the utility. At thirty, Goode was youthful or "smooth shaved," as Henry Reed, a sometime business colleague and a newspaper reporter, put it.[13] In 1902, when Morey retired from the presidency, Goode succeeded him.

48   Goode moved quickly through the ranks, rising from his initial appointment as vice president and general manager to the executive committee where he served as assistant secretary. When he

Thomas Sullivan was PGE's hydraulic engineer from 1890 until his death in 1940. He designed and built the dam at Willamette Falls and PGE's Station B, both located at Oregon City. Station B was later renamed the Sullivan Plant in his honor. (PGE collections)

Henry W. Goode succeeded Parker F. Morey in the presidency of Portland General Electric. Goode arrived in Portland in 1890, working as a manager for Northwest Thomson-Houston Company which merged with Edison Electric to form General Electric in 1892. He saw the company through its early years of growth and through the success of the Lewis and Clark Exposition. He died of pneumonia in 1907. (PGE collections)

49

accepted the presidency, he was only forty. A quiet, courtly man (he had a long line of Southern forebears), Goode was Morey's opposite in many ways. Where Morey, according to Reed, was a combative, technically oriented deal maker, always pressing his next project, Goode was calm, "unassuming, gracious, soft-spoken, and never in a hurry."[14] In short, Goode was not a nineteenth-century entrepreneur, but a twentieth-century manager.

Goode served as president for five years, until his death from pneumonia in 1907. According to Reed, the early years of his term were somewhat troubled. Although the company continued to grow and prosper, Goode was held in low esteem by its majority stockholders, the Pratt family of Philadelphia.[15] They frequently thwarted his plans for capital improvements before 1905, often canceling his orders for new machinery without discussion. Despite this, and a general economic slowdown in the first years of the twentieth century, Goode was able to add capacity and keep Portland General Electric growing. His strength was primarily in marketing and sales, and he immediately recognized how the company's future could be insured against competition. When he assumed the presidency, the company was receiving twenty cents per kwh for its electricity, which he knew was too high a price. Gradually, over the course of his stewardship, the company lowered rates to a more marketable 9.74 cents per kwh.[16]

In 1902, Station E was added to the company's capacity. The construction of the station, which burned hog fuel for steam generation, began in 1902, near 21st and Nicolai, not too far from Station C. It was the result of one of Goode's major attributes—his ardent boosterism. He understood that it was important for Portland General Electric to be a force for civic improvement and economic development. Under his management, the company began to identify itself and its product closely with local, state, and regional economic development and civic betterment. The *Bulletin* was a favored medium of this effort. The April 1906 issue, for instance, noted that the company was supporting a "Made in Oregon" display at the windows of businesses along Morrison and Washington streets downtown, scheduled for the following month. The displays would illustrate "in striking degree how largely the question of electric power enters into the true economics of domestic production."[17] A later issue in the same year featured a flattering portrait of Salem, "the Center of Oregon's Richest Valley," and pictured the State Capitol, which, not surprisingly, was fully electrified by Portland General Electric.[18] Another issue boasted that Portland used more electric light per capita than any other city in the Northwest. The article called Portland the second largest volume wheat-shipping port in the world. The "inevitable" conclusion to infer from such a fact, said the article, was that "there exists [in Portland] the true spirit of advancement, the uplift that makes for the highest attainment in commercial progress."[19] The coda exhorted readers, "At this epoch, when widespread publicity for the advertising of city and state is looked upon as the greatest factor . . . of commercial progress and civic development, it is of utmost importance to include the consideration of existent economic advantages such as . . . CHEAP electric power for manufacturing, as among the valuable features of any advertising propaganda."[20]

Goode set himself the task of making the company "a popular public utility" in the eyes of Portlanders.[21] The new generation station was critical to fulfilling this goal, as it would enable the company to light the world's fair scheduled for the spring of 1905 in Portland. The fair's planners had anticipated that the generation of electricity would be difficult, since neither of the city's two major utilities had the capacity to illuminate the fairgrounds and service its regular customers. Moreover, the organizers lacked the money to build their own electrical plant.

The civic-minded Goode boldly seized the initiative by traveling to New York, where he implored his major stockholders to invest some three hundred thousand dollars in a new plant that would initially be dedicated to meeting the electrical needs of the fairgrounds. He promised that the fair would so stimulate the local economy that, in its aftermath, even more capacity would be required of Portland General Electric to keep pace with the increased demand for electricity. He argued forcefully that it was the company's duty to the city to help the extravaganza achieve its goals. The executive committee reluctantly granted his wish, with the stipulation that he would be held personally responsible for the results.[22]

The idea for the world's fair—the Lewis and Clark Centennial and American Exposition Oriental Fair, as it officially came to be known—had germinated in the mind of Portland businessman Dan McAllen as early as 1895 as a way to stimulate the local economy, still sluggish after the disastrous nationwide depression of 1893.[23] The business community had other priorities at the time. Still, the idea held fascination for a few. World fairs enjoyed a paradoxical vogue in the last years of the nineteenth century. While they were always exciting, and frequently enhanced the prestige of the cities in which they were held, their consequences could range from the merely unprofitable to the financially disastrous. It is difficult to fathom why local business leaders were so eager to plunge into them.[24]

The idea took root in the minds of Col. Henry Dosch, a local manufacturer, and U.S. Rep. Thomas Tongue of Hillsboro. They advanced the view that a fair might be good for Portland and the rest of the state. By early 1900, the idea had gained sufficient currency for the Board of Trade to have established a committee to explore its feasibility. In December that year, the Oregon Historical Society endorsed the fair, proposed the Lewis and Clark motif, and suggested June 1905 as the appropriate date for its beginning. A pledge of financial support for the project from the state legislature was accompanied by the formation of a commission chaired by Portland's leading business figure, Henry Corbett.

Corbett, Harvey Scott, editor of the *Oregonian*, and J.W. Long of the Board of Trade led the effort to generate financial support from the business community, citizens throughout the state, and other governments in the West. The eventual response was heartening. Large local businesses, labor unions (which were promised that construction on the buildings and grounds of the fair would be performed exclusively by organized labor), and three thousand Portland citizens quickly oversubscribed the initial offering of stock in the venture, which, against all precedent, was intended as a profit-making enterprise.[25]

In 1902, the site of the exposition was chosen. Guild's Lake, a 406-acre plot of uninviting marshland in the far-northwest quadrant of the city, was selected. Already served by two trolley lines, the parcel could be leased cheaply and was vacant, except for the odd farmstead.[26]

As a leading Portland businessman whose company depended on economic development (but perhaps also because he had put so much pressure on himself with respect to Station E in its relationship to the exposition), Goode found himself inexorably drawn into the event's planning and administration. In October 1903, he became the exposition's director general—the equivalent of a general manager—at a salary of five hundred dollars a month. He served under Harvey Scott, who had assumed the presidency on Corbett's death in March 1903. Scott resigned less than a year after taking the position, and on 8 August 1904 Goode assumed the presidency, while remaining director general. In his dual role, he was responsible for almost every detail of the complex preparations and eventual operations of the Lewis and Clark Exposition. There were major and minor crises, including a strike by the building trades over the hiring of nonunion workmen at the fairgrounds and a minor flap over a proposal to keep the fair open on Sundays, a prospect that displeased the pious.[27]

The exposition's economic impact began to be felt by local businesses, not the least of which was Portland General Electric. Henry Reed, secretary to the fair's board of directors, reported on 7 July 1904 that the executive committee had let a contract "for furnishing electric current during the Exposition to the Portland General Electric Company, at the contract price of $82,000."[28] The company also rented transformers and generating equipment to the exposition and contracted to supply "30,000 or more regular frosted incandescent lamps, at 16¼¢ each . . . [and] 5,000 or more spherical incandescent lamps, frosted, for 53¢ each."[29] It might be surmised that Goode's preeminent position in the fair's hierarchy, and the fact that its electrical engineer was James R. Thompson of Portland General Electric, gave the company an edge for the electrical business, but there is no evidence that the company was anything but the lowest, and in some cases the only, bidder for the contracts it won. Indeed, where the electrification award was concerned, Portland General Electric, owing to its generating capacity, was the only possible provider.

The exposition was operating under some major handicaps. More than half of Guild's Lake was under water when it was leased. The U.S. Congress, tired of throwing away federal funds on the grandiose but invariably money-losing procession of world fairs of the late nineteenth century, grudgingly appropriated a mere 22 percent of the exposition's original request. Despite such difficulties, the Lewis and Clark Exposition became a success, financially as well as aesthetically. Although the scale was less grand than that of Chicago's Columbian Exposition of 1893, the grounds and buildings recalled the White City of the earlier event. Mainly in a Spanish renaissance style, the structures were temporary in nature and appealing, if not beautiful, by day. At night, they blazed with electrical lights. Proudly, Portland General Electric called attention to this fact in the *Bulletin*. Describing the effects of the lighting that outlined the various shapes of the exposition's edifices, the publication labeled the scene "a marvelous twentieth-century picture."[30] It went on to note smugly that this was also "a striking object lesson of the tremendous resources of the Portland General Electric Company . . . [and] a demonstration of the absolute reliability of the service."[31]

In the end, the exposition returned a profit to its backers of $84,461, an unheard-of outcome for such an enterprise. Speaker of the House "Uncle" Joe Cannon remarked of this feat, "Mr. Goode has done what no other man has done."[32] The historian of the Lewis and Clark Exposition, Carl Abbott, has estimated that it brought $8 million into Portland. He calculated that it created some six thousand jobs, five thousand of them in services and a thousand in construction.[33] It also catalyzed a real-estate and general economic boom which saw extraordinary growth between 1905 and 1913. Goode and Portland General Electric could take much of the credit. And, as Abbott has also noted, their role in the exposition was a harbinger of a dawning era in the city.

As contrasted with Corbett and Scott, his predecessors in the presidency of the exposition, Goode was a man of the new century with a professional approach to business. Like the nationally famous entrepreneurs they resembled—Vanderbilt, Rockefeller, Huntington, Fiske—Corbett and Scott were "operating owners," as the historian Thomas Cochrane has called them. Their identities and egos were inextricable from their business. Their civic-mindedness battened ultimately on the potential it had for personal gain and stature in the eyes of the community. Men like Goode, on the other hand, were managers, "career men," in the telling phrase of Mabel Newcomer. Their methods and motives were at the service of the modern large-scale corporations they ran. Their job was to enhance what a later age would call the "image" of the businesses they oversaw, not their own reputations. Thus, where his predecessors saw personal triumph in the fair, Goode saw a possible corporate triumph in civic leadership.[34] His company was a new one in the infant industry of electrical power. Speaking at the fair's opening ceremonies, Charles Fairbanks, vice president of the United States, echoed the late William McKinley in remarking that "expositions are the time-keepers of progress." In the case of Portland's world's fair, the event was a vision of the city's emerging future.

Goode had brought credit to himself and his company at the exposition. According to Reed, this fact was not lost on the Pratts of Philadelphia, who thereafter exhibited more faith in Goode and stopped countermanding his orders.[35] Ironically, there was a stiff price to be paid for the company's immersion in the fair's preparations. Minutes of the Portland General Electric Board of Directors' meeting of 13 December 1904 note that the company's work on lines for the fair and repairs to existing lines to downtown Portland in preparation for the anticipated influx of visitors precluded expansion into the less settled suburban areas of the city.[36] Residents of St. Johns complained that they were being neglected. They had been waiting for electrification impatiently for some months since the work had begun, while other parts of Portland and the vicinity had already received service.[37]

The year after the exposition ended, in 1906, a firm retained to examine the company's books found Portland General Electric's accounting system in serious disarray. "Generally speaking," said the examiners in the opaque language of auditors, "the accounts are not upon such a good basis as in the prior two years; the business has increased beyond the staff and matters of moment come before our notice."[38] In other words, the company had required the full attention of its chief, who was still beset with the details of closing the exposition. Fortunately, these problems were easily corrected, and in the report on the 1907 audit the accountants were able to give a more sanguine overview of the company's condition.[39]

In any case, these were minor problems that indicated as much that Portland General Electric was busy and growing as that it was temporarily ill managed. Goode was generally an able manager, especially where labor relations were concerned. At one point, soon after he resumed full-time management of the firm following the fair, a labor organizer appeared in Portland to

Commemorative engraving for the Lewis and Clark Exposition. (OHS neg. OrHi 21913)

Souvenir ticket from the Lewis and Clark Exposition. (OHS neg. 68660)

Entrance to the fairgrounds. (OHS neg. 25733)

Visiting dignitaries to the Lewis and Clark Exposition. Vice President Charles Fairbanks is the tallest man in the front row. To his right stands Thomas Edison. To Fairbanks' left stands Henry W. Goode, president of Portland General Electric and director general of the exposition. (OHS neg. 48986)

THE EXPOSITION used one hundred thousand electric lamps, two hundred fifty miles of wire, one hundred fifty transformers.

Oregonian, 2 January 1905

PRESIDENT H.W. GOODE contributed an electric sign to the exposition that said "1905," and was placed on the summit of a hill. Its dimensions were 30 feet by 110 feet, and it could be seen from thirty miles away.

A night picture of the Lewis and Clark Exposition taken from Cornell Road. (Ashford Collection, OHS neg. 28077)

A view from the Grand Stairway of the Bridge of
Nations and the U.S. Government Building.
(Ashford collection, OHS neg. 28733)

The amusement arcade at the Lewis and Clark exposition was called The Trail. This dancing girl was from the "Streets of Cairo" exhibit. In the background, a salesman holds a light aloft, the better to show his wares. (OHS neg. 25123)

The Fair Japan Exhibit on The Trail at the Lewis and Clark Exposition. (OHS neg. 36789)

prepare a strike against the company. Goode, whose conciliatory manner made him a popular boss, halted the unrest. Essentially by the force of his personality and the apparently credible promise of fair treatment, he convinced the workers to decertify the union and to form a company union with himself as its head.[40] American workers of the day were not anxious to join militant labor unions and resisted organization unless pressed by recalcitrant bosses.

Goode's health, during and after his grueling years at the exposition, was fragile. When he resumed his full-time duties with the utility he had only a short time to live. He presided over some of the company's most ambitious undertakings, which involved decisions that shaped it for years to come. For instance, Portland's enormous growth, occasioned by the success of the exposition, had created an extremely tight financial picture for the company, whose principal investors could not raise sufficient funds from their own local sources to seize the opportunities afforded by the city's expansion. As a result, in 1905 they were forced to seek capital from Wall Street. Thirty-year bonds aggregating $8 million at 5 percent were sold.[41]

Goode was also instrumental in the massive merger that eventually subsumed Portland General Electric and occurred over the years 1905 to 1907. This event brought together (under the new name of Portland Railway Light and Power) Portland General Electric; the Portland Railway Company; Citizens' Light and Traction Company of Salem; the Vancouver Light and Traction Company; the Union Light and Power Company of Silverton, Mt. Angel, and Woodburn; and Oregon Water Power and Railway Company, and the Oregon City Locks, which were owned by Portland General Electric. The *Oregonian* of 4 May 1906 speculated that it was the biggest merger ever in the history of the Pacific Coast, and certainly in the annals of Northwest business. The combined $30 million value of the companies was huge by the standards of the day, especially in the region. The paper described the real meaning of that figure: "Every electrical light, power and traction company in the lower Willamette Valley has been merged into one vast consolidation of interests. Every mile of electric railway and every horsepower of electric energy generated within a 50-mile radius of Portland have been brought under the same ownership and will be operated by one management." Portland General Electric alone owned the whole electric power and lighting system of Portland and its suburbs, the paper claimed. The merger, too big for local investors to bring off, was funded by a syndicate of what the *Oregonian* called "Eastern capital."[42] E. W. Clark and Company, Philadelphia investment bankers, secured the controlling interest in the venture, with New York banking houses, J. and W. Seligman and the Portland General Electric principal, Charles Pratt and Company, participating. The Clarks, previously minor stockholders in the company, had assumed the lead in Portland General Electric's affairs as the Pratt family's interests had receded.

In the context of the times, this apparently staggering transaction was actually evidence of a trend toward consolidation in American industry generally and in utilities in particular. Although the Sherman Antitrust Act had been on the books since 1890 and large firms were still a tiny minority of American enterprise, "bigness" was the dominant mode, especially between 1898 and 1904, when the majority of the great American trusts were formed. In this period, some 234 trusts were organized; 5,288 concerns merged into 318 industrial combinations; over 1,000 railroads allied with 7 major cities; and 111 utilities gained control of 1,336 generating plants.

Station	Type	Location	Dates of Operation
A	hydro	Willamette Falls (Oregon City)	1889-1897
B	hydro	Estacada	1895-
C	steam	21st & Sherlock (Portland)	1901-1911
D	steam	Chapman St. (Portland)	1905-
E	steam	adjoining "C" (Portland)	1904-
F	steam	E. Lincoln St.	1906-1911
G	hydro	Cazadero (Faraday)	1907-
H	steam	Salem	1906-
I	steam	Vancouver	1906-1911
J	hydro	Silverton	1906-1933
K	steam	Boring	1903-1917
L	steam	Portland	1910-
M	hydro	River Mill (Clackamas)	1911-
N	steam	Portsmouth	1911-1922
O	hydro	Bull Run	1912-
P	hydro	Oak Grove	1924-
Q	hydro	Scott Mills (Oak Creek)	1917-1953
R			
S	hydro	Salem Ditch	

THE MAN RESPONSIBLE for bringing the first eastern capital into a Portland General Electric predecessor was a Portland banker named Abbott Mills. Born and educated in the East, he moved West, and within a few years cofounded the Security Savings and Trust Company, a bank closely allied with the First National Bank.

One of Mills' financial interests was in transportation. He was heavily involved in financing early streetcar companies and in 1904 was instrumental in preparing the merger of the Portland Railway Company with the City and Suburban Railway Company. In preparing this consolidation, Mills corresponded frequently with his cousin, the New York investment counselor and banker Augustus White. The latter was to be responsible for recruiting eastern investors when the railway merger deal had closed.

On 18 October 1904, the merger was completed, and the resulting company was incorporated as the Portland Consolidated Railway Company.

White then began his search for someone to purchase the new company's assets. At that time, in 1905, the huge increase in passenger traffic to and from the site of the Lewis and Clark Exposition boosted the company's revenues, making investment attractive. Whether White pointed out to prospective investors that this traffic was of a temporary nature is uncertain, but he soon found an interested New York underwriter, Seligman and Company. In turn, Seligman and Company found Percy Clark of Philadelphia, who was interested in purchasing the majority of Portland Consolidated Railway Company's stock. On 13 October 1905, a new Portland Railway Company was incorporated, and the next day the company bought all the assets of Portland Consolidated Railway Company. Clark maintained control, and it was he who, a year later, began the merger to consolidate all of the area's power, light, and traction companies into the gigantic Portland Railway Light and Power Company.

63

Much of the consolidation occurred at the local level in the utilities as huge telephone, telegraph, traction, and power and light companies emerged preeminent in their regions.[43]

This trend was a result of the rapid diversification and expansion of capital markets that after the Civil War, had begun to address the more sophisticated financial needs of the maturing U.S. industrial economy. It featured the development of a variety of new investment institutions which included revamped trust companies, insurance companies, and private investment banks of the kind that underwrote the Portland Railway Light and Power merger. The investment banks, of which J.P. Morgan; Kuhn, Loeb; and Kidder, Peabody are the best known examples, were prepared to infuse vast sums into large-scale businesses in which reinvested corporate income was inadequate to the needs of their owners and managers. The banks were virtually indispensable, particularly in industries like utilities, which experienced great growth in the general expansion of 1904-1907 and therefore had greater needs for fixed capital.[44]

This perfectly describes the situation of the constituents of the Portland Railway Light and Power merger. Between 1905 and 1906 (the first years for which comparative figures are available), Portland General Electric's total kilowatt-hours generated rose about 13 percent (from 50,278,520 kwh to 56,759,119 kwh). From 1906 to 1907, they rose about 27 percent (from 56,759,119 kwh to 72,326,057 kwh).[45] Accurate figures for the expansion of ridership and trackage in Portland before 1906 are unavailable, but a Portland Railway Light and Power prospectus of 1911 indicates the extent of railway growth in the period between 1900 and the first eleven months of 1910. The number of passenger cars in the Portland Railway Company increased from 100 to 487; the number of employees went from 450 to 2,900; 182 freight cars, 75 work cars, and 8 electric locomotives had been added; and the number of cars "passing a certain point in a given length of time" increased by a factor of eight.[46] In other words, the line was experiencing a huge increase in ridership and, consequently, in scheduled trains.

There is plenty of general evidence to reinforce what these statistics suggest: that costs for capital improvements for railways in an expanding economy were enormous. There were new cars to purchase and new tracks to lay. Expansion required a number of station buildings (freight sheds, dispatching offices, and car barns), waiting rooms or sheds, as well as specialized construction equipment and vehicles, such as dump cars, which were trolleys used for hauling away dirt from construction sites. In addition, by terms of the franchise awarded to the railway, the city required that the company pave between and outside the rails for varying distances, depending on which kind of trackage—single or double—was employed.[47] The railway was compelled to expand by the city's tremendous growth. The continued growth of suburban centers such as Albina, St. Johns, and Fulton Park owed a great deal to the construction of the various bridges across the Willamette, which made railway travel between the two banks of the river not only feasible but necessary in order to sustain the economic and physical expansion of the metropolis.

If Portland General Electric was built through a process of judicious acquisition and refinement of its component parts, the Portland Railway Company was put together through relentless pursuit of the available trolley franchises at whatever cost. The reason was simple. Monopoly assured a fixed price in the face of the great overhead expenditures requisite to the business of running a railway. Economic historian Harold Vatter claims that utility owners accepted "that

*Interior of a trolley car that roamed Portland's
streets in the early 1900s. (PGE collections)*

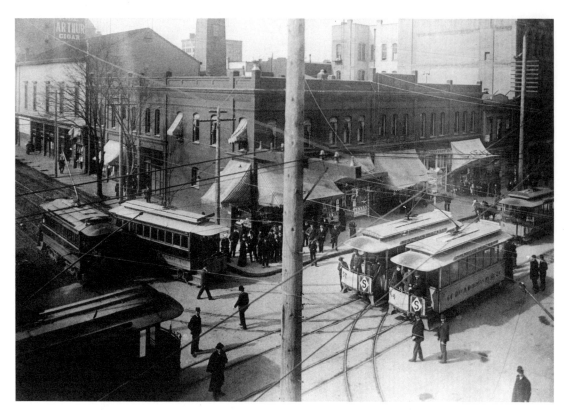

City and Suburban Railway cars prior to the merger in 1905 that formed Portland Railway Light and Power Company. The trolleys are on Third and Yamhill in downtown Portland. The city's current trolley system, the Tri-met MAX trains, continues to travel along Yamhill. (OHS neg. Or-Hi 13267 OPS)

the long-run cost curve continued to slope down at output rates so large that the expansion of the enterprise eventuated in a 'natural' monopoly of the market for several publicly essential services."[48] In this context, "natural" (a term used extensively at the time) referred to control over a coherent geographical area. In business's mental climate one great change from the late-nineteenth-century era of laissez-faire business philosophy to the early-twentieth-century era of bigness in enterprise was that businessmen tended to be uneasy about the idea of competition, ostensibly the animating force of laissez-faire capitalism. They worried about the competition in which their predecessors had reveled because it frequently became so intense that it made long-range stability in their markets impossible.

In other quarters across Portland, the huge new presence was greeted with enthusiasm. The *Oregonian*, summarizing the views of those to whom bigness was no sin, wrote, "The molding of all-electric power, light, and traction interests into one great machine will give increased service at a minimum cost." Carrying its justification further, the paper pontificated, "The benefits of great trolley and lighting systems being the manufacturers of their own power are apparent." The report's optimistic conclusion was that, "Great economies will be effected and reductions in fixed charges can be put into improvements and extensions."[49]

No less a personage than the occupant of the "bully pulpit," President Theodore Roosevelt, agreed. Although a forthright and vigorous foe of pernicious monopolism, the president and many others in the American political and business communities saw nothing inherently threatening in large corporations, so long as they used their size with restraint toward the public and within the limits of "natural" development.[50]

But the benefits of bigness were by no means universally admired. Many Americans, led by the activist lawyer, Louis Brandeis, among others, were deeply suspicious of large-scale business and believed that monopolies must be broken up or restrained in the interests of the public. Roosevelt himself was anxious that bigness be policed through rational regulation. In his annual message to Congress in 1905, he observed that, in an "age of combination," the need was not for "sweeping prohibition of every arrangement good or bad, which may tend to restrict competition, but such adequate supervision and regulation as will prevent any restriction of competition from being to the detriment of the public."[51]

Roosevelt's speech was the pragmatic aspect of the reformist reaction to the excesses of monopoly capitalism. The movement encompassing this reaction was known as Progressivism, a broadly national but locally focused industrial and political force with strong roots in the middle class. Deeply conservative, yet determinedly innovative in its approach to government and the economy, the Progressives' self-assigned mission was to save capitalism and democracy from ruin at the hands of a plutocracy. Progressives scrutinized the activities of big business with particular interest and waged a valiant struggle at the local level to curb its abuses. Throughout the country at the local level, the foremost heroes of reform were politicians and other activists who militated aggressively against abuses of the public trust by monopolies. Privately owned trolley and utility companies, which, once granted exclusive franchises, could misuse them by charging excessive rates and otherwise misbehaving, were a prime target. Mayors Tom Johnson of Cleveland, Hazen Pingree of Detroit, and Sam "Golden Rule" Jones of Toledo founded successful political

THE PERIOD IN AMERICAN HISTORY following the Civil War, in which industrialization was proceeding at its most rapid pace, was known as the Gilded Age. The American government—whether local, state or federal—was unprepared to handle the changing economic and political climate, and many people, fearing the potential of unregulated big business to abuse its considerable wealth and power, banded together under the term "Progressivism" to put forth their own reformist political agenda.

The Progressives may have been suspicious of big business, but they were aware that the conglomerates were henceforth a permanent fixture in American economic and political life. Rather than attempting futilely to return to the age of small business, they sought to preserve American democracy by creating and enforcing regulations on corporate behavior. Their goal was to inject responsibility and economic and political parity into the enormous economic and technological boom of the time, and especially to cope with the power of industrial monopolies.

Just as monopolies were forming in other industries such as rail and steel, in the first decades of the twentieth century many utility companies in the United States consolidated, forming huge power conglomerates. The eastern financial backers of Portland Railway Light and Power favored developing the company into a monopoly; by 1908 the company was proposing to merge with yet another, Northwestern Electric. Portland's Progressive mayor, Harry Lane, opposed the merger, and fought to have the city's lighting contract, which until then had been negotiated solely with Portland Railway Light and Power, opened up for competitive bidding. The proposal was put to a popular vote, and was defeated. Portland Railway Light and Power had successfully resisted the Progressives' attempts at regulation.

careers by ending such practices. Portland, no less than other large American cities, had a full complement of reform-minded citizens. They regarded the Portland Railway Light and Power merger with undisguised distaste.

The three railways that joined together in 1906 to form the Portland Railway Company had been built by some of the city's most important entrepreneurs, among them individuals already associated with Portland General Electric. The assets of no fewer than thirty-six earlier railway companies and properties had been subsumed by two of the surviving three. The Oregon Water Power and Railway Company was descended from eight of these predecessors. In its penultimate incarnation as the Portland City and Oregon Railway Company, which lasted a little more than a year between 1901 and 1902, the line's owner, Fred Morris, imported a superintendent and dispatcher from Oakland, California. The new team was not adequate to the task of managing the line efficiently, let alone safely. The new dispatcher, exercising a proclivity to have cars rendez-vous where there was no siding, thereby arranged several head-on collisions. In 1902 the compa-ny's crews, not amused by such mix-ups, struck. The superintendent, a man named Tiffany, was forced to handle the Oregon City run. The *Oregon Daily Journal* deadpanned that, with only the one car on the Oregon City Line, Stuart, the dispatcher, had "so far prevented Tiffany from running into himself."[52] Eventually the strike was settled, and customer confidence returned when the luckless Stuart was himself dispatched—to California.

Morris and three other backers changed the name of the Portland City and Oregon Railway and its corporate charter in June 1902. The new Oregon Water Power and Railway Company was now empowered to build a rail line to Cazadero, in eastern Clackamas County on the north fork of the Clackamas River. The purpose of this was, in part, to construct a hydropower facility there. Operating franchises for Portland were secured, and Oregon Water Power and Railway made an agreement with Portland General Electric to buy power for its cars.[53]

By 1906, Oregon Water Power and Railway had been transformed into a viable company. A thirty-two-mile standard-gauge railroad had been built from Portland to Cazadero. Under con-struction was a branch line from Linneman Junction to Fairview and Troutdale, in eastern Multnomah County. The Cazadero project, which was on the donation land claims of an early settler named John Zobrist, was completed in February 1907. In addition, in January 1904, a plat for Estacada, a town of some three hundred people near the Cazadero site, was filed at Oregon City, the Clackamas County seat. The Oregon Water Power and Railway had built a hotel, the Estacada, in the town and proclaimed it to weekend tourists as a desirable destination for outings with attractive fares and inducements. The railway was also envisioned as a solution to the unexploited yellow-fir resources of the region around the upper Clackamas River. Natural ob-structions on the river and steep terrain had precluded the use of log rafts, which were a common method of getting logs to mills or logging roads where they could be hauled from forests. Because the principals had remade this once hapless line into an attractive package from a number of perspectives, Portland General Electric acquired it in October 1906.[54]

By 1906, the other major railway component, the Portland Railway Company, had crafted a company that had subsumed twenty-eight predecessor lines, going back to 1882. Among the most important of these was the Multnomah Street Railway Company incorporated in 1882 to run along B Street (now Burnside) west into the hills.[55] The company began with horsecars. Another forebear was the Portland Traction Company, which started business in August 1887. After several false starts, including a plan to operate as a cable company, the owners, a wealthy young financier from Philadelphia, George Markle, Jr.; the recently elected mayor of Portland, Van B. DeLashmutt; and another investor named Duff F. Sherman, inaugurated their line in 1888. This railway also operated on the west side, downtown. The Transcontinental Street Railway Company, formed in 1882, included among its backers Henry Corbett, William S. Ladd, and Tyler Woodward, who served as president of the U.S. National Bank from 1895 to 1902. (If nothing else, the company had the city's most prestigious investors.) The line ran through Portland's main business district along Third Street. The Willamette Bridge Railway Motor Line, incorporated in 1887, initially ran horsecars, but secured a franchise to operate a steam train to the Sunnyside district in the southeast. The Waverly Woodstock Electric Railway Company came into existence in March 1891, enjoyed a brief half-life in the near southeast of the city until September, and was then bought out by the Willamette Bridge Railway line, which shortly began using electric cars. It was said to be the first double-truck electric-car operator in the western United States.[56] The Portland and Fairview Railroad Company, which ran out to the vicinity of Gresham, was incorporated in 1890. The Portland and St. Johns Railway Company, begun in October of 1903, eventually became the Portland, Vancouver and St. Johns Railroad Company in October 1905.

The two key companies in the merger that eventuated in the formation of the Portland Railway Company on 13 October 1905 were the City and Suburban Railway Company, incorporated in June 1891, and the Portland Consolidated Railway Company, which subsumed City and Suburban on 18 October 1904. City and Suburban, whose major investors included Corbett, Swigert, the estate of Henry Failing, and the First National Bank, had strengthened itself with the lines of seventeen predecessors. Its successor, Portland Consolidated Railway Company, was a combination of the lines of ten previous companies before it swallowed City and Suburban.

The Portland Consolidated Railway Company was capitalized at $5 million. Charles Dolph and the ubiquitous Swigert were named vice presidents. John C. Ainsworth was the owner. The company president was Abbott Mills, also president of the First National Bank and the prime mover in the two years of complex negotiations that led to the formation of Portland Railway Light and Power. By putting together Portland Consolidated Railway Company, into which had been folded the original Portland Railway Company (started in 1896 to serve north Portland), and then creating a new Portland Railway Company (set up in October 1905 as a holding company expressly to absorb Portland Consolidated Railway and Portland and St. Johns Railway companies), Mills formed better than half the package of public service companies that went into the formation of the 1907 colossus. As a businessman in tune with his times who also had impeccable connections in the eastern financial markets, he knew precisely what would appeal to the east's largest investors: bigness, monopoly. He delivered it.

70

3 THE ANNALS OF BIGNESS

ENRY GOODE LEFT A STRANGE LEGACY when he died in 1907. He had worked diligently in the presidency of the Lewis and Clark Exposition to bring distinction to the city of Portland and to promote the best interests of Portland General Electric. He had seen these goals as mutually beneficial to city and company, and the prosperity following the fair confirmed that assessment. When the exposition ended, Goode also worked hard to arrange the deal that resulted in the formation of Portland Railway Light and Power. Yet, by helping Abbott Mills to bring about the huge new utility, he created an institution so large, so cumbersome, and at times so remote from the citizens and rhythms of Portland's life that the goodwill he had built for the company among the populace was strained almost to the breaking point.

What emerged from the marriage of eastern capital and Northwest business was a collection of public service companies that, by 1910, numbered nineteen and held some forty-three franchises. That year, the *American Banker*, stating the obvious, called Portland Railway Light and Power a monopoly.[1] In its initial years of life the company seemed to run efficiently and profitably, although trying to standardize the various gauges and car sizes of all the rail lines that had been bought up was a nightmare in itself. Nevertheless, so far as its investors were concerned, the fundamental personality of the company confirmed the reasons for which monopolies were formed: it was profitable, and it completely controlled its market.

Goode's successor was Benage S. Josselyn, known in the fashion of the day as "B.S." Imported from Baltimore where he had run a trolley company, the new president had been an investor in the Oregon Water Power and Railway Company in 1902 and was thus already somewhat familiar with the railway business in Portland when he arrived. He catapulted himself immediately into the upper reaches of Portland society by joining the most exclusive clubs and by acquiring the Massachusetts state building from the exposition grounds, which he then had transported across the river to a site close to Mt. Tabor, where it served as his mansion.[2]

Josselyn was unmistakably a proponent of bigness and a creature of the eastern investors who dominated Portland Railway Light and Power's executive board. His major interests appear to have been a drive for absolute control of the markets he dominated, as well as the pursuit of maximum profits, and his methods and manners were sometimes shockingly arrogant. Throughout his presidency, he fought a running battle with Portland's Progressive mayor, Dr. Harry Lane, and the small but hardy band of critics of Portland's business leaders and their allies in municipal government. Chief among Lane's allies was the evening paper, the *Oregon Daily Journal*, which rallied to the mayor's reform standard with stinging critiques of Portland Railway Light and Power and other franchise holders.

In fairness to Josselyn, some of the most prominent names in the city were on Lane's list of evildoers—men such as Mills and Swigert, who had much longer associations with the city. It needs to be said also that terms like "conflict of interest" and "social responsibility" had little meaning in the context of early-twentieth-century business practice. Men like Josselyn, Mills, Swigert, Corbett, and even to some extent Goode saw the city as an arena of economic opportunity, not public service, so far as business practice was concerned. They were still sufficiently imbued with the laissez-faire and political values of the late-nineteenth century to believe that, if competition needed to be controlled, at least the control should not apply to the businesses in which they invested. Control was for markets, not businesses, and was asserted by strong companies over weak ones, not by government over enterprises. These attitudes help to explain why Portland's early development bore the hallmark of commercial opportunity rather than rational planning.[3] It must also be said that, although the rise of Portland Railway Light and Power required a relatively supine municipal government to succeed, by the standards of other American cities of the day, Portland was a paragon of civic virtue.

Still, Josselyn's regime couldn't be called a public relations victory for the company, if only because a persistent drumbeat of criticism of monopolies by Progressive reformers, including the journalists Lincoln Steffens, Ida Tarbell, and Ray Stannard Baker, had alerted a wide audience to the symptoms and evils of municipal corruption. When linked to the specific charges brought against Portland Railway Light and Power by Mayor Lane, Dan Kellaher (another Progressive politician who served in various capacities), and the *Journal*, these views frequently brought vigorous disapproval and determined action from reform elements.

The nature of Josselyn's style and intent as a manager was quickly revealed in both his internal and external dealings. Shortly after the incorporation of Portland Railway Light and Power, the Amalgamated Association of Street and Electric Railway Employees tried to organize his motormen. Josselyn ignored the union, raised his carmen's wages on his own, and formed a company

Benage S. Josselyn was imported in 1908 by the Clarks from Baltimore, where he had run a trolley company. He had earlier invested in Oregon Water Power and Railway Company so he was somewhat familiar with Portland's railway business. He bought the Massachusetts Building from the Lewis and Clark Exposition for a home and moved it to Mt. Tabor. He fought with Portland's Mayor Harry Lane in various municipal battles over what the city could and could not make his company do. He retired from the presidency in 1913. (PGE collections)

Mt. Tabor streetcar passing the former Massachusetts Building from the Lewis and Clark Exposition. B.S. Josselyn used this building to serve as his residence while he was president of Portland Railway Light and Power. The building later became a sanitarium. (OHS neg. OrHi 24669 OPS)

union, the Brotherhood of Electric Railway Employees of Portland Railway Light and Power, with himself as its head. This organization supplanted Goode's old union, which had ceased to exist with his death. In September 1908, Josselyn wrote to the executive board of the municipal government, rejecting its request that Portland Railway Light and Power help the city pay for the rebuilding of the Madison Street Bridge, which its trolleys used extensively. He said he would not negotiate with the board over the matter because it had no power to compel him to do so. [4]

Not surprisingly, by the spring of 1908 the company had acquired a reputation for corporate arrogance among the general public. This image was nurtured by the reportage and editorializing (frequently in the same space) of the *Oregon Daily Journal*, whereas the *Oregonian* usually portrayed the company favorably.

The reputation of Portland Railway Light and Power as a ham-handed, selfish giant was reinforced for many Portlanders by the events of 1908 and 1909 when the city's streetlighting contract came up for renewal. Mayor Lane and his allies on the city council alleged that the company was charging about one-third too much on the city's lighting bill. [5] When Josselyn predictably resisted any downward rate revision in the projected agreement, Lane proposed opening the new contract to competitive bidding. Although Portland Railway Light and Power was the only utility capable of providing electricity to the city on the expiration of the contract, another company, Mt. Hood Railway and Power, had assured the city that, when the contract ran out on 31 December 1908, it would be ready to provide service. [6] An alternative proposed enthusiastically by some council members, and cautiously endorsed by the *Journal*, was municipal ownership. [7] The *Journal*'s lukewarm support of the idea rested on the assumption that local political hacks would be no less corrupt than grasping businessmen where utility operation was concerned. [8] "The objection to municipal ownership in the United States is based on a disbelief that there would be either competence or honesty in the management," its editorialist said flatly. [9] He advised waiting at least ten years to see if the city fathers could discharge their responsibilities honestly and effectively before attempting a buy-out. [10]

There was ample evidence to support the *Journal*'s view that Portland politicians were soiled. On 7 April 1908, Josselyn, in the mistaken belief that his influence would cow the mayor, informed Lane that certain city council members received free railway passes from his company. "All honest councilmen," said the *Journal* with tongue in cheek, "will probably turn these passes in if the report be true. No public servant can serve two masters." [11]

On 8 April, Councilman George L. Baker, later one of Portland's most colorful mayors, stepped forward to confess unashamedly that he was one of those who had accepted passes. "For ten years I have been getting these tickets and I want to say right now that such a favor from the company does not and could not swerve me from my duty as a public official." [12] He went on to castigate Lane for vetoing the council's ordinance of the previous day directing the executive board to complete a new contract on the old terms with Portland Railway Light and Power. "I want municipal ownership of [a] lighting plant," he said in justifying his vote for the contract, "but we cannot get one short of several years." [13]

Citizens' groups denounced the company and the council majority. Both west-side and east-side interests spoke out against the new contract. The North Albina Improvement Club threat-

*Construction to put cables underground in 1909
on First and Madison streets in downtown Portland, with the Hawthorne (formerly the Madison)
Bridge rising in the background. (PGE collections)*

Linemen raise steel transmission tower on Portland Railway Light and Power line from River Mill to Portland. The line was built in 1911. (PGE collections)

ened to circulate a referendum petition to put the contract to a vote of the people if the council overrode Lane's veto. A representative for the groups claimed that its members would rather have dark streets until an alternative to Portland Railway Light and Power could be secured than be at the company's mercy. Not only was the contract too expensive, but the company moved at its leisure in providing service. As the club's representative noted, "Thickly settled residence districts are without lights."[14]

For his part, Josselyn used the disarray at city hall as the basis for a tough stance toward Lane in the negotiations for a new contract. He demanded one of no less than five years in length. At the same time, he was making certain that no competition could weaken his position. The Mt. Hood threat had faded by late 1908, but a new entity, the Clackamas Land and Electric Company, had entered the picture. The new firm sought to locate a power plant on the Clackamas River, but Portland Railway Light and Power's hydraulic engineer, Thomas W. Sullivan, filed a competing claim to the riparian rights at the site. The owner of the new company, F.S. Morris, intended to litigate if necessary to secure his rights, but his comment that he could not seek a franchise in Portland until his plant on the river was completed, within fifteen months, indicates that the immediate purpose of the Portland Railway Light and Power counterclaim had been fulfilled.[15] Morris had been effectively precluded from competing for the new contract.

As the year ended, the cost aspect of the controversy took a new twist that went against Lane and his allies. The city attorney delivered an opinion to the council's lighting committee that the city's light bill from 1908 should not be one-third lower, as the mayor's allies on the council charged. The opinion was based on the presumption that the city was paying for illumination, not energy. Earlier in the year, Portland Railway Light and Power had gained permission to replace the old street lamps with a more advanced type that, though brighter, required less energy. The council argued, in effect, that, as the city had contracted with the company on the basis of overhead costs for a certain amount of electricity, and the company used less electricity, resulting in a lower cost than that agreed upon, the savings should be passed on to the city and not kept by the company.[16] Consequently, the council had been withholding some $166 per month from its regular payments to Portland Railway Light and Power.

On 30 December, the city had not signed a new lighting contract. Because the head of the council lighting committee, Thomas Greene, was out of town until after the new year, it looked as if no agreement for lighting would be reached before the old contract expired on 31 December. "City May Be Left in Dark," the *Journal* headlined its story on the situation.[17] The newspaper reported that the Portland Railway Light and Power board of directors had voted to cut off service on its expiration if the city did not offer a new five-year agreement. Lane asserted that the city would buy lighting by the month. "I don't think the company will let us go home in the dark," he said.[18]

Josselyn, enjoying the discomfiture of the mayor and his friends, recalled that when St. Louis had neglected to renew its lighting contract, "the thugs and crooks of two continents collected in the dark city and established a reign of terror. The citizens went to city hall . . . and threatened to hang the mayor."[19] He mused that something similar might happen in Portland and noted that there were those in the city who thought Lane's sanity should be examined by a specially appointed commission.

SAYS CITY LIGHTS COST TOO MUCH — MAYOR LANE DEPLORES CONDITION GOVERNING ILLUMINATION OF PORTLAND STREETS — *Writes Letter to People—Says Power Company Has Monopoly and Lighting is Only Half-Way Adequate—* Favors Municipal Ownership of the Plant
Oregonian, 22 March 1908

DOES LANE SEE SHADOW OF GRAFT? — MAYOR POINTEDLY PAYS RESPECTS TO METHOD IN THE MADNESS OF SOME OF THE CITY'S ALLEGED REPRESENTATIVES — *Advocates Municipal Electric Plant and Derides Effort to Foist Antiquated Light System on the Taxpayers*
Oregon Daily Journal, 22 March 1908

MAYOR LANE'S MESSAGE OCCASIONS MUCH TALK — CITY IS AT THE MERCY OF ONE LIGHTING COMPANY — *City Executive Making Every Effort to Safeguard Rights of City on the Bull Run River*
Oregon Daily Journal, 23 March 1908

SAYS CITY COULD SAVE ON LIGHTING — MAYOR WILL TAKE MUNICIPAL OWNERSHIP IDEA BEFORE THE PEOPLE — *B.S. Josselyn's Figures— President of Power Company Declares Concern Has Lost Money Under Existing Contract—* Councilmen Oppose Mayor
Oregonian, 24 March 1908

GIVE BODY BLOW TO MAYOR'S PLAN — ENEMIES IN CITY COUNCIL REJECT MUNICIPAL OWNERSHIP RESOLUTION — *Decline to Investigate—Defeat Proposal to Look Into Cost and Feasibility of Installing Street Lights—* Declare for Contract System
Oregonian, 26 March 1908

CALL FOR NEW LIGHTING BIDS — MAYOR FINALLY WINS AGAINST COUNCIL IN FIGHT FOR COMPETITION
Oregon Daily Journal, 26 March 1908

EAST SIDE CLUBS FAVOR MUNICIPAL LIGHT PLANT — PROPERTY OWNERS ASSERT COMPANY OVERCHARGES AND FORCES CONSUMERS TO PAY EXORBITANT RATES FOR PUTTING IN WIRES — *Company Says It Only Wants Money Back*
Oregon Daily Journal, 30 March 1908

MAYOR ASKS CITY TO BUY LIGHTING PLANT — ADDRESSES LETTER TO PORTLAND CITIZENS SETTING FORTH FACTS OF INTEREST TO TAXPAYERS — *Lane Anxious to Save Company "From Again Losing Money"*
Oregon Daily Journal, 31 March 1908

SEEKS TO LEASE STREET LIGHTS — MAYOR LANE MAKES PROPOSAL TO THE PORTLAND RAILWAY, LIGHT & POWER COMPANY — *Also Suggests Purchase–Head of Corporation Intimates That Matter Will Not Be Considered—*Executive Also Writes a Letter to People
Oregonian, 1 April 1908

REPLIES TO MAYOR — JOSSELYN
REJECTS PROPOSAL TO LEASE PLANT —
Offer Is Far Too Low—Head of Power Company
Questions Lane's Sincerity and His Authority
and That of Council to Make Contract
Oregonian, 3 April 1908

MAYOR LANE APPLIES LASH
TO CITY COUNCIL — GIFTS FROM
A PUBLIC SERVICE CORPORATION —
*Vetoes Lighting Contract Because City Is Not
Getting Rebates That Would Mean Thousands a
Year to Taxpayers*—Corners Oskar Huber in
Office and Swears Him
Oregon Daily Journal, 3 April 1908

YOU MAY HAVE IT, YES, YOU
MAY — NOT — CITY AS LIKELY TO
LEASE PLANT AS PLAY MARBLES WITH
THE MOON
Oregon Daily Journal, 6 April 1908

COUNCIL WILL NOT SUPPORT
LANE — INSIST THAT LIGHTING
CONTRACT SHALL STAND — *George Baker
Admits He Travels On Passes and Explains His
Position; Thinks Veto Is Political Trick*—City's
Executive Will Not Back Down
Oregon Daily Journal, 8 April 1908

ATTACK MAYOR'S LIGHTING
POLICY — PRESIDENT JOSSELYN SAYS
CITY WOULD GAIN NOTHING BY OWNING
PLANT — *Cites List of Facts Head of Power
Company Seeks to Show That Municipal
Ownership Has Failed in Many Instances*
Oregonian, 12 April 1908

CITES FAILURES OF
MUNICIPAL OWNERSHIP —
PRESIDENT JOSSELYN OF THE LOCAL
ELECTRIC COMPANY — *Presents Arguments
to Mayor Lane Against the Executives's Plan for
Lighting the City*
Oregon Daily Journal, 12 April 1908

ONE MUST YIELD WITHIN 48
HOURS — QUESTION OF LIGHTING
CITY STREETS HAS COME TO ACUTE
STAGE — *Lights May Be Turned Off–Board of
Directors of Company Resolves to Shut Off
Current at Midnight Tomorrow*—Five Year
Contract Is Not Signed
Oregonian, 30 December 1908

BUY LIGHT BY DAY, SAYS
MAYOR — CITY WILL HAVE TO PAY IN
ADVANCE UNDER SUCH A PLAN, SAYS
PRESIDENT JOSSELYN OF THE LIGHT
COMPANY
Oregon Daily Journal, 31 December 1908

AGREE ON TERMS FOR CITY
LIGHTS — JOSSELYN AND LANE
FAVORABLE TO PLAN THAT WILL AVOID
CRISIS — *City To Back Old Claims*—
Kavanaugh's Plan for Municipal Warrant
Accepted After Stormy Session, at Which Bitter
Personalities Are Exchanges
Oregonian, 10 January 1909

AUTHORIZES MAYOR TO
SEEK A COMPROMISE —
COUNCIL DIRECTS EXECUTIVE TO
APPOINT A SPECIAL COMMITTEE TO
CONFER WITH THE EXECUTIVE BOARD
AND THE ELECTRIC COMPANY ON CITY
LIGHTING CONTRACTS
Oregon Daily Journal, 10 January 1909

Throughout December, the fight had dragged on as the newspapers and city council chambers brimmed with the fulminations of both sides in the issue. Lane, constantly dramatizing the situation, proclaimed that he wanted the council to break the grip the "trust" had on Portland. Councilman Cellars, speaking for the company, accused the executive board of acting in a high-handed manner.[20]

On the last day of the year, the issue was still stalemated. Lane refused to sign a new contract for longer than a year, while Josselyn insisted on a new contract of from three to five years. From 1 January, he said, the city would have "ten days' grace" to reach a decision. After that, Portland's streets and its municipal offices would be plunged into darkness. Lane countered by reassuring citizens again that "we will not have to go in the dark."[21] He said the city would pay for its lighting by the day. Josselyn demanded that each day's payment be made in advance.

By mid-January 1909, the fight was over. Each side engaged in various face-saving operations, including a ritual advertisement by the city for competitive bids, but the outcome was that the adversaries signed a new contract in March that was essentially the same as the old contract.[22]

Lane's term ended in 1909, and he retired to the sidelines. The new mayor, Joseph Simon, was much more sympathetic to business and proved to be an ally of the utility. Other politicians, such as state Sen. Dan Kellaher, Lane's old ally, would continue to attack Portland Railway Light and Power, but their intensity and effectiveness could never match Lane's.

BREAKING OUT OF THE GILDED AGE

If electrical generation and distribution was a business that seemed nakedly monopolistic to many Portlanders, Portland Railway Light and Power's trolleys represented a more benign—even pleasant—aspect of the two giants in their midst. The presence of the trolleys on city streets and in the countryside, at least for the first fifteen years of the new century, represented convenience, adventure, and freedom. Trolleys did what machines should do—they made life easier and better. They were quick, clean, and cheap. By all accounts, Portland Railway Light and Power owned one of the best, most complete railway systems in the country.[23] Throughout the first two decades of the twentieth century, there were random complaints about poorly maintained roadbeds and cars, inadequate service on some lines, and surly conductors. But on the whole the railway was the jewel of the company's operations in the eyes of its investors and its public.

The company relied on the growing leisure of the urban dweller to boost railway ridership. In its publications, it encouraged the use of trolleys for travel to recreational destinations and promoted picnicking along its more scenic lines. Engaging in the flack's license for hyperbole, the *Bulletin* of April 1907 touted the upper Clackamas, "where there are innumerable picnic spots perfectly secluded and where a city's recreation-seeking population might lose itself" in "the long and glorious Oregon summer."[24] The company owned or promoted some fourteen recreational sites on or near its lines. The most famous were the Oaks and Council Crest amusement parks, which attracted thousands of fun seekers each summer. The Vaughn Street Baseball Park was also a favored destination of Portland Railway Light and Power riders.

From *Ten Rules for the Prevention of Accidents*:
4. Always spit behind the controller or elsewhere on the vestibule car. You are liable to
cause a slick rail by spitting out the door or
window.

Carman, 11 February 1911

CONDUCTORS CARRIED pounds of pennies to
give change when fare was raised to 6 cents.

Oregonian cartoon, 16 January 1918　　81

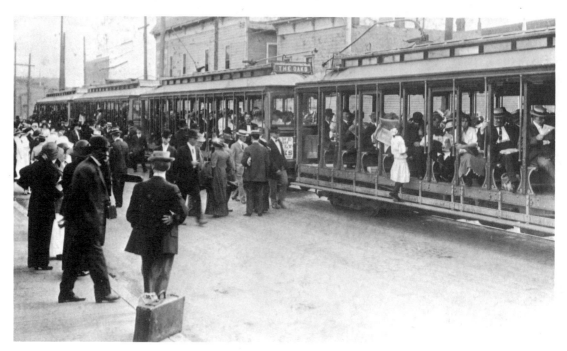

The Portland train to Oaks Park circa 1915. (OHS neg. OrHi 1604)

John E. Johanson, an employee of the Portland Railway Light and Power Company, circa 1910-1912. (OHS neg. OrHi 84700)

82

This woman is getting on a twin car. She is probably entering the exit because it is closer to the ground and easier to ascend considering the skirt she is wearing. (OHS neg. PGE 129-75)

The waiting room of Portland Railway Light and Power's Milwaukie Station, 1915. Bill Hayes collection (OHS neg. 54094)

The company worked hard at maintaining good relations with the public in the railway division, where the greatest number of its employees came into daily contact with a huge segment of Portland's population. It published paid, half-page, numbered "bulletins" in the *Oregonian* and its archenemy, the *Oregon Daily Journal*, even as the newspaper attacked it in its columns over the lighting issue. The bulletins dealt with the problems the public encountered in riding the railway. They tried to assure passengers that the company was working as hard as possible to solve the problems about which they most frequently complained. "The Rush Hour Problem," for instance, explained the obstacles the railway encountered in its daily attempts to move riders from place to place during the busiest parts of the day. After pointing out that in 1908, the company had put 30 percent more trolleys to work during rush hour, it implored riders to "try not to kick if you don't get a seat in the evening or if some one [*sic*] casually walks over you. Think it out, and realize some of our difficulties."[25] Another message explained the transfer system. Again, it ended with a plea for calm. If it turned out that a transfer was invalid on a certain line, "do not blindly censure us; think out the reason for yourself, and you will find . . . that in every case the reason is not an arbitrary one."[26]

Another bulletin proclaimed the trolleys to be an agent of orderly social and economic development. Instead of the crowding common to large cities of the nineteenth century, the street railways allowed less density by making the cities readily accessible from the suburbs.[27] Conscious of its contribution to Portland's public coffers, in a June 1908 bulletin Portland Railway Light and Power tried to explain why citizens should make sure the railway was not overtaxed. Arguing that the company paid an annual tax bill larger than most street railways in the country, the essay asked not for "unreasonable reductions" in railway taxes, but rather "to be let alone until we 'catch up.'"[28]

Catch up to where? Many Portlanders must have asked the same question of themselves while rustling the pages of the evening paper and sipping their after-dinner coffee. Reading between the lines, a perspicacious individual might have noted in the essay not just a brief for tax restraint (a familiar corporate refrain), but a muted cry for financial help. Yet even the discerning could be forgiven for not recognizing, in the heyday of the electric streetcar, the earliest signs of trouble down the track.

Josselyn retired from the presidency of Portland Railway Light and Power in 1913, to tend to his own business affairs—presumably his private investments. Curiously, he left his post immediately after being reelected to it by the company's board of directors. The *Oregonian*, remarking on his leave-taking, characterized Josselyn in words usually reserved for the retirement of statesmen: "The public was not prepared for news of the resignation of President Josselyn of the Portland Railway, Light & Power Company; nor has it been received anywhere with satisfaction."[29] His old adversary, the *Journal*, shed crocodile tears over his departure, noting his role in the company's growth, which the paper described as "unexampled in the history of such enterprises on the Pacific coast," a thing, the article's tone suggested, which was not all to the good. In lukewarm terms, it extolled his interest in the welfare of Portland Railway Light and Power employees and his activities on behalf of the Commercial Club and the Oregon Development League.[30]

A 1913 PGE line crew in Salem takes time out to pose with their handiwork for the camera. Soft hats, knee-high boots, and safety belts were all part of the linemen's uniform. (PGE collections)

Raising a utility pole on State Street, in Lake Oswego, Oregon, December 1913. Despite difficulties in other areas of the company, the region's need for electric power continued to grow. (PGE collections)

The load dispatch office in 1913. A telephone system connected the dispatcher to each generating station and substation. This room was adjacent to the office of the operating engineer. There had been no load dispatcher prior to the set-up of this room. (OHS neg. PGE 137-2)

It was left to the *Evening Telegram*, a small, liberal daily of the time, to put Josselyn's influence in perspective. "If there is a criticism to be made of his administration, it would take the direction of his relation with the public," the paper said, charitably modifying its assessment a little in adding that "even in this direction he was often much more harshly criticized than he deserved."[31]

In fact, Josselyn had operated with a good deal less discretion than many Portlanders knew. The executive committee of the Portland Railway Light and Power board during his tenure was made up mostly of easterners and controlled by the majority stockholders, the Clarks of Philadelphia. There were actually few Portland Railway Light and Power stockholders of any kind during Josselyn's term of office. Through the first fifteen years of the company's existence, fewer than nine hundred persons had about two hundred fifty thousand shares of stock, with one hundred twenty-six thousand shares owned by Philadelphians and another seventy-two thousand possessed by New Yorkers. Thirty-one Portlanders owned only one thousand three hundred ninety-six shares in 1916. Thus the company was closely held, with nearly 80 percent of the outstanding stock in the hands of easterners.[32] The majority holders, so distant from the site of their investment, clearly thought of the utility less in terms of its relationship to the community it served than in terms of its relationship to their pocketbooks. With so much power in their hands, remote as they were from the nuances of the day-to-day business, they ran the company as a personal fiefdom, regarding Josselyn as a mere retainer.

A letter from Charles Clark, chairman of the executive committee, to Josselyn survives from 1911. In it, he scolds Josselyn for "squandering" money on what was to become the Oak Grove hydroelectric development and a railroad extension on the upper Clackamas.[33] The missive, its subtext a barely concealed fury at the way the company's Portland-based management had used its own judgment in allocating funds for the project, is hard evidence of the extent to which Portland Railway Light and Power and its management at this time were in thrall to outside forces.

Unquestionably, Josselyn's somewhat poor public image and that of the company can be attributed to the impersonal objectives of the eastern ownership. If the gaiety and fascination associated with the trolleys somewhat softened this aspect for Portlanders, the sense of the company's huge and sometimes problematic presence remained with most as well. Josselyn had not ignored the boosterism and public-spiritedness in the affairs of the community that was part of that era's role of the business leader and the large corporation. From time to time the company's electrical publication, which changed its name to *Public Service*, carried on Goode's tradition of extolling Portland. To a more limited degree than under Goode, the company was civic-minded. In 1910 the company donated seventy-five hundred dollars to the city's Rose Festival Association. But under Josselyn it continued to be perceived by many in the community as little more than a selfish and powerful monopoly.

That altered rather dramatically in 1913 with the installation of the forty-three-year-old Franklin T. Griffith in the presidency of Portland Railway Light and Power. The change in the company's transportation affairs was attributable to his personality, as well as to developments in

LETTER FROM C.M. CLARK TO
B.S. JOSSELYN

October 21, 1911

Dear Mr. Josselyn:

Your letter of 16 inst. concerning Oak Grove
Development partially answers my night letter of
17th inst. but is not at all satisfactory or pleasant
reading to me. You have been spending $4,000 a
month on a wagon road, and for the life of me I
cannot see what you want with it, particularly as
in your letter you stated that the Government
would not accept that work as part of the development expense which they require. I understand,
of course that you are following a policy which
you consider to be forced upon you by the government's requirements, and perhaps it is, but it
looks to me as though you are continuing a policy
which we have been following during the past
two or three years of wasting our money in advance of accurate knowledge as to what we really
ought to do. By this I mean that we have squan-
dered upwards of $200,000 on the Upper Clack-
amas and somewhere around $100,000 in build-
ing a railroad extension to the Upper Clackamas
which we might just as well have saved until we

know better what was the best thing to do.

My position now is that I am going to find out
what is the best and right thing to do and I am not
going to squander money even if the United
States government requires it. Moreover, I do not
think they will require it when the situation is
properly presented to them, to apply this new
policy if you choose to call it such, to the Oak
Grove Development—I do not consider that we
have as yet determined upon a single detail of our
plans for this development, and yet we have been
spending $6,000 a month. Without any question
this will be a tunnel and flume development with
high heads. Tunnels and flumes can be constructed in the back woods with a comparatively
small force of men and without either road or
railroad communication. And possibly we will
never require such communication. In other
words, a pack trail is all that is necessary. A very
large part of the construction work can be done
before we reach the point where we will need
either wagon road or railroad communication. In
other words, the building of timber diverting
dams, timber flumes, tunnels through the hills,
or canals, will not require such communication.
The situation may be somewhat different if you
require cement for dams or canals or flumes, but
that is not yet determined. It may be from three
to five years before we will need power from this
Oak Grove Development and as the putting in of

the hydraulic and electric machinery will be the last thing to be done, it certainly seems folly to spend a large amount of money now on building a wagon road which may not be required for three years. As a matter of fact, I think it is folly to spend money on these water power developments anyhow until we know what we want, and unfortunately in our water power developments at Portland I am afraid that ignorance has been more in evidence than knowledge, and I am willing to accept my share of the blame and acknowledge my ignorance. As a matter of fact, the trouble has been and still is, that we go ahead too fast and do not wait until we have before us the facts necessary to arrive at a correct conclusion. Before I make up my mind in regard to the Oak Grove or Upper Clackamas or Clear Creek Development or the high head Estacada Development, I am going to have an amount of information from Mr. Heweine and Mr. Crane, and after we get their reports we may want a large amount of still further information, and I want you and Mr. Griffith and Mr. Coldwell to appreciate that I will not come to any conclusion until I am satisfied that I have enough information to arrive at a reasonably correct conclusion, and that until I do reach such a conclusion that any money that you spend may be absolutely wasted and can only be justified by the legal requirements of the situation, and that personally I feel that Mr. Griffith

may be mistaken in his feeling that the legal requirements are as great as far as cash expenditures are concerned, as indicated by what we have been doing lately. In other words, I do not believe the United States Government representative, or the Forest Service representatives would for one minute ask us to throw away money. At any rate you can instruct Mr. Griffith and Mr. Coldwell that they will have to work on a different policy from now on and that they can take this letter as the outline of the new policy.

C. M. Clark

P.S.   I have been looking through the files to find what justification you have for the expenditure of $6,000 a month on the Oak Grove and as far as I can see, you have taken the responsibility of these expenditures without referring them to me, in fact, my letter of August 6th to you from Manchester, was very emphatic in asking you to spend just as little as possible. In the future I wish you would instruct Mr. Coldwell that when an estimate is submitted for my approval covering investigation expenses such as Estimate #1626 appropriating $25,000 for the Oak Grove investigation, that I want the estimate detailed so as to show me what it is proposed to do.

C. M. Clark   89

railway economics. These developments forced upon the Portland management a much greater role in decision making, as the company was compelled to respond to a series of crises that gave Griffith the opportunity to exert the kind of leadership lacking in his predecessor.

Griffith was born on 6 February 1870 in Minneapolis.[34] His father, a financially troubled building contractor, moved the family to Oakland, California, where Griffith attended the city's public schools and, for a time, a private one. Apparently strapped for funds, he quit before graduation, taking a cashier's job in the payroll office of a paper company.

His biography at this point begins to read like the classic American tale of the self-made man. In the late 1880s, he began a self-directed course of legal studies. Although he never entered law school or read law with a practicing attorney, he was able to pass the bar exam. In 1890, his employer built a mill, Willamette Pulp and Paper, at Oregon City, and Griffith came north as cashier, but soon left to practice law in town. When he was retained by Portland General Electric to represent the company in Oregon City in 1894, there began a long relationship in which he eventually became Portland Railway Light and Power's corporate counsel and, on 1 July 1913, the firm's president.

During his career at the head of the company, Griffith moved easily among the various levels of Portland society. He was definitely a figure of the local business and social leadership, with directorships in a number of corporations, influence in Republican councils, the rank of thirty-second degree Mason, and memberships in the Arlington, Waverly, and Multnomah Athletic clubs, as well as the local and national bars. Throughout his life he also received approbation from Portland's more liberal newspapers—the *Telegram*, the *Star*, and, of course, the *Journal*. A life of concern for, and activism in, the city's social-welfare causes was in part responsible for this. Perhaps even more significant was his sense of the company's responsibility toward the city, the utility's energetic participation in economic development during his regime, and his pacific relations with his work force in particular and organized labor in general. During his stewardship, there were no strikes, walkouts, or lockouts.

Griffith's determination to induce a change in the company's attitude toward the public, and in public sentiment toward the giant in its midst, was immediately apparent. Proclaiming "a new era of understanding between corporations and the public," he called for "an open air policy at Portland Railway Light and Power." "Public service corporations," he said, "are no longer private enterprises."[35] Griffith, even more than Goode, was the modern executive. In fact, the modern utility executive, understanding the implication of the recent merger and the attack on it by the reformers, knew that he must henceforth walk a narrow line between competing responsibilities to his investors and his public. He seems to have realized that, while he could never neglect the interests of his stockholders, the advantages conferred by size had to be balanced by a respect for the newly awakened intent of American communities to govern their relations with the monopolies in their midst. This was an understanding illuminated by the Progressive journalist Herbert Croly, who, in 1909, published *The Promise of American Life*, a popular book that emphasized the twentieth-century shift of moral initiative, where business was concerned, from the entrepreneur to the citizen. He wrote:

90

*Portland General Electric began its long associa-
tion with the Portland Rose Festival in 1910. This
truck is Portland Railway Light and Power's contribution to the 1912 parade. The driver has not yet
entered into the festive mood. (OHS neg. OrHi
49665)*

The 1914 Rose Festival Queen, Thelma Hollingsworth (later Mrs. Wade Williams) waits patiently in "The Garden of Rosaria" for the Electric Parade to begin. (OHS neg. PGE 138-27)

"Apple-blossom Time in Oregon." (OHS neg. PGE 138-24)

"The Gift of Many Waters," complete with electric cherubim and utility poles. (OHS neg. PGE 138-21)

"Portland, the Land of Roses." (OHS neg. PGE 138-25)

"The Wedding of the Oceans," guarded over by a miniature battleship Oregon. *(OHS neg. PGE 138-26)*

"The Food of Kings and the King of Foods." The salmon queen is not amused. (OHS neg. PGE 138-23)

Born in Minneapolis in 1870, Franklin T. Griffith
came to Portland from San Francisco in 1891 to
work as a cashier for the Willamette Pulp and Paper Company in Oregon City. He studied law in
his spare time and was admitted to the bar in 1894,
the same year he was retained as legal counsel to
Portland General Electric. He became president of
the company in 1913. This portrait was taken in
1906. (PGE collections)

94

Wherever, as is so often the case, private companies now enjoy a complete or a substantial monopoly of any service, and do so by virtue of permanent franchises, every legal means should be taken to nullify such an intolerable appropriation of the resources of the community. Persistent and ruthless war should be declared upon these unnatural monopolies, because as long as they exist they are an absolute bar to any thoroughly democratic and constructive system of municipal economy. Measures should be taken which under other circumstances would be both unfair and unwise for the deliberate purpose of bringing them to terms. . . . Permanent commissions should be placed over them. . . . Taxation should be made to bear heavily upon them.[36]

Griffith's dramatic transformation of Portland Railway Light and Power's attitude toward the public began with his own employees. His first official act as president was to raise the wages of all four thousand Portland Railway Light and Power workers by one percent. But this was only a beginning. He faced grave challenges at the core of the company's business. Those challenges, as much as any comprehension of the public mood, were responsible for the company's new humility. Perhaps foremost among them was that the railway's position as the preeminent mode of urban transportation had quickly begun to erode. The apogee of the electric-streetcar era in Portland had been reached by 1912, when the city's population of 257,490 was mostly on foot.[37] As early as 1908, other forms of transportation, especially the automobile, aided by the appearance of an increasing number of paved roads and streets, had begun to take riders away from the trolleys, as Portlanders, like Americans everywhere, started their long love affair with the vehicle that conferred on them both privacy and individualism on the same trip. The impact of the automobile on the city lines was almost immediate. Between 1911 and 1912, there was a 3.8 percent increase in trackage, from 172.13 miles to 178.89 miles, and a 4.3 percent increase in ridership, from 85.9 million to 89.5 million; but from 1912 through 1913 there was an 8.4 percent increase in trackage, linked to a .4 percent decrease in ridership.[38]

In 1912 a severe snowstorm and silver thaw during early January compromised operations.[39] Still, the company's first historian, Roy R. Robley, noting that ridership on the interurban division had also begun a sharp decrease (from nearly 15 million in 1911 to just over 4 million in 1915), said that the drop resulted mainly from the transferral of all the city lines of the interurban division to the Portland Railway Company in 1914.[40] This means that the Portland figures just cited for 1914 to 1920 should be considerably discounted, if the real dimensions of the railway's decline are to be properly appreciated. Robley further wrote that interurban ridership after 1912 declined because of the completion of two Portland Railway Light and Power hydroelectric projects, River Mill (Station M) and Bull Run (Station O) in that year; construction workers were a substantial proportion of the ridership on those lines.[41]

Other factors in the streetcar's decline were just as threatening as the automobile. From 1914 to 1916, jitneys (small motor carriers, mostly Ford automobiles or delivery trucks with home-built bodies shaped like washtubs), which operated beside the trolley tracks, carrying off passengers who alighted and might otherwise transfer to another railway car, began to make inroads on Portland Railway Light and Power's business. As they were unregulated by any ordinance, they

1916 silver thaw. This utility pole was on East Sixtieth Street between Stark and Glisan streets. Ice storms in this period were blamed for taking away riders from Portland's trolleys. (OHS neg. PGE 139-10)

could do as they pleased. In 1915, motor buses appeared on Portland's streets.[42] They, too, took away trolley ridership, as did a series of snow and ice storms and floods in January and February 1916, at the time said to be the worst in Portland's recorded history.[43] Naturally, this episode had a profound impact on the company's balance sheet.

In all, the years from 1910 to 1920 were to present Portland Railway Light and Power with a troubled portrait of its railway divisions, although 1918 showed a large city increase in ridership over 1917, from more than 84 million to over 95 million. In 1919, the city lines carried more than 100 million passengers. These increases reflected only a momentary respite from the division's ailments, as the jitneys were brought to heel by regulations imposed by the city council and as a huge influx of out-of-town workers crowded into Portland to work in the city's World War I shipyards.[44] The trolleys delivered them to their jobs every day, but with the armistice, the yards and the workers disappeared almost overnight.

Another problem for the entire company was that from 1913 to 1915 there was a depression of major proportions on the West Coast that made business sluggish. In Portland there was about 20 percent unemployment.[45] Electricity sales fell off because of the economic downturn and because of the competition of Northwestern Electric, which started generating power to Portland on a twenty-five-year franchise granted by the city council. The company was started by the owners of a paper mill in Camas, Washington, who built an electrical-generating plant on the White Salmon River. The plant was to power the mill, but the excess energy was sold in Portland at rates lower than Portland Railway Light and Power's.[46]

Griffith's commentaries on company operations in the annual reports of those years illustrate the range and extent of the difficulties Portland Railway Light and Power suffered at the time. The anxieties betrayed by the president's notes form an index of the increasingly problematic nature of railway operations, even in good years. The notes also reveal the growing awareness that the fate of the utility was inextricably entwined with the economic health of the city and the region. Lurking in the background of Griffith's comments is a twin realization of great significance to the company's future. Bigness, even bigness as monopoly, could not forestall, much less preclude, competition, nor could it make a company proof against the vagaries of the economy, human events, or even something as ephemeral as public opinion.[47]

Griffith wrote of 1914:

> The total decrease of gross earnings from all causes . . . [amounted] to $450,571. There were indications in August of the unsatisfactory results . . . and owing to that fact and to the unfortunate financial situation brought about by the European war [World War I had begun in August 1914, and the Allies were borrowing heavily from U.S. banks, leading to a scarcity of loan capital and higher rates for American borrowers] the Directors decided . . . to suspend payment of dividends on the stock.[48]

"Decidedly unsatisfactory" and "distressing conditions" were the descriptions of 1915. They were attributable to the "general business depression prevailing in . . . the territory in which the company operates." The unlicensed and unregulated competition from the jitney automobiles and the continued competition of Northwestern Electric were the other major problems the company faced.[49] Although a large number of new customers had signed up in the last ninety days of the year, there had already been about a 9 percent loss of electricity customers, from 42,062 to 37,938, in the previous year.[50]

Nevertheless, the report said, there were some glimmers of hope for economic conditions in 1916. The lumber industry, Oregon's most crucial economic activity, severely crippled by soft demand over the preceding two years, was reviving, with railroads placing orders for wood for ties and new cars coming into the state's mills. "The improving conditions in lumber will directly benefit this company through increased freight tonnage on its interurban lines and through the general business improvement naturally following a revival of our chief industry."[51] But again, in 1915, no dividends were paid.

In the next year, the hope that had been kindled about the local economy was still alive in December, despite what Griffith called a "revived depression" that had lasted the summer. What was more, the European fighting was beginning to have a positive economic effect. The Allies' need for lumber was producing activity in the forests, a boon to the freight department of the Portland Railway Light and Power interurban lines. But a shortage of railroad freight cars on the West Coast, as well as cargo ships, had slowed business and actually forced the closing of some mills. And, he wrote, a loss of population in Portland of "not less than ten percent . . . during the year ending with August 1916 . . . of course, directly affected the earnings of all public service corporations."[52]

If 1916 held mixed success, Griffith was nonetheless able to call his stockholders' attention to economic news that portended great things for Portland Railway Light and Power's future. He observed:

> Since the last annual report Portland has developed an entirely new industry, that of steel and wooden shipbuilding . . . firmly established and rapidly growing. Our shipyards now have contracts for twenty steel steamers . . . and twelve composite or wooden vessels. . . . We are supplying electric energy to all . . . shipyards in operation and have just closed a ten-year contract with two additional yards. It is estimated that our sales of energy for ship-building purposes during the present year will approximate $100,000.[53]

Griffith may have been personally delighted about the growth of the industry because he was a principal in one of those yards, the Heath Shipbuilding Company, on the city's south waterfront. Clearly, he relished the vigor the new yards brought to the Portland economy. They would create new opportunities for everyone.

Other fronts showed improvement. The jitney threat was now playing itself out as municipal regulations, promulgated in 1915 after a legal battle that ended in the Oregon Supreme Court, took their toll on the guerrilla cars, as did simple economics. The company, recognizing the threat the cars represented, had waged an intense, sometimes demagogic campaign against them in the election campaign. The drivers of jitneys were mostly men left unemployed by the depression. They picked up used cars cheaply, thanks to the glut triggered by the Model T's popularity.

Whenever Wheels Turn Electric Motors are Needed

SAVE POWER ✒ REDUCE EXPENSE ✒ INCREASE OUTPUT
IMPROVE THE PRODUCT ✒ KEEP THINGS CLEAN ✒ SILENT
ARE ALWAYS READY

THEY ARE GOOD FOR

Bakers, Blacksmiths, Bottlers, Butchers, Dentists, Confectioners, Contractors, Doctors, Dressmakers, Grocers, Laundrys, Housekeepers, Jewelers, Wood-Workers, Founders, Machinists

Power Users Can Profit by Consulting

Portland Railway, Light & Power Co.

WILLAMETTE VALLEY DIVISION

1910 advertisement. (PGE collections)

This coupon from October 1913 was good for $11 off various $50 groupings of appliances. The groupings included such appliances as the Simplicity Sweep-Clean, the American Toaster and a series of El appliances—El Tosto, El Chafo, El Perco, El Bako, and El Teaballo. (PGE collections)

THIS COUPON IS GOOD FOR $11.00

$11.00

PORTLAND RAILWAY, LIGHT & POWER CO.

THIS COUPON IS GOOD FOR $11.00

$11.00

TO APPLY ON THE PURCHASE PRICE OF ANY ONE OF THE GROUPS OF APPLIANCES DE-
SCRIBED ON THE OTHER SIDE OF THE CERTIFICATE. GOOD ONLY DURING THE MONTH OF
OCTOBER, 1913. THE APPLIANCES ARE MADE BY THE LEADING MANUFACTURERS OF THE
COUNTRY AND HAVE OUR GUARANTEE BEHIND THEM. BY PRESENTING THIS COUPON
WHEN YOU PURCHASE YOUR CHOICE OF THE GROUPS, YOU ARE GIVEN THE PRIVILEGE OF
EASY PAYMENTS; $3 DOWN AND $3 A MONTH. THOSE WHO WISH TO AVAIL THEM-
SELVES OF THE EASY TERMS ARE THUS GIVEN PLENTY OF TIME IN WHICH TO PAY FOR
THEIR APPLIANCES.

THIS COUPON IS GOOD FOR $11.00

99

In December 1916, Portland Railway Light and Power celebrated Electric Week. This photo shows an electric genie hovering over the corner of Sixth and Morrison streets. (PGE collections)

IN THE MID-NINETEENTH CENTURY, Portland's city streets were lit by flame from fish-oil lamps. These were later replaced by gaslights, but it was the advent of electric street lighting that really changed Portland's night life.

PEPCO's Chief Illuminating Engineer, F.H. Murphy, developed and improved many of Portland's outdoor and commercial lighting displays, until by 1928 the PEPCO *Synchronizer* was able to proclaim that the city by night was "more pleasant, safer," and "beautiful." Broadway was Portland's brightest street, and much was made of the fact that four times as many window shoppers were attracted to the business districts as before electrification. Window displays paid careful attention to the use of electric light in their promotions.

That same year, the *Synchronizer* announced that the city would hold its second Christmas outdoor-illumination contest, sponsored by the Advertising Club of Portland. The company bulletin called it an "excellent advertising idea [that] in addition seems to be a wonderful way to show and share the Yuletide sentiment."

Night picture during Electric Week looking south on Broadway. (PGE collections)

Outline lighting of bridges was popular during the early part of the century. This picture of an illuminated Broadway Bridge was taken from the Steel Bridge. (PGE collections)

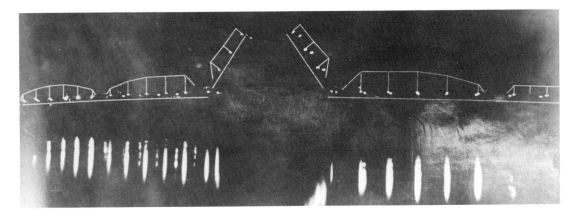

101

But Portland Railway Light and Power, ironically, had treated them in the campaign as links to the public's old bugbears, the trusts and their operators, the avaricious captains of industry. Thus, according to the company's propaganda, behind the rise of the jitneys were the petroleum and rubber trusts. Illustrating its claim that the jitney men were tools of eastern capital, the company published a graph purporting to show that, while three-fourths of the nickel fare for a streetcar ride stayed in Portland, only one-fourth of the same nickel spent for a jitney would. Portland Railway Light and Power charged: "Little Johnnie Rockefeller gets a big slice of the nickel for gasoline and oil," "The Rubber Barons come in for another fat part of the coin [there were no tire factories in this locality]," and, "Repair parts bought from the Eastern auto manufacturers absorb a little more."[54] Many of the jitney drivers could not afford the new licensing fees, and in heavy weather were unable to operate, forcing those working out of pocket out of business. The numbers of jitneys went from a high of 363 in December 1915 to a low of 152 in the beginning of 1917.[55] Indeed, by the end of 1917, jitneys ceased to exist. They were replaced by taxicabs operated under the strict auspices of a city ordinance.[56]

In the 1917 report, Griffith discussed two linked problems that more than ever showed the precariousness of the railway operations and the threat they represented to the overall health of the company. The first was that the railway workers—both platform workers and mechanics—demanded, and received, pay increases to keep pace with the cost of living. In August they also won the right to an eight-hour workday. Griffith, always sensitive to the workers' situation, wrote that he recognized "the necessity for increased wages to meet the higher cost of living."[57] His concern only partly explains why he felt compelled to grant their requests. Like other cities after the United States entrance into World War I in early April 1917, Portland was suffering a labor shortage. Griffith might not have been able to replace striking workers had he refused their demands. The subsequent loss of revenues to a paralyzed railway division would have been devastating to the company's health. He had been forced to accede to the higher pay and shorter hours.

The second problem rose directly out of the wage demands. Despite the earlier demise of the jitneys, increased ridership, and higher freight receipts, Griffith believed that the company could not cover the railway raises from current revenues.[58] Coinciding with the earlier drops in ridership was a three-year trend of falling revenues, which in some months saw cash on hand in the merest amounts and even at deficit levels in March 1915 and February 1916.[59] The solution, as Griffith put it in starkest terms, was "to increase streetcar fares sufficiently to meet the higher operating costs and to preserve the solvency of the company."[60]

At this point, Griffith's views on public candor about company policies underwent a severe test. On accepting the presidency of Portland Railway Light and Power, he had enunciated a more thoroughgoing attitude toward the public than that of his predecessor. No doubt he assumed that the light of public scrutiny would be directed at the company on his own terms. But in 1913, the year of his promotion, the city charter was refashioned along Progressive lines. One of its requirements was that franchise holders must file an annual financial statement with the city auditor. Griffith and other franchise holders railed against the provision, alien as it was to their usual practice.

Members Of Our Organization WITH THE Army & Navy

Emanuelson. P.H	Piedmont	Babb. B.E.	Savier	Hamer. E.I.	Sellwood	Sievanus. E.G.
Jones. W.	"	Crowley. A.R.	Piedmont	Butcher. C.E.	"	Wells. V.H.
Nelson. G	"	Olsen. C.A.	Sellwood	Lile. T.A.	"	Hainline. L.B.
Church. S.A.	"	Huckins. A.R.	"	Roberta. W.	"	Olson. R.F.
Kendall. F.		Warmath. G.W.	Piedmont	Cornwall. C.M.	"	De Carr. M.
La Fountain. C.	Savier	De Wert. E.E.	Savier	Howard. D.J.	Piedmont	Scott. J.A.
Charters. E.W	Piedmont	Boucher. C.R.	"	Fitzlaff. L.A.	Savier	Morris. A.D.
Fetters. W.C.	"	Nelson. J.B.	"	C.H. Willison	Maint. of Way Dep	Lilley. L.R.
Grindrod. O.E	"	Fuchs. J.M.	"	Novak. S.	Bridg. & Bldg. Dep	Danforth. M.
James. F.C.	"	Overlook. W.H.	"	Callen. E.	Maint. of Way Dept.	Le Tourneau. E.H.
Powelson. C.R.	Savier	Walsh. G.W.	"	Dunn. F.	" "	Wakeman. H.R.
Ashlock. G.C.	Sellwood	Worrell. L.E.	Sellwood	Olsen. C.W.	" "	Jett. G.H.
Van Coelen. H.A.	Savier	Phillip. S.L.	Savier	Dyer. H.C.	Purchasing Dept	Morrow. P
Selway. F.	Ankeny	Thornton. P.L.	"	Eklund. G.	" "	Gillard. F.
Jones. E.R.	Piedmont	Clarey. T.M.	Piedmont	Gorrie. T.	" "	Tice. A
Lindsay. R.O.	"	Robson. J.A.	Ankeny	McMahon. A.B.	" "	Rilea. T.E.
Phegley. B.E.	"	Crawford. C.F.	Savier	Huggins. C.C.	Treasurer Dept.	Strong. R.T.	TRANSPORTATION DEP
Williamson. P.	Ankeny	Simms. W.H.	"	Dyer. C.J.	" "	Wood. T.C.	SALEM OFFICE
Smith. R.E.	Savier	Harrison. C.M.	Piedmont	Evenson. O.M.	" "	Mason. F.
Schwartz. A.A.	Piedmont	Inkster. J.M.	"	Wertz. C.W.	Traffic Dept.	Schwab. E.S
Nelson. E.	Sellwood	Ranes. E.A.	"	Leer. O.	Interurban Div.	Bain. R.	Savier
Koon. H.G.	Sellwood	Tatreau. R.	"	McMurren. J.E.	" "	Rockey. Dr. A.E.	Chief Surgeon Medical Dept.
Hubbard. C.O.	Savier	Anderson. G.	"	Dirrim. G.R.	" "	Rockey. Dr. Paul	Medical Dept.
				Murnahan. E.L.	" "	Scupham. H.S.	Light & Power
				Brace. F.L.	Cont. Dept.	Skiff. H.B.	" "
				Vickery. H.P.	" "	Charters. H.J.	" "
				Firch. T.W.	" "	Quanstrom. G.	Savier
				Shell. J.L.	" "	Weeks. T.S.	Light & Power
				Brumbaugh	Master Mech. Dept.	Finney. W.A.	Savier
				Reinke. H.	" "		
				Atwood. E.W.	" "		
				Wadsworth. E.	" "		
				Evans. W.M.	" "		
				Dungan. J.H.	" "		
				Phillips S.L.	" "		
				Smith. F.A.	Light & Power Div.		

Honor Roll of Portland Railway Light and Power workers who served in the Great or First World War. (PGE collections)

IMMEDIATELY AFTER the United States had entered World War I in 1917, the country's industry turned to war production. The need for power in the shipbuilding, lumber, machinery, and woolens industries in the Northwest greatly strained Portland Railway Light and Power to meet its load demand. In addition, rising prices of supplies and operating costs, and demands from workers for higher wages and shorter hours created internal problems, taxing the resources of the company "almost to the limit," according to the 1917 *Annual Report.*

Throughout the war years, Portland Railway Light and Power's publications emphatically pointed out that while the prices of most foods and other necessities were rising, the cost of electric power was actually going down. However, the company pushed vehemently for an increase in streetcar fares—attempting to show that its proposal for an increase from five cents to six cents was insignificant compared with the prices in other cities, where fares were being raised to six, seven, eight, and even twelve and fourteen cents.

Portland Railway Light and Power was apparently not affected by labor shortages. Although company bulletins note the service of women as conductors and other officials elsewhere in the States, no mention was made of women's filling in for Portland men who had been "called to the colors."

The company did more for the war effort than supply power to its industries. Early on, besides selling Liberty bonds through its main office, it announced that some of its land holdings, unused for other purposes, would be put into food production. It urged all citizens to start their own "victory gardens."

When he formally petitioned for a fare increase on the railway lines to meet his rising labor costs, he attracted even greater governmental scrutiny of the conduct of his business—scrutiny that proved profoundly unsettling to Portland Railway Light and Power. Although under the charter the council's role in ratemaking was unclear, the Public Service Commission of Oregon —yet another manifestation of the reform impulse in Oregon's politics in the early years of the twentieth century—stepped into the case. The relatively new regulatory organization, which had evolved as a utility watchdog from the early Railroad Commission, undertook lengthy deliberations on the company's right to an increase, based on an extensive examination of its books. Following established legal precedent, the commission determined that it would grant the company a rate guaranteeing a "fair return" on the value of its assets. After some debate on both sides concerning what the value of the assets actually was (the commission said $50.9 million, a figure derived from business in the recession years of 1915 and 1916; the company said $60.8 million), a compromise of $55.3 million was reached in April 1917.[61] Based on the company's original figure and Griffith's opinion that the company was entitled to a 6 percent return on its assets, the one-cent increase he sought seems justified. But the compromise figure made any decision problematic. As a result, the commission's deliberations dragged along.

By late spring 1917, the company's fiscal situation was critical. Wage increases and rising fuel prices were driving operation costs inexorably upward. The pressure on Griffith to solve the financial mess was immense. In desperation, he appealed to both the city council and the Public Service Commission for a fare increase. Both bodies kept their own counsel and the deliberations dragged on through the summer. Kellaher, the company's old legislative foe, now a city commissioner, spoke heatedly against an increase.

On 5 October 1917, the Public Service Commission rejected the fare increase while approving a wage raise for Portland Railway Light and Power workers. The company could cover its higher costs by reducing expenses, said the commission, especially if it would consolidate service on unprofitable lines to the better Portland neighborhoods where ridership had declined. The commission also recommended, with a cavalier disdain for reality, that the city reduce franchise fees and reduce the bridge tolls paid by the trolleys.[62] This would have required a popular vote to amend the city charter.

Griffith had kept his composure through the fall. But in December, as the company books hemorrhaged red ink, he publicly stated that Portland Railway Light and Power faced bankruptcy unless relief were granted. He appealed to the commission for a reconsideration of the rate decision. Testifying before the commission himself, he successfully demonstrated that wartime inflation was killing the company. The one-cent raise was granted.

The new fare was met with equanimity by the public, if not by Portland reformers, and for a time materially improved the company's balance sheet. But Kellaher and Judge Henry McGinn, a Republican jurist of a ferociously Progressive bent, were outraged, and they marshaled opposition to the increase. One of the most colorful figures in Portland's history, McGinn was an erratic crowd pleaser, at his best when the crowd was bellied up to the nearest bar. Working the local political halls, lodge meetings, and newspaper letter columns, he teamed with Kellaher, who kept pressure on his city council colleagues to examine the company's books in February 1918 and to sue the Public Service Commission to enjoin it from enforcing the new fare.

The suit charged that the commission had usurped a council function in granting the increase, but the circuit court decided for the commission, and in March the state supreme court affirmed the decision on appeal.[63] The council, however, was not finished. Taking up the commission's original suggestion that the city abolish the various charges levied on the company, in May it referred to the people an ordinance dropping the utility's obligation for street improvements, bridge tolls, license fees, and free rides for policemen and firemen. Instead, it levied a tax, in the hope that passage would force a fare rollback.

Griffith's response indicated his understanding that the fare increase was only a temporary expedient, a short-term solution to the company's long-term problem. He embraced the ordinance, and the company campaigned vigorously for its passage.[64] The voters, however, following the lead of McGinn and Kellaher, defeated the measure.

Griffith's instincts were proven correct in the next year. The jitneys were gone from Portland's streets, the Public Service Commission and not the city council held the fate of the company in its hands, but the company's situation remained precarious. A wage increase for railway workers granted by the National War Labor Board added a 6 percent increase to the company's books in 1919. More significantly, from January 1917 to September 1919, the wage for interurban trainmen alone had risen some 89 percent, as wages in that period went from 35 to 66 cents per hour.[65] Street railway platform workers had received wage increases in roughly the same period from 29 cents per hour to 61.7 cents per hour.[66] In October 1918, there had been a 20 percent increase for electrical workers.[67] In June 1918, an ordinance modifying the bonding provisions on for-hire automobiles was passed. Out of this relaxation of the regulations came the United Motor Bus Company, which was purported to control one hundred automobiles, nearly all of which were operating as taxicabs.[68] There were also more than thirty thousand private automobiles operating in Portland in 1919.[69]

The company had experimented with Pay As You Enter or one-operator railway cars for several years, and by 1919 it was running forty-five of them to mixed reviews. The public, if not enchanted by the lack of a conductor, was not hostile to the cars, but the cost savings of less labor were offset by other things, such as the impracticality of using them on heavily traveled lines.[70]

From 1917 to 1919, revenue passengers had increased despite all of these considerations, yet the company remained in poor health. The Public Service Commission, recognizing the gravity of the situation following the defeat of the city ordinance on tolls and fees, granted Portland Railway Light and Power a further fare increase, from six to eight cents, effective 15 June 1920.[71] Even this was a mixed blessing. In his *Annual Report* of 1919, Griffith noted that the higher charge would place upon the company "the responsibility of improving and increasing its ability to serve the public."[72] This meant money spent on maintenance and improvement of rolling stock and trackage. In some cases, there was much to do because the lack of funds had left much undone. Over the years dating back to the Josselyn regime, there were continued complaints from both the public and government about poorly maintained cars, erratic service, and neglected rights-of-way. The president felt confident that the restoration could be accomplished under the new rate structure with no financial strain. Experience should have argued otherwise.

4 THE HARD LESSONS OF PROSPERITY

T HE AMERICAN UTILITY INDUSTRY was substantially affected by the great social and economic changes that swept over the United States after World War I. In significant ways, the country in the twenties was different from the one it had been even a few short years before. The census of 1920, for example, revealed that most Americans now lived in cities and towns. Since only 1915, much of the predominantly rural majority had moved off the settled, producing land and out of the nearby villages that dotted the landscape, migrating to true urban areas.[1] This alone had a tremendous impact on consumption patterns, particularly the consumption of electricity. The isolated, independent, largely self-sufficient rural American gave way to the urban, prosperous, mobile consumer who increasingly depended on manufactured and processed goods for day-to-day existence.

For electric utilities this change was symbolized by the rise of the automobile, household appliances, and mass entertainment. These three things were interlocking phenomena that propelled the new urban society and the economy of what was to become a prosperous decade. By 1927, the automobile industry in this country had manufactured about twenty million cars. Middle-class automobile owners and their families had greater mobility than ever before. The new institution of the Sunday drive opened the eyes of a generation to the great variety of life to be sampled and embraced.

The first radio broadcasting station opened in Pittsburgh on 2 November 1920. By 1922, radio had become a nationwide phenomenon. Totally subsidized by advertising, it offered entertainment and information that shaped national tastes, and it constantly badgered its listeners to buy this or that product that would save time or effort, liberate the mind, or transform the inept into the socially acceptable. Enraptured Americans took the voice emanating from the box in their parlors at its word. They bought not only mouthwash and soap, but new electrical appliances such as vacuum cleaners, washing machines, toasters, sewing machines, refrigerators, and, of course, radios themselves. Sales of these items soared during the decade.

Manufacturers were also making greater use of electricity. Between 1919 and 1927, more than 44 percent of the steam engines in the United States were replaced by electric motors. In 1914, some 30 percent of American industry was electrified; in 1929, 70 percent.

Under the circumstances, the light and power industry grew rapidly. Between 1902 and 1929, the output of electric power increased about twentyfold. Almost as much hydroelectric power was developed between 1920 and 1930 as in previous years. In general, the huge expansion of electricity's consumption spelled great profits for the industry and another round of concentration. Between 1919 and 1927, more than thirty-seven hundred utilities disappeared—merged into a few large corporations. By 1930, in excess of 70 percent of America's electric current was generated by the plants of ten holding companies. At a time when Progressivism was, if not dead, then dormant, and the businessman had risen to the status of a cultural hero, the public's response was not to decry concentration and windfall profits, but to invest in utilities themselves. The only fly in the ointment for utilities was the passage by Congress of the Water Power Act of 1920, which established the principle of federal regulation of hydroelectric power. By itself, however, the act was ineffective.[2]

The national trends in electrical generation in the twenties were reflected in the experience of ordinary middle-class families in Portland in the years just before and during the twenties. From 1910 to 1920, their use of electrical energy increased only slightly from an average 252 kwh per customer to 345, but by 1930 it had shot up to 901 kwh, an increase of over 250 percent. What had only recently been first a curiosity, then a novelty, then a convenience, was, by the end of the decade, a necessity of life.[3]

The swift assimilation of electricity's use by the typical Portland family was striking. George Bracher, memoirist of one such family, recounts this development. When his family moved into the new suburb of Rose City Park in northeast Portland in 1908, their house was lit by gas jets supplemented by kerosene lamps.[4] At that time electricity was unavailable to the area. It was soon introduced, and young George's father, a lumber broker, had the wiring strung along the gas pipes to a double outlet with a gas jet on one side and an electric light socket on the other. This arrangement was intended as a hedge against the wavering dependability of electricity. Eventually, as the new power source proved its reliability, homeowners, including George's father, sealed off the gas pipes or perhaps had them removed altogether. Residents still kept matches and candles ready, just in case the electricity failed.[5]

On the street, electric arc lights, far superior to the old gas streetlights, which cast little light except to a spot directly below their lamps, "hummed and sputtered as the current jumped across the gap between two carbon electrodes."[6] The spent electrode sticks, found at the foot of the light poles, were picked up by small boys, who kept them for their own secret purposes.

Portland Railway Light and Power, like other utilities, encouraged the use and acceptance of electricity in the home, energetically marketing the appliances that required it. From its early days the company sold irons, washing machines, electric chafing dishes, and other home appliances. A company publication, *Public Service / Watt's Watt*, and other communications to employees, customers, and the general public featured recipes, household hints, commercial advice, and general information that centered on the time- and labor-saving virtues of electrical devices.

The progress of the laundry ritual at the Bracher home illustrates the expanding consumption of electricity in one household. At first, clothes were washed by Mrs. Bracher and an immigrant woman who came on Mondays to help. They used galvanized steel washtubs and a copper wash boiler set on gas burners. The clothes were washed "by scrubbing them up and down in soapy water on corrugated surfaces."[7] As soon as the first electric washers became available, Mr. Bracher purchased one. Moving arms jerked a top-mounted wooden tub to and fro, sloshing the clothes with water. A hand wringer completed the works. The noises emitted by the contraption were frightening, but it worked. The family's next machine featured a stable tub with "two copper plungers, like the plumber's friend, which stomped up and down, alternately sucking and swishing the water around the clothes."[8] This machine was topped off by a power ringer which could run either forward or backward. The successor to that washer was characterized by a "tumbling cylinder in which the clothes took a squirrel cage ride through soapy water."[9]

If, from the vantage of the late-twentieth-century washday, these appliances call up Rube Goldberg contraptions rather than technological advances, it is important to remember that the savings in time and human energy that such devices brought were real. In significant ways, appliances changed life for the better and were irresistible to urban, middle-class Americans such as the Brachers, who valued leisure and progress. Increasingly comfortable in their city homes, the Brachers and similar families in Portland and throughout the United States in the twenties wanted appliances in whatever form they took and at every opportunity purchased them one after another. By 1924, the electric range had become a coveted addition to the modern kitchen. The Portland Railway Light and Power Annual Report of that year observed that nearly fifteen hundred electric ranges had been installed in the homes of residential customers, bringing the total to forty-eight hundred exclusive of ranges in apartment houses. Revenues from electric ranges in that year were one hundred ninety thousand dollars and the company anticipated they would climb to two hundred fifty thousand dollars in 1925.[10] By early 1929, 13,263 customers were using electric ranges and electric iceboxes were beginning to appear in Portland's kitchens as well.[11] In that year, three men incorporated the Portland Stove Exchange, a company designed to trade in used cooking and heating appliances that had been replaced by electric ranges. Half the company's stock was owned by Portland Railway Light and Power (by that time known as Portland Electric Power Company or PEPCO) and half by Northwestern Electric.[12] While the venture proved short-lived (it lasted only until 1931), it indicates the great expansion of electric ranges over the decade.

The 1909 "Home Comfort" model of the 1900 Ballbearing Junior Washer. It featured an electric motor to actuate the washer. The machine was constructed with ball bearings and an improved guide board on the wringer which was designed to "spread the clothes" as they went through the wringer. (PGE collections)

The electric range was promoted in this ten-story ad on the side of the Electric Building on the corner of Broadway and Alder. The Electric Building was the site of PGE's main offices from 1910 through 1975. (PGE collections)

Westinghouse stove sold in PEPCO appliance stores during the 1920s. (PGE collections)

In an effort to help Portlanders to upgrade to an electric stove, PEPCO offered trade-ins on outdated stoves. The company also ran an essay contest on the virtues of electric stove. The prize for the winning essay was an electric stove. PEPCO *Synchronizer, October 1927. (PGE collections)*

Tape for wrapping packages from the PEPCO Electric store. (PGE collections)

The showroom of PEPCO's St. Johns office with the mighty Thor washer front and center. The photo was taken on 26 December 1929. (PGE collections)

During the twenties, the generating capacity and service area of the company was greatly expanded. In 1920, the need for increased steam power capacity had become acute. The growing population of the service area and the consequent demand for more electricity, coupled with the industrial development of Portland, had begun to strain the company's generating capacity. In the summer of 1919, the company's hydro plants had operated at full throttle, using all the water available. As a result steam-generated capacity was so overtaxed that steam cost per unit of power generated was not covered by the rate paid for that power. A 2,500-kw General Electric steam turbine generator was therefore installed at Station L. Because this turned out to be insufficient, a 12,500-kw turbo generator was also installed. The capacity of Portland General Electric's steam-operated generators was thus 35,000 kw. Meanwhile, Station N, a steam-generating plant in North Portland, was moved to Salem to supply the growing demand in the company's Willamette Valley district, as well as to supplement its two transmission lines connecting Salem with its other plants.[13]

By the end of 1923, 7,461 new consumers were hooked up to the Portland Railway Light and Power system.[14] Portland's growing population had passed three hundred thousand as 1924, dawned and called for yet greater expansion of steam capacity. Consequently, another turbo generator of 61,000 kw was installed at Station L. In 1926, this was supplemented by a 20,000-kw turbo generator.[15]

For all the growth of steam capacity, the company saw itself as primarily a hydroelectric company.[16] The steam plants were necessary for reserve, but the foundation of the utility's generating capacity was to be hydroelectric current. The headwaters of the Clackamas River were therefore to be exploited and added to the Cazadero facility's capacity, to the extent of 35,000 HP. The first unit of the Oak Grove development, as it was known, came on line in August 1924. Earlier, great capacity had been added to the Bull Run hydroelectric facility, bringing the installed capacity of that station to 21,000 kw.[17] This greatly enhanced the dependability of service to the region's customers. By 1926, the company's effective generating capacity totaled 170,000 HP, of which 110,000 HP was in hydro plants and 60,000 HP in steam.[18]

Transmission and switching were a critical aspect in the company's efforts to improve its electrical service. In 1924, a new central switching station was built at Lewis Junction on the northern outskirts of the city. After an exhaustive study of the system's load conditions, the company's engineers had determined that this facility should, in essence, be the nerve center of the entire transmission system. About $150,000 was spent for additional switching and transformation equipment to allow the station to handle that task. In 1925, a 57,000-v line was constructed between Portland and Salem by way of Newberg, on the west side of the Willamette River, in order to give Salem and the Willamette Valley district two entirely independent sources of power from the company's main system, thereby greatly enhancing the dependability of service to the region's customers.[19] The line was also intended to service an interconnection with the Mountain States Power Company, which provided power to a territory in the upper Willamette Valley south of Salem.[20] In 1925, the Jefferson Street substation, one of the largest and most critical in the city, was increased in capacity, and its switching equipment modernized.[21] The company was committed to providing underground ductways for its more important intermediate   111

"A table stove that matches your silver. With its gleaming aluminum bowl and its rubbed mahogany base, this charming electric table stove adds to the satisfaction of table cookery the delight of using a tool that is in perfect harmony with its surroundings. Table cookery may become a delightful art, but not so long as its utensils retain the stamp of the kitchen. And this graceful little stove is a step in the right direction." Electrical Merchandising, February 1923. (PGE collections)

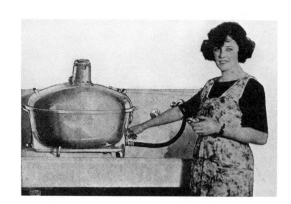

A dishwasher for a small kitchen. "The motor on top drives the fan that churns the water that washes and dries the dishes." From Electrical Merchandising, February 1923. (PGE collections)

My mother says she's never tired
Since father had the house all wired.

First thing she percolates and toasts,
And afterwards she boils and roasts.

The clothes are washed and on the line
Before the kitchen clock strikes nine.

The ironing's done and put away
Lots quicker than the sad-iron way.

Her vacuum makes the rugs like new
And cleans the dust from corners, too.

She sews for miles on her machine
And sharpens knives to edges keen.

She turns on switches everywhere
To light the lamps and curl her hair.

And when the weather's hotter than—
My mother has her electric fan.

from 1929 Pepco Synchronizer

"A versatile electric maid-of-all-work. It works as a meat chopper, coffee grinder, vegetable slicer, strainer, dough mixer, and ice cream freezer! The illustration shows how to slice a potato." From Electrical Merchandising, *February 1923. (PGE collections)*

Electricity Can Give You the Joy of a Cool Kitchen

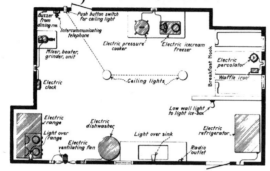

The electrically organized kitchen. The Home Electrical, *June 1923. (PGE collections)*

Although the stated intent of the burgeoning electrical appliance industry was to bring Mother out of the kitchen, there were now so many new conveniences crowding her workplace that she may not have been able to make her way out. This was from an ad campaign promoting electric ranges in the PEPCO Synchronizer, October 1927. (PGE collections)

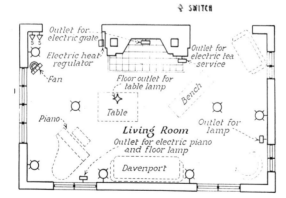

The electrically organized living room. Triangles show switches, rectangles show convenience outlets, and circles show side wall or ceiling outlets. Electrical Merchandising, *April 1923. (PGE collections)*

transmission lines connecting distribution centers in Portland. In the same year, it completed an extensive subway on Portland's east side, installing two 11,000-v transmission lines.[22] In 1926, the Jefferson Street substation was renovated and its equipment rearranged in anticipation of further load growth. Added transmission capacity was supplied by a large-capacity armored submarine cable which connected it to the company's Lincoln Street steam station. In 1926, more than $1.1 million was spent on the extension of wire lines and services to meet new demand, a fairly accurate index of the city's growth in the decade.[23] In 1927, a synchronous condenser with a capacity of 10,000 kilovolt amps was installed to maintain a constant voltage on the light and power system.[24]

A proud symbol of the power and sophistication of the system was the company's installation in 1925 of a "White Way Lighting System" along Broadway, the city's main downtown thoroughfare. One hundred seven steel posts, each equipped with two 750-w lamps, "made this one of the best lighted streets in the country," the 1925 *Annual Report* boasted.[25] There were other indications of the significance to the city of the company's power grid. At the end of the decade, the company's biggest customer was the Hawley Pulp and Paper Company. In 1928, the mill contracted for a block of power of more than 4,000 HP. In 1929, the entire pulp and paper industry hooked up to the company's lines in Portland consumed more than 100,000,000 kwh.[26]

A number of system acquisitions were made by the company in the twenties, adding to generating capacity, service area, and the total number of customers served by the company. In 1926 the company bought most of the Oregon and Southern Washington holdings of the Puget Sound Power and Light Company. The most significant aspect of the purchase was the assets in Washington County, which gave the company control of the Hillsboro franchise for electrical generation.[27] The same year, the company also acquired the Oswego Electric Light System.[28] The properties and service area of the Molalla Electric Company were acquired in March 1927.[29] By that time, the company was serving some seventy-two communities in Oregon and Washington.

THE TRIALS OF TROLLEYS

If the electrical side of Portland Railway Light and Power's operations prospered during the twenties, the railways remained a seemingly intractable problem. Ironically, the same thing that was driving up the usage of electricity—modern life—was at the heart of the streetcar's lingering malady. Nevertheless, despite the increase in private cars and the railway's operating losses, Griffith was optimistic about the railway's prospects, believing that Portland's growing population augured well for the health of rail transit. He saw little chance that the automobile would replace the trolley as the leading mode of urban transportation.[30]

On 15 June 1920, cash fares on the trolleys went to eight cents, tickets in strips of six to forty-five cents, and tickets in books of fifty to three dollars and sixty-five cents. The reality of 1920's balance sheet had forced Griffith to campaign for the raise with the Public Service Commission. He had conjured up the possibility of receivership if the company could not balance its books with greater fare revenues. Tracking ridership from 1917 through 1920 in that year's *Annual Report*, he noted that the three-cent fare increase resulted in only a minor loss in traffic for 1920, after three straight years of growth, and concluded that this fact demonstrated that "the street railway business is an industry essential to the development and growth of our municipalities."[31] Amazingly—at least in terms of the earlier brouhaha over the six-cent fare—the new increase was not met by politicians or the public with particularly loud complaint.

On the other hand, Griffith also said that revenues on the interurban lines were down for the year because of the depressed lumber market.[32] The interurban lines continued to be weak links in the railway operations, even though both gross and net earnings in 1920 were larger than in any recent year. The reason, apart from the lumber slowdown, was the failure "to secure terminal rates from the transcontinental railways covering lumber shipments originating on our lines."[33] In other words, the railroads were charging lumbermen higher rates for logs shipped to their terminals by Portland Railway Light and Power and then to their final destinations by the railroads, than if the loggers had hauled them directly to the transcontinentals' own railheads. After repeated attempts to secure such agreements the company appealed to the Interstate Commerce Commission, with a favorable result. But the victory, which was not complete until midyear, had no positive effect on the interurban's books in 1920, and it only serves to remind us that this segment of the company's activities was constantly beset by troubles.

The pattern of chronic problems in the railway department repeated itself through the decade, frequently manifesting itself in different, if no less exasperating guises. These problems tell us much about Portland Railway Light and Power and social change in Portland. In 1921, ridership on the city lines fell off from 1920's figures because of unemployment resulting from a decrease in industrial activity in Portland. Revenues were actually up for the city railway because of the fare increase, but Griffith's nervousness over the decrease in passengers was apparent in the 1921 *Annual Report*. Street railways in general were sensitive to hard times, he noted, for the simple reason that the unemployed stayed home instead of riding to work.[34] At the same time, he remained optimistic. Cut costs to cover losses, maintain service in anticipation of the return of prosperity and job growth, and the company could expect to prosper with the local economy; this was his prescription for 1922.[35]

But the story of 1922 had its own negative motif. By the end of the year, the wages of railway department employees were 100 percent higher than the scale of January 1917. This had contributed to what the 1922 *Annual Report* called "an inadequate return on equity."[36] As a result, instead of expanding the system, there would be a moratorium on extension of the city's lines, coupled with a campaign to keep passenger satisfaction high, and an effort to build up traffic on the existing lines. In keeping with the strategy of holding costs down, the company bought twenty-five one-operator cars it had been leasing from the U.S. Shipping Board, which were left over from the World War I industrial boom.[37]

Griffith's commentary in the report of 1922 is revealing not just for his strategy in dealing with his onerous railway division, but for his view of the company's relationship with the public and his understanding of the entire railway industry. He knew that across the nation street railways were struggling against popular opposition to fare increases. He obviously realized the precarious nature of the enterprise from his own and other companies' experience. Yet he predicted confidently that, given the facts, the public would treat the railways fairly.[38] While Griffith was by that time too sophisticated to think that a little fine-tuning of the fare structure would cure a struggling industry, he believed firmly that his own equitability would be matched by the public. His employees could then provide suitable service in an efficient manner and his stockholders could gain a fair return on their investment.

As the report of 1923 showed, Griffith's simple faith and his earlier predictions were not to be vindicated any time soon. Over the year, Portland's recent population increases had been "fully offset" by the increase in the number and use of private automobiles. That development was reflected in the slight decrease in the gross revenues for the city railway department compared with those of 1922.[39] Freight revenues for the interurbans had increased as hoped, and their passenger count was slightly ahead of the previous year's because of the return of prosperity to the lumber industry, but the picture remained one of only limited good health.

In the struggle between the trolley and the automobile, the company's president grasped at straws. Noting that it was "no longer always possible to park the private automobile in close proximity to the business center," and that automobile use was not indicated by proportionate decreases in railway ridership, he concluded that population increases would eventually show up in greater street railway traffic.[40]

This goal was not reached in 1924. Just the reverse occurred: increases in Portland automobile traffic, which appeared not to have approached saturation, resulted in a year-end decrease in railway revenue of one hundred fifty-seven thousand dollars.[41] Still, Griffith continued to hold out hope. Traffic congestion in downtown Portland had become serious, and parking restrictions consequently were stringent. The economy and convenience of the streetcar would surely return it to public favor in due course.[42] In the meantime, however, powerful evidence argued ever more persuasively that this faith was unwarranted, for on the other front, the interurbans were being seriously compromised by competition from the automobile in its other incarnations— buses and trucks. In the course of the year, they had carried off both railway passengers and freight. The freight side had been further hurt by another downturn in the lumber industry. In both departments, only "substantial reductions in operating expenses . . . saved the situation from disaster."[43]

If Griffith was doggedly sticking with his railways, he was not obtuse. Board minutes for April 1924 show that the company name change to PEPCO (for Portland Electric Power Company) was voted on and approved. It was felt that the new name more adequately reflected the company's services. It may also have been a device for distancing it from the railway connections. Indeed, in a classic case of "If you can't beat 'em, join 'em," in 1924 the company started Oregon City Motor Bus Company. Operating between Portland and Oregon City on the new west-side Pacific Highway, the buses served what was labeled an "attractive territory" on a half-hour schedule.[44] PEPCO also put into operation "six modern motor buses purchased for East 39th Street cross-town service."

In the next year, the company obtained a franchise for five new bus feeder lines on the east side, in addition to the 39th Street service. It also opened new territory with a line on the west side   117

The result, interior. (Ralph D. Wiles Collection)

The result, exterior. (Ralph D. Wiles Collection)

118

CAT COSTS $50,000   A sleek gray tabby cat caused one of the most expensive freak accidents PGE has ever sustained. This feline was responsible for the complete rebuilding of the entire substation at Northern Hill in the Peninsula district, at a cost of $50,000. It also nearly cost the life of one of the assistant operators.

On the evening of 22 March 1920, this mama cat stalked leisurely into the substation and dashed across the 11,000 v bus bars, blowing up the station.

Brigadier-General Thomas Rilea of the Oregon National Guard was then operator at the Northern Hill station, and declared he didn't even have time to say scat before the adventurous cat had darkened most of the city and had given the company a three-week repair job to restore the damage done. W.B. Jett, now of the operating staff of the company, buried the cat with proper ceremonies, and he remarked the other day: "That is the only $50,000 funeral I ever conducted and I don't want any more."

The owner. (Ralph D. Wiles Collection)

The victim. (Ralph D. Wiles Collection)

119

to Marquam Hill. By the end of 1925, it had twenty-two buses running in Portland and nine operating intercity. [45] The new buses were the result of the city's growth. In the early twenties, for example, the Laurelhurst subdivision had begun to take shape, with an interesting mix of handsome, large houses and attractive, moderately priced California bungalows, and arts-and-crafts and Cape Cod-style dwellings. The construction of the new Greeley Street railway line also contributed to bus growth, indicating that if Griffith and his executives could read the handwriting on the wall, they still had not finished the essay. Actually, it was believed that the bus lines would assuage the public's plea for better service on the entire system. In 1925 the railway sustained the smallest decrease in revenues in several years, apparently because of the acute traffic congestion in downtown Portland, suggesting that automobile drivers would soon become trolley riders once more. [46] The real state of the city's railway business was revealed when decrease of thirty-nine thousand dollars was counted a triumph of sorts.

The story of the interurbans was no happier in 1925, with passenger numbers and freight revenues still declining. According to Griffith, the continued recession in the lumber industry and the advent of several new intercity bus lines, as well as growing automobile use, were to blame. Altogether, the railway division lost one hundred seventy-one thousand dollars from 1924 in its own operations. But "an unusual increase in fixed charges for the system as a whole occasioned by the completion of the Oak Grove [hydroelectric] Project [on the Clackamas River was] . . . responsible for the reduction of approximately $249,000 in net surplus under 1924." [47]

By 1926, both the ills and their alleged remedies were crippling the railway division. The automobile, so far from strangling itself in devoutly wished-for traffic jams, was still stealing patrons, while the new bus service was incurring greater operating costs.

"Taxes and other imports ate heavily into your company's net income," Griffith told stockholders in the *Annual Report*. Still, in the face of mounting evidence of the preference for the auto, the report spoke of prospects of further congestion downtown and more stringent traffic regulations, with particular reference to what was called "the parking evil," as harbingers of "increased patronage" for the trolleys. [48]

By the end of 1927, forty PEPCO buses were operating in Portland, eight vehicles having been added to the Powell Valley line. "The traveling public," it was said, had made this route popular, the ten-cent fare notwithstanding. [49] The line, servicing the far southeast of the city and unannexed areas, carried passengers into the central business district. It was an index of the direction of Portland's physical growth in the twenties.

It was also an index of the involuted predicament of the railway during the decade. All but one of the seven bus lines PEPCO operated in those years were feeder lines, Powell Valley being the exception. In better times the company would not have hesitated to extend rail service to the area. Putting in a bus route was a tacit admission of the greater convenience and cost-effectiveness of bus service. Even the feeder lines would have been railway extensions had it been thought in any sense profitable to build them. Thus, in a moral sense, PEPCO was competing with its own railway and beating it at the transportation game.

The rest of the decade continued the litany of decline in the railways. In 1928, the company saw the seventh straight year of dwindling gross revenues, a situation made ironic by the fact that

The growing demands on PEPCO power required new innovations and more lines laid. This photo shows line crews laying underground cables on Union Avenue in 1926. The working attire still called for knee-high boots and hats. (PGE collections)

Underground construction on Cherry Street, with boys of all ages enjoying the process. (PGE collections)

The first PEPCO buses came in 1924 when interurban bus service was added. This forced the company's trolley division to compete with the bus division. (PGE collections)

Construction on Sixth and Alder streets in down-town Portland. In 1927, a sudden rainstorm flood-ed streets and sewers so that water backed up through sewer connections into manholes. The wa-ter covered underground cables and caused a burn-out in the underground network at Sixth and Al-der. Temporary repairs were made by laying cable in a wooden trough in the gutter. Charles Lindberg came to town shortly after the burn-out and the parade honoring his Atlantic crossing bumped over the ramp built over the cables. (PGE collections)

the buses' continuing high operating expenses were eroding the railway's net earnings. Indeed, 1928's net earnings showed a drop of half a million dollars from 1924.[50] Both the city and interurban lines showed ridership decreases, and the interurban lines suffered where freight was concerned because of a particularly bad year for the lumber business. By 1927 the depression that was to affect the rest of the American economy in the next decade had already begun in the construction industry. This explains the chronic nature of the decrease in freight on PEPCO interurban lines in the last years of the twenties.[51]

The decade ended for the trolleys with the blunt and ominous note sounded in the 1929 *Annual Report*: "The situation with respect to the city railway lines is rapidly becoming acute."[52] This was despite a fare increase from eight to ten cents, effective from March 1930, and some fairly brutal economics which had been made during the year. These included curtailing service on some of the less traveled lines, which, in turn, reduced ridership. Meanwhile, the interurbans continued to lose both money and riders. A decade of optimism in the face of hard realities had changed nothing.

CREATING A COMPANY FAMILY

In the second half of the twenties, PEPCO matured. The youthful, split personality that was the legacy of the "bigness" era when the company was part railway and part electric utility was finally integrated. It was still part railway and part utility, but there was a new sense of solidarity and mutual allegiance to a common entity. This had been missing earlier, especially when the railway had been such a large and important operation in its own right. The company had lost the callow arrogance of its early years as a monopoly, or at least an oligopoly. Since his ascension to the presidency, Griffith had labored mightily to reverse that image, but only began to make headway in the twenties.

His ultimate triumph was owing in part to his own persistence and to changing circumstances. The railway's precipitously declining fortunes made its employees feel less like an elite than a besieged minority. The growth of competitors, such as Portland Gas and Coke Company, and Northwestern Electric, formed in 1910 and 1911, respectively, and the coalescence of a small but vocal and persistent opposition to investor-owned utilities all contributed to this. No longer were there guarantees of the company's preeminence. It was becoming obvious that PEPCO would have to compete for customers, and sometimes for its very life.

The *Synchronizer*, an internal publication that began in November 1925, documented and helped shape the change. In its pages, which were for trainmen and electrical employees alike, the company's mature character emerges. The jocular, frequently gossipy editorial tone common to earlier company magazines remained, but there were also many serious articles. A constant theme was that employees should be aware of the threats to the company's well-being and take action whenever possible to propitiate them. A contest for women employees honored the essay most ably advocating investor ownership of utilities. That in itself was an important stage of corporate adulthood: the company had been forced to come to grips with the fact that it had enemies and must deal with them. Characteristically, Griffith counseled openness, honesty, and

124

ON 1 JANUARY 1926, at the banquet of the Twenty Year Club, the first woman member of that club, Anna I. Warnock, was introduced.

Synchronizer, February 1926

WONDER WHAT Charley Grable was dreaming of when he walked off the street car the other day in his sleep. Think our Safety Engineer might suggest that Charley hit the hay a little earlier in order to avoid walking off a moving street car while asleep.

Synchronizer, November 1927

I ALWAYS WEAR MY BADGE in plain sight so people will not think I am prowling, but sometimes it serves other purposes, too. The other day I knocked at a back door. I noticed the shades were drawn and I was about to leave when some one pulled the curtain aside and then hastily left. There was a great commotion inside the house and much running around. Presently the door opened and a girl stuck her head out. I told her I wanted to read the meter. She looked very much surprised and turned and called, "Hell, mother, it's just the meter reader." Seems as though they had just been bottling a batch of home-brew and when they saw my badge they thought I was a cop and dumped it down the sink. I'll bet all the pickled herring aren't in wooden tubs!

Synchronizer, December 1927

THE INCREDIBLE CASE OF
THE MISSING METER
Back in the comparatively dim year of 1920 an incredible thing happened which probably hasn't happened since and probably won't happen again . . . one of PGE's sister utilities forgot to install a meter when an eastside Portland dwelling was first wired for electricity. For 30 years, the owner had been supplied with free electric service.

When the company finally did come out to investigate, the resident said: "I wondered how long it would take you people to discover it."

More incredible . . . the man had been laying aside what he thought the monthly bill would be.

The company reportedly settled for half the estimated bill.

125

confidence. This was the only way, he said, to survive and gain the community's acceptance.

The *Synchronizer* gave monthly evidence that this was possible. One article proudly listed about two hundred thirty employees who had been on PEPCO's payroll for twenty years. "We challenge the electric industry to equal our record," read the headline over their names.[53] Other articles and notes focused on longtime employees. Billy Oldham, conductor on the East 28th Street car line, had spent half his life in the company by 1926, having begun on horsecars in 1888. Andy Richmond, a civil engineer, had been with the company for thirty-six years, including the Lewis and Clark Exposition. These and other veterans of the company, such as Frank A. Smith, who could remember the first St. Johns car line in 1892, were keepers of a rapidly growing store of corporate memory. Their presence and their stories of the company's troubles provided a foundation for its emerging shared memory.

The *Synchronizer* documented the activities of a company of busy people, but people with plenty of the new twentieth-century commodity, leisure. It was a pleasant irony that leisure was something that their product, electricity, had helped to create. The magazine reported extensively on company-organized outings and recreation leagues for baseball, basketball, bowling, tennis, and golf. In 1928 it undertook an explanation of talking pictures, which employees would be taking in at movie houses, and reported on the activities of the company's male chorus as well. Clearly, the message from the *Synchronizer* in the twenties was that the company and its employees could thrive and prosper if workers would do their part: be courteous to customers, be confident of the company's motives and value to the community, be alert to commercial opportunities. A. A. "Abe" Hoss, crackerjack salesman, advised: "Get your range prospects cards . . . talk ranges to your friends and turn in their names. Out goes a salesman, and if he closes the deal —you get $3.00. Should you run on to a real hot one, that might not keep in hot weather, sell him an electric refrigerator."[54] Of course, one had to be careful of the company's reputation when aggressively courting the public. "Let's be doubly careful that by no deed or act are we in any way a party to a transaction which can work into a real or fancied grievance toward the company," wrote Hoss.[55]

This was a different attitude from the one held under Benage Josselyn's administration, when a studied if correct indifference toward the public had been cultivated from the top to the bottom of the company. A 1910 issue of the *Portland Carman* carried an article by Josselyn that makes the point. (The essay was actually a reprint of an address given to the graduating class of Holmes Business College.) "When called upon to make an address to this graduating class, I replied that . . . I could not comply, but as I have a very great interest in all mankind . . . I consented to deliver you such remarks as may be given without devoting too much time thereto, as you know I am an extremely busy man."[56] Likewise, cartoons that appeared in the *Carman* usually depicted passengers as the railwayman's enemy—demanding, childish, helpless, rude, or ignorant. They should not be antagonized, but they were not to be catered to, either.

The attitude Griffith cultivated was different. An essay insert to one issue of the *Synchronizer* was entitled "Relation of Public Service Men to Public." It was, said Griffith, "a most intimate one." "We are, in . . . perhaps one of the highest senses, public servants. . . . Our job is to do everything we can for the people we serve, because by serving the people we succeed or we fail."[57]

126

IN NOVEMBER 1925, the first issue of PEPCO's in-house publication appeared. Called *The PEPCO* (later the *Synchronizer*), it contained a Women's Page which appeared regularly in ensuing issues. The page primarily reported on the activities of the Women's Committee, a group whose objective was "to formulate and put into effect plans for the education of women of the country on the fundamental economic principles of the electric light and power business and the interdependence of the public and industry." The committee, formed by the National Electric Light Association in 1921, was a national organization made up of women from each utility company. Franklin T. Griffith appointed Marguerite Butler to represent PEPCO, and it was she who edited the *Synchronizer*'s Women's Page.

PEPCO's women employees heard and read many double messages about their role as workers. On the same page that set down the admirable objectives of the Women's Committee appeared a report that "the Social Club [had] asked the girls to handle the February dance. . . ."

A further example of such messages came in an announcement of an essay contest for women employees on the subject of public ownership of utilities. At the end of the announcement, written presumably by the Women's Page editor herself, read the admonition: "if the men don't watch out, some of these girls are going to know much more about the public ownership issue than they do."

One of Portland Railway Light and Power's early publications (*Watts Watt*) had two suggestions for women wishing to aid in the World War I effort. In 1917, it proposed that women "help our country conserve its resources by preserving vegetables, fruit and other edible things for use when Winter comes." In the same issue, which was devoted entirely to the "fair sex," the bulletin advanced the hope that women pursuing their "pet diversion—shopping" would return home before 5:00 P.M., the rush hour at which working men were returning home—men who, it seemed, deserved a seat on the streetcar after their hard day's work.

IN 1921, *Watts Watt* heralded the new fashion of knee-high skirts, reporting that 50 percent fewer accidents among passengers boarding streetcars occurred than when skirt hems had been at shoe-top length.

It was a view of the company and the public that would seem more compelling in the light of subsequent events.

The inaugural issue of the *Synchronizer* had carried news of the company for external as well as internal consumption. In his remarks, Griffith stated that the publication's purpose was to answer the question all PEPCO employees must be asking themselves: "How can I personally do my bit to foster the proper relations between the public and the company when I lack pertinent and exact information on many of the company's major activities and aims?"[58] The president also took the opportunity to make some observations about what he called "another of my pet hobbies." (It should be noted that the term "public" was used in a favorite locution of the industry at the time to mean, in effect, "private.") This was to foster the impression that the utility, no matter how closely held, was in reality a custodian of the public weal, rather than simply another for-profit enterprise. It occurred to him, he wrote, that:

> Of late years, through the customer ownership movement, much has been accomplished toward dispelling the prejudice which unfortunately in some cases exists against public utility enterprises. We have found that human nature is so constituted that when one has a financial interest in any public matter, one is far more apt to give fair consideration to matters involving the welfare of that particular interest than when one is considering an abstract proposition of fairness disassociated from selfish interest. Our company, in common with many other public utilities throughout the country, is fostering and encouraging this idea through an offer to the public, in the territory we serve, of Preferred Stock, and our employees can be of great assistance to the company and profit to themselves by assisting in this movement.[59]

If the president's insight into human nature was not earth-shattering news, it nevertheless revealed his growing concern about a matter of fundamental importance to the enterprise over which he presided. Combined with his initial comments indicating that employees should be active public-relations emissaries of the company, the vigorous new campaign for greater public financial participation in the utility was part of a company strategy to deal with the strengthening threat of public takeover.

The Progressive movement, somewhat enervated in the aftermath of World War I, had receded from many of its most cherished issues during the twenties. In some instances it had already won conclusive victories, stopping further action, but at the same time spoiling the strength of the reform impulse. In other cases, the horror of the war had catalyzed public cynicism and indifference to the remaining elements of the reform agenda. Then there was the conservative mood of the decade, which encouraged admiration rather than suspicion of the activities of big business.

Conversely, the growth and the use of electricity and the concomitant growth of utilities in the twenties, coupled with the extension of electric current to rural areas formerly without it, gave rise to a slowly building dissatisfaction with the private utilities. For utilities throughout the Pacific Northwest and the nation, this was a dangerous development. While companies such as

PEPCO did business in a straightforward manner, others, particularly those operating in the countryside of the Northwest, overcharged their customers or otherwise abused their franchises and therefore attracted the attention of reform elements. As a result, the entire industry, honest as well as dishonest operators, became the target of talk of public takeover.[60]

In the Northwest, the early and persistent leaders of the utility reform movement were the state Granges. After the war, American farmers began to experience new difficulties that threatened their existence. Among the most prominent of their problems was inelastic demand. During World War I, the farmer thrived because both demand and price rose. Afterward, with European agriculture back in production, the American farmer's output flooded the market and prices fell 40 percent from 1920 to 1921. Yet lower prices did not translate into greater consumption. As farmers saw their income dwindle, they also saw skyrocketing taxes (up to 70 percent over the decade) and a doubling of their cost of living, including their mortgage payments.[61]

In the state of Washington, public power had been a reality since the turn of the century. The cities of Seattle and Tacoma had run their own plants for most of the time. They proved to be reliable and cost-effective operators. But it was not a foregone conclusion that they or other publicly owned utilities should be allowed to supply power to citizens throughout the state. These were years of controversy over the issue in Washington politics. The Grange, a farmers organization with a long populist history, was a forceful advocate of public ownership. The private utilities, led by Puget Sound Power and Light (which was owned by Bostonians), were strongly opposed to the idea and worked hard to prevent the spread of public utility districts (PUDs). This was a difficult task, as the state constitution allowed cities to go into debt to finance municipally owned utility systems.[62]

Just across Washington's southern border, the level of debate over private versus public ownership was comparatively muted in the first two decades of the twentieth century, although Washington's controversy alone kept the issue alive in Oregon. The private utilities, including PEPCO, had maintained a strong political presence in the state legislature and had succeeded in heading off legislation that might compromise their position. With the coming of hard times to the agricultural sector in the mid-twenties, the issue had begun to heat up in Oregon as well.[63]

Where there was smoke, there was fire. Seattle City Light had long since set the standard for regional rates. Private utilities had to meet its rate of six cents or less.[64] PEPCO had done so through much of the decade of the twenties, but other private utilities in both states had not.[65] In addition, although the Public Service Commission permitted rates that would give utility investors a reasonable return, some private companies used questionable accounting practices to inflate their book value, drive up their rates, and fatten their profit margins.[66] Thus, with popular discontent over the performance of some private utilities rising by the twenties, and the economic populism of the Oregon State Grange increasing, private utilities like PEPCO began to grid for the titanic political war that loomed ahead.

The company's strategy by mid-decade had taken the two lines already noted. The first, to involve individual citizens in the company's fortunes through stock ownership, had a dual motivation. It had always been Griffith's view that a locally owned company would function on a sounder basis than one controlled outside the state. While he had been a faithful servant of the

129

Clarks in Philadelphia, he knew that only local investors with a stake in the economy of Portland and the rest of Oregon would understand and condone the necessity for policies that might not yield immediate benefits but would nonetheless be positive in the long-term context of Oregon life. The drive to expand stock ownership among Oregonians would therefore serve that end and not incidentally, enhance the company's capital base. At the same time, he also hoped to strengthen PEPCO's hand for the coming political struggle with legions of loyal, self-interested stockholders voting their pocketbooks in whatever showdown lay ahead.

Consequently, the stock-ownership marketing plan implemented throughout most of the twenties was an earnest—some would say grim—drive that swept up all PEPCO employees in an enterprise of military complexity. A February 1927 memorandum on the subject reveals a distinctly martial flavor. In it, R.R. Robley, "Colonel," Division C, advises "captains" and "members of the teams" in the division of January's record: "The Blue Army of General Fred Cooper led the field with a sale of 1,186 shares; the White Army under General [A.C.] McMicken came next with a sale of 642 shares . . . total sales for the month, including sales by the Investment Department, were 3,268 shares."[67] As stock purchases brought the seller a commission, employees were enthusiastic purveyors, and by the end of the twenties, well over eighty-six thousand shares of all classes of stock were held by Oregonians out of a total of more than four hundred six thousand outstanding.[68]

Stock-selling campaigns with less soldierly themes lay behind and ahead of that one, but the other strategy of the defense against takeover was constant. It was a vigorous public-relations offensive against public ownership of utilities, led by Griffith himself. It aimed to argue as persuasively as possible, using a deluge of facts, sentiments, attitudes, and opinions held by Americans in general and Oregonians in particular, that government intervention in the utility business was economically indiscreet and politically immoral. Thus publicly owned utilities were decried as "socialistic" and inefficient, wasting tax dollars, costing ratepayers more per kilowatt-hour than privately generated current. One pamphlet of 1929, actually published by the Puget Sound Power and Light Company but used in Oregon by PEPCO, called itself *The Truth About the Higher Rural Electric Rates in Ontario: Photographic Facts From Official Records.* Exhibiting Canadian rural customers' monthly power bill, the pamphlet showed that they were paying more for publicly generated power, by as much as $14.65, than Washingtonians.[69]

Throughout the decade, the campaign for reform of the utilities took a number of different shapes. A constant drumbeat of criticism from those militating against public utilities kept not only PEPCO, but the state's other privately owned utilities on their guard.

An index of the determination of the Grange was the amendment to the Oregon Constitution and companion law that it offered by initiative petition in the election of 1926. The proposed amendment essentially would have given a newly created state water board the authority to construct power plants and waterworks, to regulate and control Oregon's water supply, and to loan money to local bodies for the creation of PUDs.[70]

The Oregon Public Utilities Committee, a campaign organization funded by the private utilities to which PEPCO was a heavy contributor, fought the amendment zealously in press releases, briefing papers, and radio spots. One such paper, "The Czarists of Oregon," drew on sarcasm and the specter of political tyranny to combat the Grange and the Portland Housewives Council, a co-sponsor of the measure. The utility publicist wrote in his message that the reformers called the power companies monopolists, "never realizing that they are planning a much more drastic political dictatorship to Oregon than any economic combination of interests involved by private business. It all depends on whose foot the shoe squeaks."[71]

Alluding to the example of the Canadian province of Ontario, which had elected a socialist administration, the broadside attacked an old nemesis, "Housewife Dan Kellaher," by then an adviser to the council. It also targeted a new one, George Joseph, who was to be a major adversary of PEPCO four years later. These "hydro-electroliers" were pushing Oregon toward what "Ontario has . . . wished onto itself . . . nothing more or less than one of the worst tyrannical political administrations any province, commonwealth, or dominion has ever had yoked to its pliant neck."[72]

If such hyperbole was wasted on the Oregon electorate (largely conservative and traditionally unimpressed with the more radical elements of the reform agenda), this initiative, which predictably lost at the polls, nevertheless illustrates the chronic problems posed by the reformers. In a few short years, it would create new complications for PEPCO. And it would never go away.

THE MOVE TO MERGE

As PEPCO moved ahead to the rapidly approaching thirties, it did so with optimism, but it was the perilous optimism of the late twenties. Through the last years of the decade, the company's overall finances were precarious. While the railway continued to sap much of the company's fiscal vigor, light and power had also begun to experience difficulties. Electrical generation was (and remains) a highly capital-intensive business, dependent on large infusions of money to purchase new equipment and facilities and update the old ones in order to meet load growth efficiently. Thus the quest for investment was constant, tight regulation of the company's rate structure generally preventing a high enough return to satisfy existing investors and new capital requirements. Added to the pressure of investors and regulators was the possibility of the emergence of new competitors, conversion to gas by consumers, public takeover, and even heavier regulation by the Public Service Commission or the Portland City Council. For a number of reasons, PEPCO had not entirely risen to the challenges as the twenties drew to a close.

The special problems of utility operation at the time came into focus in the spring of 1928, when on 12 April, a special election was scheduled by the city council to secure voter approval for the proposed merger of PEPCO and Northwestern Electric. When Northwestern began generating power in 1912, it had gone into competition with the then Portland Railway Light and Power in the heart of its service area, the downtown Portland business district. Northwestern's electricity, which was essentially the excess of current primarily generated for manufacturing purposes, could be, and was, sold at a much lower rate than Portland Railway Light and Power's. The result was that the older company lost more than half its business in the one concentrated area of the city where maximum potential revenue could be obtained against each unit of service cost.[73]

Oregon Journal, 5 April 1928. (OHS neg. OrHi 84265)

Oregon Journal. (OHS neg. OrHi 84264)

Oregon Journal, 29 March 1928. (OHS neg. OrHi 84261)

Oregon Journal, *11 March 1928. (OHS neg. Or-Hi 84260)*

Oregon Journal, *9 April 1928. (OHS neg. OrHi 84259)*

Oregon Journal, *1928. (OHS neg. OrHi 84257)*

This resulted in a disparity between the downtown rates of Northwestern and those charged in the rest of the Portland area by Portland Railway Light and Power. The situation was corrected by the Public Service Commission when, in 1916, after an appraisal of Portland Railway Light and Power properties, it ordered identical rates for both companies inside the city of Portland. For twelve years thereafter, neither company was able to lower rates to achieve a further competitive advantage; nor could they achieve adequate returns on investment, a fact confirmed by the failure of the Public Service Commission itself to mandate a rate reduction that could be sustained in court.[74]

For all practical purposes, the two utilities were stalemated competitively. Northwestern had locked itself into low rates in its territory by initially establishing such a small fee for its service. It simply could not make a big enough profit for meaningful reinvestment that would have attracted eager outside investors. This was particularly vexing for utilities generally. On the average, manufacturers in the major industries of the twenties turned over invested capital about three to four times annually. Gross sales totaled three to four times the investment in plant and equipment each year. In the utility industry, such a turnover occurred only once in six or seven years. A company like PEPCO required from $3-3.5 million yearly in new capital for investment in replacement, improvement, and expansion of plant and equipment.[75] This problem was compounded by the fact that the Public Service Commission allowed no more than an 8 percent return on investment as the basis for utility rates. The companies generally paid 7 percent interest on borrowed money for capital improvement and expansion. After operating expenses, small companies in the situation of Northwestern could be in precarious circumstances.

Northwestern's predicament was matched by its larger competitor, which had more capital at its disposal but was unable to recapture its most lucrative territory. In themselves, these were powerful arguments for merger. Moreover, the impulse to consolidate was an almost congenital urge of the industry, perceived as a panacea for utilities' ills.

The companies had obtained the permission of their stockholders and the city council to merge (Northwestern's franchise of 1912 contained a provision that its properties could not be sold to a competitor without the council's consent).[76] Thus, they could have proceeded with the consolidation without any further ado. However, the apparent feeling of the officers of the two companies was that, because of the suspicion with which utilities were characteristically regarded by the public, and despite a solid promise of lower residential power rates throughout the city (in some cases a reduction of as much as 33 percent could be anticipated by homeowners), the voters should be consulted in a special election.[77] A ballot, sanctioned by the city council and subsidized by the utilities to the extent of forty thousand dollars, was therefore scheduled on 9 April 1928. "Our Red Letter Day," the editor of the *Synchronizer* called it, evidently looking forward to the revitalization of the company's revenue and rate structure to be ushered in by victory at the polls.

The executives' fear of public distrust of the motives of the two utilities was well founded. Opponents of the proposal campaigned vigorously against it. Led by Sen. George Joseph, they aroused broad opposition. "Beware of the Greeks, even when they come bearing gifts," Joseph warned the voters, referring to the promise of lower rates embodied in a pledge to the public by

Griffith and Guy Talbot, president of Northwestern. Other opponents used a more pungent ethnic allusion, which became a theme of the campaign. "There's a nigger in the woodpile," went the constant refrain. Griffith, ever the gentleman, told the Realty Board there was no "Ethiopian" in the fuel supply. Joseph and his allies made a counterproposal: that the city purchase Northwestern. The terms of the Northwestern franchise offered this possibility. The city, however, was not interested.

Griffith was incensed by Joseph's attempt to discredit his promise of a rate decrease. The *Oregon Journal* had quoted two Public Service Commission members to the effect that the consolidated utility was bound to its promise and that the commission would, in any case, issue an order requiring the decrease following the election. But Griffith was offended by the attack on his and Talbot's integrity. "Even if our personal word meant nothing," he told the *Oregon Journal*, "the people could still be sure of obtaining the savings to be made from the elimination of duplication." The merger was really an attempt to follow the major trend of the electrical industry, he added. The idea was to stimulate consumption by lowering rates, which could have been achieved earlier had Northwestern not entered the picture. "We have submitted this proposal as the way to grant the lower rates that the public demands. We are acting in absolute good faith and have made no promise which we will not keep," he said emphatically.[78]

In the brief but intense campaign that followed, strong opposition emerged to the consolidation. The two largest local newspapers, the *Oregonian* and the *Journal*, generally editorialized in favor of the merger. Editorial cartoonists had a field day caricaturing both sides in the argument. The mood of the public rapidly took the form of opposition to the idea. A typical letter to the *Journal* summed up the attitude of the majority of ratepayers. W.J. Gregor wrote:

> The editorials in the *Journal* as well as the news article . . . comparing the electric power rates in the Pacific Coast cities are bearing fruit. Now that the PEP company promises a cheaper rate if we grant a complete monopoly over Portland . . . let us go back a few years, to the time when the Pacific States Telephone Company bought out the Home Telephone Company under exactly the same circumstances. The people then voted to let the Pacific buy the Home Company by doing away with duplication . . . it will be seen that the power trust is using the same line of propaganda. At the time, I paid $225 for my telephone, and I have never been able to get it for that price. And the promises from the electric companies are no better . . . and I, for one, shall not accept their promises. . . .

Griffith's comments to his employees regarding the inevitable defeat were typically high minded.

> Although we were unsuccessful we may all have the satisfaction, as I have, that we presented a clean, open fight to correct an unsound economic condition; that every statement officially made was true and that the benefit to the public resulting from the merger would be exactly in accordance with our official statements.
>
> I deeply regret the decision of the voters, but we have no right to question the motives of any adverse voter, and I hope that you will all feel as I do, that we should neither feel

nor express any resentment against those opposed to us, and that we all remember that our duty as public service men and women is to give the highest grade of service of which we are capable, and that our effort shall in the future, as in the past, be to steadily increase the standard of service, and so far as practicable, to reduce the cost thereof. [82]

In a significant, if unconscious, way, this letter closed the twenties for PEPCO. The attempted merger and the subsequent election had shown that the company's fiscal problems were not entirely on the railway's side of its books. The hard-fought campaign had revealed that, despite the relatively halcyon period that had passed internally for the company, with the development of a warm corporate tradition and memory, there was still a world outside the walls of the Electric Building that could be suspicious and hostile. The issues that challenged the company in the twenties—the intractability of the railway, the threat of public power, and now the ossification of the light and power division's rate structure—had not been resolved. But the innocence and blithe self-confidence that had marked the attitudes of many Americans in the twenties was beginning to dissipate. As disappointing as the hard lessons of prosperity must have been, it was a good thing they were being taught. The lessons of the times ahead were to be harder still.

5 THE PERILOUS YEARS

G LOWING WITH THE INCANDESCENCE of a decade's prosperity, the stock market flickered through September and the first three weeks of October, only to burn out spectacularly on 23 October 1929.[1] Stock prices disintegrated as panicked investors attempted to salvage their wealth in the careening financial markets. The banks, organized by J.P. Morgan and Company, immediately agreed to pool their resources to prop up the financial system, but although this led to a temporary restoration of calm, stock prices opened once again in mid-November to an unchecked drop in values. By that point, the *New York Times* stock average had fallen to an unprecedented 224. The morning after Labor Day it had been 452, up more than 200 points since early 1928. This represented a loss of $26 billion on the New York Stock Exchange—over 40 percent of the value of the stocks listed. By July 1932, the *New York Times* index read a pathetic 58.

Through 1929 and 1930, President Herbert Hoover, his treasury secretary, Andrew Mellon, and leaders of the financial community tried to maintain an attitude of calm and confidence. The senior partner in the Morgan Bank observed that the rush to sell was the result of a "technical condition" and not a real problem. Hoover's first public remark following the crash was that "the fundamental business of the country . . . is on a sound and prosperous basis."

That, unfortunately, was untrue. The American economy in 1929 was deeply flawed. Criti- 137 cal economic problems cried out for solutions. On the farm there were glutted markets for America's agricultural produce. In the factory high industrial productivity went unrewarded by rising wages, while technological advancement resulted in the displacement of labor. On Wall Street there was unrestrained margin buying of securities and wild speculation that resulted in pyramided investments. In the cities across the country, a poorly regulated banking system housed the accounts of a vast number of Americans whose worth was but a small percentage of that of the wealthiest handful. In the federal government, the political leadership erroneously supposed that the economy's health could be restored by ignoring its illnesses.

Hoover, his advisers, the Democratic opposition, and most economists were quite unable to plumb the dimensions of the catastrophe at hand. The history of American business cycles in the previous century argued that prosperity was periodically punctuated by severe contractions, which, according to the laws of the marketplace, would play out eventually, opening the way to a new season of expansion. The president, therefore, largely offered the business community only advice and encouragement. It was not enough.

"We have passed the worst," Hoover said in the spring of 1930, "and . . . shall rapidly recover." But the scenes in the nation's cities and towns and on its farms told a contradictory story. By the end of 1930, industrial production was off by more than 25 percent from 1929. Four million were unemployed. The figure shot up to nearly eleven million by the fall of 1932. From 1929 to 1933, the total annual income of labor dropped from $53 billion to $31.5 billion. Industrial wages lost 60 percent and average salaries 40 percent. Farm income was cut by more than half, from $11.9 billion to $5.3 billion.

The figures do no justice to the suffering of families and individuals. People lost their homes, their savings, their insurance, their optimism, and their faith. The faith in the future that had been a hallmark of the twenties gave way to a pervasive despair as, month after month, the growing army of unemployed vainly sought the redemption of work. A nation that a few short years before had been able to envision a reality behind the president's prediction of an end to poverty in America was, by 1932, a landscape dotted with shantytowns made of packing crates and other detritus, where the homeless and hopeless had come to rest. Such settlements were called Hoovervilles.

The Pacific Northwest suffered through the Depression with the rest of the United States. Lumber, the region's key industry, already suffering from the pre-Depression construction slow-down, was completely devastated by 1932, as exports fell off more than 50 percent from 1929. Wheat sold at thirty-seven cents a bushel in eastern Oregon. Apple and prune growers pulled up their trees to avoid the cost of maintaining them and used the wood for fuel. In 1932, the canneries put up one hundred twenty million fewer pounds of salmon than in 1929.[2]

In Portland, a Hooverville sprang up in the near northeast, at Sullivan's Gulch. From Grand Avenue to Northeast 21st, where the Banfield Freeway now runs, makeshift dwellings housed those who had lost everything, including hope. By 1933, twenty-four thousand heads of families were unemployed in the city.[3] Private and public construction had virtually stopped. Desperate laborers in the building trades, congregating daily at the Labor Temple on Southwest Fourth Avenue and Jefferson Street, took to following on foot any truck that left the nearby Jones Lumber

Company yard with a load of building materials. At the jobsite, they would plead with the foreman for work.[4] Some of the city's leading business and financial institutions hung on, but only by a thread. The Northwestern National Bank, and many neighborhood banks (including the Bank of Kenton), had failed before the crash. Still others, like the Hibernia Commercial and Savings Bank, Portland's sixth largest and one of its most distinguished, declined rapidly until forced to shut their doors for good. The Hibernia Bank closed on 19 December 1931.[5]

As might be expected in a business so heavily dependent on the health of the overall economy for its own well-being, the Northwest utility industry was severely affected by the financial panic and subsequent depression. For PEPCO, the results of the gathering disaster were apparent as early as 1930, when total kilowatt-hours generated by its plants increased less significantly than in any year of the previous decade.[6] In 1932, the total kilowatt-hours generated from the previous year declined (from 610.5 million to 515.4 million) for the first time since the company had begun to keep such statistics in 1905.[7] Although revenues for the whole company were not adversely affected in 1930, the *Annual Report* of 1933 was a profile of financial decline. This could be discerned in one figure: gross earnings plunged from $13 million in 1930 to $10 million in 1933.[8] Energy sales alone had plummeted by more than nine hundred thousand dollars in the twelve months ending on 31 March, compared with the previous two years.[9]

As the economic adversity deepened, Griffith was required to enforce operational economies that kept the company's books in a relatively stable state. On 30 April 1933, however, he was forced to issue a memorandum announcing that, as soon as the labor agreements expiring on 10 May were no longer in force, the company would reduce wages and salaries.[10] All officers and employees of the company would be affected. Those making over two hundred dollars per week would receive a 17.5 percent cut, while those earning between sixty and seventy-five dollars a week would take a 5 percent cut.[11] Hard times had arrived for the company's work force. In the executive suite, hard times had long been a reality. They had sneaked in while those in business, both inside and outside the utility industry, had been mesmerized by the lush present and attractive future that had seemed, in the twenties, to be the nation's birthright.

THE SPECTER OF BANKRUPTCY

The tendency toward consolidation was a powerful one for American utilities through the first part of the century. This was attributable to what amounted to an article of faith among operators: to be profitable, a company had to be a monopoly, or at least an oligopoly. In the twenties, the increasing demand for electricity put pressure on utilities to add to their generating capacity. At the same time, expansion in the financial markets meant that a new system of providing large amounts of capital to industry had to be devised. Wall Street's answer was the holding company. Unlike the trusts of the nineteenth century, the holding company (which appeared in a number of industries besides utilities) was designed not to control local competition, but to unite small companies in different communities managerially, financially, and technologically. For American utilities, the holding company was, in theory, a brilliant business stroke. At a time when

April 30, 1933

TO ALL EMPLOYES:

The earnings of Portland General Electric Company have been declining during the past two years. During the last several months the rate of decrease has been considerably accentuated. For the twelve months ending March 31st, 1933, the gross earning of the company from the sale of energy declined $900,000 as compared with the similar period two years ago. Until August 1932 the company was able to effect economies almost sufficient to offset the decrease in earnings but the decline in earnings has been so pronounced during the last eight months that it has been impossible to effect economies to offset such decreases. The decreases in its non-operating revenues which have been due to the same causes that have produced a reduction in gross utility earnings. Fixed obligations of interest and taxes are beyond the control of management and the only way to improve the net earnings of the company is further to reduce operating expenses. Action to this end has been delayed in the hope that business conditions and, therefore, earnings would improve. In this hope we have been disappointed and the management, therefore, is forced to effect further economies by reducing the rate of compensation paid its employes.

The rates of compensation for a considerable portion of the employes of the company are fixed by existing agreements until May 10th, 1933. It is with regret that I advise you that at 12:01 am, May 11th, 1933, all existing wage and salary schedules of the company will be reduced as follows:

The basis of the percentage reduction shall be on monthly earnings in the cases of all salaries paid by the company and in all wage scales computed upon the monthly basis of the hourly wage scale now being paid multiplied by 204 (204 hours being the number of hours per month computed at 8 hours per day for 25½ days).

$ 60 to $ 75 per month	5%
$ 75 " $100 " "	7½%
$100 " $125 " "	10%
$125 " $150 " "	12½%
$150 " $200 " "	15%
Over $200 " "	17½%

The reduction ordered herein shall be applicable to all officers and employes of Portland General Electric Company.

Very truly yours,

[*signed*]

Franklin T. Griffith

PRESIDENT

*The PEPCO Building at the corner of Broadway
and Alder. (OHS neg. OrHi 79621)*

capital needs and technological demands were great, the holding company allowed management to leverage both money and expertise. With a small investment, holding company entrepreneurs could control the electricty consumption of whole regions and, in so doing, centralize management and engineering for the various small utilities in which it had invested. Moreover, by the twenties the concentration of large-scale technology in the industry compelled the introduction of economies of scale so that such technology could be purchased. This was exactly what the regional utility holding company offered, in linking together existing operating companies over a certain geographical area. As the preeminent utility historian, Thomas Hughes, has noted, it was no accident that engineers and technically trained managers were in the forefront of the move to holding companies. Samuel Insull of Insull Utilities Investments, Henry M. Byellsby of Henry M. Byellsby & Company, and S.Z. Mitchell of Electric Bond and Share were examples of utility holding-company executives either trained as engineers or having extensive technical backgrounds who put in place system technology and management.[12] These men regarded the small, inefficient companies of the hinterlands as ideal components of the huge systems they envisioned. Undervalued because such companies were frequently poorly run and therefore unremunerative, their stock was cheap. They could be added for a song to a central system that was controlled in New York or Chicago. The chief financing, engineering, and management could then be done from the metropolis. Writing of the holding-company phenomenon, John Kenneth Galbraith has said that the purpose was to do away with "the incompetence, somnambulance, naivete, or even the unwarranted integrity of local managements."[13] The stock of smartly managed and technologically updated utilities controlled by holding companies, and the stock of the holding companies themselves, soared during the decade.

Like so much else in the twenties, holding companies became victims of their success and excess. In many cases, the ungoverned and ultimately ungovernable financial markets of the time prompted the creation of rococo holding-company schemes in which pyramided investments accumulated to no apparent purpose. Here is a description of Insull's empire, given by the economic historian Robert Heilbroner:

> The Georgia Power Company was controlled by the Seaboard Public Service
> Corporation, which was controlled by the National Public Service Corporation, which
> was controlled by the Middle West Utilities Company, which was controlled by Insull
> Utility Investments, Inc., which was controlled by the Corporation Securities Company
> of Chicago (which was controlled, in turn, by Insull Utilities Investments), which
> presumably it controlled. Of these companies, only one—Georgia Power—actually
> produced electricity.[14]

With the financial crash of 1929, many of the largest holding-company networks were doomed, for the same reasons that they were so successful. They were subject to reverse leverage; that is, if only a little capital expenditure was required to build them, only a small disturbance was needed to bring them down, a problem compounded by margin buying of stocks. In the enormous disturbance of the crash, those stockholders who had bought their shares on the margin (credit) were forced to liquidate their securities immediately, in order to cover as much of their debt as possible before their shares became worthless. The holding companies simply collapsed in the vacuum created by the flight of capital.

In the heady days of 1928, nobody could possibly imagine the years ahead. On the contrary, the future seemed to promise greater and greater prosperity. When the Clark family of Philadelphia had retained enough stock to control PEPCO, and indicated that they were ready to sell out, the idea was greeted with enthusiasm. At that time, the family had held a financial position in the utility for some twenty-two years, since 1906. Griffith had always chafed in the harness of absentee ownership. The Clarks had largely been content to let him run the company from Portland, but the small number of shareholders (many of them longtime friends and associates of the Clark family), the fact that Clarence E. Clark was an engineer with definite—if long-distance —views, and the very idea of external control of a business so sensitive to political conditions and public opinion as an electric utility made Griffith uneasy. As we have seen, he had long advocated local control of utilities. The merger election of 1928 had been a step in his plan to strengthen the company by eliminating Northwestern's competition, thus making it attractive to local capital. The melding of the two companies' generating facilities and transmission lines would bring about greater efficiency in per-unit cost per kilowatt-hour of power generated and give the surviving company dominance in the service area. The result would surely be lower rates, happy customers, and one efficient utility—and, as a result, a highly attractive investment opportunity. This would aid capital accumulation—an absolute necessity in a company wishing to stand alone, especially one whose traction properties were so sickly. Potential investors had to be persuaded that the opportunity the utility represented was worth the risk of acquiring the transportation white elephant.

With the unfavorable ballot on the merger issue, PEPCO remained essentially unattractive to local investors, and the Clarks were forced to look in earnest for any buyer who would take over their interests. As the stock market in the first part of 1929 was enormously expansive, this did not prove difficult.

By the fall of 1929, an aggressive new holding company, Public Utility Holding Company of America, headquartered in New York, began to show interest in PEPCO, as well as in two California utilities. Public Utility Holding Company had initially wished to acquire a minority position in PEPCO by buying shares from small stockholders through a direct-mail and newspaper advertising campaign.[15] Only after this proved unproductive did Public Utility Holding Company approach E.W. Clark and Company. The Clarks responded favorably to their offer. In the deal that was eventually arranged, Public Utility Holding Company paid eighty dollars per share for PEPCO common stock, ninety dollars for each share of PEPCO second preferred, and one hundred dollars per share for a maximum of twenty thousand of PEPCO first preferred.[16]

At the Clarks' insistence, PEPCO stockholders were offered the option of taking cash or Public Utility Holding common stock, valued at thirty-seven dollars and fifty cents per share, in exchange for their PEPCO holdings.[17] The Clarks assisted in the deal by endorsing it in a letter to all stockholders. Franklin Griffith himself turned in all his common and second preferred stocks, taking cash and approximately eighteen hundred shares of Public Utility Holding Company

143

THE LANGUAGE OF HOLDING COMPANIES

ASSETS   Everything a corporation owns or has due to it: cash, investments, money due, materials, and inventories (current assets); buildings and machinery (fixed assets); and patents and goodwill (intangible assets).

BOND   Essentially an IOU or promissory note of a corporation, usually issued in multiples of one or five thousand dollars, although one hundred and five hundred dollar denominations are not unknown. A bond is evidence of a debt on which the issuing company usually promises to pay the bondholders a specified amount of interest for a specified length of time and to repay the loan on the expiration date. In every case a bond represents debt. Its holder is a creditor of the corporation and not a part owner as is the shareholder.

CAPITALIZATION   Total amount of the various securities issued by a corporation. Capitalization may include bonds, debentures, preferred and common stock, and surplus. Bonds and debentures are usually carried on the books of the issuing company in terms of their par or face value. Preferred and common shares may be carried in terms of par or stated value. Stated value may be an arbitrary figure decided upon by the directors or may represent the amount received by the company from the sale of the securities at the time of issuance.

DEBENTURE   A promissory note backed by the general credit of a company and usually not secured by a mortgage or lien on any specific property.

DEFAULT   To fail to meet a financial obligation.

DIVIDEND   The payment designated by the board of directors to be distributed pro rata among the shares outstanding. On preferred shares, it is generally a fixed amount. On common shares, the dividend varies with the fortunes of the company, and it may be omitted if business is poor or the directors determine to withhold earnings to invest in plant and equipment. Sometimes a company will pay a dividend out of past earnings even if it is not currently operating at a profit.

FORECLOSURE   A legal proceeding that bars or extinguishes a mortgagor's right of redeeming a mortgaged estate.

HOLDING COMPANY   A corporation that owns the securities of another, in most cases with voting control.

LIABILITIES   All the claims against a corporation. Liabilities include accounts, wages and salaries payable; dividends declared payable; accrued taxes payable; fixed or long-term liabilities, such as mortgage bonds, debentures and bank loans.

144

MARGIN   The amount paid by the customer when using a broker's credit to buy or sell a security. Under Federal Reserve regulations, the initial margin required since 1945 has ranged from the current rate of 50 percent of the purchase price up to 100 percent.

MONOPOLY   Exclusive ownership through legal privilege, command of supply, or concerted action.

OLIGOPOLY   A market situation in which each of a few producers affects, but does not control, the market.

PAR   In the case of a common share, a dollar amount assigned to the share by the company's charter. Par value may also be used to compute the dollar amount of common shares on the balance sheet. Par value has little relationship to the market value of common stock. Many companies issue no par stock but give a stated per-share value on the balance sheet. In the case of preferred stocks, it signifies the dollar value on which dividends are figured. With bonds, par value is the face amount, usually one thousand dollars.

PROMISSORY NOTE   A written promise to pay at a fixed or determinable future time a sum of money to a specified individual or bearer.

SECURITY   Evidence of debt or of ownership, as a bond or stock certificate.

STOCK, COMMON   Securities that represent an ownership interest in a corporation. If the company has also issued preferred stock, both common and preferred stockholders have ownership rights. Common stockholders assume the greater risk, but generally exercise the greater control and may gain the greater reward in the form of dividends and capital appreciation. The terms "common stock" and "capital stock" are often used interchangeably when the company has no preferred stock.

STOCK, PREFERRED   A class of stock with a claim on the company's earnings before payment may be made on the common stock, and usually entitled to priority over common stock if the company liquidates. Usually entitled to dividends at a specified rate—when declared by the board of directors and before payment of a dividend on the common stock—depending on the terms of the issue.

SYNDICATE   A group of investment bankers who together underwrite and distribute a new issue of securities or a large block of an outstanding issue.

TRUST   A combination of firms or corporations formed by a legal agreement, especially one that reduces or threatens to reduce competition.

UNDERWRITER / INVESTMENT BANKER   The person between the corporation issuing new securities and the public. The usual practice is for one or more investment bankers to buy outright a new issue of stocks or bonds from a corporation. The group forms a syndicate to sell the securities to individuals and institutions. Investment bankers also distribute large blocks of stocks or bonds—perhaps held by an estate.

145

common at the option price of thirty-seven dollars and fifty cents per share in settlement for his holdings.[18] Although they had wished to liquidate their entire PEPCO holdings, the Clarks were unable to do so and were left with a minority position.

Shortly after the October crash, the president of Public Utility Holding Company, Fred S. Burroughs, visited Griffith in Portland. The encounter left Griffith with the impression that, although the stock-market crisis had put Public Utility Holding Company's plans in disarray, Burroughs was optimistic about the future and planned no alteration of his firm's relationship with Griffith. But by the end of January 1930, a new deal had been all but consummated between Public Utility Holding Company and Central Public Service Corporation of Chicago, another holding company, headed by Col. Albert E. Pierce. In the end, Central Public Service paid about $21 million in cash and securities to Public Utility Holding Company for all its PEPCO stock and the controlling interest in the Portland concern. In return, Public Utility Holding Company agreed to acquire a substantial interest in Central Public Service. Although no longer directly interested in PEPCO, Burroughs and Public Utility Holding Company would remain active in its affairs. Burroughs was given a seat on the Central Public Service board. Meanwhile, Public Utility Holding Company had made a $2 million paper profit.[19]

Griffith was apprised of these developments at two meetings during January 1930, one in New York, the other in Chicago. At the time, Pierce, Burroughs, and Griffith freely discussed the future of the Portland utility. Pierce and Burroughs envisioned great expansion for PEPCO, hoping that, in time, it would emerge as a regional holding company, perhaps acquiring Mountain States Power Company, and eventually bidding for Northwestern Electric. The two men enthusiastically offered Griffith financing for such acquisitions.[20]

Despite the events of 1929, Griffith was not put off by the ambitious blueprint laid out for him. He had known Burroughs for some years, dating back to when Burroughs had been a young engineer at the Department of Public Service in Washington State. He respected Burroughs' technical knowledge and, in particular, his talent for evaluating utility assets relative to corporate structure, a skill critical to understanding the worthiness of merger targets. As he later recalled, Griffith considered Pierce's judgment sound, if only because Central Public Service's huge stake in PEPCO made it seem likely that Pierce would "do nothing by way of improvident investment which would, as an immediate result, wipe out the equity of his common stock investment."[21] Like most business people and politicians, Griffith was confident that the American economy was essentially healthy. The stock market slide was just an aberration. Symbolic of the three men's optimistic agreement on the new, larger purpose of PEPCO was the decision to change the firm's name once again, this time to Pacific Northwest Public Service Company, a name intended to indicate the greater scope of the company's activities.[22] As events unfolded, the only scope in the utility's future was the scope of disaster and of Griffith's misjudgment of his partners.

On 18 February 1930, the PEPCO board of directors ratified the sale to Central Public Service. Shortly thereafter, the electrical generating division, Portland General Electric, and the streetcar division, to be known as Portland Traction Company (the third of that name), were set up as independent operating companies. All Pacific Northwest Public Service electric utility property, and nearly all other property other than traction, went to Portland General Electric. A third

Fred F. Burroughs, Franklin T. Griffith, and
C.M. Clark in Chicago. This meeting would have
a profound effect on the future of PEPCO. (PGE
collections)

147

company, Seattle Gas, was due to be added to the Pacific Northwest Public Service holdings upon its purchase at cost from Federated Utilities. The latter was a subsidiary of Central Public Service, which had acquired the company from a Chicago banking group headed by Charles Dawes, who had been vice president under Calvin Coolidge.

Both Burroughs and Pierce assured Griffith that the gas utility, formerly known as Seattle Lighting Company, was a great bargain. A backward, poorly managed company, it was nevertheless a profitable one, paying dividends on both its common and preferred stocks. According to Burroughs, who had monitored the company during his tenure at the Washington Public Service Commission, its profit margin could be fattened simply by trimming its excessive operating costs and exploiting its essentially undeveloped market. By comparison, Burroughs noted that Portland Gas and Coke Company was doing twice the business of the Seattle firm, in a smaller community.[23] Griffith and his board appear to have been easily persuaded of the soundness of the deal. Pierce and Burroughs were men of sound reputation, and opportunities like Seattle Lighting were exactly the reason for which utility holding companies existed.

On 14 March 1930, Pacific Northwest Public Service purchased 29,990 shares of Seattle Lighting common stock from Federated Utilities for $6.7 million.[24] The total accumulated more than double the par value of the shares.[25] The deal was financed through Harris Forbes and Company of Wall Street, an investment banking firm. Devised by Pierce, it called for Pacific Northwest Public Service to sell 6 percent debentures totaling $16 million to a syndicate headed by Harris Forbes and Company. The net proceeds of the issue, including interest, were to be deposited with Harris Trust Company in Chicago, with part being used to cover the price of the Seattle Gas stock and the rest to be put in an account in Chicago to be used for other financial obligations of Pacific Northwest Public Service. The debentures, in actuality, had been converted into Central Public Service stock to give them greater marketability.[26] Central Public Service was thus a chief signatory and beneficiary of the agreement.

The catalyst of all those maneuverings, Seattle Lighting, underwent a name change, to Seattle Gas Company, and a new general manager, James F. Pollard, was hired to vitalize the company. According to Griffith, Pollard "entered upon his managerial career with considerable enthusiasm and . . . the production cost of gas was materially lowered," even if his attempts to enhance his market were less successful. The deepening Depression and the competition of well-established electrical utilities initially gave Pollard's superiors reason to suppose that market building could be a long-term effort for Seattle Gas. They therefore united partially for positive results from their investment.[27]

Instead, they were destined to suffer in the entire venture, of which Seattle Gas was only a small part. The Depression was the backdrop for the episode that unfolded. The hardships engendered by the economic crisis produced great nobility and courage in some, in others, avarice and deceit. Unfortunately, the initially impressive Colonel Pierce and his associates at Central Public Service gave in to their baser instincts. They proved less interested in helping Pacific Northwest Public Service to grow than in looting it.

The first glimmer of this intent came almost immediately. In March 1930, Griffith was instructed to sign a management contract, like the one made by all other Central Public Service subsidiaries, with the parent company. The contract called for the payment of a management fee of 3 percent of Pacific Northwest Public Service's gross revenues. Griffith and Burroughs had previously agreed to waive the fee in the case of Pacific Northwest Public Service, known in the industry as a well-run company that would not require outside expertise. Griffith reminded Chicago of this fact, and the contract was withdrawn. Yet, in 1931, Central Public Service demanded that, beginning on 1 January 1932, such a fee be paid by the Portland firm. On that date the practice was begun, only to be discontinued, by order of Charles Thomas, the Oregon public utility commissioner, in August of the same year. [28]

At the same time, Pierce, who had a policy of having substantial or majority representation on the boards of his subsidiaries, larded the Pacific Northwest Public Service board with seven of his associates—one short of a majority. He became chairman of the board. It was clear that the Colonel intended to play a major role in the Portland utility's affairs.

Pierce also followed a policy of aggressively seeking local shareholders for Central Public Service wherever the company had a presence. Once he secured control of Pacific Northwest Public Service, he quickly set up an office in the Electric Building for his own private brokerage firm, Albert E. Pierce and Company. His sales force then began an energetic campaign to sell Oregon residents Central Public Service preferred stock and to effect exchanges of the old PEPCO preferred in the hands of Oregonians for the Central Public Service preferred. Griffith had been presented with credit reports on the financial condition of Central Public Service, and the company appeared to him to be sound. He not only unhesitatingly endorsed the purchase of Central Public Service stock, but became convinced that the Central Public Service preferred was a better investment than the outstanding PEPCO shares. [29] For that reason, he sent circulars to his employees, urging them to sell Central Public Service preferred stock to the public or to elicit, from old stockholders, exchanges of Central Public Service for PEPCO preferred at fifty-eight dollars per share for Central Public Service at the call price of each class of stock. In 1930 and 1931, about seventy-eight thousand Oregon-held shares of PEPCO preferred were converted, and about nineteen thousand shares of Central Public Service preferred were sold in the state, for a total of approximately one hundred fifty-three thousand shares. [30] The stock-selling campaign of Albert E. Pierce and Company, which had figured prominently in achieving those figures, was meanwhile characterized by high-pressure salesmanship and dubious practices, such as targeting recently widowed women whose defenses were down.

By the fall of 1931, Griffith was feeling ambivalent about the possibility of an early economic recovery. While he remained somewhat optimistic, his native intelligence and conservatism refused to ignore hard evidence of continued deterioration. When he reflected on the future and weighed its unhappy portents against the record of dividend payments on Central Public Service preferred stock, he became concerned that, although the Chicago holding company had an unblemished past, it would not be able to sustain regular dividend payments much into the future. He found it curious that Pierce's agents continued to sell Central Public Service preferred at a price considerably higher than street quotations, and regular brokerage prices for that and similar stocks, as if all were well with the economy. He protested this practice to the head office, but received no response. Consequently, he traveled to Chicago in October to urge Pierce to stop the sales and exchanges.[31] It was not until December that the campaign was halted, but in the meantime Pierce and his associates continued to encourage purchases and to spread rosy forecasts about Central Public Service and the economy.

In 1930 and 1931, Pierce initiated other practices that were to have far-reaching consequences for Pacific Northwest Public Service. In February, the directors of Seattle Gas Company met in Chicago and issued $450,000 worth of Seattle Gas 5 percent bonds against net unfunded betterments (capital improvements). These were credited, at par value, against the open account for Seattle Gas of its parent, Pacific Northwest Public Service. But on issuance the Chicago officers of Pacific Northwest Public Service, who were also officers of Central Public Service (not to mention Seattle Gas), sold the $450,000 worth of bonds, together with $589,000 in Seattle Gas preferred stock, to Central Gas and Electric Company, yet another Central Public Service subsidiary, for $1,039,900. Until Central Public Service sent the promissory note of Central Gas and Electric to Pacific Northwest Public Service, the Portland-based management of Pacific Northwest Public Service knew nothing of this transaction.[32] The note of Central Gas and Electric was held by Pacific Northwest Public Service, and interest was collected on it, but like so much else in the world of finance during this decade, its ultimate worth was hostage to an increasingly obdurate fortune.

In retrospect, one of the most distressing events of the relationship turned out to be the accumulation of a debt owed by Pacific Northwest Public Service and its Portland General Electric subsidiary to Central Public Service through 1930 and 1931, which totaled more than $3 million. The funds were applied to the Portland company's long-term operations and more money was thought to be required. By the end of 1931, Central Public Service was in growing difficulties, and Pierce was anxious to draw on its Pacific Northwest Public Service open account to inject much-needed cash into his own organization. At the same time, he was not ready to throw his Northwest investments to the wolves. He therefore prevailed on Griffith to go into the short-term money market to sell an issue of gold notes aggregating $7.5 million at 4.5 percent for eighteen months. These were held by Chase National Bank in New York. The proceeds of the sale would be used to pay the current indebtedness of Pacific Northwest Public Service and Portland General Electric to Central Public Service, with the balance to be deposited with Central Public Service for future disbursement to the Portland firms. Pacific Northwest Public Service would get the interest on the deposited funds and, before the note's maturation, Central Public Service would buy a block of Pacific Northwest Public Service preferred stock, the revenues to be used to pay off the debt.

Griffith had agreed to this with the hardy faith that, in the familiar litany of the day, prosperity was just around the corner. By early 1932, he had learned that Central Public Service was in deep financial trouble. As a result of its problems, the Chicago company was prepared to suspend dividend payments on its own preferred stock.[33] His concern grew that the interest that had accrued on the $7.5 million in notes ($2.75 million as of 1 April 1932) and held in Central Public Service accounts for Pacific Northwest Public Service was jeopardized.

Griffith's fears were confirmed in February 1932 when Central Public Service proposed a byzantine deal involving Pacific Northwest Public Service, Portland General Electric, Central

Public Service, and Central Gas and Electric. Execution of the transaction would have left Portland General Electric with an investment approaching $4.8 million in Central Gas and Electric preferred stock, an obligation of over $3.7 million to Pacific Northwest Public Service, and one of $1 million to Central Public Service. Griffith, his Portland officers, and the local directors of the two companies rejected this scheme out of hand and demanded immediate payment of the debt owed Pacific Northwest Public Service by Central Public Service.

Alert to what was unfolding in his own boardroom and the apparent desperation and unscrupulousness of his midwestern associates, Griffith traveled to Chicago to protect the Pacific Northwest Public Service funds. As he left Portland, he was well aware that Central Public Service could not pay the nearly $3 million it owed Pacific Northwest Public Service, but he hoped to salvage something of the debt. In Chicago, he found that the unencumbered assets of Central Public Service included only twenty thousand shares of second preferred Central Gas and Electric stock.[34] Central Gas and Electric, he also discovered, was in debt to Central Public Service for more than $20 million. Faced with this harsh reality, Griffith was forced to negotiate the kind of complex, four-cornered deal that Central Public Service had tried to foist on him earlier. It boiled down to this: Central Public Service increased its holdings of Central Gas and Electric stock, bought about twenty-seven thousand shares of Pacific Northwest Public Service common stock, and assumed Pacific Northwest Public Service's debt to Portland General Electric (nearly $5.9 million); Central Public Service further sold to Portland General Electric a total of one hundred twenty-seven thousand shares of two classes of Central Gas and Electric preferred stock to satisfy the Pacific Northwest Public Service debt. With the subscription of Pacific Northwest Public Service common stock, Central Public Service then owed Pacific Northwest Public Service $5.4 million. Portland General Electric, in the meantime, began collecting dividends on its Central Gas and Electric stock.

This, however, was only a temporary victory. On 1 August 1932, Central Public Service declared bankruptcy and filed a reorganization plan that featured the creation of a new corporation to be known as Consolidated Electric and Gas Company. All of the stocks and bonds of its subsidiaries that the former Central Public Service owned would be transferred to the new company. Consolidated Electric and Gas Company, in return, assumed the funded debts of those companies.[35] Another company, Central Public Utility Corporation, was started to hold all of the common, class A, and preferred stock held by Consolidated Electric and Gas. Under the bankruptcy plan, all the preferred stock of Pacific Northwest Public Service held by Central Public Service went to Consolidated Electric and Gas, and all Pacific Northwest Public Service common went to Central Public Utility.

These developments were taking their toll on Oregonians' confidence in Pacific Northwest Public Service. In particular, the suspension of dividends on Central Public Service preferred elicited great resentment among shareholders. The most agitated were those who had been persuaded to trade PEPCO for Central Public Service shares. For, while Central Public Service preferred was virtually worthless, PEPCO (by then Pacific Northwest Public Service) preferred continued to pay regular dividends. Albert E. Pierce and Company, Central Public Service, Pacific Northwest Public Service, Griffith, and other officers of Pacific Northwest Public Ser-

151

vice, and even other employees of the Portland firm who had participated in the conversion campaign, became the targets of lawsuits charging misrepresentation and fraud.[36] If the accompanying vilification and indignation were painful to Griffith, who had worked so hard to establish the utility's trustworthiness, it nonetheless opened his eyes to the true dimensions of his own and his company's predicament. The lawsuits alone were a serious threat to Pacific Northwest Public Service. He began to see that its fiscal difficulties were due not only to the failing economy, but also to the nefarious practices of Pierce and his cohorts. Later, from the remove of seven years, he was to write:

> The resentment against foreign control grew steadily and I became convinced that at least some of the charges of misrepresentation and the promise of repurchase from stockholders were founded in truth and that the only way that confidence in the Pacific Northwest Public Service Corporation could be restored and the original PEP stockholders recover their investment was to insist upon the restoration of PEP preferred stocks to all holders of Central Public Service preferred in Oregon and to remove the control of the Pacific Northwest Public Service Corporation from the Chicago group.[37]

Griffith had also concluded that Seattle Gas was worthless. The nearly thirty thousand shares of its stock held by Pacific Northwest Public Service was so much paper. Urgent action on all fronts was required if Pacific Northwest Public Service was to be saved from collapse—and, not incidentally, if he and his colleagues were to stay out of jail.

The first step Griffith took was to set up a separate corporation to receive all Pacific Northwest Public Service's holdings of Seattle Gas common stock. The corporation, Consolidated Securities Company, was then to acquire all the Pacific Northwest Public Service prior preferred and first preferred stock held by Consolidated Electric and Gas (consisting of all the holdings of the former Central Public Service), in order to return them to former PEPCO preferred stockholders who had converted to Central Public Service preferred through Albert E. Pierce and Company. These investors would then be asked to sign releases from all claims of fraud and misrepresentation by any of the corporations and persons who had participated in the original exchange campaign.[38]

The Portland business community watched tensely as this drama unfolded in the late summer of 1932. Despite all these adversities, Griffith still had many supporters. A conservative local periodical, the *Oregon Voter*, acknowledged that he was "on the spot," but pointed out that Griffith himself had so far "lost much of his lifetime accumulation in the general deflation and specifically in the Central Public Service deflation." The *Oregon Voter*'s editor further wrote, "We are ready to stick by Frank Griffith through thick and thin . . . we believe that his stockholders will find it . . . far better for their own interest in the long run, to stick with him; better to travel up the uphill road with him than to try to obstruct him or to turn against him."[39]

Griffith's job was, however, far from done. His next task was to convince Pierce and his executives to accept his plan. With one of his law partners, Maj. Cassius Peck, he hurried to Chicago to meet with them. E. Kimbark MacColl, in *The Growth of a City*, has given a colorful account of the meeting that took place, relying in part on the memory of Burl A. Green, the attorney representing disgruntled Central Public Service investors. Green, who had been pressuring Griffith on behalf of his clients, reported that Griffith said he had finally persuaded the Chicagoans to accept his reconversion scheme by promising, if they rejected it, to help indict them, even at the cost of a jail term to himself. "I like to play bridge," he said, "and there will be enough of you fellows in Salem [site of the Oregon State Penitentiary] to always make a foursome."[40]

Apparently this dose of reality worked. Griffith emerged from the meeting with an agreement to proceed with the exchange and with the right to appoint a voting trust for the stock consisting of Portland's two most prominent bankers, John C. Ainsworth of the U.S. National Bank (who was also on Pacific Northwest Public Service's board) and E.B. MacNaughton of the First National Bank. They were given full control of all rights under the stock for ten years, until 1 November 1942.[41] The impromptu nature of the negotiations is illustrated by the fact that neither Ainsworth nor MacNaughton knew beforehand that he would have such a duty thrust upon him, but each later acceded to Griffith's request.[42]

The last step was to gain respite from the crushing weight of debt that had been thrust on Pacific Northwest Public Service by its Chicago investors. Traveling to Wall Street, Griffith and Peck arrived in New York on 8 November 1932. They met with officials of the Chase National Bank and the investment house of Chase, Harris Forbes. The critical issue was the $7.5 million, 4.5 percent note due to mature on 1 January 1933. Griffith wanted an extension. The bankers tried to stall him, but he demanded a meeting with the president of Chase National, once again, according to Green, raising the specter of jail terms for them all.[43] This had a special resonance to the bankers, as Fred Burroughs of Public Utility Holding Company was also a vice president of Chase, Harris Forbes, which was in turn intimately linked to Chase National. Since Chase, Harris Forbes was an aggressive promoter of utility financing, the bankers could easily be made to appear to an Oregon jury as unscrupulous loan sharks, colluders who, through the machinations of Burroughs, had delivered up the victim, Pacific Northwest Public Service. In addition, the loans for the all-but-worthless Seattle Gas deal that had been forced on Pacific Northwest Public Service had been financed by the New York institutions. Charles Thomas, Oregon's persistent public utility commissioner, was mounting an investigation of Pacific Northwest Public Service's financing, which lent credence to the group portrait in prisoners' stripes that Griffith painted for the Wall Streeters.

Griffith's goals for the meeting were really quite modest. Still believing that the Depression could not get any worse, he hoped for an extension on the note of Portland General Electric, held by Chase, which was due on 1 January 1933. If Portland General Electric was forced to default, it would collapse and, he expected, the stockholders' lawsuits would be pressed. An extension, on the other hand, would give Portland General Electric valuable time, while the PEPCO preferred stockholders would be made whole again, defusing the potential legal problems. In the meantime, he felt, Pacific Northwest Public Service would have no problem paying the debt service on the debentures.

Since at the time there was no question of a new stock issue with the market in disarray, Chase

National was forced to offer Portland General Electric a one-year loan to cover the old notes, which were to be paid at maturity. Other, more complex problems were resolved at the meeting, but the effect of the Chicago and New York agreements was to decouple Pacific Northwest Public Service and its subsidiaries from Central Public Service, restore the confidence of stockholders and the public in the Portland utility, and buy time for fiscal healing to occur in the wounds inflicted on Pacific Northwest Public Service by Pierce, his accomplices, and the Depression. The crusading Charles Thomas best described the Chicagoans a short time later to a Portland audience, calling them "pillagers on the high seas of frenzied finance . . . armed with every conceivable instrument of modern immoral financial method including depraved and poisonous tongue."[44]

Griffith, who despite his efforts might have been pilloried anyway, returned to Portland virtually a hero. Newspaper after newspaper hailed him for defeating the rapacious Pierce and the formidable Wall Street financiers. "The state could not have a happier Christmas present," the *Oregonian* rhapsodized. He had prevented his company from "crumbling" into bankruptcy, "and nearly fifteen thousand Oregon families have received hope that their securities . . . will be restored at a fair market value." The newspaper observed that management responsibility at Pacific Northwest Public Service now rested "entirely upon the shoulders of Franklin T. Griffith, John C. Ainsworth, and E.B. MacNaughton—men whose lives are bound up with the fate of this state. If they cannot be trusted, no one can be trusted." The paper closed its story with the comment that one of the bankers at Chase, "this largest bank on earth is reported to have closed the negotiations with the remark that Mr. Griffith was the best financier to have come out of the west in recent times."[45] The Oregon City *Banner-Courier*, the *Downtown Review*, the Linnton *Public Ledger*, the *Oregon Journal*, the *East Side Enterprise*, the Portland *Spectator*, the Portland *Bulletin*, and the *Oregon Voter* joined the *Oregonian* in praising Griffith. The periodicals were an index of the widespread fear and subsequent relief the company's plight had caused in Portland and around the state.

The euphoria was to be short-lived. The company resumed its old name, PEPCO, in 1933, but things could never be as they were. The Depression's insidious effects, the plundering of Pacific Northwest Public Service, and the debt burden imposed by the relationship with Central Public Service could not be so easily defeated. Griffith's enduring and critical victories had been to free his company from Pierce, to restore its integrity, and to buy some time. Unfortunately, by 1934, the time was up.

From 1932 onward, PEPCO had no operating net income, and its only source of income was Portland General Electric dividends. On the 1 March 1934 due date of its debenture coupons, the company was unable to meet its interest obligation, and it defaulted. This opened the way to foreclosure. Subsequently, and ironically, Percy H. Clark of the Philadelphia Clarks, who owned substantial blocks of the company's preferred stocks and debentures, filed a complaint in the U.S. District Court at Portland, forcing PEPCO into receivership.[46] The reorganization plan approved by the court on 5 March 1935 converted the debentures into income bonds by a two-thirds majority vote of the debenture holders. This would essentially distribute interest payments over a longer period.

A service truck with Pacific Northwest Public Service Co. painted on its side. The PEPCO name appears in a small diamond at the right. (PGE collections)

ALTHOUGH PORTLAND'S FINANCIERS had little choice at the turn of the century but to appeal to eastern investors (since there was no significant local capital on which to draw), many Oregonians were dismayed at the prospect of outside ownership of the company. The *Oregonian* called the 1906 sale "political jobbery."

President Franklin T. Griffith essentially served as a manager during his first eighteen years as president of PEPCO. He dealt uneasily with the demands of the eastern owners, but when the Clark interests sold out to a holding company (Central Public Service) in 1929, and the holding company in turn plunged the utility into debt and financial uncertainty, Griffith responded by pulling the company back under local control,

reminding the Central Public Service officials of their legally suspect behavior if they tried to object to demands.

Local newspapers were exultant. The *Oregonian* reported on 19 December 1932 that PEPCO was "freed from . . . evil eastern control" which had "played Oregon for a sucker." On 6 January 1933, the paper applauded Griffith's "single-handed fight that wrested control of the Pacific Northwest Public Service company utilities from Central Public Service company hands." Later in the year, Oregonians were assured that matters had been settled, that Griffith had been supported by a shareholders' vote of confidence, and that PEPCO would no longer be assaulted by "outside interference."

155

Even this was insufficient to solve the company's problems. The unpaid interest on the income bonds accumulated to 30 percent of the value of the bonds in a period of five years. This constituted another default, although neither the bonds' trustees nor bondholders had pressed a default action.[47] In the circumstances, the board of PEPCO itself filed for reorganization under the provisions of Chapter X of the Federal Bankruptcy Act of 1938. The officers felt that, as the value of the company's assets comfortably exceeded the claims of the holders of the income bonds, the bondholders' interests would be best served by a reorganization that would give dividends to PEPCO preferred stockholders who had been frozen out by the 1934 reorganization. This was, in fact, simply a device to stimulate the market in PEPCO securities of all kinds, for if stockholders were once again receiving regular payments, new investment would be stimulated, and all PEPCO financial instruments, including bonds, would become more attractive. Bondholders could thus, if they wished, liquidate them at favorable prices, rather than being forced to hold onto them. The company's capital would increase as well, instead of staying static. In some ways the 1939 reorganization was a hopeful sign in the long, painful road back from the morass of the Depression years.

POWER, PORTLAND, AND THE NEW DEAL

The company's fiscal problems were reflected throughout this period in the slow pace of development and improvement of its generating, transmission, and distribution capacities. The almost flat curve of load expansion was also a factor. For an industry in which constant improvement was both the norm and the necessity, the retarded economy made simple survival, let alone enhancement, a challenge.

In 1930, Pacific Northwest Public Service operated a super-power system providing light and power to one hundred twenty-five thousand consumers in Portland, Salem, Oregon City, Hillsboro, St. Helens, Silverton, and eighty other towns in western Oregon. The total population of those cities was four hundred twenty thousand. The generating capacity of its system aggregated 227,850 HP—126,650 HP from hydro and 101,200 HP from steam. The energy produced traveled over nearly eight hundred miles of high-tension lines, interconnecting all the generating plants and communities served.[48] As the decade opened, the Pacific Northwest Public Service generating system was an integral part of the super-power system of the Pacific slope, having established interties with other large power systems of the region.

In 1929, consumption of the company's electricity was 421.9 million kwh. In 1930, the figure was 422.3 million kwh.[49] The minuscule gain indicated the lengthening shadow of the Depression on the land. By 1934, with the economy in a state of virtual collapse, and a quarter of the American work force unemployed, industry in the Northwest had either cut back drastically on operations or shut down entirely. Conditions were reflected in the ever-declining figures on consumption of the middle years of the thirties. In an effort to reverse the trend, the company went on the offensive where it could have the most effect. Portland General Electric targeted residential, farm, commercial lighting and small power consumers in an intensive campaign to expand sales of load building appliances. Thus, in 1934, 1,318 electric ranges were added to Portland General Electric households.[50] in 1935, the total rose to 2,529, refrigerator sales totaled 6,350, and water heaters 744, both of which were also above the 1934 figures.[51] On the last day of 1935, the total number of customers reached 123,001, considerably lower than the 128,515 disclosed by the 1931 *Annual Report* but ahead of the number for 1934.[52] By 1935, the Portland General Electric residential customer was using 1,010 kwh in the home, and the company's revenue was $31.29 per home per year for the service. The cost to the consumer for each kwh was 3.21 cents.[53] At the end of the decade, in 1939, the company generated a total of 603.3 million kwh. Of that total, 468.3 million kwh were generated by the hydroelectric facilities and 135 million kwh thermally.[54]

The company made giant strides in expanding its generating capacity or bettering its transmission and distribution systems, although it struggled to improve where it could or where it was necessary to do so. In 1930, before the true ramifications of the economic decline were known, a 20,500-kw steam turbine generator unit with a large pressure boiler was added to Station L, and a record unit rated at a 35,000-HP capacity was installed at the Oak Grove hydro station. The wisdom of the Station L project was clear in the fall and winter of 1930, when a dangerously low water supply for the hydro plants made it necessary to rely on steam generation to meet demand. Without the new boiler, this would have proved impossible.[55]

In April 1931, Oak Grove was the site of a project known as the "Big Bottom Tunnel." The purpose of the tunnel was to permit diversion of the main branch of the Clackamas River to the Oak Grove fork. This would increase the capacity of the Oak Grove power plant, especially during the low water season. The work on Big Bottom, which reached thirty-five hundred feet, was halted at the end of the first phase because of the company's financial crisis. The 1932 *Annual Report* somberly notified shareholders that management was rigidly curtailing expenditures on system betterments of all kinds except for "necessary service extensions which the companies are required to provide by law and the replacements and improvements essential to maintain proper standards of service."[56]

In one area, the company was forced to keep abreast of expansion for its own survival. The New Dealers had targeted extension of electricity to rural residents as a particular goal, in the belief that it was a key to regional economic development and a more efficient agricultural sector. Private utilities in some areas had dragged their feet in extending rural lines because of the high cost of serving sparsely populated areas. The passage by Congress of the Rural Electrification Act (REA) of 1935, and the threat of the creation of PUDs, spurred the private utilities. The company had been slowly building service to its potential rural consumers when the economy collapsed. After REA, it made a concerted effort to reach farmers and other rural residents. During the thirties, Portland General Electric strung 558 miles of new transmission lines, primarily to rural customers.[57] By 1935, it could boast that its power was serving, or was available to more than 85 percent of possible customers in its service area.[58] By 1937, only a few small, sparsely settled areas remained unserved, although the annual report of that year said the company was "prepared to give service when economically practicable."[59]

The irony was that, mightily though Griffith had labored to wrest control of the company

157

PEPCO'S EFFORTS to establish a sense of family among its employees began in the first issue of the *Synchronizer*. In it, company President Franklin T. Griffith expressed his desire to engender a sense of cohesion and familiarity among employees about each other and about the company itself. He believed that PEPCO staff who knew the workings of their company would present the best public image and would most ably serve the company's customers.

Although part of the intention in fostering this sense of family was for public-relations purposes, it was also to benefit the employees. In 1923, company veterans assembled to form the Twenty Year Club, devoted to creating a "fraternal bond" among employees with twenty or more years of company service. In addition, PEPCO sponsored dances and picnics for its employees and devised and built its own float for the annual Portland Rose Parade.

In 1935, R.R. Robley, a longtime employee, wrote the company's first history, *Portland Electric Power Company with its Predecessor and Subsidiary Companies 1860-1935*. For the first time, the PEPCO family had a life story.

Minor White's photo of the boiler of PEPCO's Station L. (OHS neg. OrHi 9391)

A group portrait of the 1935 PEPCO baseball team. (PGE collections)

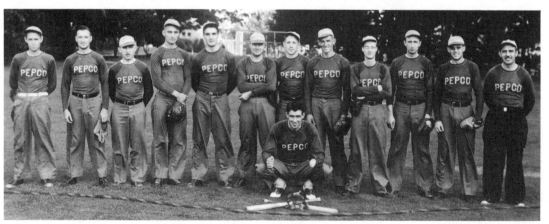

This 1935 photo shows PEPCO employee Delmar Brown testing boiler water from Station L. (PGE collections)

Adventures in fine dining in the hog fuel combustion chamber in Station L. The banquet was part of the dedication of the new station in 1930. (PGE collections)

The Rural Electrification Act brought the possibility of motors doing work that men, women, children and animals had been doing for centuries. It also brought new voices and new visions into the lives of many rural families in the United States. (National Archives)

This posed picture shows a farm family intently watching the radio as they relax for a few moments. (National Archives)

THE RURAL ELECTRIFICATION
ADMINISTRATION (REA) was created in 1935
to encourage electric utilities to extend service
into rural areas by providing the companies with
low-interest (2 percent) loans. Although the effort
was quite successful, and was one of the New
Deal's most popular achievements, it was marked
by wariness on the parts of both private utilities
and the government. Private utilities worried that
the REA's ultimate goal was the socialization of
electric systems, while the government openly
criticized many practices of the utility industry,
particularly the abuses perpetrated by its holding
companies. Some private companies extended
what were called "spite lines" into rural areas:
haphazard extensions of service into districts
targeted by the REA. Districts riddled with such
lines had some customers who received electric
service and some who did not. Utilities financed
by the REA found their operations rendered inefficient and disorderly, since they were forced to
put in the same amount of equipment for fewer
customers as for electrifying the whole district.

By 1937, PEPCO had extended service into 86
percent of the rural area in its territory. That
same year, only 19 percent of the entire nation's
rural areas had electricity, of which 46 percent
were in Oregon. PEPCO was justifiably proud of its
accomplishment.

Between 1945 and 1949, REA borrowers connected two million consumers. In the Northwest,
virtually all such borrowers supplied their customers with power purchased from the Bonneville
Power Administration, whose low rates allowed
the Northwest to continue to lead the nation in
rural electrification.

I HAD SEEN FIRST-HAND the grim drudgery
and grind which had been the common lot of
eight generations of American farm women. I
had seen the tallow candle in my own home,
followed by the coal-oil lamp. I knew what it was
to take care of the farm chores by the flickering,
undependable light of the lantern in the mud and
cold rains of the fall, and the snow and icy winds
of winter.

I had seen the cities gradually acquire a night
as light as day.

I could close my eyes and recall the innumerable scenes of the harvest and the unending pun-
ishing tasks performed by hundreds of thousands
of women, growing old prematurely; dying before
their time; conscious of the great gap between
their lives and the lives of those whom the accident of birth or choice placed in the towns and
cities.

Why shouldn't I have been interested in the
emancipation of hundreds of thousands of farm
women?

Sen. George W. Norris of Nebraska,
Cosponsor of the Rural Electrification Act

from external forces, another influence was taking shape that was to play a role in the utility's future. It was the force of nature itself—the Columbia River. The fulcrum of its power was at Bonneville Dam. The contest for leverage over Bonneville energy brought together the New Deal, the advocates of public power, and regional private utilities such as PEPCO.

The thirties were paradoxical years. A time of collapse and despair, the decade was also a time of renewal and hope. Defeat mingled freely with triumph, while intellectual bankruptcy, matching the threadbare economy, coexisted with blazing innovation and economic renewal. Thus, the heartfelt but hidebound allegiance of Hoover and his advisers to an economy structured to benefit business was supplanted by the passion and creativity of the New Dealers, who wished to orient the economy toward the welfare of all classes. Reformers of the right and left as disparate as Huey Long, Francis Townsend, and Father Coughlin competed for attention by trumpeting ideas designed to uplift and galvanize the masses. In the course of the decade, the nation changed from laissez-faire capitalism, with a passive federal government, to welfare industrial capitalism, with the government playing an active role in the economy and society.

Some deplored the change, but it was clear at the time that the economy as planned was not working. In the election of 1932, the relatively unknown governor of New York was elected president over the hapless Herbert Hoover. Franklin D. Roosevelt was himself an exemplar of the ironic oppositions of the era. A patrician, he was a Democrat; crippled by polio, he had great vigor; according to Justice Oliver Wendell Holmes, he was intellectually second rate, yet he gathered around himself a collection of brilliant minds—the so-called "Brain Trust." Together they set out to rally Americans from the malaise of hard times and took on the monumental task of restoring the nation's broken economy, society, and dreams. The Roosevelt administration offered a "new deal" to the American people.

Under that New Deal, Roosevelt and his advisers moved rapidly on a variety of fronts after the 1932 election to restore public confidence and lay the foundations for recovery. It is necessary to understand that the New Dealers hoped not simply to "jump-start" the economy, but to effect fundamental changes in the American economic and financial structure that would protect the nation against the kind of malfunctions that had led to socioeconomic catastrophe. They had a formula: relief, recovery, and reform. To effect recovery and reform, they scrutinized the entire economy and drew up plans in order to address problems wherever they found them. Furthermore, they took inspiration from the largely unfulfilled reform agenda of the twenties. They sought to strengthen and rebuild, not only in the traditional centers of industry, commerce, and agriculture, but in the more isolated and underdeveloped regions of the nation, including the Pacific Northwest.

Roosevelt had first seen the Columbia River in 1920, during the ill-fated Democratic presidential campaign of that year, when he was the running mate of James N. Cox. He was deeply impressed with the river's potential, which he thought the federal government should develop.[60] By the Depression, he had also become alarmed by the abuses of the utility holding companies. Not surprisingly, in a campaign speech for the presidency in Portland on 21 September 1932, he spoke of the evils of utility abuses, of the vast possibilities of power development on the Columbia River, and of the government's duty to protect the people against inefficient service or exorbitant

163

THE FEDERAL POWER COMMISSION (now known as the Federal Energy Regulatory Commission) was created in 1920 under the Federal Water Power Act. The Federal Power Commission was originally responsible for the general administrative management of waterpower sites on navigable rivers, public lands, and reservations. In 1930, Congress broadened its jurisdiction to include authority over rates, services, and operations of electric-power facilities. Five years later, Title II of the Public Utility Holding Company Act assigned the FPC supervision over all utilities generating electricity that would be transmitted over state lines. The FPC became the major regulatory authority over utility rates, securities, accounting systems, property, physical operations, and services. It also promoted power-pooling projects and conducted rate surveys to aid consumers in choosing the kind of utility—public or private—that would serve their area best.

A 1944 *map showing rural electrification administrations in Oregon. (PGE collections)*

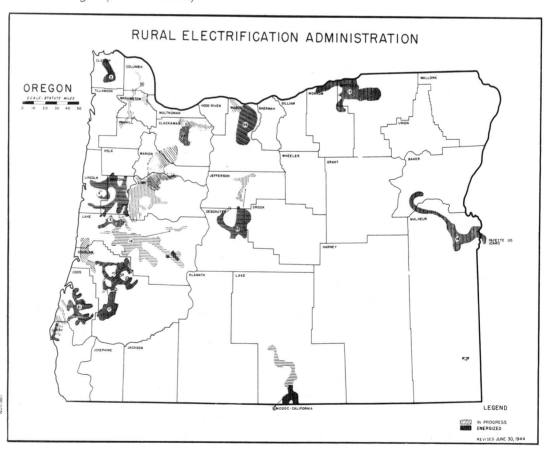

charges of the holding companies. He said, "I state in definite and certain terms that the next great hydroelectric development to be undertaken by the federal government must be that on the Columbia River."[61]

The idea of federal regulation and generation of power predated his speech. It had been nurtured by Sen. George W. Norris of Nebraska throughout the twenties. In 1920, the Federal Power Commission was created, but Norris, fixing on a government facility at Muscle Shoals, Alabama, which generated electricity and sold it to a private company, wanted the government itself to market power regionally. Presidents Coolidge and Hoover both vetoed bills to that end. In May 1933, during the famous First Hundred Days of his administration, Roosevelt signed into law the Norris-Morin Resolution, which created the Tennessee Valley Authority (TVA) with the Muscle Shoals facility as its centerpiece. The TVA was a regional public agency, but a unique one, with both public and private administrative features. In this hybrid form, it was probably the most striking innovation of the First Hundred Days. Under its exceptional administrator, David Lilienthal, the agency could, and did, act with alacrity to build, own, and run power facilities, as well as to market electricity. It also had purview over navigation, flood control, land management, and reclamation in one of the nation's most depressed areas. The ambitious scope and objectives of the TVA had an immediate economic effect. The region benefited from the agency's construction projects for dams, dikes, levees, and roads. The TVA appeared to achieve the Roosevelt administration's goals perfectly.

Many influential persons in the Northwest, especially from the dry lands of eastern Washington, had lobbied since the end of World War I for federal assistance in exploiting the irrigation and hydropower potential of the upper Columbia River in order to attract industry and immigrants. By the twenties, the focus of attention was a plan popularized by the editor of the *Wenatchee World*, Rufus Woods, among others, to construct the largest man-made structure ever built at Grand Coulee on the river about eighty miles northwest of Spokane.[62] Strenuous lobbying and the evolving attitude of the U.S. Congress toward the exploitation of the nation's resources resulted in House Document No. 308-69/1, published by the War Department in 1926. This paper called for comprehensive surveys by the Federal Power Commission and the U.S. Army Corps of Engineers and Flood Control on the country's navigable streams. The River and Harbor Act of 1927 empowered the agencies to undertake such surveys, and on 29 March 1932, a "308 Report" (as the surveys became known) was issued on the Columbia by the Corps. Entitled *Columbia River and Minor Tributaries*, the report envisioned eight dams on the river (later changed to ten) and was in essence the culmination of the struggle to achieve a development policy.[63]

Roosevelt's promise made in Portland was then translated into action once he took office, amid widespread support from the Northwest public. Many clearly saw it as the occasion for the start of the region's own TVA. On 16 July 1933, ground was broken for the first project, Bonneville Dam, thirty-five miles east of Portland. The Works Progress Administration's first project guaranteed not only power, but jobs. Almost everyone in the region was pleased.

Among those who were not were the private utilities of the Northwest, who were most intensely concerned about Bonneville. They were understandably uneasy, because the Roosevelt administration and Northwest public power advocates were bent on setting the lowest possible rates for the energy generated by the dam. Those rates would then set a standard for the rest of the nation. The only constraint on price would be the need to retire the debt for the construction of the plant.[64] For the private utilities, the competition that such a rate guaranteed seemed to spell their doom. A more troubling and immediate unknown was the structure and authority of the agency created to manage the power. Would it be another TVA or would its writ be more limited? The answer to these questions was crucial to private utilities.

The proponents of public power in the region, as well as their allies such as the Granges, organized labor, and other Progressive groups and individuals, argued for the creation of a Columbia Valley Authority (CVA). As its name suggests, the agency was to be modeled on the TVA and would be supervised by a board of governors. To all intents and purposes, it was to be independent and self-sustaining, operating on revenues from power sales. In the Senate James Pope, an Idaho Democrat, introduced a bill (S. 869), and in the House Knute Hill, a Washington Democrat, offered legislation to create such an agency in 1935. Supporters of the CVA proposed that it sell its power at preferred rates to public utilities and cooperatives.[65]

The private utilities, chambers of commerce, and those opposed to the extension of governmental authority disapproved of the CVA. The city of Portland was also skeptical. Many in the city felt that Bonneville could supply Portland more cheaply alone than if it were part of a CVA system. Still others felt that existing federal agencies, like the Corps of Engineers, would be adequate to the task of running the Columbia River dams. The senators from Oregon, Charles McNary and Frederick Steiwer, countered the CVA bills with one of their own (S. 330), which more nearly reflected the interests of business. But the two Republicans were actually representing the interests of the Corps of Engineers and the Bureau of Reclamation, which wished to retain control of the dam.[66]

A major fight loomed over the various pieces of legislation until, in the next session of Congress, a compromise, sponsored by the Senate delegations of both Oregon and Washington, was hammered out. Senate Bill 4695 of May 1936 offered the Corps of Engineers the authority to generate power and build the high-voltage transmission lines. The Federal Power Commission was, under the terms of the bill, empowered to market the electricity and set rates.

Hearings on the issue in 1936 substantially centered on two differing sets of expert opinions embodied in testimony and reports given to President Roosevelt and the congressional committee conducting the investigation. One view, represented by the work of the Pacific Northwest Regional Planning Commission, a group made up of the region's state planning bodies, was largely influenced by a Reed College professor named Charles McKinley. In McKinley's view, a CVA was not appropriate for the Pacific Northwest because the region was not so severely underdeveloped as the Tennessee Valley.[67] In his opinion, the development of hydroelectric power and its distribution were primary, not the special social function of a TVA. On the other hand, he and his allies called for the creation of a new agency under federal control to dispense Bonneville's energy, at postage-stamp (uniform) rates, throughout the dam's service area and for the creation of a three-member administrative board, similar to TVA's. McKinley also advised a central-grid system for the region, in the shape of a triangle, with Portland, Spokane, and the Puget Sound areas at the corners. He envisioned it extending eastward and northward to encompass the entire Columbia

INVESTOR-OWNED UTILITY   Also known as a "private" utility. Because the term "private" sometimes conveys the image of a company that does not necessarily act in the public interest, the term "investor-owned" has nearly replaced it. An investor-owned utility such as Portland General Electric is financed by the sale of securities on the free market. Such a utility is a tax-paying business, administered by officers elected by shareholders. The activities of an investor-owned utility in Oregon are regulated by the Public Utilities Commission.

PUBLIC UTILITY   This term includes municipally owned electric systems as well as state and federal power projects. The Bonneville Power Administration is a public utility, administered by the federal government under the jurisdiction of Congress but not under the jurisdiction of the Public Utilities Commission.

PUBLIC UTILITY DISTRICT (PUD)   A public utility district is a political subdivision serving an area larger than a municipality, established for the purposes of generating, transmitting, and distributing electric energy. A PUD is administered by a board elected by the voters in the district and does not fall under the jurisdiction of the Public Utilities Commission.

"Glossary of Electric Utility Terms," Edison Electric Institute

Construction work on the high towers for the Bonneville Dam. (Bonneville Power Administration)

167

River drainage basin, as far south as California, with Grand Coulee hooked up on completion.

McKinley's position called for a fully realized blueprint for the distribution of Columbia River power before the opening of the dam. Although he put hydroelectric generation, transmission, and distribution before the system's socioeconomic attributes, he sympathized with the New Dealers' desire to advance that aim. He felt that the goal of cheap regionwide electricity would be lost if not affirmed at the outset.

The opposition was led by the Corps of Engineers. Supported by the private utilities and the Portland Chamber of Commerce, the Corps expressed skepticism about McKinley's plan, charging that uniform rates for the entire region were not economical. There was too small a population base and too few industrial customers in the region ever to pay off the construction costs of the system. William D.B. Dodson, of the Portland Chamber of Commerce, testified that Bonneville ought to be left to private enterprise. He condemned the plan of McKinley and the Pacific Northwest Regional Planning Commission as "too visionary" and said that a regionwide transmission system without special rates for the private utilities and industries (which would be the biggest consumers) would be economically unsound. Given the modest population base and the enormous cost of the proposed system, the rates would have to be prohibitively high. The Corps' report to Congress confirmed this view. Its basic argument was that high rates could engender a vicious circle: no new industry would be attracted to the region because of them, no one would migrate to the region because of lack of industry, unused capacity would keep rates high, and the pattern would repeat itself endlessly.[68]

Through 1936, Congress failed to act on all this information and legislation, although the Corps of Engineers' report found favor with the House committees on rivers and harbors and navigation. During the stalemate, the issue was put to a test at the polls. In Roosevelt's 1936 reelection campaign, his views on power policy (which obviously tended to favor a role for government) became a focus for Northwesterners. He won bigger pluralities in each of the Northwestern states than he had in 1932. So did those members of the region's congressional delegations who were running at the time, and since they represented various positions across the board on the issue, no clear mandate on the administration of Bonneville power could be inferred. On the other hand, the event created the conditions under which the matter could be resolved.[69]

At headquarters in Portland, the debate over Bonneville was followed with fascination and apprehension. While joining the lobbying effort against government control of the power, PEPCO publicly followed a policy of studious evenhandedness against all possible outcomes. In practice, this meant welcoming Bonneville into the region's power supply system, but plainly stating the company's fears about the effect of public power in private utilities. Stockholders were told in 1934 that Bonneville would be able to produce power at a lower cost than any other hydroelectric development in the United States and that this electricity might disastrously affect the business of the privately owned electric utilities.[70] If the proponents of public power won the day, and state or municipally owned systems "financed by low cost federal funds and with complete freedom from taxation in competition with the existing privately owned electric utilities" were to arise while the private utilities were forced to continue bearing their regular tax burden, the private utilities might ultimately collapse, for "no private business . . . can successfully compete with a tax exempt enterprise having behind it the treasury of the United States to finance it with low cost funds and to absorb its losses."[71]

If, as some believed, most or all of Bonneville's power was reserved for use by electrochemical and electrometallurgical industries which required cheap, abundant electricity, then the dam would be a welcome addition to the Northwest. "The management of your company," the *Annual Report* of 1933 said, "believes the establishment and successful operation of such . . . plants would be of great advantage to Portland and . . . the entire northwest."[72] Here was the reiteration of the familiar theme of Griffith's administration. The company's fate was intertwined with that of the city and the region. The company would promote the common good, but expected to enhance, not erode, its own position.

That position was elaborated in an interview of Griffith that appeared in the *Synchronizer*. "If electric energy can be purchased by PEPCO [from Bonneville] at less cost than . . . [from] new, privately owned plants," Griffith said, "PEPCO will willingly buy it and pass on the benefit in still lower rates to consumers, already benefiting by one of the lowest rates in the nation. I am certain that our full cooperation with state and federal agencies will not only preserve the value and earning power of the investments of our security holders but continue to provide the lowest practicable rates to consumers in keeping with fair investment returns and adequate salaries for employees."[73]

Throughout the years until Bonneville Dam began generation in 1937, PEPCO's position remained the same. But the lingering congressional battle over the nature of authority over Bonneville and the extent of its operations was reflected in the nervous prose of the 1936 *Annual Report*. Griffith wrote, "We are unwilling to believe that either the Congress or the Federal Administration will enact or adopt a policy of deliberate confiscation."[74] Again, an emphasis was placed on PEPCO's willingness to assist in making Bonneville a success.

As the whole region waited, the Bonneville legislation began to take shape early in 1937, with the completion of the dam itself only a few months off. President Roosevelt's own preferences for the shape and objectives of Bonneville's administration began to emerge. He wanted the dam's power and that of the private utilities to be separate; he wanted preferential rates for public and cooperative distribution systems; the basic transmission (or "backbone") system should be built by the federal government; and he desired that a new civilian agency market Bonneville power and be a part of the Department of the Interior, under the purview of his trusted lieutenant, Secretary Harold Ickes, an ardent public-power advocate.[75] Coupled with the lobbying of the "Commonwealth Federations" of Oregon and Washington (organizations of liberal to radical elements, including the Granges and American Federation of Labor and Congress of Industrial Organizations labor unions), the two states' delegations began to move toward a compromise.

The bill that Congress passed as the Bonneville Power Act on 20 August 1937 was a reconciliation of the Senate and House versions. The House bill contained the famous "Bone Formula," named after Sen. Homer T. Bone of Washington. This was a compromise to all interests, creating a balanced and segmented sharing of authority and preference over the power and rates of Bonneville's energy. It became the essence of Bonneville's operation. The Bonneville administrator, a civilian, would fall under the jurisdiction of the secretary of the Interior, who distrusted the Corps of Engineers, but the Corps would actually run the dam. The administrator would market the electricity and set the rates. The champions of public power had lost on the CVA concept, but won preferential rates. The private utilities and their allies lost the right to construct the dams and transmission lines and to share in preferential rates, but they avoided what they most dreaded: another TVA. Moreover, according to Philip Funigiello, an astute historian of this episode, in the course of the political infighting that characterized the crafting of the legislation, and in order to break the impasse that was looming over the completion of Bonneville Dam, Roosevelt undermined his own advisers and turned his back on the chance to fashion an enduring national power policy.[76]

The structure of Bonneville's administration was set, although the language describing it implied that there might be changes on the completion of Grand Coulee. It was hoped by public-power advocates that the energy from that dam (whose essential purpose was irrigation) would be wrested from the Bureau of Reclamation and added to the Bonneville power pool through a provision that allowed no intertying of federal projects.

In the boardrooms of the Northwest's private utilities, as well as the offices of the various public-power lobbies, little comfort was found in the settlement. A new fight loomed ahead. Who would be the Bonneville administrator? This was a crucial decision, because that individual would not only set all the rates for Bonneville power but essentially set its policies.[77]

President Roosevelt dedicated Bonneville Dam on 28 September 1937. At his speech, vocal supporters of J.D. Ross, the respected head of the Seattle City Lighting Department and an advocate of "municipal socialism," greeted Roosevelt with calls for their favorite's elevation to the position. The president's speech called for the widest distribution of power at the lowest cost, a sentiment shared by Ross, who seemed to be the inevitable choice for the job. The candidate and his allies soon became the focus of attacks by Northwest utilities, the Portland business community, and the Oregon Democratic leadership. Oregonians were afraid that, as administrator, Ross would initiate the dreaded postage-stamp rates that would eliminate the city's trump card in the economic-development sweepstakes. That is, if rates were pegged to the distance from the source of transmission rather than on postage-stamp rates, Portland's close proximity to Bonneville would give industries that settled there a lower rate than if they settled, say, in Seattle. Ross, for his part, refused to declare his interest in the job, but went on the offensive against the utilities and Portland commercial interests. He accused the utilities and their friends of trying to limit Bonneville's generation of energy in order to protect the high rates of the private concerns.[78] In October 1937, Ross, a close personal friend of the president, was appointed as the Bonneville administrator.

The new administrator was empowered to make wholesale rates, locate and construct transmission lines, give preference to municipalities and PUDs in allocating power, and reserve one-half of Bonneville's installed capacity for the public bodies up to 1 January 1941. However, he was free to sell power to private utilities for resale on contracts not exceeding twenty years. The contracts could be canceled on five years' notice if the administrator judged part of their energy was likely to be needed by the public bodies or cooperatives.[79]

WHEN FRANKLIN ROOSEVELT was elected president in 1932, it was on the basis of a campaign that emphasized the development of electric power as a national concern, criticized the practices of utility holding companies, called for better regulation of private utilities, and supported the right of the public to choose public utilities over private. Roosevelt believed that waterpower belonged to all Americans, and that such a resource should be developed in accordance with the national interest.

Although many people thought Roosevelt was actually seeking the socialization of utilities, PEPCO's president, Franklin T. Griffith, perceived his real goal, a system in which hydro projects would be operated by the government and power responsibly transmitted and distributed by private industry. Roosevelt wanted to curtail the abuses by private industry, not put it out of business.

Griffith believed that private utilities should cooperate fully with federal power developments. He heralded the government's proposal to build Bonneville Dam, because, although PEPCO could not afford to construct the project itself, he recognized the opportunity for the company in transmitting and distributing Bonneville power. Most importantly, however, he brought the company to understand that it should, and would, serve the public interest and that it could still prosper while cooperating with federal power agencies.

171

For PEPCO, the completion of the dam and the appointment of Ross marked the end of a long period of watchful waiting. It had long since become abundantly clear that Bonneville's energy would be offered preferentially to publicly operated bodies and that their partisan would be named its head. PEPCO had prepared itself for this. Under Griffith, the company had aligned itself with the moderate range of conservative opinion on the controversy. It could reconcile itself to government construction of dams. Like many private utilities, since the passage of the Federal Power Act of 1920 (which gave the federal government purview over navigable streams), it had abandoned plans for generation facilities on the Columbia and moved to the Clackamas.[80] With the dam in place, PEPCO and its allies wanted business rather than government to take control of its energy at the "bus bar," a term that became industry jargon for the point at which power leaves the generating plant. The utilities' view was that federal paternalism should be discouraged once the power was manufactured, while the nation's driving principles—individualism, free enterprise, investment for profit—should be encouraged. For conservatives, the specter of regional planning (which haunted the testimony of the public-power advocates in the congressional debates over the issue) was particularly troublesome, as it portended future limitations on traditional paths of development.[81] Still, the dam was tolerable to the company because it represented a positive force in Portland's development through its offer of abundant and cheap energy to the big users in the chemical and metal industries. Their location in the city would inevitably be a great load-building opportunity for PEPCO, if what Oregon Gov. Charles Martin liked to call Portland's "God-given advantage" (its proximity to the dam) was protected by measured rates. Because the postage-stamp rates advocated by the public-power people would harm these possibilities, PEPCO had aligned itself with the Corps of Engineers (which, throughout the hearings, had wrung its hands over what it took to be the inadequate replacement schedule of the dam's construction costs through uniform rates) and the Portland Chamber of Commerce.

These stances had been thwarted by Congress and the president, but there was reason to be optimistic. The freewheeling political environment of Washington State may have nurtured the growth of public power, but the conservative voters of Oregon were not to be easily seduced by "the free-power-for-nothing-boys," as some called Oregon's public power advocates. On 8 April 1937, the voters of Clackamas, Polk, Washington, and Yamhill counties, all of which were served by PEPCO, as well as those in two other locales, rejected a public-utility-district measure that would have relied on Bonneville's energy. The margin of victory was three to two.[82] The voters vetoed the idea because, in a well-financed campaign, the utilities had argued persuasively that, as the state did not tax PUDs, the revenues ordinarily available from taxation of electrical generation would be absent from the counties' coffers, lowering the quality of service by local governments.[83]

This and other events led some to question the size of the market for Columbia River power. "Kilo-what?" the *Oregonian*'s editorial of 1 October 1937 was entitled. Directing itself to those on both sides of the issue who feared they would be cut off from cheap Bonneville energy by the appetites of the preferred customers, the paper scolded the alarmists. There would be plenty of electricity to go around. It was probably safe to assume "that the practical engineers," as opposed to the "political engineers," would be "selling Bonneville power to whatever customers will take it."[84] Even the advocates of planning offered olive branches. The job of ratemaking, said Roy Bessey of the Pacific Northwest Regional Planning Commission, "cannot be completed without compromise of the extreme views on either side."[85]

These developments allowed Griffith to reiterate PEPCO's long-standing attitude of cautious optimism that a workable relationship with the Bonneville administration could be achieved. In the 1937 *Annual Report* he wrote:

> The company is now, as at all times since the beginning of Bonneville construction prepared to cooperate fully with the Administrator in the utilization of energy produced at Bonneville to the extent that Bonneville energy can be used in our system to the advantage of the company and its customers. We have agreed that any and all savings resulting from our purchase of Bonneville energy will be passed on to the consumers. It is our earnest hope that a basis of fair cooperation can be established . . . to the end that steadily increasing quantities of Bonneville energy can be utilized in our system with increasing advantage to our customers.[86]

Before the election of April 1938, Griffith gave what amounted to a campaign speech before a friendly audience, the Oregon City Chamber of Commerce, concerning the Clackamas County public-utility-district measure. The speech not only captures the views of a conservative and a utility executive on the issue of public power, but also illustrates the keen analytical turn of mind that allowed Griffith and PEPCO to maintain a fairly serene, moderate posture in the controversy when others on both sides were losing their composure. The speech begins with another constant theme of Griffith's outlook, an article of faith in his operation of the company: that the company would observe the equities in its relations with the public, and the public would reward such conduct by doing likewise. In so doing, mutually satisfactory goals could be achieved.

Recalling PEPCO's roots in Oregon City, he said, "I want you to appreciate the fact that many things of the electric industry were done for the first time right here in Oregon City." In his folksiest manner he observed: "What this old company has done, it pioneered. It really entitles us to some consideration from the people in the territory in which it has its entire being." Turning directly to the issue of public power, he said: "I don't believe in the engagement of government beyond the legitimate field of government. That is a basic principle." Yet, he said, the right of the people to form a PUD was not an issue. It was their legal right. PEPCO, he recalled, had once made a study to determine whether it could cost-effectively build a dam and produce power on the Columbia. The answer was no. The government could draw on the Treasury of the United States (interest free) to finance construction and charge all operating costs to navigation (a lock was built at Bonneville). The rate it could therefore charge for power would be among the lowest in the nation. Under the circumstances, he was reconciled to the undertaking. Then he took his listeners on a tour of the future of BPA, warning them of the dangers of Ross's "municipal socialism." Comparing the cost per kilowatt-hour of Ross's Seattle City Light, TVA, and PEPCO, he found that it was about equal. Nothing was to be gained, he asserted, by forming a PUD to distribute Bonneville power.

Toward the close of this speech, Griffith revealed clearly why, at bottom, he had always viewed the coming of Bonneville with equanimity. His remarks explain the mild approach that PEPCO took toward the battle over federally generated power. Griffith asserted that candidate Franklin Roosevelt, in his Portland campaign speech of 1932, had said:

> I do not hold with those who advocate government ownership or government operation of all utilities. I state to you categorically that as a broad general rule the development of utilities should remain, with certain exceptions, a function for private initiative and private capital . . . state-owned or federal-owned power sites can and should properly be developed by government itself. When so developed private capital should be given the first opportunity to transmit and distribute the power on the basis of the best service and the lowest rates to give a reasonable profit only.[87]

Holding a stenographic transcript of the speech to verify his claim, Griffith confidently charged that Roosevelt's views on public power were largely misunderstood. The president was not "in favor of public ownership and against private ownership.[7] "The worst he has ever said about utilities," Griffith pointed out, "is to correct abuses."

> I think I may say this much in quoting him directly, within the last few months he said that to me personally, that he had no reason to change the opinion he expressed in 1932. He believes that it is entirely practicable for the government to cooperate with private operating companies.[88]

Griffith's old law partner in Oregon City, Joseph E. Hedges, had introduced the speaker to the chamber luncheon group. In giving the audience some intimate glimpses of their guest, Hedges recalled a case they had tried together as young lawyers in their salad days. The case was in the federal court system, which neither knew much about. But Griffith, Hedges said, "had a most wonderful memory . . . and a wonderful mental capacity . . . he bought two books, one of pleading and one of procedure in the United States District court, and studied night and day for two weeks. He went into the court and, upon his own pleading, won the case."[89] Listening carefully and studying assiduously had always been the way of Franklin Griffith. His studious, lawyerly approach to the power policy of Franklin Roosevelt explains why this self-taught and independently minded man was one of the few people in the Northwest to understand where the president stood on the issue of Bonneville and the private utilities. The president's gingerly, sometimes ambivalent, approach to the role of government in hydroelectric generation and marketing has been well documented, particularly with respect to the Bonneville project, but in the thirties it was not generally understood.[90] On the power problem, as on so many other issues of the New Deal years, Roosevelt was a reformer rather than a revolutionary. He wished not to destroy private enterprise, but to preserve it in its most equitable form.[91] Griffith's comprehension of this fact made it possible for PEPCO to hew to the same policy toward Bonneville through the decade: the company welcomed federal hydroelectric development on the Columbia and promised to cooperate with it so long as the largesse of federal power was used to benefit all private and public utilities alike.

This rational approach was rewarded on 1 December 1939 when Paul J. Raver, who became Bonneville administrator after the death of J.D. Ross in March 1939, signed a contract to supply PEPCO with wholesale power for one year. The agreement called for the utility to receive 10,000 to 20,000 kw of prime power, as well as some "dump" or surplus power. By 1 December 1940, the company had actually received 40,700 kw.[92]

The company had requested a contract from BPA before the completion of transmission lines and, as a token of its intent to honor Griffith's policy of cooperation, had offered use of its lines to serve three municipal systems within its service area, Canby, Forest Grove, and McMinnville. The administrator made use of rights-of-way for transmission lines owned by the company, including the Oregon Electric Railway right-of-way, over which it had exclusivity.[93] If the relationship between the agency and the company would, over time, prove spikey, it was nonetheless starting on a note of amicability.

THE RIGORS OF RAILWAYS

Clearly, there were enough problems inherent in the operation of a railway system in relatively plush times. Trying to run one in a depression of unparalleled proportion was nearly impossible. By 1933, PEPCO, the parent of Portland Traction Company, was in complete control of the railway, which had no mortgaged indebtedness. There was therefore virtually no extraneous outside pressure for competing views of management strategy. By 1933, the interurban system had "suffered severely," as that year's *Annual Report* put it, and the department was "not earning operating expenses and taxes." In 1933, the worst year of the Great Depression, Portland Traction as a whole "suffered a severe decline in earnings because of the general business conditions prevailing and . . . failed to earn operating expenses, taxes, and depreciation." Curiously (in the midst of the economic agonies of the time, surely nobody could have thought otherwise), the 1933 report stressed that the company had no surplus earnings with which to pay any dividends to PEPCO.[94]

In the wider spectrum of the railway's miseries, the increased patronage for 1933 was insufficient to offset the wage increase granted railway employees by a federal arbitration board convened to settle a labor dispute. The increase was set to take effect in February 1934.[95] The board had been constituted under the National Industrial Recovery Act of the New Deal to help administer the Transit Code of the National Recovery Administration. The act (the brainchild of Gerald Swope, president of the General Electric Company) was designed as a way for private business rather than government to regulate itself (in the hope that stable production and prices would result) during the economic crisis. The Roosevelt administration's plan hoped that this, in turn, would encourage stable wages and wider employment.[96]

PEPCO had argued that the weekly earnings of street-railway employees could be increased by raising their working hours to forty-eight per week as allowed by the Transit Code. In the view of

PEPCO's management, this was the only way to address the code's requirement that the weekly earnings of employees paid wages in force on 1 January 1934 should exceed the weekly earnings of employees hired at an earlier, higher scale, who worked only thirty-six hours per week. The conditions of the street railway industry nationally, and especially of Portland Traction Company, Griffith wrote, "will not permit payment of weekly wages desired by the employes if the Company is required to maintain on its payroll 25% more men than are required to operate its system on the basis of hours of work permitted by the Transit Code."[97] Here was a case in which the cure was at least as devastating as the disease, if not worse. Although this was a not-unusual consequence of the act, it could be particularly painful to industries and companies with fundamental problems, not simply problems caused by the Depression—industries such as the nation's street railways.

The maladies so apparent in the twenties—the automobile with its counterparts (the truck and bus), and the social changes they all wrought, and the growing decrepitude of the track system and the rolling stock—still haunted PEPCO's railway in the thirties. But Griffith and Portland's political leaders clung to the view that the trolleys were both essential to the life of the city and potentially profitable. Consequently, as the decade opened, both sides began a joint struggle toward a mutually satisfactory agreement on its operation. All the street railway franchises expired on 31 December 1932. Negotiations on a new agreement started in 1931. The company's main objective was to secure terms in a new franchise so attractive as to suggest to prospective lenders and securities underwriters that the company was solid enough to be granted the huge credits necessary to undertake a "substantial modernizing program."[98]

In this regard, Griffith exhibited the same dogged optimism as in the previous decade. In various cities throughout the United States, he said, railways had shown that programs of modernization could boost ridership from 7 to 40 percent. His opinion was that regaining lost patronage would restore revenues and control of the cost curve, thereby stabilizing the company's balance sheet.[99] The measure of the romanticism of this view lies in the observation that in every annual report since 1915, including the one (1934) in which this opinion was aired, the automobile was said to be a major obstacle to the reestablishment of the trolley's preeminence. How, one wonders, could fixing the tracks and purchasing new cars alter what was by then the well-established and still-growing preference of Americans for the private automobile as a commuter vehicle?

As early as 1928, the Portland City Council had commissioned a study by the Carey and Harlan Company, engineering consultants, to determine whether the railway was receiving a fair rate of return on its investment and, if it was not, what could be done to ensure that it would. On 20 January 1930 the consultants responded with the "Carey and Harlan Traction Plan." The report had been commissioned because the council had wished to prevent the levying of the ten-cent fare, which was granted anyway by the Oregon Public Service Commission. In its letter of transmittal of the plan to the council, the consultants wrote that they found "that the impending increase in fares will solve the problem and that increases in the rates of fare will not be accompanied by a corresponding increase in revenues, and therefore that some other solution to the street-car problem must be found."

"We have reached the conclusion," the letter further stated, "that a plan must be evolved which radically departs from the present operating conditions and financial setup of most street railway utilities throughout the country."[100] The plan had fourteen points. The most important of these were:

1. That the company furnish street railway service to the city of Portland on an actual service-at-cost basis.

5. That the city acquire solely out of car fares the portions of the city lines which are in reality a part of the street surface, such as ties, rails, rail fastenings, and pavement. . . .

6. That a new company be organized at once to take over, operate, and maintain all necessary facilities for operation, except the track and pavement, to the end that an adequate transportation system be furnished the city. The new company to be required to operate the cars on an actual service-at-cost basis. Such a new company would allow only legitimate operating expenses to be charged to the street railway.

7. That the newly organized company be required to take over all equipment (rolling stock) and overhead structures, operate and maintain the same on an actual service-at-cost basis.

12. That the franchise taxes or fees now paid by the utility be hereafter removed because such tax is under present conditions paid for solely by the car rider.[101]

The plan also called for the mayor and council to appoint a "City Street Railway Commissioner" to supervise operations of the new company and for a member of the city to sit on the board of directors of the new company. It further called for the purchase of sixty new "safety cars of attractive and approved modern design," as well as the conversion of "at least two hundred fifty of its present cars to attractive, modern-type safety cars" and to refurbish them thoroughly. The safety car was an undersized, all-metal trolley, as opposed to the older, wooden cars still in use on many PEPCO lines at the time.[102]

There was strong opposition to the Carey and Harlan plan. In the general public, it came primarily from the prestigious City Club, the public-affairs forum of the community civic leaders. The committee assigned to analyze the proposal issued its report on 30 January 1931. In an exhaustively researched and closely reasoned document, the committee concluded that there was "no evidence that the financial results which Carey and Harlan Company set up as attainable under the proposed service-at-cost franchise will be realized." The report went on to say, "The proposed plan for the city acquiring and maintaining the streetcar tracks brings divided responsibility as to ownership and operation with almost certain increased costs and decreased quality of service."[103]

The City Club report was a blow to the Carey and Harlan plan. The report cited plenty of evidence that fares would inevitably increase, even though it was designed to prevent that. It also reported that, across the United States, streetcar ridership was on the decline, while bus ridership was increasing rapidly. "Public favors buses," the report captioned one section, while nonetheless maintaining that:

> Notwithstanding all these data indicating the shift from streetcars to buses, all those whom we consulted here in Portland who are best qualified from experience to advise as to what transportation method should be employed, have reiterated the contention that buses could not be used in large metropolitan areas in lieu of streetcars, and most streetcars are inherently cheaper and therefore should be continued.[104]

Partisans of the plan included the Portland *Evening Telegram*, which editorially endorsed the Carey and Harlan proposal with whole heart. "The limit has been reached of the number who will patronize the kind of streetcar service that is offered at the price of eight cents," said the paper. "If a higher rate were demanded, the . . . company would be up against the law of diminishing returns and find itself worse off than it is today." Better service at cheaper fares, the essence of the consultants' plan, would, the paper suggested, increase the company's income far more readily than "a higher price for niggardly service to a smaller number of dissatisfied, disgruntled customers."[105]

The city council, meanwhile, had resumed hearings on the ten-cent fare. One commissioner, John M. Mann, was assigned to evaluate the consultants' proposal. He, in turn, directed the city engineer to make a study of the plan. In late February, Mann reported that the engineer had found the plan to be "impractical" and founded on "too many assumptions and not enough facts." He further claimed that Carey and Harlan had done slapdash work, merely perusing the accounts of PEPCO and the Public Service Commission instead of "making a physical valuation of the streetcar properties." Such a review, he asserted, would have revealed the folly of the city's purchasing the company's worn-out tracks, which would have required a substantial investment by the city.[106]

Mayor George Baker, always an ally of the company since his earliest days in politics, nevertheless backed the plan and instructed Carey and Harlan to prepare its proposal for a November 1930 vote. The council (left little choice in the matter) also embraced the plan. Griffith, however, was now caught in the middle of a bizarre situation with his traction company. He was suffering what in effect was an embarrassment of riches. He was saddled with a controversial plan that, if endorsed by the voters, would end his railway's financial miseries. But at the same time, the Public Service Commission had granted the fare increase anyway. The city had requested a delay until the "service-at-cost" plan could be implemented. The commission had refused, saying the city could not justify withholding the raise and the company needed it to survive. Griffith had warned Baker that, if the commission acted favorably, he would be in no position to decline the increase.[107] But the result, he knew, would be to make the company seem to be manipulating events.

The ten-cent fare, far from being the solution, had become a major problem and a liability for everyone concerned. Carey and Harlan had been shown up in the City Club report and in the press as sloppy, lackadaisical analysts. Petitions were circulated for the recall of Baker, and the city council, who, the petitioners asserted, had failed to prevent the fare increase. Not even the chairman of the Public Service Commission, Frank J. Miller, was immune from criticism. Governor Albin W. Norblad publicly castigated him for not cooperating with the city and its consultants to work out a service-at-cost plan.[108]

For PEPCO, the controversy had both short- and long-term consequences. On the short-term side, the Carey and Harlan plan lost at the polls, and the increase was only a temporary panacea, as it was clearly always destined to be. Its immediate impact was to cause a decline in ridership. The real solution to the railway's problems lay elsewhere. But these problems were not going to be addressed frankly any time soon. In the long term, the controversy helped to unleash forces that would cause the company trouble on the political front. Already a focus of the suspicion of some activist groups, PEPCO became the object of an energetic reform campaign. The Progressive Citizens' League papered the city with broadsides calling for stricter law enforcement, a reformed city government, more jobs, and lower power rates and streetcar fares.[109]

Forced back on its own resources, even though enhanced by two cents per ride, the company struggled on. Lengthy negotiations ensued with the city for a franchise agreement that the railway, the public, and the politicians could live with. The issues remained unresolved for approximately four more years, until 1936, when the company was once again granted franchise rights.

Even then, the company had to pass one more test. In 1934, Mayor Baker empaneled a commission of fifteen Portland citizens to report on the mass-transit problem and offer a solution. The group's subsequent report said that Portland Traction Company should be granted a franchise, on the condition that it meet certain requirements. The main one was that within a year, the company should spend more than $3 million on a modernization program, with most of the money to go to a fleet of electric trolley coaches and additions to the existing gas-powered buses. The report said, further, that the city's main arterials should still be served by rail.[110]

With the publication of the committee's recommendations, a second company entered the picture. Portland Motor Coach Company, a local enterprise, made a strong plea for a franchise to control the buses in the mass-transit system. The strongest aspect of its proposal was that, if the new company was granted the rights it sought, Portland Motor Coach would then be purchased by a subsidiary of General Motors Corporation, the automobile giant. The successor company, with the resources of General Motors behind it, would then finance the purchase and operation of all equipment. Needless to say, this was an attractive proposition to council members tired of dealing with the shaky finances of Portland Traction. Still, the decision was not easy, because it called up the issue of local control of the city's vital transportation system and the possibility of exploitation by an impersonal absentee ownership. In the way of politicians, the council found an escape. It called a referendum on the issue.

Griffith considered the Portland Motor Coach application a vital challenge to the health of the railway. To his mind, should Portland Traction lose its bid, the value of the company would be destroyed.[111] The year 1935 passed tensely as the special election, scheduled for 31 January 1936, approached. In the end, the voters affirmed a twenty-year franchise for Portland Traction, permitting operation of streetcars, trolley coaches, and motor buses.

The election was the culmination of a five-year effort to achieve the security that would allow

179

the company to modernize its traction system through the purchase of new rolling stock. Amazingly, the process had involved exhaustive studies of the efficiency of the street-railway system by every affected group—the company, the public, and the city. Predictably, the results of each study showed that the street railway was rapidly losing favor with the public. Each also showed that the system should be modified by the introduction of the trolley's chief rival—the bus—in order to achieve a modicum of operational efficiency. Yet the railway remained the centerpiece of each group's plan, largely because, on paper, the electric railway remained the most economical form of mass transit.

In announcing the victory to stockholders, Griffith's relief was almost palpable. The company would purchase at least one hundred twenty coaches and thirty-six motor buses. "The management confidently believes," he wrote, ignoring the facts, "that with the cooperation of the public in patronage of a modernized system, the Portland Traction Company is entering upon an era of profitable operation and that ultimately a substantial portion, at least, of your investment in traction properties will yield a return."[112]

It was not to be. Despite an energetic program of modernization that included the purchase of one hundred forty trolley coaches and sixty-eight motor buses; the installation of new overhead lines specially designed for the new coaches; alterations to the railway stops, car barns, and service facilities; and the abandonment of more than eighty-two miles of track, Griffith's goal was unachievable. In the first seven months of 1937, there were increases in both ridership and revenue. But then the realities of a depression economy set in. A "general business stagnation," "jurisdictional labor disputes," the closing of Portland's lumber mills, and a 15 percent wage increase to the carmen granted by a board of arbitration all contributed to an overall decline in revenues that was lower than the figures for 1936. The circumstances also conspired to create serious problems for the company as the first installment on more than $3 million worth of equipment purchases fell due in October.[113]

By January 1938, the railway was operating in the red, even though it had vigorously attacked its problems with various cost-saving measures, including service cuts. It had, moreover, defaulted on the first installment for the cars. The *Annual Report* of 1937 observed that, even after $13.3 million worth of write-offs, the city and interurban lines had failed to earn any net income for the last seven years.[114]

When the decade ended, the railway was still PEPCO's patient rather than its partner. The 1939 *Annual Report* noted tersely that the railway "for several years will continue to require . . . all available cash of the Traction Company in excess of direct operating expenses." The disease was catching. "The decline in transportation income has been largely responsible for the inability of PEPCO to provide for interest accruing upon its income bonds or dividends upon its preferred stocks." But faith dies hard. Griffith closed out two decades of traction torture with a familiar litany: "With the improvement of traffic reasonably anticipated from better general employment conditions, it is believed that the urban transportation system will, after it has provided for the cost of its rehabilitation, again become a source of net income for the Portland Electric Power Company."[115]

180   Before the close of the decade, in 1938, Griffith was named Portland's First Citizen by the

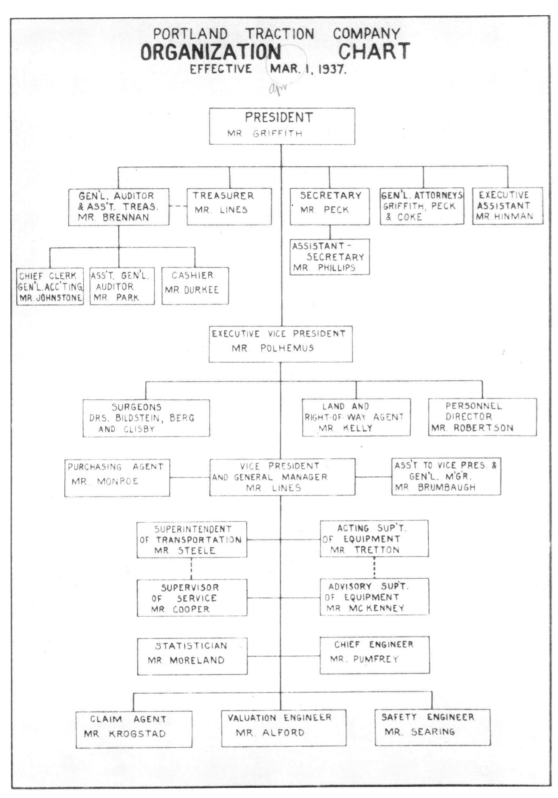

PORTLAND TRACTION COMPANY
ORGANIZATION CHART
EFFECTIVE MAR. 1, 1937.

PRESIDENT
MR. GRIFFITH

GEN'L. AUDITOR
& ASS'T. TREAS.
MR. BRENNAN

TREASURER
MR. LINES

SECRETARY
MR. PECK

GEN'L. ATTORNEYS
GRIFFITH, PECK
& COKE

EXECUTIVE
ASSISTANT
MR. HINMAN

CHIEF CLERK
GEN'L. ACC'TING.
MR. JOHNSTONE

ASS'T. GEN'L.
AUDITOR
MR. PARK

CASHIER
MR. DURKEE

ASSISTANT -
SECRETARY
MR. PHILLIPS

EXECUTIVE VICE PRESIDENT
MR. POLHEMUS

SURGEONS
DRS. BILDSTEIN, BERG
AND CLISBY

LAND AND
RIGHT-OF-WAY AGENT
MR. KELLY

PERSONNEL
DIRECTOR
MR. ROBERTSON

PURCHASING AGENT
MR. MONROE

VICE PRESIDENT
AND GENERAL MANAGER
MR. LINES

ASS'T. TO VICE PRES. &
GEN'L. M'G'R.
MR. BRUMBAUGH

SUPERINTENDENT
OF TRANSPORTATION
MR. STEELE

ACTING SUP'T.
OF EQUIPMENT
MR. TRETTON

SUPERVISOR
OF SERVICE
MR. COOPER

ADVISORY SUP'T.
OF EQUIPMENT
MR. MC KENNEY

STATISTICIAN
MR. MORELAND

CHIEF ENGINEER
MR. PUMFREY

CLAIM AGENT
MR. KROGSTAD

VALUATION ENGINEER
MR. ALFORD

SAFETY ENGINEER
MR. SEARING

The reorganized Portland Traction Company.
(PGE collections)

181

The clean simplicity of the interior of car 267 belies the snarls and difficulties of the transportation side of the company. Photo by Judy Hartman (PGE collections)

Portland Realty Board. At a banquet on the night of 4 January 1939, he was honored by the board and other Portland business and social leaders.[116] Telegrams from well-wishers who could not attend the banquet poured into the Electric Building. These communications, the speakers at the banquet, and the Portland newspapers on the following day heaped praise on Griffith, who responded with characteristic modesty. The esteem in which he was held was astonishing, considering the grueling decade he had put in: the travails of the railway division, the fight over public power, the wrangling on the Bonneville issue, and the continuing financial problems, including bankruptcy, which would not be resolved until the end of the 1940s. Griffith's activities in one or another of these spheres were bound to alienate large numbers of people at any given time. That he nevertheless was granted the award and the accompanying encomiums seems almost miraculous, a testament to integrity, courage, intelligence, native shrewdness, and will-power, not to mention an apparently dry, but telling, wit.

Griffith had become chairman of the board of PEPCO upon reversion to local control, for twenty-six years having served the company in one or both of the primary leadership positions. As he stood to receive his due, he was sixty-nine years old. He had achieved a long-held goal for the company—complete local control—but in a way he would never have chosen and at great cost to himself and others. Had the merger election of 1928 turned out differently, the price might never have been paid. The Clarks might have been able to attract a better suitor than Central Public Service. On the other hand, once the deal was made, Griffith had consistently misread the economic trends and stayed the course with Pierce, who, in return, led Pacific Northwest Public Service into financial thickets while nurturing Griffith's misplaced optimism about the Depression. Only when the results of chronic economic decline and Pierce's pillaging of PEPCO became painfully evident did Griffith act.

At the same time, he had led the fight against public power, and he had been reviled by skilled politicians and ordinary citizens alike. The same fight in a slightly different guise—the struggle over private access to Bonneville energy—had elicited a similar response from sections of the political community and the general public. In these arenas he had triumphed, not necessarily because he had superior skills in waging his battles. The tools he brought to any contest were formidable, yet he sought only equity for his company and its stockholders. He consistently judged the mood of his fellow Oregonians correctly, and he understood—frequently better than his adversaries—their own arguments and the realities behind them. Bonneville was a case in point. While public-power advocates pinned their hopes on a rigidly antibusiness reading of New Deal philosophy and the friendship between Ross and Roosevelt, Griffith absorbed the president's commitment to free enterprise and did nothing that might disappoint it, even as other Portlanders and private-utility executives derided the public purpose of the dam.

In essence, the night Franklin Griffith received his award, he was like the America of the thirties. Like the nation, he had misjudged and stumbled, but with admirable agility had recovered a semblance of balance and moved forward.

6 A HAZARD OF OLD FORTUNES

T HE HISTORICAL PROCESS UNFOLDS not only in unbroken lines, but frequently in more erratic patterns. There are often large gaps or discontinuities between episodes otherwise contiguous in time. In an overlapping sequence of events, what appears to be chaos is often the birth of a new era before the death of its logical antecedents. For distinctive groups and individuals there are different ends, different beginnings. Thus the history of PEPCO in the thirties ended with Franklin Griffith's civic canonization in 1938. But the history of PGE, the company that emerged in the forties from the financial rubble of the Great Depression and the Central Public Service Corporation misadventure, really took shape in 1936. At that time, the structural reorganization that accompanied the rigorous fiscal rehabilitation arising from the bankruptcy proceedings began.

A study of the options for reorganization of the company was made in 1937 by Frank M. Warren, Jr., a young man with a Stanford University engineering degree and a Harvard MBA. Warren, who had joined the firm in July 1937 as assistant to the president, was the son of a PGE board member, Frank Warren, Sr. The Warren family was one of Portland's wealthiest and most prominent. The senior Warren was a close friend of Griffith. The junior Warren presented to the board of directors a plan that would streamline the company structurally and reduce operating costs, while improving customer service and relations.[11]

The recommendations of Warren's study, accepted by the board in November 1937, were in some ways dramatic and wide-ranging. For example, the responsibilities of PGE's general sales manager, A. Craig McMicken, were greatly reduced when he was given charge of the Portland Service District to build the load there. This was not so much a demotion for McMicken as a recognition by the directors that Portland was the company's greatest and most profitable electrical market and needed intensive attention. At that time also, George Sullivan took charge of PGE's six operating divisions and the two subsidiary electric utility companies, Molalla and Yamhill. In May 1938, the assets of PGE's wholly owned subsidiaries were merged into PGE's Yamhill Electric, Molalla Electric, Electric Supplies and Contracting, and Electric Appliance and Construction. Another subsidiary, Clackamas Power and Irrigation, ceased to exist. Yamhill and Molalla became divisions of PGE. Arthur L. Strickland was appointed manager of both divisions. By 1940, Sullivan had been appointed vice president and assistant general manager. Another consequence of the reorganization was to concentrate customer relations under one manager, Ernest Brede-meier. He had charge of three separate functions: customer accounting, credits and collections, and service.[2]

Meanwhile, on the financial front, structural changes and modifications occurred that were significant in the activities and decisions of the forties and the ensuing years. The most important of these changes was that, as a result of the financial reorganization of 1939, the voting trust arrangement of November 1932 was vacated, meaning that Griffith, John Ainsworth, and E.B. MacNaughton would no longer exclusively control PEPCO, Portland Traction, and PGE. Judge Alger M. Fee appointed two independent trustees, Thomas W. Delzell, a Portland lawyer, and Leslie M. Scott, partial owner and vice president of the Oregonian Publishing Company. Early on, Scott resigned and was replaced by Ralph L. Clark, a leading Portland businessman. Griffith remained operating trustee. In ordering these appointments, the court directed the new trustees to investigate thoroughly "the acts, conduct, property, liabilities, and financial condition of the debtor . . . the operation of its business, and the desirability of its continuance thereof, and report thereon to the judge of this court." In this way, Delzell became intimately familiar with the company, which made him indispensable later in the decade.[3]

A further structural change was the addition of Walter W.R. May, former manager of the Portland Chamber of Commerce, in the post of director of industrial development in 1938. May and his assistant, Ralph H. Millsap, who came to the company early in 1940 from *The Dalles Chronicle*, were hired to expand the load by aggressive marketing in the industrial sector, in anticipation of the opportunity afforded by low-cost BPA energy and of upcoming public-utility-district elections.[4]

At the outset of the reorganization, Griffith, anticipating great hydroelectric development, recruited James H. Polhemus for the position of executive vice president of PEPCO, which he assumed on 1 September 1936. The company made an emphatic commitment to hydro generation as a key to competitive rate structures, which had developed in the twenties and thirties with the rise of the PUDs and Bonneville. The preemption of the Columbia River by the federal government, coupled with the company's long-held riparian rights along the Clackamas, meant that it had to begin serious planning for hydropower construction if it was to maintain rate parity

CHAPTER TEN OF THE BANKRUPTCY ACT
of 1938 made provisions for corporate reorganization in the event that a creditor of a financially
troubled company filed a successful claim. The
chapter enumerated the terms of such a claim
and laid down the procedure to be followed to
take the claim to hearing and to examine the
officers and property of the company under scrutiny. Under Chapter Ten, if the claim was approved, the court was authorized to appoint a
trustee to develop a plan to reorganize the company. This plan was directed to deal with the distribution of property, the cash settlement of claims,
the execution of the plan itself, the manner of
selecting officers, and the terms of selling securities. The court reviewed and approved the plan,
oversaw its implementation, and, upon its con-
summation, entered a final decree closing the
estate.

THE SECURITIES AND EXCHANGE
COMMISSION (SEC) was created in 1934 and
given jurisdiction over the 1933 Securities Act,
which required corporations and banking syndi-
cates to file detailed financial statements before
they began to sell securities. The SEC was also
directed to implement the Public Utility Holding
Company Act, compelling the reorganization of
holding companies for the purpose of regulating
their questionable financial structures. The SEC
had control over such aspects of the reorganization as the limit of total capitalization, capital
structure, terms of security sales, and protection
of utility assets.

with the PUDs. River development required a manager with a specialized engineering background; Polhemus had been general manager and chief engineer at the Port of Portland, in charge of the Port's dredging projects. As a young man, he had been responsible for field engineering on The Dalles-Celilo Canal on the Columbia from 1911 to 1914, and later had laid out and superintended the Port construction of the Swan Island Airport in 1927-28 and had designed a widely imitated diesel electric dredge.[5] As manager, he had worked with Frank Warren, Sr., who was president of the Port Commission in the late twenties and thirties. It was Warren who brought Polhemus to Griffith's attention.

Griffith had greater responsibilities in mind for his recruit. Polhemus was his hand-picked successor for the presidency of the utility. As administrative head of the Port, Polhemus was already a man of consequence in Portland's business and economic community, and his connections and knowledge would be of great value to the company.

Polhemus served under Griffith until 1940. On 10 February 1940, Griffith stepped down as president. He retained the chairmanship. "I have for some time felt that I should be relieved of the active duties of president," he said, "particularly as respect to operations . . . I think the present an opportune time."[6]

With that announcement, an era ended for PGE. A generation of men whose influence on the company's day-to-day operations had been primary, as well as on its policy decisions, passed from the scene. The process had begun in 1935 with the death of Charles Swigert, one of the original investors. In 1937, Clarence Clark died and, at the end of the decade, E.W. Clark. Orin B. Coldwell, who had served the company as vice president and written extensively on the early history of electricity in Oregon, retired in 1940. He remained as a consultant to company personnel, who often visited his office in the Electric Building for advice and counsel. Coldwell had worked at PGE for almost the entire existence of the company, beginning as a very young man. The legacy of Coldwell and of other key employees was preserved by Supt. R.R. Robley, who wrote a detailed history of the utility's technical and business development. But by 1940, Griffith remained PGE's sole link to its beginnings. Operating from the chairmanship, he functioned as a link to the past and as a subject of PGE's current history. To all intents and purposes, the company was in the hands of Polhemus and a newer generation of managers. The problems they faced in the next years were not so different from those that Griffith had tackled (many were legacies of his era), but his successors encountered them in a different economic and social context and from the vantage of different backgrounds. Remarkably, the solutions they offered were consonant with the spirit of Griffith. This was not so much a mark of his continued influence as an acknowledgment of the durability of his methods and values.

PGE AND THE SECOND WORLD WAR

For all Americans, an era of a different kind ended at 1:50 P.M. Eastern Standard Time, on 7 December 1941, when word reached the White House of the dawn attack by the Japanese Imperial armed forces on the U.S. Pacific Fleet, riding at anchor in Pearl Harbor, Hawaii. Until

James Henry Polhemus was born in Newport, Oregon in 1887, and was a graduate of Stanford University. As manager of the Port of Portland from 1920 to 1936, he was credited with making Portland the first city in the United States with a paved airport. He joined Portland General Electric in 1936 as an executive vice president. In 1942, he was instrumental in locating the Kaiser shipyards in Portland. He was a member of the Masonic Lodge in The Dalles, the Al Kader Shrine, the Royal Order of Jesters, the Arlington Club, and the Bohemian Club in San Francisco. Photo by the Gladys Gilbert Studio. (PGE collections)

then, the familiar tensions of the interwar years had pervaded the nation. A dread of the conflict everyone knew was coming saturated even the languor of a Sunday morning. Nevertheless, at 1:51, the United States found itself in a changed world. As one newspaperman put it, "between cockcrow and catastrophe" on Sunday morning, America was "a portrait of a world about to be destroyed." The afternoon was war, he recalled, "but the morning lies in the years between wars."[7]

At the outbreak of war, the wracking economic wounds of the thirties were by no means healed. In 1941, the GNP figures were tangible evidence that America's long national convalescence was ending, thanks largely to massive spending for defense dating from 1940. Like a patient recovering from a trauma, the United States moved with deliberation into the sunshine once again. The patient's former vigor had returned, even if it had not quite regained all its old confidence.

For PGE, 1940 and 1941 were good years, exemplifying the recovery's impact on the Pacific Northwest. The *Annual Report* of 1940 seemed to herald a brighter outlook. Sporting a new royal blue-and-orange bullseye logo with the initials "PGE" superimposed over the target at a jaunty upward angle, the publication for the first time included drawings, photographs, and other graphics and was printed on slick paper. It supplanted the austere, no-nonsense reports of past years. Revealingly, in the blue outer circle of the target, beneath the full name of the company that ringed the upper half, was the legend "Bonneville Power Distributor."

In the last days of 1941 and the early part of 1942, the revitalized PGE found itself serving a vast array of defense plants in its fifteen-hundred-square-mile service area as the American war machine geared up.[8] One of the most important such plants was the Iron Fireman Manufacturing Company, the largest outside source of machined parts for Boeing, the Seattle aircraft maker. PGE's 1941 report proudly noted that Iron Fireman parts went into the "Famous Flying Fortress —the plane that is blasting aggressors from Berlin to Tokyo."[9]

The utility's role in the war effort was obviously critical. Speaking of its function, J.A. King, director of the Office of War Utilities, War Production Board, said that PGE was to deliver power, "this 'life blood' to 67,000 war jobs."[10] The company sent 250,000 HP to local war industries and other concerns engaged in activities vital to the war effort. At the great Kaiser Shipyards on Swan Island and at other plants along the Willamette and Columbia rivers, liberty ships, aircraft carriers, minesweepers, "commando" landing barges, cargo barges, seagoing tugs, 2,500-HP steam engines, and fifteen-ton stern frame castings for liberty ships were made; plywood spars for all-wood training planes were fabricated in other locations; tank, truck, and tractor parts were cast in the Portland area; woolens for uniforms and blankets were made in Salem and Portland; production of food by farms in the service area was stepped up; and refrigeration for food-processing plants was increased. The *Annual Report* of 1942 boasted that war industries on PGE's lines were enjoying rates that were among the lowest in the nation.[11]

The war effort gave an unprecedented boost to PGE. In 1944 it recorded an 11 percent increase in sales of electric energy over the previous year and a 75 percent increase over 1940. The company sold over 1.2 billion kwh of energy in 1944.[12]

Like all American cities, Portland was caught up in the patriotic fervor that usually accompanies wars. Seven men set themselves adrift in a life raft on the Willamette River, refusing to return to shore until the city fulfilled its quota of bond purchases.[13] PGE and its employees actively supported mobilization. By the end of 1942, 91 percent of the 1,137 company employees were signed up for payroll deductions for the purchase of war bonds.[14]

The ramifications of the conflict were immense for individuals and institutions everywhere. In the case of PGE, the effects of the war were felt in a number of different and unexpected ways. Copper was in desperately short supply in the opening months of the war. The company, like other utilities, was put under a "Share the Copper" plan devised by the War Production Board, the government's industrial watchdog and planning agency. Under this program, in roughly the first year of the war, PGE turned over to the federal government some two hundred thirty-five thousand pounds of scrap copper and over two hundred seventy-four thousand pounds of new copper, which had been stored away primarily for use in line extensions to new customers. As the editor of the *Bullseye* (successor to the *Synchronizer*) put it a little wistfully, it was enough copper to build a single-conductor electric line from Portland to Juneau, Alaska. (Problems with this program arose when sixteen families moved into a newly developed Gresham neighborhood. An average of thirty-eight and a half pounds of copper was needed to wire the new houses properly, but the "Share the Copper" plan limited each home to thirty pounds. The houses could not be wired, occasioning a blast from the editor of the Gresham weekly, accusing the utility of being "arbitrary.")[15]

The company made a concerted effort to turn over as much vital scrap and new metal besides copper to the War Production Board as possible. This led to the creation of a special division of the PGE Salvage Department, whose only job was to handle scrap materials. In the first quarter of 1944, the department shipped 742,140 pounds of steel and iron scrap, 31,255 pounds of copper wire scrap, 10,872 pounds of yellow and red brass scrap, and 22,723 pounds of lead.[16]

The urgency of home-front industrial production was dramatically illustrated by an occurrence at the Kaiser Swan Island Shipyard. The yard was perhaps the most productive in the nation, achieving an astounding record when it lowered the production time for liberty ships from 329 to 10 days.[17] In 1943 PGE needed to do extensive work on the two 57,000-V lines serving the facility. The lines had to be worked "hot" in order to keep the yard, which operated round the clock, running continuously. A hand-picked crew of workers was assembled and a "general staff planned the job as if it were a military operation," as one observer put it. A detailed plan was committed to paper, with each step in the repair process meticulously mapped out. The plan was then submitted for the approval of PGE's general superintendent, the business agent of the International Brotherhood of Electrical Workers, the union to which the participating line workers and the PGE safety engineer belonged. Specially constructed tools were used and a ladder was built to hang on the top crossarm of the key power pole, to extend below the bottom high-tension arm. The actual work was done in one day, in a painstakingly deliberate fashion, and the job was completed without ever having to shut down the lines.[18]

A special wartime problem for utilities was the enforcement of a dim-out on the Pacific Coast ordered in August 1942 by Lt. Gen. John G. DeWitt, head of the Western Defense Command of

A lineman at work in March 1944. Spikes strapped to his legs enabled him to climb up the pole. The hard hat was not yet part of regulation gear, although the cigarette was probably not an uncommon accessory at the time. (PGE collections)

191

LATE IN 1942 it became necessary for the Gresham Division to hire girls as meter readers to replace men who were being taken into the armed forces. Most of the meter reading in this territory has to be done in a car because of the distances involved; and in the Mt. Hood, Squaw Mountain, Corbett, and Sandy areas the roads are difficult to travel, and some doubt was expressed as to whether the girls could handle the job. At the end of 1943, the division had the same three girls that started on this job more than a year earlier.

Bullseye, June 1944

PGE did pioneering work in repairing hot lines so that area shipyards could remain open around the clock during the war years. Instruction on working hot lines is given by Jack Armfield in this photo. Roy H. Wolford, photographer. (PGE collections)

This photo shows a safety demonstration of pole-top resuscitation for a knocked out lineman from January 1941. (PGE collections)

Present and past presidents of Ladies' Auxiliary PEPCO Post #104 of the American Legion. PEPCO contributed to the war effort with more than electricity. (PGE collections)

BECAUSE COPPER IS NOT AVAILABLE, 40,000 tons of silver—yes, TONS—are being turned into bus-bars for use in aluminum plants. This quantity represents approximately one-half the United States' silver reserve. The silver is being loaned by the treasury to the Defense Plant Corporation, and will be replaced by copper after the war. The Defense Plant Corporation has announced plans to supply General Electric and other manufacturers with silver for use in place of copper in building transformers."

Bullseye, August 1942

USES OF COPPER IN WAR INDUSTRIES

in bands on shells: copper prevents shells from wobbling in the air, keeps them moving at the target.

percussion primers: used to ignite gunpowder (primers, as well as cartridge shells, are made of brass, which is made of zinc and copper).

gun mechanisms: parts of mechanisms made of bronze, an alloy of tin and copper.

Liberty ship propellers: tons of copper for each propeller; props weigh 21,500 lbs. and are 2 stories high.

Bullseye, August 1942

From the 21 November 1942 Oregon Voter. *(OHS neg. OrHi 84729)*

THE WAR YEARS

IN OCTOBER 1944, PGE began sending a newsletter to employees in the armed forces. The company wanted to "tell them they were missed on the job, give 'em some company news and let 'em know the home guard was pulling for a safe return." Called "Vick's Chatter," the newsletter was edited by Harold P. Vickrey. Its publication continued until after demobilization.

1 February 1945   Bob Beecroft, formerly of the Salem Line Department who started in the army as a supply clerk and ended up as a corporal and radio operator with Co. B, 136th Ordnance Maintenance Battalion, is now somewhere in France. The fellows in the outfit are doing a swell job keeping the equipment rolling while Bob sits and listens to the radio squawk. He is inclined to agree with a GI who, when they had landed, stood on the dock, looked around and said, "So this is France. All right, I've seen it; let's go home." Bob was struck by the marked resemblance of the open country in France to familiar scenes around home in Marion County. Somewhere along the line, he attended four operas and sent home a program of "Faust." If he is going to see more of the country, he concludes it will work out more satisfactorily to let him choose his own itinerary.

1 April 1945   Probably there are only a few employees that remember Esther Rae, who was Frank Test's secretary on the 4th floor, Electric Bldg. in 1937-38. She resigned to become Mrs. Rankin and later went to Manila. The reason for bringing it up is that she was interned by the Japs in Santa Tomas concentration camp in '41, and remained there until the 1st Cavalry smashed in the gate and set several hundred internees free.

1 April 1945   MAJOR WARREN IN PHILIPPINES
The Philippines is the present address of Frank Warren, Jr., perambulating vice president. He explains that he is getting along all right since he managed to steal a canvas cot and found a spot to park it under a tent. Sleeping on the ground and eating K rations out of a cardboard box were a bit rugged. The surroundings were considerably banged up with shellfire, and a battery of Long Toms in the vicinity almost rolled him out of bed when they cut loose. There are artesian wells in his particular area, and Frank speaks of the joy in finding a shower bath that works and has plenty of water.

1 April 1945   BELGIUM DOGS DON'T BITE
Suggestions concerning meter readers' equipment comes from Lester Smith who left a reading job in Portland for tank corps service in France and Belgium. He noticed that dogs over there are very well behaved. They rarely bark or growl and never snap. There are no meter readers; only soldiers with guns and canines respect guns if they have little consideration for those who carry them. Smith remembers that dogs are the bane of a meter reader's existence and opines that tommy guns would be helpful in getting over the routes at home. Just observes it—that's all.

1 April 1945   Civilians use this recipe to make the butter ration stretch. They mix a pound of butter with a pound of lard and you can't tell the difference. It all tastes like lard.

1 April 1945   NEW KVA. CIRCUIT   Work has been started on clearing a right-of-way for a new 57-thousand kv line from Harborton to Burlington. The new three and a half mile piece of construction has been approved by Federal agencies, and rated essential to maintain continuity of service to the industrial loads in the St. Helens area.

At the present time, there is one 57-kva. line from Harborton to Burlington, while there are two beyond Burlington to St. Helens. The new tie fills the gap and substitutes for a smaller capacity circuit that comes over the hills from Beaverton. In event of serious trouble, the old Beaverton line may not be able to carry the load.

The proposed line calls for two-nought copper and about sixty new poles. Most of the poles are 50 and 60 foot sticks, but there are a few that run up to 75's and 80's. A pair of 100 footers are included to give the crew a taste of higher altitudes. They clear the railway trestle.

1 May 1945   PGE USING NEW TYPE RADIO
New frequency modulation mobile transmitters are being installed in 15 PGE cars and by the N.W. Electric. The net effect will be that trouble rigs can remain under high lines and in other noisy locations and transmit effectively to the dispatcher. Most of the noise and static will be screened out. Bill Leidigh hasn't been able to get stationary apparatus so the dispatchers can send FM and they will continue to use amplitude modulation now installed. Bill needs better priorities to get new radio apparatus that is necessary to finish the setup. The FM equipment is the first that has been used in the Portland area.

1 July 1945   A fellow who makes his living with a sharp pencil and a slip stick, came up with these figures. There are 1,032 employees on the PGE payroll—a decline from 1,300 as of 1941. The reduction has been offset by having a substantial number go from a 40 hour to a 48 hour work week. Two hundred and thirteen employees were given a leave of absence to join the armed forces. Fourteen of them have returned and gone back on the job.

1 July 1945   Occasionally an unusual letter comes into the office. An elderly customer wrote this one in recently: "Will you do me a favor? A robin built a nest directly over and obscuring my light meter. Mamma Robin is now setting. Would it be possible to estimate my electric bill until the family is out of the nest? We like the birds around and would like to avoid disturbing them until the family is raised."

The letter was acknowledged and the meter reader instructed to skip the reading until notified.

1 November 1945   The trouble in every line department office on the PGE system is that work comes in twice as fast as it can be handled. If a line extension requires an installation of an appreciable number of new poles, it may hang on the hook for a long time before the crews can get at it.

During the war years, federal agencies denied formal requests to use material for extensions and a heavy back log of unfinished business piled up. When they took off the halter, all this business flocked in at once. Meanwhile no one became an apprentice in anyone's line department. Adolescent youths were getting much more pay in war plants or Uncle Sugar put the finger on 'em in uniform.

The material situation isn't a happy one either. Aluminum wire, for instance, that was ordered in March came along in September with the reminder that the next order would be filled in rotation and could be expected eight months hence. Cedar poles have been a short item also.

So far as the public is concerned, the war is over and utilities should get 'em lights, telephones and water service with the speed of a fire department answering a call. It doesn't work that way and they don't understand it. Line department headmen grew grey haired quickly in the old days. If you want a 'rush' job now, you better see them personally, and take along a 10-inch piece of lead pipe, a pair of brass knuckles and a small bundle of midget hand grenades, just in case. The only time the construction gang smiles these days is when a lineman gets back from the armed service. It's no time to tantalize them by sending 'em more jobs; they're getting awfully tired of looking at the ones they have already.

1 December 1945   The Newberg office will look prewar before long. Durell Belanger expects to be back shortly and will be out with the line crews again to help clean up the pile of rush construction. He has been a flier in Texas. Bill Garvin wrote from an airplane carrier in Tokyo Bay that he had a chance for Thanksgiving dinner in the Yamhill Valley if he got the breaks. This will bring all of that division's service men home except one. Larry Weissert, formerly of the Sheridan office, is still parked in China the last anyone heard.

the Fourth Army. The entire West Coast was declared a military zone at the outset of the war, in the belief that it was vulnerable to invasion by the Japanese. The Army did not think a total blackout necessary, but the reflection of light from a large city on the clouds above might be visible for up to one hundred fifty miles. At a certain point at sea the glow thus cast would be visible close to the horizon, like the sun at its rising or setting. A ship would be silhouetted against the background, making it an inviting target for a lurking Japanese submarine. While all coastal lights were to be extinguished at night for the same reason, the dim-out of inland cities entailed shielding or painting over the tops of streetlights, the restriction of "spilled" light from stores, restaurants, other public establishments, and homes to one footcandle, and no light source could be visible from outside above the level of the fixture. Home porch lights were reduced to 25 w and shielded; parking-lot illumination, properly shielded, could be as much as 60 w, 15 feet above ground, 15 feet apart, to produce one footcandle of light. The marquees on theaters could display lighting of 25-w lamps, 10 feet apart, or 15-w lamps, 7.5 feet apart.[19]

In Portland, as a result of the dim-out, PGE experienced an immediate and precipitous drop in lighting revenues. At the end of the first week, company engineers estimated that energy normally used for lighting dropped approximately 42,000 kwh a day—a gross revenue loss of around $420 per day, or $153,000 per year. However, the impact of these figures was more than offset by the escalation of war-related industrial production, which reached a breakneck pace early in the conflict. A good index of this was the net system load, which between 1941 and 1944 (the last full year of the war) grew almost 20 percent, from 198,000 kwh to 247,000 kwh. The net system load grew from 890.9 million kwh in 1941 to 1.3 billion kwh in 1944.[20]

For PGE, as for the rest of American business and industry, the war caused a labor shortage. The *Annual Report* of 1945 listed 216 PGE employees in the armed forces by V-J Day. Two had given their lives. Apart from those few who were seriously disabled in the service, most returned to the company, responding to what was described as a "sincere intention to offer every encouragement to the veteran for resuming his former career in civilian life."[21] This gesture was both practical and generous. It was to have a delayed effect on the company's character in the years immediately after the war. By the end of the forties, the war's stimulation of the economy was to prove a double-edged sword for the company, but at the end of hostilities in August 1945, on the troopships bearing the returning veterans, in Oregon and all over America, people experienced only relief and joy. The future, like the past, was another country; the latter a stark, desolate, and forbidding wasteland, the former an indistinct shape on the horizon, a place where peace, prosperity, and repose were tantalizingly discernible.

THE END OF THE LINE FOR RAILWAYS

The reorganization of 1940 saw PEPCO recede as an integrated entity. Its function became simply that of a holding company. On the other hand, its two primary components, PGE and Portland Traction, were each henceforth required to stand alone and justify their existence on the basis of their own balance sheets. In that year, Gordon Steele, who had served through much of the previous decade as superintendent of the railway, became president of the trolley company. Although he was an able transit executive, the railway continued to struggle, even as the local, regional, and national economies emerged from the Depression. In the old structure, the trolleys would no doubt have survived as a loss against the improving fortunes of the electric utility. But when the company's balance sheet was reviewed each year outside the context of the larger format, it became evident that the railway's travails were a needless drain for its still struggling parent.

A consultant's report of 1941 that looked into the railway company made this fact and the need for stricter cost control in the traction operations quite apparent. The consultants, noting the railway's chronic deficit, urged the PEPCO board to be stern regarding transactions between PGE and Portland Traction where a lenient attitude might damage the electric utility. The consultants' calculations showed:

> an annual AC load factor for . . . [supplying power to the railway] of approximately 45 percent, which seems reasonable. Assuming average annual conversion losses of 25 percent, and allocating generating and transmission costs, our figures indicate that the actual cost to PGE, exclusive of conversion expenses, of these DC kwh on the switchboard is approximately 7½ mills [per kwh]. It is apparent that the spread above this 7½ mill cost is considerably less than sufficient to cover expenses of conversion and carrying charges, including taxes on the conversion equipment. While generally it seems undesirable to further penalize a company already operating at a deficit, or close to it, we believe the Directors should consider the responsibility which they may be undertaking if . . . the railway load is being carried at an actual out-of-pocket loss.[22]

The report also questioned other financial relationships between the two companies, such as obsolete traction company supplies owned by PGE. The consultants urged that the railway make use of them whenever possible in order to cut its expenditures, even if labor was required to make them usable. In this, the consultants were calling for the two companies to behave as one corporation, in the hope that PGE would be spared further drains on its resources.[23]

Upon becoming executive vice president, Polhemus had begun an analysis of the railway, including preparation of a technical paper entitled "Modern Trolley Coach Operation." The trolley coach, a combination of bus and streetcar, was the hope of the company on its introduction to Portland in 1936. It was cheaper to operate than buses or streetcars, as it used electricity transmitted from overhead lines rather than gas (like buses), and it ran on the streets rather than rails (like streetcars). This would cut costs for rail and street repair. After a year of operation, Polhemus noted, "public reaction to the operation of trolley coaches has been good."[24] The coaches were quieter, faster, and safer than streetcars. The average speed of the coaches in 1937 was 12.78 mph, whereas streetcars reached an average speed on the city streets of only 10.35 mph. A coach could stop as fast as, or faster than, an automobile, while a streetcar was considerably slower than either. (On occasion, this resulted in car-trolley collisions.) The paper noted that the company had started with one line and a few coaches in 1936, but a year later, in its anxiety to cure its transit ailments, it had a total of seven coach lines, one hundred forty coaches, and total route lengths of one hundred forty miles.[25] Once again, however, the pursuit of profitability was disappointed as all lines continued to lose money into the next decade.

The apparently stronger early outlook for the city lines was not matched by similar projections for the interurbans in the forties. On the contrary, they had become a genuine albatross in the last years of the thirties because of falling freight revenues. Serious efforts to sell off the interurban properties had been made since 1931, but the railroads to which they were variously offered— Southern Pacific, Union Pacific, and the Spokane, Portland and Seattle, separately and in combination—proved immune to their allure.

Perversely, the reorganization of 1940 occurred at a time when the railway's fiscal situation was reversing itself. Under the new arrangement, PEPCO kept the interurbans, which immediately began to show signs of health with the return of the lumber business. Portland Traction, however, was left with the city lines, which, despite the high taxes generated by the trolley coaches, continued to suffer—mainly from the perpetual competition of the automobile.

Both the interurbans and the city lines limped through the first few years of the decade. The freight revenues on the interurban lines remained stable, but were never remarkable. In 1944, the federal government considered restoring the abandoned line between Boring and Estacada in order to accommodate the logs being shipped out of Clackamas and Boring for war production. An investigation revealed that a better, more cost-efficient alternative was to improve the highway between the two places. Most of the trees cut in the area were being trucked out anyway.[26] This was a serious blow to the interurbans, not simply in lost revenues, but in that the improved road would further encourage truck traffic rather than rail.

The real death blow came in 1946, when the Chase National Bank, attempting to collect on its old note of nearly $6 million, forced the sale of the property. At that point, PEPCO was required to meet its obligations. It therefore rid itself of the railways in the only way to attract a buyer: it charged the fire sale price of $7.9 million in cash (against a book value of $18.2 million).[27] Both the interurbans and the city lines were sold to a California firm calling itself the Portland Transit Company. With that, an era and a saga came to an end.

THE MOVE TO MODERNIZATION

The promotion of James Polhemus to the PGE presidency was a characteristic recognition of practical fact by Franklin Griffith. With the recovery under way and the BPA and public-power issues facing the company daily, a formula for expansion and economical, technologically advanced operations was needed so that PGE might run efficiently and profitably throughout the forties. This was not merely a conundrum to be addressed at annual meetings with earnest platitudes to assure stockholders that the company was in responsible hands, but a matter of survival. It was acknowledged in the PGE boardroom that higher rates resulting from inefficient plant would bring about irrepressible competition from public-power advocates, perhaps leading to the extinction of the company. The situation was perilous at best, because the bankruptcy

198

episode and the Depression had left the company with aging facilities and equipment. Only essential replacement and innovation had been undertaken during the lean years of the thirties. Moreover, even in the early halcyon days under Central Public Service and, for that matter, under the Clarks, improvements had been held to the barest minimum. One veteran of PGE recalled that, when he came to the company shortly after World War II as an engineer in hydroelectric generation, he found a "chintzy" system held together "by chewing gum and baling wire."[28] The situation called for an aggressive response, a battle that could not be won swiftly, but that had to be joined with a technologically aware individual leading the way.

Under Polhemus, the company did begin to grapple again with modernization and to move forward, at times innovatively, if only on a modest scale. For example, in 1940 PGE was one of the first utilities in the United States to equip its vehicles with two-way radios so that line crews and repair equipment could be quickly and efficiently dispatched to emergencies.[29]

The recovery of the economy led to great opportunities for load expansion. Under Polhemus's leadership the company responded, insofar as fiscal constraints would allow, with capital construction and new technology. In 1940, PGE constructed ten new automatic outdoor substations. Two 57,000-V submarine cables were laid across the Willamette at Linnton, carrying Bonneville power into Portland's west-side metropolitan district. Probably the company's major building project that year was the reconstruction of the Cazadero dam and flume on the Clackamas River. It was the largest timber-built flume in the world at the time.[30]

The newfound health of the economy was indicated by the number of such projects and by the fact that 1940 was, as that year's *Annual Report* put it in a headline, "the Biggest Load-Building Year in the Company's History." Several things contributed to this success, including an intensive and many-faceted marketing effort. Although the company stopped selling appliances in 1938, it continued to promote them in cooperation with independent dealers. It became a prolific advertiser of their value to homemakers. It stimulated the appliances' acquisition and use through the employment of home economists. It aided in arranging Federal Electric and Farmers' Home Administration financing for appliance purchases, financed installation itself, and counseled more than two hundred retailers on sales and merchandising in 1940 alone.[31]

The result was that, in 1940, PGE enjoyed its greatest success ever in appliance sales (figuring on the basis of volume of its retail partners), with sales of electric ranges up 39 percent and water heaters up 49.7 percent over 1939. Use of such appliances on the company's lines climbed from 25.9 percent of residential customers at the end of 1939 to 28.8 percent at the end of 1940. "Refrigerator saturation," to use the infelicitous phrase of the 1940 *Annual Report*, was at 62 percent of the company's customers in the same year. In the Portland metropolitan area, electric ranges were installed in 83 percent of the new houses constructed during the year, electric water heaters in 44.8 percent, and electric refrigerators in 86 percent.[32] In that year, PGE served its 122,869 residential customers on average with an approximate 18 percent increase over 1935 and an approximate 4 percent rise over 1939. Kilowatt-hours per customer were at 1,518 in 1940, as opposed to 1,010 in 1935 and 1,390 in 1939.[33]

This greater usage was attributable not only to PGE's marketing efforts, but to technological advance in the appliances themselves, which made them less expensive and more efficient than a

IN AUGUST 1940, the Chase Manhattan Bank filed suit against Portland General Electric, claiming that the utility owed the bank $4.78 million and had defaulted on notes that had fallen due on 31 May of that year. Two months earlier, when the dispute had first come into the courts, a temporary restraining order had been granted preventing either party from changing the terms or amount of the indebtedness for a period ending 9 September 1940. The order thus prohibited the bank from selling PGE's collateral and halted PGE's plan to renew the notes. The injunctions gave the parties time to prepare their cases for hearing.

The Chase National suit followed statements by PGE Trustee Thomas W. Delzell, which questioned the validity of some of the debts PGE owed the bank. The suit demanded payment within thirty days or asked for foreclosure on PGE's mortgage. The company was forced to find the cash to cover the debt. Its sole recourse was to sell its least profitable division, the traction division. Had PGE not sold the streetcar lines, it would still be offering the services now provided by Tri-Met.

(*Oregonian*, 9 August 1940)

The first floor customer service area of the Electric Building, always ready to connect. (PGE Collections)

The customer department in the Electric Building.
Herald Campbell, photographer. (PGE collections)

The billing department in the early forties. (PGE collections)

Underground crew lifting cables from river bottom near the Hawthorne Bridge. Roy H. Wolford, photographer. (PGE collections)

IN COMPANY PUBLICATIONS produced during World War II, relatively little mention was made of appliance sales. Soon after the attack on Pearl Harbor, the War Production Board had placed strict limits on appliance sales and connections, and most of the company's efforts then went into supplying power to war industries and coping with increased load demand and a diminishing labor force. Still, in August 1942 the *Bullseye* pointed out that PGE had set a record the previous year with its sales of ranges (8,989) and water heaters (3,957). In the first half of 1942, however, after the board's regulations had gone into effect, the company sold only 2,878 ranges and 1,607 waterheaters. However, the falloff of in sales didn't worry company officials with an eye on the balance sheet. The boom precipitated by the war more than made up for the loss of sales of a few thousand kitchen stoves.

few years earlier. This had an effect on the company's load-building strategies. In the thirties, PGE engineers were fearful that the marketing of electric water heaters would have a deleterious effect on the utility, even though they would contribute significantly to load expansion. This was because the heaters were so inefficient that the amount of power they used was bound to drive up the consumers' utility bills, thereby building resentment rather than appreciation of the advantages of electricity.[34] The eventual evolution of a more energy-efficient water heater ended the strenuous internal debate at PGE over the sale of the devices.

The increase in load was responsible in part for five rate reductions that occurred in 1940. Residential rates dropped from 2.65 cents per kwh to 2.23 cents over the year, an aggregate savings of $690,000 to homeowners.[35] Commercial reductions totaled $282,000, industrial reductions $239,000, and the city of Portland's streetlighting bill was cut by $37,700 over that of 1939. All other public uses realized $209,500 in savings.[36]

The aggressiveness of the company, so recently in turmoil, made an ironic point in 1940. On the rise, it became the biggest retail distributor of BPA power. During the year, PGE bought more than 225 million kwh of the agency's power—more than the total of all deliveries to the publicly owned bodies it served.[37] The next year was one of further rate reductions and continued health on the balance sheet. As in 1940, the company made a profit, with net income growing by $313,226 over that period, from $1.2 million to $1.5 million.[38] Again, the reason for the growth was the accelerated pace of load-building in which the sale of energy climbed steadily. Once more, the increased usage was located in the residential segment of the market. Residential customers averaged 11 percent higher consumption than in 1940.[39]

The PGE decision makers, heartened by these developments, determined to continue to expand and modernize rather than rest on their laurels. They therefore moved to increase efficiency and generating capacity by plowing back profits into construction instead of dividends. In 1941, this meant the addition of 93.41 pole-line miles of transmission and distribution circuits, bringing the total to 4,871.13 pole miles. It meant the construction of eleven new distribution substations, as well as increasing the capacity of the twenty-two existing ones.[40]

At the time, one could measure load growth and the prosperity of Portland in a tangible way. At Station L, the gigantic (100,000-HP) steam plant at the east end of the Hawthorne Bridge, the turbines were fed with a combination of oil and hog fuel. The sawdust pile in good times was so high that it was named Mt. Osborne, after Charles P. Osborne, PGE's superintendent of operations. The pile could at times top one hundred fifty feet in height and reach to the bridge deck. Station L was the largest wood-burning power plant on the company's line, needing the sawdust pile because it was so heavily relied upon. It was used up in the summer months when the hydro plants were down because of low stream flow. As a publicity stunt, in 1941 the Oregon Trails Club climbed Mt. Osborne as if on a serious expedition, with the local press recording the event.[41]

World War II, with its shortages of critical materials, especially those required for construction and power generation, had effectively stopped PGE's new construction. At the war's end, the company projected a period of great demand. Its planners also recognized that the existing system still needed improvement. In 1945, Polhemus and his board of directors thus committed the company to a three-year program of new construction. The budget for this was to be $8.5 million, the largest construction expenditure in PGE's history. The plan, based on a study by the engineering department, called for major efforts in five spheres. There were to be betterments and replacements in generating equipment, budgeted at $900,000; new Bonneville interconnections were written in at $250,000; a 57,000-v transmission ring would be built for a cost of $1 million; a subtransmission network (substations) figured at $1 million; and distribution and miscellaneous construction at $5.3 million. The most significant items in the program were new substations, which would transform high-tension voltages to distribution voltages in a single step, thereby reducing both energy losses and investment costs (because of the elimination of much subtransformation and subtransmission). The program also incorporated (especially in rural areas) the use of higher distribution voltages and the automation of numerous substations and some generating plants. This entailed the installation of new supervisory and telemetering equipment, as well as the construction of a new load dispatching center; the installation of unit-type distribution substations with new automatic and safety characteristics; and the new Bonneville interconnection with 60,000 kilovolt amps (kva) capacity, which would include the required transmission line ties. [42]

The construction program proceeded at a $3.5 million clip in 1946, but it was not enough to prevent serious problems from developing during the year. These were in some ways pleasant since they stemmed from the first stirrings of the postwar economic boom. To the company, the boom was a source of stress on an already overtaxed system that created customer dissatisfaction and ran up costs. An unexpected industrial expansion had occurred immediately after the war. This depleted federally generated power reserves, reducing the amount of cheap energy PGE could sell to its domestic customers. This, in turn, had forced the company to run its more costly steam plants to make up the shortfall. [43]

In a determined effort to avoid further such difficulties, the pace of construction was accelerated in 1947 and $7 million was spent. [44] The projection for 1948 construction expenditures on the accelerated schedule was again $7 million, with $7.8 million actually spent. The company added 90,000 kva of substation capacity to its system and more than sixty miles of new transmission and distribution lines. Even on a temporary basis, this was still not enough to deal with the growth of demand, and the company planned to spend $850,000 in 1949 for another 83,000 kva of substation transformers. In 1948, two new interconnections with the Bonneville system at St. Louis, near Woodburn (capacity 8,000 kw), and one at St. Mary's, near Beaverton (at 32,000 kw), were completed. An interconnection at Troutdale, completed in mid-1949, brought the number of ties between PGE and BPA to seven. The others were at St. Johns, Harborton, Salem, and West Salem. Other projects in 1949 included the installation of 30,000 kva of capacitors to retain full power output, maintain voltages, and reduce transmission losses from power generated by new facilities added at Grand Coulee Dam. Also in 1949, the biggest project of the year was the replacement of the three-mile wooden flume that carried water from the Sandy River to the Station O plant at Bull Run. It had deteriorated to such an extent that a new creosoted flume was built at a cost of $850,000. [45]

G.E. ("Ding") Cannon, president of the Oregon
Trails Club in the summer of 1941, carries the flag
to claim Mt. Osborne in the name of Portland
General Electric. The intrepid would-be skiers
bringing up the rear are Mary Lawrence McArthur
Bennett and Lewis McArthur. (PGE collections)

THE IMPACT OF FEDERAL POWER

In 1941, PGE commissioned the Stone and Webster Service Corporation to investigate the company and its activities comprehensively and in detail. On 5 June, the consultants made their report. The document they submitted covered general policy, operations, and accounting. It made a number of strong recommendations on matters ranging from railway operation to the nature of the company's accounting practices. These, naturally, were matters of vital consequence to PGE. Most important, the Stone and Webster report of 1941 was quite clear about the public-policy issues facing PGE in the first years of the 1940s and about their significance to the utility's future.

> The most important question now confronting the company is the purchase of power from Bonneville on a basis which will permit it to reduce rates to a level which will compare favorably in competition with other agencies and permit the company to retain its property and increase the volume of business sufficiently to enable it to continue on a satisfactory earnings basis. [46]

Thus stated, the issue was relatively clear and the steps to be taken to resolve it no less obvious. First and most critically, "determination of future ownership of the property" had to be established. This would require "intensive negotiations and the formulation of a program embracing either purchase of power from Bonneville on a favorable basis, or, if this is not possible, to see whether or not a satisfactory sale of the entire properties can be made to some form of public agency." [47] If such a bloodless assessment ignored two decades of struggle against the public-power movement and against the specter of the BPA, the CVA and the PUDs, it nevertheless succinctly stated the order of battle for the forties.

In the decade following its founding on 20 August 1937, the BPA, its allies in the Pacific Northwest public-power movement, and public-power proponents within the New Deal were frequently at odds. For privately owned utilities in the region, such as PGE, this was a welcome development. The tentative rather than ironclad alliance among the public-power advocates and federal policy makers promoted some discord in their ranks instead of the kind of sustained, unified, and coordinated militance that might have won over public opinion and presented the utilities with a vertically organized opposition, from generation to marketing, and at all levels of policy, to which they would inevitably succumb.

The reasons for the dissension in the public-power ranks were several, and they are critical to an understanding of PGE's situation in the forties. The death of J.D. Ross on 14 March 1939 had left a leadership vacuum at Bonneville and in the ranks of the public-power movement. Ross was a genuine hero to the advocates of public power as well as a respected figure among private utility operators, on the strength of the authority imparted by his record and his friendship with the president of the United States, and with Bonneville Dam actually producing electricity, he might have been able to dominate the debate on the ownership issue. With his shrewd tactic of staying out of local political battles and his generally high standing in the region, he might have put the

1945 load dispatchers' office. There have been a few changes made since the picture shown in chapter 3. (PGE collections)

3 August 1934   Construction of Bonneville begins (called the Bonneville Project until name was changed to the Bonneville Power Administration in 1940).

28 September 1937   Dam is dedicated by FDR. Power generation begins in 1938.

1 December 1939   First PGE contract with BPA signed: 1 year term, to provide 10,000-20,000 kw of prime power plus varying amounts of surplus or dump energy.

30 September 1951   First PGE long term contract (five years).

18 September 1953   Twenty-year contract between PGE and BPA, giving PGE a share of power as new generating facilities come on line.

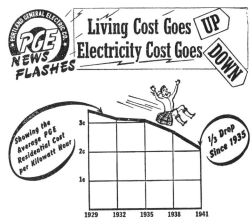

From PGE ... the Biggest Bargain in Your Family Budget!

At a time when it seems that nearly everything you buy has jumped in cost ... here's welcome news: The cost of PGE electricity keeps on going down, DOWN! Look at the chart. Notice that in 1935 our residential customers paid an average of a little over 3 cents a kilowatt-hour (a kilowatt-hour will run a typical radio for two days' average use.) By 1938, the average cost had dropped to 2¾ cents. By last year, the average cost had tumbled to 2-1/10 cents. And the reduction is continuing through 1942. Since 1935, this average cost has dropped one third! PGE electricity is the biggest bargain in your family budget!

* * * * *

Among the more than 100 parts in your electric meter, you'd find a jewel—a tiny sapphire.

PGE ... Portland General Electric Company

From 4 July 1942 Oregon Voter. (OHS neg. OrHi 84728)   207

private utilities at a severe disadvantage. A purely speculative scenario based on Ross's beliefs and actions as well as the climate of opinion at the time, would work this way: Ross could no doubt have seemed to the public the evenhanded administrator while he withheld all but token allocations of Bonneville energy from the private companies, thereby creating a significant differential between the retail price of public and private power. Such a strategy would have been difficult to execute, especially in the agency's first years, because of its need to sell the dam's power to anyone who would have it—even private utilities—until a preferred customer base of electricity-intensive industries and PUDs could be built. But Ross, revered figure, confidante of FDR, fair fighter, and public-power evangelist all in one, would have been capable of pulling it off. To reiterate, this is merely speculative. However, such a scenario indicates the precariousness of private utilities like Portland General Electric in 1939. What is clear is that Frank A. Banks, Ross's immediate replacement, was not able to assert the same degree of leadership. Banks, who had been chief construction engineer on the Grand Coulee project, as well as a member of the Bonneville advisory committee, seemed to have excellent credentials, but was identified with the Bureau of Reclamation (the agency actually responsible for Grand Coulee, the dam's main purpose being irrigation), which had poor standing among New Dealers and public-power advocates because of its well-known links with private business. From their perspective, the *Oregonian* and other newspapers against PUDs administered a confirmatory kiss of death to Banks by insisting that Roosevelt retain him permanently.[48]

Banks began his stewardship of Bonneville maladroitly, by cleaning house of Ross's appointments. He carried out his purge under the watchful eye of the Secretary of the Interior, Harold Ickes, a stout foe of the Bureau of Reclamation and private utilities with an apparent ambition to dominate federal power policy from Interior. Banks set himself against the Oregon and Washington PUDs and their supporters by refusing to campaign for new PUDs and by endorsing their goals in only the most desultory manner. He indicated that, as the administrator of a federal agency, he was duty bound to give assistance and information equally to both private and public operators. The impact of this policy had an early test in the summer of 1939, when a particularly tough election came up over the purchase of Northwestern Electric, a first step in forming a Portland-area PUD. Banks' refusal to campaign on the public-power side was a real blow to the movement, although, as already noted, Ross himself had tried to remain above local political frays.

Angered by Banks' neutrality and by his refusal to quit selling power to private utilities, Oregon public-power proponents complained to Ickes, who, early in the game, was restraining himself. Ickes rebuffed their entreaties to get rid of Banks, but he was becoming alert to the issue of the administrator's leadership. Meanwhile, Banks was exacerbating tensions within the BPA itself by calling for more condemnation proceedings against private utilities, a policy different from Ross's, and not well supported in the agency because condemnations characteristically involved long and costly legal battles. The result of all this was paralysis at Bonneville as his subordinates accused Banks of trashing Ross's legacy. Shortly, the administrator found himself besieged from within and without Bonneville. Sniping by his staff, much of it well grounded, became known to Ickes.

208

Ironically, Banks' activities and views bought him no credence with the private operators. They thought him dilatory in negotiations to sell them power from the second of the Bonneville generators to be installed. Banks had indeed been proceeding slowly on this issue, but for good reason. The contracts he made would become benchmarks, precedents for future federal power contracts. Ickes had admonished him to be careful in setting rates and crafting surrounding policy that would shape the government's relations with the entire utility industry for the foreseeable future.

By the end of the summer of 1939, Ickes had lost whatever enthusiasm he may have had for the embattled Banks, and he dismissed him on 21 August. Eventually the secretary settled on his replacement. Paul J. Raver, a professor of engineering and public utilities at Northwestern University, was an obscure figure among public-power advocates, but Ickes knew him as the former head of the Illinois Commerce Commission and as part of the movement that had brought down Samuel Insull and Middle West Utilities. (Insull had been by far the most visible of the utility holding company magnates, his empire the most extensive, and its collapse the most spectacular of the crash and ensuing Depression.)

Raver's appointment met with a variety of responses in the rest of the nation and the Pacific Northwest. Eastern and business-oriented newspapers that generally favored private power, such as the *Wall Street Journal*, endorsed the new man as a potentially conservative force at Bonneville, but at least one public-power advocate in the region construed such encomiums as a subtle attempt to undermine the new administrator with Northwest progressives. Generally, the private utilities and the public-power advocates adopted a posture of watchful waiting.

Behind the scenes, Raver began his tenure as the beneficiary of a tidal wave of advice and pressure. William Martin, the BPA counsel, advised that he should go forward with the BPA-PGE contract that Banks had negotiated, but should discourage long-term contracts. The administrator of the Rural Electrification Administration (REA), Harry Slattery, charged that he was neglecting attempts by the Washington Water Power Company to sabotage cooperatives east of the Cascades. Another official in that administration, Dr. Harlow S. Person, criticized him on his handling of rates and rate revenues in the BPA's relations with cooperatives financed by the REA. The Bureau of Reclamation sniped at him over rates, public-utility-district commissioners expressed unhappiness over a perceived lack of support from the BPA except on technical matters (Raver had assured the region's power companies that he would not use his authority to undermine them), and Ickes, in the meantime, worked toward the day when he would have complete control of national power policy and the agency's administrator would be his cat's-paw.[49] Raver, for his part, reacted strongly to criticism by his erstwhile allies, further exacerbating tensions.

Such circumstances, coupled with the extremely unfavorable statutory conditions for the creation of PUDs, made Oregon voters less than receptive to public power. Voters were required to pass on the PUDs in two separate elections—one on the principle of a PUD and a subsequent election to fund it if it passed. The struggle, for the most part, centered in Washington. Between 1934 and 1942, fifty-six elections were held in Oregon over the issue. Only eighteen districts were created as a result of those ballots, and two of the districts defeated later bond levies.[50]

This was the background against which PGE began its relationship with BPA, the voting public, and the forces of public power in the forties. With its initial half-million-dollar contract for BPA energy (which subsequently grew into the distribution of more of the agency's electricity than any other agency, public or private, and, at one point, more than all its public-agency distribution combined), PGE was able to charge its residential customers the fourth lowest rates in the nation.[51] Yet the circumstances and figures were not enough to end the fierce battles for the company's turf with the persistent advocates of public power. As a result, during the forties, there were eight elections in PGE's service area.

The Stone and Webster report had correctly stated the dynamics of the issue in 1940. It said the "ability of . . . [the] company to retain its key territory, instead of losing it piecemeal to public authorities," was the crux of the PGE problem. The consultants observed that the critical element to both retention of service area and bargaining leverage with regard to price in any condemnation proceeding was continued rate reduction. Territorial loss, they said, was threatened from four sources: municipal ownership; PUDs, which had to be voted on by citizens; cooperatives; and REA projects. The co-ops would be the most difficult to oppose "in that they undoubtedly require more extreme rate cuts to slow down their development." The report noted that the company had thus far done "a remarkable job in holding its territory against projects requiring a popular vote and . . . with reasonable rate reductions, the territory can still be held against projects requiring votes."[52]

At PGE in 1940, expectations for the company's survival were low. Alan Hart, later a prominent Portland lawyer who was a BPA legal adviser at the time, recalled that E.B. MacNaughton, acting as an emissary for Franklin Griffith, called the BPA to request a meeting. Griffith was concerned that the utility's system would slowly be reduced to a worthless remnant by condemnation proceedings initiated by PUDs, municipals, and co-ops strengthened by the rise of the federally nourished public-power movement. He worried that eventually only the company's distribution system would be left, in itself useless, once the generation and transmission capabilities were stripped away. Although the BPA could not itself buy electrical systems, the two executives, facing what they perceived as the hard realities, wondered if the agency would be interested in purchasing the PGE system if it seemed that raiding by the public bodies would begin. The agency was interested, and explored the possibility of seeking from Congress an amendment to its charter to allow it to acquire PGE's assets. Hart went so far as to draft a contract, but difficulties developed over the asking price—$58 million—and the BPA's offer of $50 million. The issue was finally laid to rest by the bankruptcy trustees, Delzell and King, who refused to entertain the notion of a sale.[53] With the demise of this possibility, the utility was left to the vagaries of the rapidly developing politics of public power.

The actual record of PGE against the public-power movement during the forties remained good, largely because of the company's adherence to the Stone and Webster strategy, as well as the relative disarray of the opposition and the structural difficulties inherent in Oregon law. In 1940 there were ten elections in the PGE service area. They involved all, or portions of Marion, Clackamas, Columbia, Yamhill, Washington, and Polk counties and the cities of Portland, Woodburn, and West Salem. The only successful challenges were at Woodburn, where a twenty-two-vote margin ratified a sixty-thousand-dollar bond levy, and Columbia County, where a Columbia River public-utility-district proposal embracing rural areas of the county, and therefore offering attractive rates set by the REA, passed by ninety-two votes. Altogether, in the 1940 elections, 115,339 votes were cast against public ownership and 67,119 in favor, a ratio of nearly two to one against.[54] By all accounts, this was an accurate index of the general attitude of Oregonians toward the issue of public ownership.[55]

The record of 1940, however, did not prevent supporters of public power from taking their case to the voters at every opportunity in the next nine years. Over the course of the decade, PGE won four public-utility-district elections and an unopposed franchise renewal polling in Hillsboro in 1949.[56] Even the few defeats the company suffered were not severe. The municipality of West Salem, the only locality where PGE operated without a franchise, dealt the company a blow in a cooperative election that took two hundred fifty customers off PGE's lines in 1944. In 1949, however, the town merged with the city of Salem, where PGE operated a secure franchise, having won a public-utility-district election there in 1946. In one spectacular effort, Guy C. Myers, a financier with excellent Wall Street connections and a close association with the public-power movement, attempted through the Hood River PUD to acquire not only PGE's entire system, but those of Northwestern and Pacific Power and Light (PP&L). The scheme was thwarted as usual by the Oregon law calling for a bond election, where its futility was exposed. Myers asked a handful of voters to take on a massive debt out of all proportion to their electricity needs, and on 7 January 1944, a total of 1,417 voters defeated the $175 million levy by 865 to 552.[57]

If the issue of PUDs remained a matter of grave concern to the PGE leadership in the forties, it was no doubt because of two other problems that were also apparently intractable. As they had the possibility of playing directly into the hands of the public-power advocates, they had to be taken seriously by the company. In hindsight, it seems obvious that the first—the question of a CVA— was a tenacious, if remote possibility. The second—the inability of PGE to reach terms on a permanent contract with BPA for firm power—was a critical issue, but one to which the company brought little leverage against the policy of the agency's administrator.

The concept of a CVA for the Northwest was attractive to a variety of the region's legislators and policy makers by 1939-40. As noted earlier, it received some consideration in Congress at the onset of the Bonneville project, but fell by the way in favor of other possibilities. As the forties proceeded, several attempts to revive the idea were made in Congress, and there seemed to be a ground swell of support in the region. PGE and other private utilities in the Northwest lobbied vigorously against the idea, but they were not decisive in the defeat of the CVA in its various guises. The proposal really met its end in the social and political climate of the Pacific Northwest. The region's voters (not even those favorable to public power) and its key policy makers (David Eccles, Oregon's representative to the Pacific Northwest Regional Planning Commission and a vocal opponent of the CVA, is a good example) failed to warm to the idea because it seemed to represent an extension of federal authority in an area where, on most all important issues, citizens preferred local control. Thus, of the many attempts to institute a CVA during the forties and early fifties, none was ultimately appealing to the electorate or threatening to the utilities.[58]

Of greater moment to PGE was the real problem of a permanent contract with the BPA for firm power. The issue nagged the PGE leadership throughout the decade. Griffith and Polhemus felt they had to have a permanent contract in order to remain competitive against the threat of takeover and, especially in light of the findings of the Stone and Webster report, had been forthcoming where rate reductions were concerned. They always felt it could not be argued that PGE had made excessive profits on the basis of low BPA wholesale rates that were not passed on to the consumer. The company, in their view, thus deserved a permanent contract for a reliable quota of BPA power.

The first three of the agency's administrators—Ross, Banks, and Raver—were in no particular hurry to make such an agreement. Each played his cards slowly, stalling PGE, and, for that matter, all the other private utilities in the region, with temporary, yearly contracts for the reasons already discussed. They apparently hoped that the public-power movement in the Northwest would reach critical mass, through a gathering tide of public-utility-district victories at the polls, municipal condemnations of utility properties, or the passage of a CVA bill in Congress that would give the agency's administrator himself the power to condemn and distribute to municipalities, cooperatives, and PUDs the assets of the utility companies.

In PGE's case, the situation was essentially stalemated in that both sides needed each other. While Washington's public-utility-district movement was successful, Oregon's never really developed. When Bonneville Dam came on-line, even during the height of war production, the agency had excess, or "dump," power to sell. Thus, it could hardly refuse the initial half-million-dollar contract with PGE in 1939. The measure of the agency's misreading of the utility's reluctance for its power is seen in Ickes' instructions to Banks for the first PGE contract. The secretary advised Banks to force progressive rate reduction on PGE. If the utility resisted, he should drop negotiations and contact Electric Bond and Share, which owned Mountain States and PP&L and was a company already familiar with the concept.[59] PGE, of course, wholeheartedly embraced the conditions. Even before the Stone and Webster report, it had been clear to Griffith that the company needed BPA power to survive and must do whatever was rational to get it.

The frustration of the decision makers at PGE with the foot-dragging at Bonneville over a permanent contract was reflected in the combative tone of public utterances on the company's relationship with BPA in the forties by both Griffith and Polhemus. Even the usually circumspect Griffith disputed Raver publicly, a practice he had mostly avoided in the thirties in his relations with Ross and Banks. On the other hand, the dominant note he and Polhemus struck remained "Cooperation not Antagonism," which happened to be the title of a speech Griffith delivered to the Progressive Business Man's Club of Portland on 11 March 1943.

In his address, Griffith was critical of Raver, who, once settled in office, struck a militant pose toward the Northwest's private utilities. For the administrator, this was in keeping with his own views and politically correct, but it frustrated Griffith, who complained that Raver's bill of particulars against the companies included accusations of nefarious practices outlawed by the Public Utility Holding Company Act of 1934; those practices had, therefore, long since ceased. Such accusations, Griffith intimated, simply constituted a pretext for denying the private utilities the power to which they were entitled. By the spring of 1943, said Griffith, Raver controlled in excess of 700,000 kw of energy. By the end of the year, he noted, that figure would increase to about 1.3 million kw or 1.75 million HP with the installation of additional generators. The demand requirements of all the PUDs on BPA's lines totaled less than 6 percent of the agency's current capacity and less than 4 percent of the predicted year-end capacity. Moreover, the energy requirements of the war effort, which the administrator constantly held up to the private operators as his first priority, were, according to Griffith, adequately served already. Only about twelve concerns were directly connected to the BPA lines. All other war industries were served by the region's major public and private utilities.[60]

Raver's delaying tactics on a permanent contract for PGE had, in reality, been keyed to two propositions. The first was that PGE withdraw its demand for condemnation proceedings on portions of its property coveted by Woodburn (in Oregon) and Vancouver (in Washington) and simply sell them at the price the public agencies were willing to pay. The second was that he required future transactions of a similar kind to be validated and, therefore, expedited by the power contract. PGE was unwilling to make such a concession, since to do so would have been to eliminate its best defenses against takeover—the lengthy and intrinsically failure-prone double-election process and the long-drawn-out, and inherently costly condemnation proceedings, which called up court battles with platoons of judges, lawyers, and accountants. To acquiesce in such a demand would have been tantamount to self-liquidation. Griffith, meanwhile, insisted that the agency administrator had no authority to require that the company sell its properties on any basis.[61]

Griffith had questioned Ickes in June 1941 for his view on these issues. In discussing the future of the BPA and the Northwest's private utilities, the secretary of the Interior had warned Griffith that the CVA bill (by then before Congress), if passed, would give the agency's administrator the authority to acquire private utilities in the Pacific Northwest. He also said that, since nearly three-quarters of Washington State was served by public-power agencies, and the developing capacities of Bonneville and Grand Coulee would surely dominate the supply of raw power in the region, to his mind public ownership throughout the Northwest was inevitable. Ickes was inclined to believe that arrangements should therefore be made to effect the swift transfer of all of PGE's properties to public entities, looking to the time when the company was finally engulfed by the public movement.[62]

Ickes nevertheless felt that, until the passage of the CVA bill, a joint dominion between the company and the BPA would be worked out, unless the company was giving its customers inadequate service. The secretary was otherwise not in favor of "forcing public ownership down the throats of an unwilling public," Griffith reported. The BPA and PGE representatives should therefore be able to come to an agreement on the fair value of the company's properties, and until such time as it was authorized to acquire them, BPA should cooperate with PGE and in the secretary's words, "not stir up trouble for it." Under those conditions, Ickes "would approve an indeterminate contract protecting PGE's supply of energy until the United States should take over the entire property of the company which he expected would be parceled out to various public agencies wishing it," according to Griffith.[63]

Because Ickes had stopped well short of demanding the enshrinement of the administrator's right to take company property before the coalescence of the widespread demand that Oregon utilities go public, in June 1941 Griffith was able to achieve agreement with Raver on the outlines of a permanent contract. It would include a permanent and adequate supply of energy to the company and options on the company's property exercisable by BPA when the agency was legally authorized and financially able to purchase it and the voters of the affected area demonstrated their desire for public ownership. It also included BPA's recognition of the company's right to continue to function as a private utility under state regulation until the options were exercised.[64]

A month later, talks were halted while Griffith turned his attention to PEPCO's reorganization. This left the company without the assurance of a power supply. The independent trustees insisted on the importance of negotiating one with BPA, and the company soon renewed its efforts to secure a permanent contract.[65] However, the moment had been lost. Raver returned to his stalling mode, which he deemed appropriate because of the war. The administrator simply did not wish to tie up a significant block of power while the war continued.

Griffith was left to point out that Raver himself had said Portland rates were among the lowest in the nation, as evidence that the company had complied with the agency's wishes and passed on its savings from the purchase of BPA power to the consumer. Raver's counterargument was that the company was, in any case, making a profit on the federal government's investment. Griffith responded that, between 1939 and 1943, BPA had provided PGE with 1 billion kwh of energy at an average rate of approximately 2.5 mills per kwh. The cost of producing energy in PGE's hydro and steam plants was approximately 5 mills per kw. Over the period, the company had passed along the differential savings so that PGE's customers had saved a total of $2.5 million. "We have not reached the limit of rate reductions," Griffith promised.[66] His argument, that it mattered little if the company profited from the government's investment as long as the people were fairly served, fell on deaf ears at BPA.

In the battle for permanence in the relationship between BPA and the private utilities, aid came to the companies from an unexpected source in the summer of 1942. In July, the War Production Board issued Order I-94, directing BPA to interconnect with all the other major electrical systems in the Pacific Northwest. Thus inaugurated, the Northwest Power Pool linked more than 3.3 million HP of electric generating capacity in Oregon, Washington, Idaho, Montana, and Utah. The result was essentially that entities with surplus energy would pump it into the pool; those requiring energy would be able to draw it from the pool for their needs.

Ironically, Raver, a member of the National Power Policy and Defense Committee, had taken the lead in making Grand Coulee and Bonneville linchpins in the region's wartime power network. In so doing, the BPA administrator seriously compromised—at least in the eyes of public-power enthusiasts, the possibilities of a CVA.[67] In the national emergency, honorable men such as Raver could hardly ignore the imperatives of efficient production. The Northwest Power Pool, which remained operative after the war, certainly weakened the case for the public agencies, as it gave the private utilities physical linkage to cheap Bonneville energy, undercutting the claim of the public-power forces that only PUDs and cooperatives had a right to the government's power. At the same time, the very concept and practice of pooling indicated to the general public that there was harmony and coordination among public- and private-power agencies. The idea of a superagency and of the right of one kind of power entity over another's to BPA energy seemed superfluous or wrongheaded.

This did not stop strong competition from developing between the operatives of BPA and private utilities like PGE. Many PGE employees of the era have indicated that a wide ideological gulf separated them from their BPA counterparts when it was necessary to deal with each other.[68] Although the consensus among them is that the agency's personnel never behaved less than fairly with the company, the sentiment for public power at BPA intensified the difficulties inherent in the various negotiations undertaken over the decade.

The tensions between BPA and PGE and other private companies are encapsulated in an exchange of letters from 1948 between Raver and Polhemus and the presidents of PP&L (which had bought out Northwestern Electric in 1947 and now operated in Portland), Washington Water Power, Puget Sound Power and Light, and Mountain States Power. In the letters, the same nagging problems—the size of the companies' temporary allotment of BPA energy, and the lack of a permanent, or at least long-term, contract—were at issue.

Raver opened negotiations:

> Loads have increased generally beyond expectations and your present estimates are far in excess of the estimates [for energy needs] made by you several years ago. In addition, the program of installation of new [Bonneville] capacity . . . has been . . . delayed. . . . As a result . . . it is . . . not going to be possible . . . to supply you with all of your . . . requirements over the next five years or more unless water conditions . . . are at least as good as average.[69]

The letter went on to enumerate the conditions under which the utilities could have BPA energy.

> Bonneville Power Administration will—
> 1. Extend the existing contracts with your companies for a period of one year from September 1, 1948 to August 31, 1949, with such adjustment in firm power commitments as may be required in accordance with presently estimated loads and resources. We estimate at this time that we will be able to increase the 335,000 kw of peaking capacity made available to your companies under existing contracts to something over 400,000 kw; or
> 2. (a) Incorporate the above extension into new contracts for a period of five years from July 1, 1949 to June 30, 1953, with a firm commitment to supply on the basis of average or better water conditions the presently estimated requirements of the private utility companies in excess of generation available to them;
> (b) Under water conditions less than average, Bonneville Power Administration will agree to supply such firm power as it has available after taking care of existing commitments and public agency loads required to be served by the Bonneville Power Administration under the preference and priority provisions of the Bonneville Act. At least ninety days prior to July 1 of each year of the contract, the amount of firm power to be available during the following year would be determined in the same manner as for the presently existing contract and would be embodied in a supplemental agreement;
> (c) To the end that no unused transmission capacity would stand idle, any new transfer

arrangements would be worked out at the time of each annual review and embodied in the supplemental agreement in accordance with provisions to be negotiated in the contract.[70]

The reply of the utility presidents, plaintive and frustrated, perfectly captured the relationship they had endured since the BPA's origin and which they would continue to endure until 1953. Collectively, they wrote:

APRIL 21, 1948
We are disappointed at the terms and conditions you propose for what you designate as a new contract for five years. Among other objections, it is only a one-year contract, because the provision for a review each year of the amount of firm power to be delivered leaves us without any firm commitment from you. Such a contract would be of little or no assistance to us, either in planning or financing.

The undersigned companies have for a period of years endeavored to get from you a long-term contract for power. We have done so in pursuit of our responsibility properly and adequately to take care of the requirements of our 770,000 customers. They have a direct and active interest in the transmission facilities under your jurisdiction, and also in the dams and generation facilities which have made federal power available in this region. Our customers, and the business enterprises we represent, are taxpayers and share responsibility for the funds which made the Bonneville and Grand Coulee projects possible. Fair dealing demands that these customers receive their just share of power from these projects. To refuse to grant contracts to the privately owned agencies serving them, on a basis comparable with contracts given to other distributing agencies and industrial consumers, constitutes an obvious discrimination.

Our contract negotiations with you have been frequent, prolonged, and exhaustive, and show clearly our willingness to cooperate in securing the widest distribution of Bonneville power, having particularly in mind the predominant number of our rural and domestic customers.

Current negotiations, covering a period of more than three months, for a reasonable, long-term contract, have been no more successful than those in the past. Your letter of April 2, 1948, closes the door to our obtaining such a contract. We, therefore, reluctantly conclude that, in order that our customers may have some assurance of service during the next year, we must accept your proposition for an extension of our present contracts for another year. To this end we stand ready to confer with you at your convenience.

The letter was signed by James H. Polhemus; Paul B. McKee, president of PP&L; K.M. Robinson, president of the Washington Water Power Company; Frank McLaughlin, president of Puget Sound Power and Light; and Z.E. Merrill, president of Mountain States Power Company.[71]

THE CHANGING OF THE GUARD

Something was missing from PGE's 1946 *Annual Report*. It was the listing, usually present at the front or back of the document, of the board of directors and officers of the company. It was again present, in 1947. But it had a different look. For perhaps the first time in living memory, the name of Franklin T. Griffith was absent from the list of PGE management. Instead, as chairman, Thomas W. Delzell was listed. Griffith had retired.

Griffith's leave-taking was the occasion of great regret by his colleagues at PGE, in the business world generally, and among the city's editorial writers, who wrote glowingly of his service to the company, the city, and the state.

Characteristically, however, Griffith did not retreat to a life of leisure. Bob Lee, who started as an electrical draftsman in 1948 and went on to become the general manager of hydro production until his retirement in 1988, recalled that at one time in the late forties or early fifties, he and another man put in a lot of overtime on a certain project. They frequently found themselves at the Electric Building on a Saturday or a Sunday, or even both. Invariably there was also "old Franklin T.," as he was known, working diligently at his desk, solving some problem or other, unable apparently to spit the bit from between his teeth. "He was there more than we were," Lee mused.[72] He continued that habit and his law practice almost to the day of his death in 1952, at eighty-two years of age.

When Griffith retired, he had much to be proud of. One of his proudest accomplishments was the transformation he wrought in PGE, especially after the Central Public Service episode, in making it a local company, as opposed to a locally operated, but essentially colonial, concern. By the end of World War II, the company could say that it was "a venture pioneered by local citizens" and was "today a 'home-grown' institution directed by men who, without exception, are Oregonians."[73] Even the company's top management were nearly all natives, and the few who weren't, including Griffith himself, were longtime residents. To Griffith, this was not a boast, but a statement of necessity. He had always known that local control was essential to the company's survival.

When Delzell assumed the PGE chairmanship on 23 January 1948, he recognized the importance of Griffith's commitment. He brought in a completely new board of directors, perhaps because, as independent trustees, he and Ralph L. Clark (who was a member of the new group) had often clashed with the old board over company fiscal policy. The *Annual Report* of 1947 noted that the new board of directors was still composed entirely of Oregonians.[74] As Delzell and Polhemus observed in their joint message opening the report, "PGE, historically the pioneer of electric public service in Oregon and operated solely within the state, is directed by men all of whom possess long experience with Oregon problems and who can provide close-at-hand attention to management of the company's business."[75]

Whatever else the selection of the new eleven-member board represented, it was a complete break with the recent past. Choosing new people without ties to PEPCO was a deliberate way of signifying the end of the utility's holding-company era. On 2 February 1948, an exchange of PGE

Born in Chickasha, Oklahoma in 1901, Thomas Delzell moved to Klamath Falls at the age of four. He attended Oregon State College and graduated from the school of Civil Engineering in 1922. He served as assistant public utilities commissioner for the state of Oregon from 1938-39. He was asked to serve as one of two trustees to oversee the reorganization of PEPCO in 1939. He was made a director of PGE in 1948 and chief executive officer in 1955. He retired 31 May 1966. He was a member of the Shriners, the Masons, the Waverly Club, the Arlington Club, the University Club, and the Multnomah Athletic Club. (Photo by Logan Markham)

218

stock for the securities of the parent was begun in order to dissolve PEPCO. No longer would PGE be the subsidiary of a holding company or itself a holding company.[76]

The latest reorganization had resulted from the sale of Portland Traction at the bargain price of less than $8 million. With the cash from that transaction in hand, Delzell and Clark, then still trustees, developed a "Second Alternative Amended Plan of Reorganization, as Amended," to replace an earlier plan that had been filed in 1942, in light of the company's improved financial condition, which included settlement of disputes with its biggest noteholder, Chase National Bank. In 1944, the Securities and Exchange Commission had rejected the 1942 plan, but the U.S. District Court, under Judge Fee, decided the twice-amended version, with the Portland Traction funds and other cash available to subsidize the $10.9 million the plan required to be disbursed to pay off PEPCO bondholders and other costs expected in the transition, was workable and approved it.[77] The new structure was designed to save all the interest owed to PEPCO bondholders, and to give PGE securities greater attractiveness to potential investors, undergirded as they would then be by a sounder, more profitable balance sheet. As the 1948 *Annual Report* put it, "earnings and dividend potentialities can better be evaluated by the results of the last three years."[78]

Yet another improvement in the company's financial character brought about by the reorganization was the broader base of stockholders that emerged from the attractive prospectus of the strengthened company. Some fifteen thousand persons owned 1.25 million shares of PGE common in 1949. Of those, some 33 percent lived in Oregon and 85 percent on the Pacific Coast. They held about 70 percent of the company's stock. No individual owned more than 3 percent of the common stock. PGE had become a public company, owned largely by those who could understand the conditions in which it operated.[79]

Yet another period of the company's history had passed. PGE was now ready to face the shimmering future of the prosperous America of the postwar era.

7 THE QUEST FOR KILOWATTS

I N THE YEARS AFTER World War II, there was an unprecedented surge of pent-up demand from American consumers. As the United States was the only major industrial power with its physical plant intact at the close of hostilities, the means of satisfying consumer desires was in place, and the swift conversion to peacetime production kept available foreign goods out of the domestic market. By the same token, the onset of the cold war kept defense production at record peacetime levels, which also favorably affected prosperity. Although there were recessions in 1947, 1953, and 1958, an expansion quickly took hold and became moderately buoyant in roughly the first fifteen years of the postwar era.

Between 1948 and 1960, the U.S. population rose from 139.9 million to 180.6 million, and the birthrate (per thousand live births) in the same period went from 20.4 to 23.7. From 1948 to 1960, GNP (in 1982 dollars) expanded from $1.1 billion to $1.6 billion, or from $7,544 to $9,200 per capita.[1] Over this span, motor-vehicle registrations grew from 41 million to 73 million, and advertising expenditures exploded as billings mushroomed from $4.8 million to $11.9 million.[2] Americans were on a consuming binge. Meanwhile, the Pacific Northwest kept pace with the national trends as the region grew in population, from 3.3 million in 1940 to 5.2 million in 1960, and industrial and commercial expansion proceeded apace.

For utilities like PGE, the economy in the postwar period presented an unprecedented opportunity, as well as a perilous challenge. The Pacific Northwest was generally acknowledged by observers to be ripe for growth.[3] As early as 1943, PGE had recognized this potential. A memorandum of that year by a PGE research analyst, prepared for the attorney representing PEPCO preferred stockholders, projected a shining future for the region in general and Portland and the rest of Oregon in particular. Alluding to "a magnificent opportunity with promising potentialities for industrial capital," the report said that it was well known that "industrial development means new population, and new population requires public utility service." With copious, specific examples, and expert testimony in Portland's economic promise, including what the author took to be the commitment of the resources of Washington, D.C., to the future of the state and the region, the report asserted flatly that "the Federal Government [through the work of various agencies] has, in effect, set itself to the task of developing the Pacific Northwest to bring its heretofore unbalanced economy into balance on what may be considered to be a continuous, long-range program that practically underwrites continued peacetime development."[4]

It was one thing to recognize opportunity and quite another to seize it. Ironically, PGE was to find that prosperity, even unprecedented prosperity, could be as rigorous a challenge as depression and war. The crux of the problem through the fifties remained what it had been during and immediately after World War II: the nature, amount, and cost of the power supply to which the company had access and the generation facilities.

By the fall of 1947, the Northwest's power situation had become critical. On 6 September the *Oregonian's* front page reported that Bonneville and Grand Coulee dams "marked up a new power production record in August as demand of the Northwest for electrical power required operation of their generators 'up to the hilt' on every day of the month," as one BPA official put it. The region's peacetime economic robustness was evident in the figure for power generated by the two government facilities for August 1947—909,821,000 kwh—as against the highest one-month record of the war years—899,641,000 kwh—for March 1944.[5] Remarkably, good economic health had become a problem.

By September the situation had become distressing enough for the press to be reporting the possibility of regional brownouts. "Faced with winter power load estimates hitting in excess of two billion kilowatts a month through December," the *Oregonian* said, "utility executives and engineers were advised that at peak periods full operation of all available generating capacity, both hydro and steam, will be required."[6]

Eventually, brownouts did occur in Central Oregon in the winter of 1947, when sub-zero temperatures brought dramatic increases in demand.[7] This was simply a symptom of underlying problems in generation and consumption in the region. A closer look at census figures for Washington and Oregon will tell a more complex story. The population of Washington increased by 37 percent from 1940 to 1950, as numbers went from 1.7 million to 2.3 million.[8] Oregon's growth was similar in that the state's population expanded from 1 million to 1.5 million persons over the period.[9] General growth did not cease in the 1950s. Perhaps more important, trends in population and the nature of economic establishments began to take a new shape in the region. Between 1940 and 1960, the number of places in Oregon with concentrations of population over twenty-five hundred went from 86 to 104 for a growth rate of about 8 percent, while Washington experienced a similar pattern, with such centers growing in number from 90 to 121, a rate of more than 9 percent.[10]

What was important here was that urban dwellers used significantly more electricity than rural dwellers. At the same time, there was steady growth in the vaunted electroprocessing industries as well as in the more traditional kinds of manufacturing. For example, in 1950, a major National Biscuit Company plant costing $10 million opened in Portland. The Northwest economy and society had changed greatly, and would continue to do so. Furthermore, these were structural changes, meaning that the strain on the Northwest's pool of power would be permanent.

Despite the spectacular Vanport flood of 30 May 1948, a series of low-water years in the late forties and early fifties drastically affected electrical power supplies in the region. The combination of high demand from an ever-increasing population and inadequate generation facilities promised to be a deadly recipe for the region's economy. Chester K. Sterrett, manager of the industrial department of the Portland Chamber of Commerce, had reported in the fall of 1947 that the power shortage was so serious that the chamber had been forced to "tone down . . . promotion work on industries requiring large blocks of power." At the time, the best hope for relief seemed to be more generators for Grand Coulee and the completion of McNary Dam on the Columbia. But, according to Sterrett, they required "continuous annual appropriations" from Congress in order to bring them to timely completion.[11]

In formulating its response to the gathering crisis, PGE faced complex political, economic, demographic, technological, and environmental realities, both nationally and regionally. This was especially true where its relationship with the BPA and the agency's power supply were concerned. The results of the 1946 elections left the Congress in the hands of the Republican Party for the first time since 1928. A particular target of Republicans was New Deal power policy. Bills were introduced in the eightieth Congress to curb the Federal Power Commission's jurisdiction to severely restrict the power components of the government's reclamation program and to require the Corps of Engineers to sell power from its hydroelectric projects outside the BPA area at the bus bar. From the House Appropriations Subcommittee came a large cut in the BPA budget request, accompanied by a committee report decrying the "unAmerican" efforts of Washington State's PUDs in condemning private electric-utility distribution systems.[12] Each of these bills was eventually defeated. Meanwhile, the BPA budget was raised for fiscal 1949 as the result of fierce reaction from the Northwest's congressional delegation, which had been pressured to resist the measures by the region's editorial writers, its utilities, and the electricity-consuming public.

A more dramatic lobbying tool was the Vanport flood. This disaster killed 15 people, left 18,700 homeless, forced evacuation of 100,000, destroyed 5,000 homes, covered 251,000 acres, and caused $103 million in damages. In the process it erased from the map Oregon's second largest city, as the Columbia River raged over its banks near Portland.[13] The flood, the Truman administration's narrow victory in the 1948 elections, which emboldened the president to push for a CVA in a special message to Congress, and the outbreak of the Korean War were decisive in spurring Congress to sign the River and Harbor and Flood Control Act of 17 May 1950. This law empowered the Corps of Engineers to proceed with a record number of Columbia Basin hydro

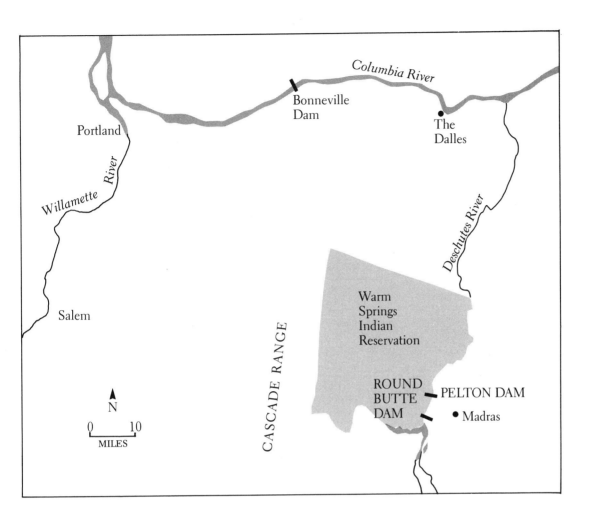

projects, including Albeni Falls, Libby, Priest Rapids, John Day, and The Dalles dams. For good measure, the act reconfirmed the Chief Joseph Dam on the Columbia, first authorized in 1946.[14] The sweeping program headed off sentiment for a CVA, which some thought could solve the region's power shortage. Yet the extent to which the act was a triumph for private Northwest hydropower interests like PGE, as well as public bodies, was mitigated by uncontrollable circumstances. Delays in building the facilities necessary to absorb the region's demands for electricity, which were occasioned by congressional wrangling, were to be so lengthy as to postpone relief until well into the next decade. No matter what there was to be said about the future, immediate needs were to remain unmet during the fifties, even as pressure to address them grew daily.

In time, PGE's leadership crafted a series of responses to the facts of life in this paradoxical decade wherein shortages seemed to be dictated by abundance. They were responses shaped by the interplay of an array of variables over the course of the decade. These variables included the company's image of itself and its sense of its role in the regional economy; the political agendas of Congress and the national administration, the Northwest public-power lobby and PGE's private-utility brethren; the goals of the state of Oregon, its Fish Commission, and the U.S. Supreme Court; and the patterns of the natural environment. They formed the basis for a decade that could have been set to a fox-trot: two steps forward and one step back; two forward, one back.

DAM BUILDING

From the end of World War II to the close of the forties, the company spent $32.8 million on construction and system betterments. This was not enough. In 1950 new construction reached a total of $7.3 million, the highest annual postwar figure to that point. Most of this construction consisted of new substation capacity, but one of the larger projects of the year was reinforcement of service in the underground area of downtown Portland. This gave commercial customers greatly improved network service in both reliability and capacity.[15]

There was a slight increase in the construction budget for 1951. As in 1950, a little more than $10 million went for interconnections with BPA.[16] In the next year, the construction budget increased to $8.5 million, most of which went to new substation construction, while some $2.3 million went to new generating capacity. For example, 5,000 kw were added at River Mill by installing a new generator, and modernization and improvements at the Willamette Falls hydroelectric plant promised to bring 15,400 kw on line in 1953, boosting capacity there by a factor of three from the prior 5,000 kw.[17]

The pace of PGE's growth accelerated in mid-decade as the regional and national economy continued to expand. A $10.9 million budget in 1954 brought postwar capital construction to about $69 million. The expenditures had netted a 98.7 percent increase in the utility plant. One of the biggest expenses of the year was for the development of the Timothy Meadows reservoir above the Oak Grove hydro plant on the Clackamas River. Its completion was expected to add an average of about 10,500 kw to the company's three plants on the stream during the cooler months when electricity was most needed. The expansion included additions to the transmission and distribution systems that would accommodate PGE's ever-growing loads. Even though 1954 was a year of economic recession, PGE added 3,477 new residential customers, as well as 423 new businesses.[18]

The pressure on load growth came not just from domestic and commercial consumers. Agriculture had grown in the postwar era to become Oregon's second largest industry. PGE experienced the impact of this growth on energy demand when, in 1953, the company had a 20 percent increase over the previous year in its irrigation load, bringing the total power for that purpose to 32,000 kw. The company was unprepared for this surge and had to "cut over" rural distribution lines to 12,500 V in order to meet farm needs.[19]

PGE's construction budget grew again in 1955 when the company allocated some $11 million to it. The biggest cost item was the new $1.4 million service center located at 3700 Southeast 17th Avenue in Portland. The facility was considered one of the most efficient in the country. Once again, the largest category of construction expenditures was in distribution and transmission necessary to keep pace with growing loads.

By 1956, normal construction was augmented by the accelerated pace of hydro facility construction. The company was pursuing Pelton on the Deschutes, and a North Fork dam project on the Clackamas, begun in late 1956, as well as modernization of the Faraday plant with the addition of a 34,500 HP-turbine generator. These three projects were completed in 1958, with the addition of 189,000 kw of generating capacity.[20] Though augmentation of generating capacity by a figure of that magnitude was impressive, PGE President Thomas Delzell was not satisfied. In 1958 the company filed a plan with the Oregon State Hydroelectric Commission to build Round Butte Dam, also on the Deschutes. This promised to bring an additional 300,000 kw into the PGE system. Round Butte was uncompleted by the end of the decade, but from 1950 to 1960, PGE's plant grew from an $80,896,510 investment to one worth $210,666,374, and its generating capability increased by 234,620 kw.[21]

Pelton Dam was an example of the complexities of postwar power supply. The problems associated with regulation and control began to manifest themselves almost immediately. In the winter of 1948-49 water levels were low in Columbia Basin rivers, and peak-load demand exceeded the capabilities of the Northwest Power Pool's generating capabilities.

A large part of the solution was thought to lie in the campaign of capital construction that the company undertook in earnest after the war. For a company emerging from the nightmare of bankruptcy, it might have been a daunting prospect, but for a utility, it was essential. The "General System Planning Study" of January 1948, performed by Westinghouse Electric Corporation engineers for PGE, estimated that peak load would increase over the period from 1938 to 1950 by 300 percent.[22] The expectation was that it would continue to grow at a high rate.

While the consultants expected that the company would be supplied with power from BPA and the Northwest Power Pool for the foreseeable future, they were concerned about PGE's own generating capacity. They viewed the company's generation system not as a source of base power supply, but as being a critical value in another role. They wrote:

> The sources of generation within the [PGE] system, will perform the function of regulation and control rather than one of base power supply. These plants will become fully as important in the role of reducing the peak demands of purchased energy, or in

225

Artist's rendering of PGE's North Fork Development. (PGE collection)

The completed North Fork Hydro Project on the Clackamas River, March 1959. Photo by Western Ways, Inc. (PGE collections)

226

*Working on the foundations of the powerhouse.
(PGE collections)*

Construction of the spillway. (PGE collections)

227

This crew is working on a temporary river barrier, which will be pumped to keep out the water so that the dam can be built. A hole is drilled with a pneumatic rock drill, dynamite is placed in the hole, and detonated which crushes the rock. The boxes strewn about the area contained dynamite. (PGE collections)

Construction of the North Fork Dam. The base of the dam is in bedrock. (PGE collections)

Spillway in the foreground appears to be complete while work continues on the dam in the background. (PGE collections)

229

This photo shows the three basic elements needed for generating electricity. At the top are the two stator units, which will serve serve as the magnet. Next to the lower stator, with a ladder leaning against it, is the turbine which serves as the power source. Near the bottom of the picture, waiting to be placed within the stator, is the rotor unit, which serves as the coil. There is an elegant simplicity in these three basic components of electricity, even with all the complexities of construction. (PGE collections)

The valute (or snail) distributes water around the turbine connected to the penstock at the bottom of the dam. Only one of the two generators is in place in this photo. (PGE collections)

231

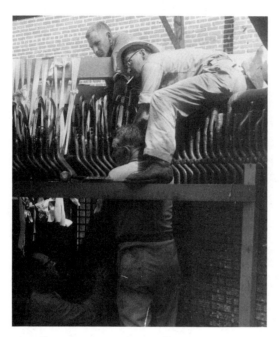

Installing the stator. (PGE collections)

Moving rotor unit no. 1 to begin the process of installation. (PGE collections)

Maneuvering unit no. 1 rotor into place inside the stators. (PGE collections)

Rotor unit no. 1 is lowered inside the stator. The crew is stationed at the rim to make sure it is a good fit and that nothing goes crunch. (PGE collections)

An aerial view of the not yet completed North Fork Dam. Photo by Western Ways, Inc. (PGE collections)

234

Membership in the Clackamas River civil engineers kibitzing society is bestowed on Dave Horner (left), president of Estacada city council, and Jim Anderson, editor and publisher of the Clackamas County News, *by Ralph Millsap, Portland General Electric Company vice president. (PGE collections)*

the control of reactive power flow, as they are at present in supplying base power. The possibility of expanding the PGE hydro or steam generation should not be overlooked in any farsighted program, since such expansion may well be justified when viewed from the standpoint of power control.[23]

This was why in 1948 the company began what would turn out to be an almost decade-long struggle over Pelton Dam. To be located on the Deschutes River in Central Oregon, the dam was projected as a concrete-wall structure about 205 feet high, creating a reservoir with normal pool at an elevation of 1,580 feet, a side channel and funnel spillway, three short penstocks, and an "outdoor-type" powerhouse with three 52,000-HP generators. The turbines were to be connected to three 36,000-kw generators. The dam was planned from the first as a peaking power facility, available for precisely the purposes recommended in the Westinghouse report.

Apart from the search for new sources of power, the company had been led to the decision to build Pelton by a number of seemingly favorable circumstances. The site, near Madras in Jefferson County, was a choice one from the engineering standpoint. Its geological configuration would be easy to capitalize upon for a quick and relatively inexpensive construction period. The project also attracted two other investors. PP&L and Washington Water Power Company joined PGE. They formed the Northwest Power Supply Company, an entity under the direction of a PGE consultant, Gen. Thomas Robins (formerly of the Corps of Engineers), in order to capitalize the undertaking. The three utilities agreed to share Pelton's energy output. In addition, the dam would use the PP&L central Oregon transmission line to send its power out. In short, Pelton promised significant returns on an apparently minimal and risk-free investment.

The project's preliminaries were too easy. Even the advance engineering reports had been prepared years before, so that Northwest Power Supply had only to resubmit them for approval to the Federal Power Commission, rather than prepare them itself. Under Federal Power Commission License No. 57, granted in 1924, a company called Columbia Valley Power had undertaken preliminary work for construction of a dam on the river, with a view to selling the electricity produced in Portland. The Depression and the erection of Bonneville and Grand Coulee dams quickly reduced the project's attractiveness, and Columbia Valley Power dropped it. In 1936, the Federal Power Commission canceled the Columbia Valley Power license. Thus, when Northwest Power Supply filed on the site, the commission granted the license with alacrity. However, this was not the start of a solution to the precarious power situation for the company and the region, but the beginning of a long battle over the utility's right to build the dam at all.

An informal hearing before the Oregon Hydroelectric Commission on the Northwest Power Supply application for a state-granted license to build Pelton resulted in a decision directing the concern to apply to the state's Fish Commission. That body, after ten months of apparent deliberation, denied the permit. If the decision was a shock to the utilities, it should not have been. Antidevelopment forces (including the Fish Commission) had introduced two subsequently defeated bills in Oregon's 1948 legislative session that would have denied exploitation of the Deschutes and Metolius rivers for the purpose of power generation.

Still, the Pelton project had at least two boosters. One continued to be the Federal Power Commission, which was then encouraging hydro production. The other was the National Security Resources Board, a federal agency created to oversee the allocation and use of critical resources in wartime. With the advent of American involvement in the Korean conflict in 1950, this body greatly favored Pelton's construction. Unfortunately, the Oregon Fish Commission, the U.S. Fish and Wildlife Service, and the Oregon Hydroelectric Commission remained among its opponents. In the context of the Northwest's evident power shortage, the case for the dam seemed overwhelming, yet the Fish Commission would not reconsider.

The problem for the commission was that the very traits that made the Pelton site so attractive to the company made it unacceptable to commission biologists. For the company, the site's natural advantages included narrow, solid rock walls rising more than a hundred feet above the riverbanks. These would make rapid economical construction possible. To the scientists, on the other hand, the site's geology precluded the use of fishways or ladders for passing anadromous fish upstream and downstream. Moreover, according to the commission's experts, the fast-flowing Deschutes offered no place below the dam site to hold adult salmon until their spawning time (salmon cannot be held in rapid water).[24]

By 1951, delays by the Fish Commission had caused PP&L and Washington Water Power to drop out of the project. PGE, for its part, pressed on. There followed a six-year controversy over the issue of fish versus power that culminated at the U.S. Supreme Court. Amazingly, the issue had transmogrified from salmon and dams to states' rights versus the powers of the federal government. PGE had been granted a fiscal permit for Pelton by the Federal Power Commission, in defiance of the Oregon Supreme Court which on appeal from PGE had decided in favor of the state agencies. The commission based its decision on the necessity of alleviating the Northwest power shortage, arguing that the government had not surrendered jurisdiction over nonnavigable waters, such as the Deschutes, in the Desert Lands Act of 1877. Nevertheless, the U.S. Ninth Circuit Court of Appeals, in February 1953, ruled on the contrary, that the Desert Land Act gave states power over such streams and rivers running through arid or semiarid federal lands.[25]

At the U.S. Supreme Court, the issue was over whose sovereignty controlled the water on federal lands (the part of the Deschutes on which Pelton was to be built touched public lands on the east bank and the Warm Springs Indian Reservation on the west)—the states' or the federal government's. Oregon's case was joined, *amicus curiae*, by twelve states. The court, with Justice Harold Burton delivering the opinion for the majority, decided in favor of the company on the basis that, since the reservation had given consent to the project, the problem of reserved lands (which were different from public lands) was not germane as the state contended and that the Federal Power Commission thus had authority to grant the license to build the dam.[26]

There were strong dissents. Justice William O. Douglas based his on his fear that tampering with the water rights of western states by the executive branch might eventually cause "vast dislocations in the economies of the western states." Herbert Lundy, an *Oregonian* editorial writer and a knowledgeable commentator on regional power policy, advised Oregon's governor, Elmo Smith, to order his attorney general to "proceed in court to stop construction of the dam

The proposed site of Pelton dam. (PGE collections)

238   *The proposed Pelton Dam site with inklines to show the outline of the dam. (PGE collections)*

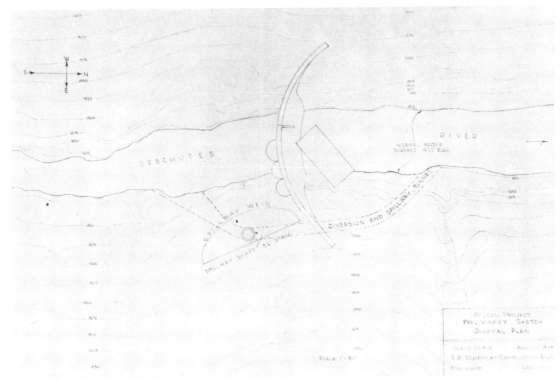

A preliminary sketch of the Pelton project. (PGE collections)

At water level on the Deschutes River. The inklines show the the approximate outline of the dam. (PGE collections)

Charles "Charlie" Jackson, chairman of the Warm Springs Tribal Council signs the agreement for the building of the Pelton and later Round Butte Dam in the company of Ralph Millsap, vice president–public relations for PGE (standing) and J.W. Elliott, superintendent of the Warm Springs Indian Agency. (PGE collections)

TO THE EDITOR:

This is an open letter from the Chinook Indian Nation to the Warm Springs Indians and to all of the citizens of the Northwest.

We, the members of the Chinook Indian nation have never relinquished our aboriginal rights that we have held since time immemorial extending for centuries into antiquity.

It is our opinion that Portland General Electric company of Portland has misled the Warm Springs Indians into accepting an amount for a dam site on their land that is equivalent to about one fortieth of the annual value of the salmon and steelhead runs that spawn in the Deschutes River system and may be destroyed by it.

Many members of the Chinook Indian Nation have made their livelihood from fishing in the Columbia River and its tributaries for centuries and still do and with proper conservation we expect to be able to do so for many years to come.

We have never surrendered our hunting and fishing rights to the U.S. government or to any other person or groups. We have no treaty so we still retain our original fishing grounds, which extend from ocean to Celilo, including the spawning grounds.

The steelhead, salmon and all other natural fish were our living, so we will fight to protect our rights by every legal method that is available to us.

The white man has exploited our fishery and has found it necessary to enact laws of conservation to try and perpetuate the fish runs. It seems to us that all will be in vain if the dams on the Cowlitz River and the Deschutes River are built and that the white man as well as the Indian will suffer.

The Chinook Indian Nation wishes to make it understood that all tribes of Indians living in the Columbia River watershed have a right to partake in its fishery and we believe that the Warm Springs made a sad mistake in selling out to PGE.

We do not condemn them for this as we believe that they have been misled and so we beg of them to reconsider and deny the PGE the right to build a dam on the Deschutes.

J. Grant Elliott,
Chairman Chinook Nation
Skamokawa, Washington

Oregonian, 5 March 1956

240

TO THE EDITOR,

Being a member of the Warm Springs tribes of Indians, I am naturally greatly interested in the development and utilization of the Deschutes River. The Warm Springs tribes recently entered into an agreement with the Portland General Electric company, whereby the tribes grant to the electric company the right to use tribal lands of the reservation in connection with the development of hydroelectric dams at the Pelton and Round Butte dam sites. This contract, which runs for a period of 50 years, guarantees the Warm Springs Indians a substantial income for this period of time. This contract was recently ratified by the eligible voters of the tribes by an overwhelming majority.

I have read in recent issues of the Portland daily newspapers, various editorials and letters written to the papers by various sportsmen organizations, and citizens of Oregon. None of these publications that I have read takes into consideration the rights and interests of the Warm Springs Indians in the Deschutes River. In fact the interests of the Indians in these projects are never even mentioned, and it would appear that the writers of such articles either are ignorant of the existence and terms of the treaty of June 25, 1855, between the Confederated Bands and Tribes of Middle Oregon and the United States, or for reasons known to themselves, find it convenient to ignore its existence. Most of the editorials and articles which I have read dealing with the development of the Deschutes river hydroelectric potential are bitterly opposed to such development, and offer many reasons why no dams should be constructed in this river. They completely ignore the fact that the Warm Springs Indians have a very valid interest in this river, and that its hydroelectric potential is one of their most valuable resources.

One organization known as the "Save the Deschutes committee" seems to be determined to do as the name implies, "save the Deschutes." For whom do they propose to save the Deschutes? It seems to be convenient for all of these writers to mention the interest the Warm Springs Indians have in the Deschutes River, and the average reader, being unaware of the rights which the Indians have in this river, may readily be convinced that no dams should be constructed therein. I wish to quote below a clause taken from article I of the Warm Springs treaty of June 25, 1855:

"Provided also, that the exclusive right of taking fish in the streams running through and bordering said reservation is hereby secured to said Indians."

It is well known to many citizens of Oregon that the Deschutes River borders the Warm Springs reservation from its confluence with the Metolius river for approximately 35 miles, to a point near Nathan. The proposed Pelton and Round Butte dams are to be located within this stretch of river.

The state of Oregon has recognized that it is bound by the Indian treaties of 1855 (see Anthony vs. Veach, 189 Ore 462, 483-485, 220 p. 2d 493, 502-503). The Supreme Court of the United States also has upheld the validity of these treaties (see United States vs. Winans, 198 U.S. 371).

Many people no doubt have the understanding that the Indian reservations were simply given to the Indians by the federal government. What they do not know is that the Indians paid dearly for their reservations.

In the case of the Warm Springs Indians they ceded to the United States a vast empire which they had held and occupied for unknown generations prior to the coming of the white man to the Pacific Northwest. This area includes what is now Hood River county, Wasco county, Jefferson county, Crook county, Deschutes county, Moro county and Sherman county. They received in payment for this great and rich area the sum of $150,000 and reserved for their own use the present Warm Springs reservation, which includes an area of approximately 500,000 acres, which were it not for the stand of timber found on the higher elevations, would not support 10 percent of the population.

It will be noted that this reservation was not granted to the Warm Springs Indians by the federal government under the terms of the treaty of 1855, but that it was already theirs, and they simply reserved it for their future use.

The same thing is true of their exclusive right to take fish in the streams running through and bordering the reservation. This right was theirs at the time the treaty was signed, and the Indians reserved this right for their future use. The highest courts in our land have upheld the terms of these treaties time after time.

Linton Winishut, Warm Springs
Oregonian, 5 March 1956

242

Famed anthropologist Luther Cressman focuses camera to take a photo of petroglyphs. He was part of a scientific salvage survey team hired by PGE to look at the Pelton site. (PGE collections)

243

This certificate was created in commemoration of the torrential downpour at the dedication of the Pelton Dam. (PGE collections)

The completed Pelton Dam and powerhouse. (PGE collections)

and to force PGE to comply with state water laws." The force of Lundy's strongly worded views on the dam was somewhat vitiated by his reputation as an ardent fly fisherman. This opposition notwithstanding, the construction of Pelton at last went forward, with ground-breaking ceremonies on 1 May 1956.

The completed dam was dedicated on 22 May 1958 and began immediate service. Its importance to PGE and to the regional power grid was clear, but the controversy its construction had engendered would not disappear. Pelton was a harbinger of disputes to come, for even though the need for its energy was undeniable (at least in the logic of economic development), there were those who viewed other imperatives as equally important. For them, preservation of the environment and of wildlife for aesthetic and recreational reasons was as compelling as economic considerations. The demands of groups such as sport fishermen (who had joined forces with the Fish Commission in the Pelton case) for an accounting of the impact of such projects on nature and humans would only increase, and their ranks would swell as Americans of the postwar era enjoyed more and more leisure in an industrial age. Habituated to the myth of America as nature's nation, they wished to spend their free time at one with an unspoiled land. The fight over Pelton was both a herald of a solution to the power shortage and the opening shot in the hit-and-run battle that PGE was to wage with conservationists and elements of the environmental movement over coveted parts of the state's natural heritage.

The travails associated with Pelton never cooled the company's ardor for power from central Oregon's rivers or from any other cost-effective source of hydropower in the Pacific Northwest. On 1 May 1952, the Federal Power Commission granted PGE a preliminary license for a proposed concrete gravity dam called Round Butte, to be situated about nine miles from Pelton on the Deschutes, Crooked, and Metolius rivers.[27] Construction of the $72 million, 300,000-kw dam did not begin until 1961.

Development on the Clackamas and Deschutes rivers, arduous though it sometimes was, could not touch the problems encountered in hydro development on the Columbia in the fifties. This may seem strange, as for the first time in twenty years, PGE and other private utilities had an administration in Washington that could be expected to sympathize with their aims. To a great extent, it did. However, even in light of the chronic power shortage of the early postwar era, that was not enough.

REDEFINING PARTNERSHIP

As president of the United States, Dwight D. Eisenhower could only be described as being above the battle. A man who had made his reputation in the execution of the invasion of Normandy, in his presidential capacity he operated from the high plain beyond the killing ground where the partisans of the Congress and the various interest groups that sought to influence legislation closed in deadly embrace. His detachment was a useful political device but also a habit of mind. As a career soldier, the president had exhibited few discernible political impulses before his election. His political profile was so low that he had been approached by both the Democrats and the Republicans about running for office. His subsequent allegiance to the Republican party became genuine, but his administration proved profoundly unambitious ideologically. Following the 1952 election, when he first assumed office, he set a course annoying to the conservative wing of the Republican party in that he did not draft the agenda for which they had hoped—the dismantling of Roosevelt's New Deal and Harry Truman's Fair Deal. He set himself the pragmatic task of simply governing the country fairly and efficiently according to his lights, modifying only what he and his advisers regarded as the excesses of twenty years of Democratic hegemony in domestic affairs and leaving unmolested his predecessors' worthwhile initiatives.

Nowhere in the domestic sphere was Eisenhower's approach more evident than in federal power policy. In the immediate postwar years, it had become apparent that hydroelectric development would be crucial to maintaining the nation's growing prosperity. The president felt that the New Deal had made important strides in power generation, and he did not want to tamper with the federal role as it existed. At the same time, he wished not to antagonize the private utilities, their investors, or their political sponsors. He wanted to encourage them, as he saw a larger role for private power in nurturance of the postwar expansion. In his memoir, *Mandate for Change: The White House Years, 1953-1956*, he wrote:

> The administration's power policy had one main purpose; to get every one of . . . [the nation's 480 private power companies, 55 federal organizations, and approximately 2,000 public power agencies] pulling harness to keep up with the expanding electrical needs of the American people, and doing it in such fashion . . . as to achieve the maximum efficiency and economy, fullest local control, and fairness to consumers. The administration sided with neither private power nor with politicians who, in their zeal for pet projects, seemed to prefer federal kilowatts in the mind to nonfederal kilowatts on the line.
>
> We confronted power, developed where needed, and by methods and by agencies found most appropriate in the special circumstances of each area. We knew that the country's need for power was growing at a gargantuan rate—a rate which the federal government would not, and indeed should not, try to satisfy by itself.[28]

In his first State of the Union speech, delivered in February 1953, Eisenhower alluded to an idea that had been developed during his campaign of the previous fall to address the energy shortfall. It would become the basis for his power policy. He called for a natural-resources program for the country based on "a partnership of the state and local communities, private citizens, and federal government; all working together."[29]

Over the eight years of Eisenhower's administration, the fortunes of "partnership" followed an erratic course. As the term implied, the key to the concept in power policy was to put together financial coalitions of private and public developers in order to avoid saddling taxpayers with total responsibility for hydroelectric development and to give private utilities access to, if not control over, the nation's hydro resources.

Almost immediately the concept came under a cloud, when the administration tried to arrange for Middle South Utilities and the Southern Company to supply the city of Memphis,

Tennessee, with electricity from a new thermal plant. The plan the administration negotiated (named Dixon-Yates, after the heads of the two utilities) seemed to some to be an attack on the sacrosanct TVA (the agency that normally would have been given the job) and a "sellout" or "giveaway" of federal resources. The incident caused congressional advocates of public power to regard administration resources policy with a skepticism that questioned every detail. Under the circumstances, partnership was, at its core, suspect to them.

To manage this apparently stillborn policy, Eisenhower chose Douglas McKay, who resigned as governor of Oregon to become the nation's thirty-ninth secretary of the Interior. As governor, McKay, a moderate Republican, had been mildly friendly to private utilities, but as the president's spokesman, he tried to follow a more evenhanded course, promising to be as "tough" with the privates as with the PUDs.[30] Nevertheless, he chose as his undersecretary Ralph Tudor, an active advocate of private power and an energetic opponent of the New Deal. Tudor had learned his conservatism in the upper echelons of the Corps of Engineers where he had long served. Exacerbating the difficulties in executing the partnership principle during McKay's largely unsuccessful tenure in the department, where he served from 1953 to 1956, were the two men's temperaments. McKay was well meaning, but not always effective, while Tudor's stubborn ideology and agenda infused bias into the department's otherwise ostensibly neutral policy.

By all reasonable standards, the results of the 1952 election should have been met with glee by the private utilities. The end of Democratic dominance and the start of Republican ascendancy was certainly received in the PGE boardroom with great optimism. The brief message on the inside cover of the company's 1952 *Annual Report* indicated the relief PGE policy makers felt at the passing of dominant New Deal values from natural resources. "After 20 years, the people expressed their desire to reverse the trend toward an all-powerful centralized government," the 1952 report said. "We will anticipate history's verdict to the extent of expressing our belief that the change was for the good, for a return to constitutional government by law rather than government by men."[31]

Sedate hosannas for the restoration of free enterprise aside, PGE had long since achieved a separate peace with the Democratic regimes of Roosevelt and Truman. Griffith's tone toward BPA had been notably conciliatory. As president, Polhemus had taken a harder line against BPA policy, from time to time, but the company's approach since the inception of the agency remained one of live-and-let-live and of enjoying the inexpensive fruits of federal power generation.[32] The company's constant refrain through the forties remained the same in the first years of the fifties: that it was the region's largest distributor of federal power.

The Eisenhower administration's power policy was pleasing to Delzell. Indeed, in some ways, PGE had anticipated it. As the power-supply problem had become acute immediately after the war, the PGE leadership had stepped up its emphasis on cooperation with federal agencies. The 1948 *Annual Report* had said:

> PGE will continue to give leadership and assistance to . . . better understanding of the overall Northwest power supply problem, to the end that full cooperation and respect will become a reality among the federal, municipal, and private power company systems.[33]

In 1950, anticipating by a full two years the spirit, and to some extent the letter of the Eisenhower administration's policy, Delzell, in testimony before the president's Water Resources Policy Commission, adumbrated the features of what would become the "partnership" principle in Northwest hydroelectric development policy. Seeking to "bury the dead cat of alleged opposition within the power industry of the Pacific Northwest against appropriate Federal participation in the development of the region's water resources," he called for a point-by-point program of government/private enterprise "joint development of resources."[34] Specifically, he said that federal power projects should be only those designated "multipurpose"; that is, power should be developed by the government only in connection with improvement of navigation, control of floods, and reclamation of arid lands. All other projects should be left to states, municipalities, and private entities, which should have the prior right to develop as many of the multipurpose sites as feasible. He also said the government's role in marketing power from multipurpose projects should be severely restricted. Only those industries unable to buy power in sufficient quantities from any other source should be the customers of the federal dams. He also testified against the priority and preference clause in the federal statute governing BPA's allocation of its power. He argued, particularly, that the priority clause, which gave public bodies first access to BPA energy, created two classes of consumers among Pacific Northwest taxpayers. Those who were hooked up to public energy lines were getting superior treatment compared with the customers of private companies, even though both had subsidized the construction of BPA lines.[35]

Delzell and his colleagues at the region's other private utilities knew that their concerns were precariously balanced at a point where the views and impulses of the secretary of the Interior, the BPA administrator, Congress, and the electricity-consuming public in the Northwest converged with nature itself. Nothing better illustrates this than the power shortage of fall 1952 and winter 1953, when nature and human institutions conspired to jeopardize PGE's standing with its customers and the general public. At the same time, the episode shows the extent to which population growth, chronically low streamflows, and the retarded schedule of Northwest hydro development forced the issue of partnership as the only apparent alternative for the company in the face of accelerating demand.

In September 1952, drought conditions, which had become evident in late August, created a critical power shortage as the decreased water levels in the Columbia and other regional streams lessened water pressure on the turbines and generators at Pacific Northwest dams. The BPA therefore reduced its deliveries of nonfirm power and some seasonal energy from Bonneville and Grand Coulee to its private utilities and its large industrial customers. With no long-term contract for firm power, PGE, like other private utilities, had no choice but to fire up its steam-generating plants, as the BPA cut it off in order to honor its commitments to its priority customers.

Uniformly old and inefficient by that time, PGE's thermal plants burned expensive fuels. They were so costly to operate that the Oregon public utilities commissioner, Charles Heltzel, and his Washington counterpart allowed the utility companies to add a surcharge to their customers' monthly electric bills. Heltzel made his decision without a public hearing, an oversight that was to prove costly in the currency of public regard for both him and the private utilities. The surcharge was based on the difference between projected costs of hydro generation and those expected to accrue as the result of employing the more expensive thermal method. PP&L was granted an 11 percent surcharge based on each customer's monthly billing in order to recover $1.6 million of extra expense it estimated would be incurred over the year. PGE, which needed to recover more than $3 million, was allowed to add 20 percent to its billings.

The extent of the crisis is indicated, to some degree, by the fact that in the midst of the Korean conflict, the Federal Defense Electric Power Administration ordered the region's aluminum plants (gluttonous consumers of electrical energy) to cut back production by 10 percent.[36] A perceptible rise in regional unemployment resulted, but the government's position was that the energy cutback was necessary. The private utilities, recognizing a public-relations opportunity when they saw it, claimed that, without thermal generation, loss of production and employment would have been six times the published figures.[37]

Electricity consumers in the Northwest were not impressed. Although they tended to blame the crisis on the Congress' substantial slowdown of hydro development, citizens' perceptions of public and private utilities, as well as of BPA, were not favorable. Customers on PGE, PP&L, and other private lines, felt particularly aggrieved inasmuch as they were the only ones on whom the surcharge actually fell, even though PUDs with their own steam plants were operating during the emergency. (The PUDs came under the BPA priority clause, which gave them continued access to enough Bonneville power to minimize thermal generation.) The *Oregonian*, speaking for Portland residents, said: "The purpose of the priority clause was to encourage the early, struggling PUDs. It was not intended that it should discriminate between individual consumers."[38]

As 1953 began, the surcharge became the occasion of another heated exchange on the relative merits of public and private power and the state of ethics on both sides of the industry. Gus Norwood, executive secretary of the Northwest Public Power Association, a lobby for the PUDs, asserted that the shareholders of the private utilities should absorb the surcharge. He claimed the privates were making excessive profits—up to 8.57 percent for PGE as a rate of return on average net electrical plant investment from 1937 to 1949. Utilities like PGE, PP&L, and Mountain States, according to Norwood, had saved millions of dollars by purchasing a combination of dump and firm power from BPA at an average rate of 2.32 mills. PUDs, on the other hand, had to pay 2.8 mills for firm power and the insurance against shortage that it represented.[39]

Responding for PGE, Thomas Delzell said flatly, "We don't make a penny on Bonneville power," and claimed that the utility sent it out to consumers "at cost and all savings resulting from its purchase in past years have been passed directly to the customers." He said that Norwood's figures were "interesting but inaccurate." He also endorsed the statement of a PP&L spokesperson to the effect that the only reason private utilities brought dump power at the lower rates was that, until the five-year contracts of 1952, BPA had refused firm-power contracts on terms with which the companies could live.

Naturally, Delzell was unhappy with the adverse publicity. He lashed out at BPA as the real culprit, charging that the agency had oversold the Northwest's firm hydroelectric energy "chiefly to one type of industry [aluminum] and without regard to the prior needs of the general consuming public."[40] This view was commonly held throughout the power industry, in both the public and private camps.

249

Despite the best efforts of Delzell and his fellow utility executives, the image of the private utilities suffered. Their delicate position was vividly illustrated by the fact that the surcharge became a preferred medium of attack by public-power advocates. In February 1953, Monroe Sweetland, a staunch New Dealer and Oregon Democratic state senator from Milwaukie, initiated with others a suit to end the surcharge. The case dragged through the judicial system long after 27 May 1953, the date on which the surcharge was ordered dropped by Heltzel. In 1956, the Oregon Supreme Court found that the surcharge had been lawful.[41]

In retrospect, the surcharge episode underscores the ramifications of congressional impairment of development of the region's comprehensive electric power system and PGE's position in it during the fifties. It also underscores the uncertain nature of the Northwest's hydropower supply; the importance of that power to the region's economy; the extent to which the company, as well as Northwest society, had become wedded financially, economically, and politically to cheap hydropower; and the way in which PGE's reputation was balanced in public perception between rapacity and corporate good citizenship. Furthermore, the incident shows how the relationship established between PGE and BPA in the forties had repercussions long afterward and points to the way in which it would soon force uneasy, but long-term, joint dominion on these two antagonists.

As the period of the extra charge drew to a close, Delzell said in the PGE *Annual Report* of 1952 (not published until May 1953) that it had "enabled the company to maintain user normal earnings in 1952, and protected its credit and ability to render adequate electric service to the public." Acknowledging the "public relations scars" PGE had sustained over the period of the surcharge, he concluded, "There is hope that out of this situation will come cures for this sort of inequity in the form of fair and nondiscriminatory federal rates."[42]

Earlier, Lundy had recognized the problem inherent in the surcharge issue. Writing editorially, he laid the blame for the creation (triggered by the priority clause of the inequitable two-tier rate system) squarely at the door of Congress.[62] The politicians, he charged, had slowed the pace of hydroelectric development in the Columbia basin and now the customers of private utilities would have a "brown taste" in their mouths "long after the 'brownout' is forgotten."[43]

His assignment of blame for the surcharge notwithstanding, with Pelton stalled by chronic litigation and regional economic development pressuring deadlocked congressional factions on federal water policy, PGE's situation looked increasingly grim. The BPA continued to pursue its marketing strategy of attracting the most voracious industrial users of hydropower—aluminum plants. Even the utilities' old ally, Douglas McKay, had evidently deserted on the issue. In February 1953, the secretary signed a twenty-year contract with Harvey Machine Company of Torrance, California, for 40,000 kw of BPA firm power and 80,000 kw of interruptible energy for a smelter on the middle Columbia near The Dalles, Oregon. The BPA allotment for Harvey had been approved by the Defense Production Administration as critical to national security.

PGE, combined with PP&L, lobbied against the contract privately with McKay and in Congress. They wanted to halt the project and to acquire the Harvey energy allocation for themselves. The companies, through Marshall Dana, editor of the *Oregon Journal*, who was a personal friend of McKay's, argued to the Interior secretary that the federal government had denied other types of industry and domestic consumers their fair share of federal hydropower while lavishing it on heavy industrial consumers such as aluminum. Dana argued that the level of employment in a typical aluminum plant (six hundred to one thousand persons in each of the five facilities in Oregon and Washington in 1954) did not justify the largesse. He was unsuccessful in stopping the construction of the Harvey facility, although his militance on the utilities' behalf did result in the congressional Appropriations Committee slashing funds to BPA that would have permitted federal subsidy of the transmission lines from Bonneville to the aluminum plant. Harvey eventually built its own lines and received power directly from The Dalles Dam at a specially reduced bus-bar rate.[44]

Still, a frustrating incident like the Harvey contract was only a sidelight to the really significant possibilities inherent in PGE's situation. If the Northwest's population continued to grow exponentially, if the economy kept expanding, if congressional factions continued to deadlock over dam building on the Columbia, if there came another drought, and if the priority and preference clauses remained on the books, customers and the general public might turn on the utility. Takeovers by a PUD or the creation of a regional power authority might eventuate.

Opportunity and circumstance came together in 1953 fortuitously to allow the company to mitigate its predicament, as well as that of the region's other private utilities. The surcharge episode had hurt the image of BPA as much as the power companies', and under the influence of Ralph Tudor, whose antipathy toward Paul Raver was palpable, BPA policy came under sharp scrutiny at Interior. Despite enjoying McKay's support, Raver was under considerable pressure to show some sympathy toward the private utilities.[45] Over the winter of 1953, he was engaged in negotiations with Polhemus over renewal of PGE's power contract. Polhemus also felt pressured, inasmuch as editorialists had recently harped on PGE's rejection of long-term contract terms from BPA in 1942 and 1946 as the cause of the extra burden its customers were bearing, the unfairness of the priority clause notwithstanding. There were compelling reasons to renew the quest for a long-term firm-power contract. Polhemus broached the idea with the administrator as a way to eliminate a recurrence of the surcharge.[46] In return Raver, anxious to demonstrate to the Republican administration a conciliatory attitude toward private power, drew up a document calling for twenty-year contracts for all Northwest power companies. Formal negotiations began on the agreement on 27 May 1953.

Raver had embarked on a delicate course: he had to appease the public-power groups, his basic constituency at BPA, while at the same time accommodating the private companies. This was not easy, since elements on both sides were unhappy with the agreement for their own reasons. In particular, Paul McKee, president of PP&L, who disliked Raver and the whole idea of BPA, was allegedly contemplating the disruption of the negotiations in order to discredit the administrator with his superiors at Interior and force him out.[47] From Tudor and conservative Republicans in Congress, Raver was indeed under fire, but McKay, who had been apprised of the situation by a well-placed outside observer, refused to accede to his dismissal.[48] Instead, he encouraged the administrator to conclude the negotiations.

Polhemus and Raver eventually hammered out a contract providing for 1.5 million kw of firm energy predicated on a revised priority schedule. Current industrial customers with previous long-term contracts would still have priority over the power companies. On the other hand, the requirements of the new signatories would come before those resulting from the expansion of industrial customers or new loads. The preference list would read as follows: public-power systems, established industrial plants, power companies, and new or expanded industrial users. No power would be available for industrial expansion until the allocation of energy to the power companies equaled that of existing industries. Public and private utilities were barred from increasing their loads by more than 10,000 kw unless they could generate the excess kilowatts themselves. This was an important concession by BPA, since at the time most PUDs and rural electrification areas were wholly dependent on the agency for their power. It amounted to effectively barring short-term territorial competition with the private firms by the public agencies.

In light of the tensions involved, the contract was probably the best that could be achieved. It was submitted to the PUDs and large industrial users for inspection. They gave their approval and McKay gave the draft the administration's imprimatur. Nevertheless, after its signing on 18 September 1953 by PGE, PP&L, and Mountain States Power, there was criticism from executives of the aluminum industry, who complained of favoritism toward the utilities. Lundy, alluding to the dearth of new generating facilities, pointed out in the *Oregonian* that the contract, in effect, divided up among three heavy users "a reservoir of power which Bonneville doesn't have now, and has no assurance of getting." Calling it "a sort of Alice in Wonderland contract," he noted that the dams coming into production would be able to deliver only half the energy called for in the contract (1.5 million kw) in the scheduled peak year of 1960. Still, he said, the agreement illustrated the possibility of cooperation between the utilities and the agency.[49]

In fact, the long-term contract was a remarkable feat for its two authors. Both were at the end of their service to their respective organizations. Raver, no doubt reading the handwriting on the wall at the agency, soon moved on, to become head of Seattle City Light, while Polhemus, whose serious-minded and objective negotiating posture had catalyzed the success, would shortly retire from PGE, to be replaced by Frank Warren, then executive vice president at the utility. If their pact did not add new generation to the region's resources, as the 1953 *Annual Report* acknowledged, it gave impetus to other cooperative initiatives and provided private utilities the luxury of a clear basis for solid, long-range planning.[50] This could only be regarded as beneficial to the whole region. Moreover, the contract would "give impetus," as the report put it, "to the 'partnership' concept of hydroelectric development."[51]

This reference was not simply annual-report boilerplate. On the contrary, the company was poised to commit wholeheartedly to partnership. The policy was in substance the gospel that Delzell had been preaching since the opening of the decade. As the linchpin of the administration's power policy, it was only natural that PGE should embrace it wholeheartedly. More than that, partnership seemed to be a key to the company's timely access to a large block of federal power to be generated on the mid-Columbia. This outcome might well occur through the partnership of government and private interests in constructing a federal dam that might otherwise be stalled by the vagaries of regional and national politics. In the wake of the surcharge incident, and because of the "dry" long-term contract (what good was a twenty-year right to nonexistent power?), partnership was, at worst, a worthwhile roll of the dice in the efforts to secure a source of abundant, cheap, and reliable power. For this reason, the company not only embraced, but eagerly led the quest for a federal-private hydropower partnership.

252

PGE's venture into the thicket of partnership was initiated in a series of memoranda and talking papers prepared over the first two months of 1954 and presented to the board of directors by Polhemus and Art Porter, manager of power operations. Polhemus's views had been refined in conversations with Undersecretary Tudor, the administration's most ardent proponent of partnership, and U.S. Sen. Guy Cordon, an Oregon Republican who was chairman of the Senate Interior Subcommittee and of the Senate Appropriations Committee also sympathetic to the Eisenhower power policy.[52] While this advisory combination of Tudor and Cordon encouraged PGE on partnership, Norwood has pointed out in his history of the BPA that their political alliance essentially doomed the policy in the region.

Tudor hoped to strengthen the razor-thin Republican majority in Congress in the 1954 off year elections. His published diary makes constant reference to his intention to advance legislation that would redound to the benefit of Republican candidates where power policy was concerned.[53] But his zeal and political acumen were compromised by his blind hatred of BPA, which he hoped to emasculate. "I do not believe in the nationalization of power," he wrote emphatically of what he saw as the agency's self-assigned task. The congressionally mandated BPA construction allocation for 1951-52, a record $134.5 million, had catalyzed a 90 percent increase in employment at the agency from 1948 to 1952 (from 1,716 to 3,360).[54] Tudor saw such growth as the leading edge of hydroelectric socialism. In July 1954, he therefore directed the agency to fire 600 employees and confine its activities to marketing power. The result made unpleasant banner newspaper headlines in midsummer that seemed to indict Cordon, who was then preparing his reelection campaign for November. The victory went to Cordon's opponent, Richard L. Neuberger, a longtime supporter of the BPA and the Democrat who tipped the Senate balance against the Eisenhower administration. At the opening gavel of the eighty-fourth Congress, 48 Democrats and 47 Republicans were seated. In the House, the Democrats held a majority of 232 to 203. Although the administration pursued partnership in the ensuing years, the 1954 shift essentially lamed the policy.

On the basis of his conversations with Cordon and Tudor, Polhemus wrote, "the John Day hydroelectric project should be the next . . . started on the main stem of the Columbia River." In a fourteen-point argument, he asserted that "PGE should take the lead in . . . enactment of the necessary legislation, as it means more to PGE than anyone else . . . [as] PGE needs the largest block of power from this project."[55] He further proposed that PP&L and Mountain States be invited to pursue partnership actively with PGE and the federal government to build the project. He reasoned that John Day (about thirty-five miles east of The Dalles, authorized under the River and Harbor and Flood Control Act of 1950), along with five other projects on the Columbia, including Priest Rapids, would be the best place to start, because it was:

1. Closest large hydro plant to centers of power deficiency in Oregon.
2. It is a large block of cheap power [John Day became the second largest hydroelectric facility on the Columbia] also close to other load centers, that should minimize transmission costs.
3. There is a ready market for this power as soon as the plant is built.

253

4. Simplest plant to be coordinated and operated with the present government and private systems.

5. It is Oregon's best chance to get a large block of cheap power before all the cheap power is gone.

7. It is a splendid work project and probably is needed right now. It has been pretty well engineered and it can be started with a minimum of delay.[56]

Polhemus said the plant should be built and run by the federal government, because it would mean cheaper power for obvious reasons: lower taxes and interest rates and longer term payouts than private investors could secure. Because of the improvement in Columbia navigation it would bring, it would be a multipurpose project, especially welcome for the positive effect it would have on the regional economy and particularly the Portland area. In that respect, although he did not say so, it would meet the administration's criteria for its own participation in hydro-electric development and be a showcase of the partnership principle.

Polhemus' argument also included the warning:

8. If we or someone else do not get legislation in the hopper soon to get it started under some program, the Washington public power interest will beat us to it, by starting Priest Rapids project, which will mean a work project for the State of Washington and an assured supply of cheap power for that state, leaving Oregon out in the cold. Also, it is possible that the public power bodies in Washington might switch their interests to the John Day project, which not only is a better power project than Priest Rapids but also has less complications. Its disadvantages to them is that it is further from their load centers, and the facts of life are that it costs money to transport large blocks of power a great distance.[57]

Calling for a coalition of Oregon's public and private utilities, which would lobby vigorously for John Day, he cautioned that, as it seemed unlikely that the government would start simultaneous construction of two Columbia River projects, John Day and Priest Rapids were therefore competitive. PGE should "act promptly and decisively in this matter," he said, lest "its most advantageous source of cheap power . . . be taken away from it and the project lost to Oregon." As the superior project, John Day would, he asserted, benefit "not only Oregon, but the whole Northwest integrated power system."

If Polhemus's fervor for a John Day partnership was patent, his sense of the realities had not been distorted. Recognizing the task of salesmanship and financial acumen facing PGE, he estimated that the private partners should raise about $200 million to cover their $164 million contribution to the $325 million project. But, he wrote, "If such a sound, self-liquidating project cannot be financed in this partial manner in a partnership agreement with the federal government, then the Department of Interior's new power policy will not work."[58]

This pronouncement could almost serve as the epitaph for partnership in Pacific Northwest power. Initially, PGE's attempts to attract investors and political enthusiasm among Oregon power constituencies were fruitful. The project seemed to augur a major test of the administration's policy and to promise secure and abundant loads for everyone for the long term. The attorney for the Oregon State Grange met in May 1954 with Cordon, McKay, and PGE officials to confirm that partnership would work at John Day. The Grange, PGE's old foe, led several consumer-owned systems anxious to support the project because of its promise of future cheap power.[59] The *Oregon Grange Bulletin* had already editorialized about John Day that:

> This proposal differs from any that we had heard of in the past in that it comes close to the historic position of the Grange on this question. It appears to have more breadth and opportunity for the public power groups than any of the other proposals, providing as it does for the inclusion of the REAs, PUDs, and municipally owned plants as full partners.[60]

But disintegration of the coalition that was forming began with the introduction of identical John Day bills (SB 3135 and HR 93707, respectively) by Cordon in the Senate and Representative Sam Coon of eastern Oregon in the House. The bills were based on the PGE proposal. The dam would be built, owned, and run by the government. Part of its output would go to the investors, and the rest would be available on a preference basis to public systems through BPA. The private systems would be guaranteed John Day energy for fifty years by virtue of their investment, which amounted to prepayment for their power.[61]

In drafting the bills, Cordon had added something. A measure for a Priest Rapids and Wanapum partnership was then making its way through Congress. The project featured a partnership between Washington State public utilities and the U.S. Government. Representative Homer Angell of Portland, concerned that the Washington utilities would selfishly hoard the dams' power, elicited from Washington senators and representatives support for an amendment that guaranteed Oregon an allotment of the power. Cordon included a similar feature in the John Day bills, observing that Washington State already took 70 percent of the power produced on the Columbia, while Oregon got less than 30 percent.[62]

This brought a reaction from the Washington congressional delegation, particularly Sen. Warren Magnuson, and from the Oregon cooperatives and public-power systems that had initially favored the proposal. By June 1954, the public systems had begun to take the view that an allocation system favoring Oregon would actually work against them. They thought that the state's private utilities, with the larger (and growing) demand for energy, would control an ever-expanding percentage of the allocation, whereas the public systems—mostly in rural areas of stable population and energy needs—would in effect be partially subsidizing the private utilities' control of the state's natural resources.[63] This was a position similar to that of Oregon's other senator, the maverick Wayne Morse, who opposed the partnership principle in all instances as a thinly disguised attempt at monopoly.[64] The public systems also had second thoughts about the financial burden that private financing of their obligations would entail. It seemed to them that its high cost, compared with the low-interest federal loans and bonding they were used to, would force them to impose higher power rates, which in turn would strip them of their main advantage over their private competitors.[65] Cordon's defeat in November was the final blow. Not only was

255

his immense influence lost, but Neuberger, the bill's strong critic, was seated in his stead.

With these formidable opponents arrayed against them, the John Day partnership bills sailed into heavy weather and sank. A modified version of the bills was presented by Coon at the next session. Hammered out by the members of Congress and private-utility executives, it called for the companies to underwrite the total cost of the power component of the project, some $273 million. The government would pay for the features of the dam, including navigation locks, flood control, and so forth.[66] Again, the well-practiced opponents of partnership lobbied against the bill with the result that by 1956 it was dead.

Coon and other Northwest Republicans were swept out of office in the 1956 elections, dramatically weakening support for partnership in the Northwest. The policy of the region's Democrats was that the Columbia dams should be totally federal. When a proposal by Klickitat County PUD for financing along the lines of the Priest Rapids bill was met with interest by the administration, Democrats hardened their line, even though the choice seemed to be between some kind of joint financing or no project and possible energy shortages. (Indeed, no new projects had been recommended by Eisenhower in his first term.)

For its part, PGE remained committed to partnership. The company saw the principle throughout the decade as the key to regional power development and its own growth.[67] Its support of the policy bore bitter fruit. While the company, under Delzell, wanted nothing so much as cooperation and coordination among all elements of the power community as the best setting in which development could occur, public-utility representatives saw PGE's enthusiasm as damaging to federal development. In testimony before the House Subcommittee on Public Works, Delzell had gone so far as to endorse the Klickitat County proposal as the only way to fill the critical needs of the region in the absence of either private investment or full federal funding.[68] Norwood, of the Northwest Public Power Administration, charged that Delzell was, by such views, proving to be an enemy of public power.[69]

The truth was that PGE's chairman was desperate to bring large blocks of cheap hydropower on line in order to build the PGE load. When private partnership failed, he was prepared to take any productive tack. None of the major policy makers at PGE—Delzell, Polhemus, and Warren— were as ideologically rigid as the leading advocates of public power, or other private-utility executives, like McKee. Their position had remained consistent since the advent of BPA. They steadfastly hewed to a course of accommodation with the agency and with other regional cooperative power bodies, such as the Northwest Power Pool, on the theory that PGE loads could be more effectively built—especially in the face of the severe power shortages and population growth of the immediate postwar era—on the basis of regionwide public and private cooperative initiative.

This is not to say that PGE policy makers were not firmly in favor of private rather than government development of power sites. They most decidedly were, as sentiments cited earlier show. There was a strong sense in the upper reaches of the company of the fragility of PGE's fiscal position, given its fairly recent tumultuous financial history. This was complemented by an equally strong perception that PGE was chronically poised on the brink of public censure, despite the generally successful campaign against takeover and condemnation by public bodies the company had waged since at least the twenties, and despite the rigorous procedures involved in

A party on Christmas Eve 1950 is a chance to show just a few of the many talents of the men and women of the Hawthorne Building. Despite the company's difficulties in the fifties, PGE's employees still managed to make some music. (PGE collections)

The evening's entertainment after a company bowling dinner in 1951. (PGE collections)

The daily work of line repair continued. This photo shows the sprightly PGE logo on the car and it also poses the question, "How does the ladder stay up?" (PGE collections)

PGE'S 1940 ANNUAL REPORT announced the results of ten elections held that year calling for the establishment of PUDs or municipal electric systems. The proposals were defeated in all but two cases—in Woodburn and in a section of rural Columbia County. Of the total vote in all ten elections, the majority opposed the initiatives by 1.7 to 1.

No proposals were submitted to voters in 1941. In 1942, electorates in Columbia and Washington counties defeated public-power measures. During World War II, the promotion of public power was "largely submerged," but emerged again in 1946 when a Marion County proposal was defeated by a ratio of 3 to 2.

Between 1946 and 1959, thirty-one elections on public-power issues were held in Oregon statewide. Moves in favor of public power were defeated in twenty-nine of the attempts.

Charles Simpson, a Tualatin Valley Division employee of PGE, fiddles with his new television set in 1952. (PGE collections)

In 1951, a move into the future with the installation of IBM billing machines. (PGE collections)

258

making a reality of either option. The strong reaction of consumers to the surcharge seemed a confirmation of this attitude. It was better that the company portray itself much like the PUDs themselves, as being largely at one with the common goal of regional development and consumer service. This view, constantly reinforced in company publications such as the *Bullseye*, which was published intermittently in the fifties, and in annual reports of the decade, was not a pose but a tool of survival and, going back to Griffith, the company's actual perception of its role in the local and regional economies.

PGE's ambitions were remarkably circumscribed. By 1958 PP&L had swallowed up Mountain States Power, had always dealt aggressively with BPA, and government entities generally, and saw itself as an avatar of expansive free enterprise (perhaps because of its long-standing heritage of association with an aggressive non-Northwest holding company, Electric Bond and Share). By contrast, PGE was an unusually benign presence in the regional power community. It energetically defended its service area whenever threatened, but studiously refrained from encroaching on that of others. It thought of itself as being what its name implied—*Portland* General Electric.

A good illustration of PGE's apparent passivity is the case of the North Clackamas County Electric Cooperative, or the Sandy Co-op, as it was popularly known. The co-op was an organization financed by the REA that served nearly a thousand members in a lightly inhabited area east of the town of Sandy along the Mt. Hood Highway.[70] From its birth, the co-op had struggled to survive. It suffered inefficient and erratic management and, because of its low enrollment, uneconomical service. Rates for Sandy Co-op's electrical service were double that of PGE, which had lines running parallel and adjacent to the co-op's. The membership grew restless. A majority of the members directed their board to explore a buy-out by a larger, better equipped utility. The candidates were PP&L, PGE, and Consumers' Power of Corvallis and West Oregon Electric Cooperative of Vernonia, both of which were also financed by the REA.

Because the consumption of electricity by the Sandy membership was low, the area sparsely settled, and its terrain difficult, not to mention its debt to the REA of $1 million, the co-op was not an attractive opportunity.[71] The field of potential buyers therefore quickly narrowed to Consumers' Power and PGE. Although PGE's investigations revealed that the Sandy area's population was growing and that incentive rates could raise electricity usage substantially, the utility was a reluctant suitor.[72] It had long ignored the area as not worth exploiting. Little had changed since the early days of its electrification, except that by early 1956 the superintendent of PGE's Yamhill District was reporting that more than a quarter of the Sandy membership had petitioned for PGE to buy the co-op.[73]

The *Oregon Grange Bulletin*, wringing its hands in print over the blow to the public-power movement that a sale to PGE would represent, implored the Sandy membership not to abandon the co-op.[74] The Corvallis cooperative made an offer of $1,007,300, full membership for customers, and postage-stamp rates. The Sandy Co-op board of directors urged acceptance, but the membership turned their backs on the pleas. They voted instead for PGE's tender of $1,010,000, postage-stamp rates, full integration into the PGE system, both administratively and technically, and employment for all the Sandy staff.[75] The vote was 571 to 99.[76]

Perhaps PGE's languid pursuit of Sandy was a recognition of the mixed economic possibilities inherent in the situation, perhaps it was a shrewd bargaining ploy. As Sandy was the only co-op to have dissolved itself in favor of private service in the Eisenhower era, PGE could have promoted its success as a triumph of free enterprise. Although not unaware of its coup, the company took a decidedly low-key public-relations approach to the incident. A few lines in the 1956 *Annual Report*, a small story in the local Sandy newspaper, one in the *Bullseye*, and fleeting coverage in the *Oregonian*: that was the extent of the celebration.

One can only conclude from the evidence of the Sandy episode and from the general conduct of PGE policy makers during the decade that PGE operated out of complex motives. These were made up of PGE's own caution and small-scale ambitions, a strong concern for its power needs as well as those of the region generally, and a concern for political realities, rather than from some sort of capitalist aggression. The company took a typically Oregonian attitude toward the world. As the Northwest historian Gordon Dodds has pointed out, conservatism, modest aims, and a parochial view of the world have been the enduring hallmarks of the Oregonian's outlook.[77]

The failure of partnership at John Day still left a huge deficit of power to be made up. With the main stem of the Columbia precluded by the partnership wrangle, the interest of would-be hydro developers, both public and private, shifted to the Northwest's secondary waterways. Remarkably—given the chronic and, by all accounts, urgent nature of the Pacific Northwest power crisis—the results were only mixed.

For PGE, besides Pelton and Round Butte, there had to be active pursuit of new opportunities in combination with other companies. As a result, in April 1954 the company revived the principle under which Pelton had been started. It joined with PP&L, Washington Water Power Company, and Montana Power Company in 25 percent ownership apiece to form the Pacific Northwest Power Company. The first plans called for the new company to undertake major power developments to satisfy joint yearly needs of 800,000 kw of new plant capacity. By late summer, the company had obtained a preliminary permit from the Federal Power Commission to begin studies on a 536,000-kw dam site on the north fork of the Clearwater River in Idaho and for one at Penny Cliffs on the Clearwater's middle fork. Later in the year, Pacific Northwest Power filed for permits to conduct feasibility studies at two sites known as Mountain Sheep and Pleasant Valley on the Snake River in Idaho. Engineering reports indicated that the maximum generation potential of the two sites was 1,446,000 kw.[78]

In time, both Penny Cliffs and Bruce's Eddy were dropped for technical reasons (though the latter was built as Dworshak Dam in 1962). Pacific Northwest Power concentrated its efforts on the Snake River sites instead. When, in 1955, the company filed for a construction license to build the $213 million project, the subsequent hearings triggered 7,315 pages of testimony given by 200 witnesses in 58 days.[79] Because of controversy over the threat the dams would represent to fish and to the area's natural scenic values, and the economic impact of the projects, witnesses included the attorneys general of Idaho and Oregon (for the states' Fish and Game commissions), the Oregon and Montana National Farmers' unions, the Idaho Federation of Labor, and the National Hells Canyon Association. The Federal Power Commission examiner endorsed the application but was not upheld by the full commission. The commission ruled in January 1958 that a combination of dams on the middle Snake, including a dam at Nez Perce, which was below the mouth of the Salmon River where it flowed into the Snake, was preferable to the Pacific Northwest Power plan.

The company came back in March 1958 with an amended plan for development of the middle Snake. This application called for a 670-foot-high dam to be known as Mountain Sheep, a mile above the confluence of the Salmon and the Snake. The siting of the dam was intended to preserve the critical spawning nature of the salmon, regarded as the source of 30 percent of all salmon and steelhead passing McNary Dam on the main stem of the Columbia.[80] The dam was to provide 2.7 million acre-feet of usable storage for power and flood control in a reservoir fifty-eight miles long, extending to the Hells Canyon plant of Idaho Power.

High Mountain Sheep, as the project came to be called, was supported by the Corps of Engineers as being less damaging to the environment than a Nez Perce dam at the mouth of the Salmon. When the decade closed, the issue was not settled. A competing application in March 1960 by the Washington Public Power Supply System, a consortium of that state's PUDs, to build the Nez Perce project further complicated the matter, as the Federal Power Commission was forced to choose between the two. Thus, when the last day of 1959 arrived, Pacific Northwest Power had yet to turn a shovelful of dirt on a hydroelectric project.

If PGE's efforts—Pelton, Round Butte, North Fork, and the addition of a new generator at Faraday notwithstanding—to bring new power on-line through the use of bulldozers and jack-hammers were largely frustrated during the fifties, the company had much better luck when it employed pen and ink. During the latter part of the decade it was actually able to bring some half-million new kilowatts on-line by entering into agreements with public-power bodies. This was because the only partnership project ever approved by Congress and the administration turned out to be that of Klickitat-Priest Rapids. Eisenhower and McKay had approved public, not private, enterprise. But the other Washington PUDs were desperate for power, as most of them had depended solely on BPA for generation and had no facilities of their own. With partnership a dead letter and private development stalled, they had no choice but to finance their own dams. They therefore undertook dam building on the upper Columbia, breaking the political deadlock over hydro development on the river. But as they were typically small, rural entities serving some of the region's least dynamic population centers, in places least likely to experience much industrial growth, their dams were overendowed with generating capacity as compared with their energy needs and financial capabilities. They were only too glad to enter into long-term contracts (in most cases of fifty years' duration) with the Northwest's private utilities.[81]

If any last laugh over partnership was given, it must have been in the boardrooms of the region's private utilities. True, the dams were not close to the urban centers served by the private companies, but the Bonneville grid was probably the best transmission network in the country. True, the companies did not "own" the dams, but the length of the agreements they negotiated was such as to make the arrangements come to much the same thing, and in final terms they would not have owned partnership dams either. True, the total energy generated at the sites could not compensate for the amount of power that could have been generated at a site like John Day, but anything was better than nothing. In some sense, then, the PUDs proved to be stalking-horses

261

for the private utilities on Columbia River hydro development. The congressional allies of the public-power movement had been outflanked with the help of public power itself.

Thus, by 1959, PGE had "tied down," as its 1959 *Annual Report* put it, 583,046 kw in contracts with various Washington State PUDs. These contracts covered power from the Priest Rapids, Wanapum, and Rocky Reach projects. Wanapum alone, due on-line in 1963, promised to deliver 261,428 kw. Almost 60 percent of the total was on a firm fifty-year contract. Portions of the remainder could be withdrawn on five years' notice. Rocky Reach would initially deliver to PGE 113,848 kw, beginning in 1963.[82] At last, partnership had worked for PGE. To an extent. In a way.

POWER AND THE HOME

Through the fifties PGE remained what it had only lately become: a largely locally held company. "Westerners continue to hold the reins in this Oregon corporation, in ownership as well as in operation," the 1954 *Annual Report* said.[83] By the end of the decade, three-quarters of the company's 18,890 stockholders were concentrated in the three Pacific Coast states, with Oregonians constituting 24.8 percent and Californians 39.7 percent of the total number. While westerners held 67.3 percent of the outstanding shares of PGE common stock at the time, Oregonians owned only 16.9 percent of those shares and Californians 40.8 percent.[84] Nevertheless, the company's consciousness was strongly regional and local, compared with the years of control by the Clarks and Pierce, when Griffith fought a lonely battle to maintain what he considered to be the necessary level of identification of PGE with the economic and social well-being of Oregon and, in particular, Portland.

Under Delzell, the company, following Griffith's lead, was acutely attuned to its position in the state politically, socially, and economically. In 1953 PGE found that in the forty-four cities and towns it serviced, franchise relationships with the various municipalities were sometimes dramatically inconsistent. In a move to rationalize and regularize such arrangements, PGE offered the standard franchise payment of 3 percent of gross revenues from the sale of electricity to the twenty-six towns that had previously granted franchises on different terms. All the towns and their electricity consumers thus came onto the same footing in their relations with the company on a long-term basis. This allowed PGE to retail electricity to all consumers throughout its service area on the postage-stamp or uniform-rate basis.[85] It also provided equitable relations that proved to be politically invaluable.

By far the biggest adaptation PGE had to make in the fifties was to the changing social and economic character of its public. Thus, under Delzell, the area's prosperity continued to be a focus. The 1951 *Annual Report* cited statistics indicating how closely PGE's success was allied to that of the Northwest. The "swelling economy," as the report put it, had led to an 18 percent increase in kilowatt-hour sales from 1950, as individual residential consumers made ever greater use of electricity. That figure did not even include the more than eight thousand new customers of all lines added to the PGE line.[86] The statistics thus indicated not only a quantitative increase in electricity use, but an improved standard of living for Portlanders. In all types of consumption, there was a 9 percent growth from 1950 to 1951.[87]

One sign of this greater affluence was the addition of television to the growing list of postwar Portland's consumer luxuries. On 30 September 1952, the city received the initial broadcast of the nation's first commercial UHF station, KPTV, Channel 27. The station itself was powered by PGE. The utility's planners, in preparing for the introduction of television, thought that load growth from switched-on sets alone would be negligible. Rather, they reasoned, significant increases would come as a result of changes in living patterns imposed by the presence of TV sets in countless homes. Lights, space heating, ranges, and water heaters would all be "affected by the last show and the midnight snack," they figured.[88]

The enormous postwar prosperity of the United States, which Oregon shared, had in many ways created a new society. High employment; expanding disposable income, with a greater discretionary percentage than in any prewar period; unheard-of mobility, better housing, and a vast increase of affordable consumer products, including home appliances such as TV; and the appearance of young, affluent, and fertile couples changed the face of the nation. One feature of this transformation was that the nuclear family living in a single-family dwelling (usually a tract house) became the prevalent social unit.[89] With the popularity of television, the postwar home's so-called family room, in which the set was customarily placed, became a social center, disrupting traditional visiting patterns, crippling movie attendance, and generally keeping Americans indoors more.[90] The result was that the young mother—the "homemaker," as the popular magazines and business executives who sold her their wares liked to style her—became more than ever essential to the economy generally, and to utilities specifically. Residential use of electricity through the decade accounted for a greater and greater share of the utilities' sales, and the homemaker had unchallenged hegemony of the home. A husband might bring home the bacon, but the homemaker fried it, washed the appliances and utensils with which it was served and eaten, and, more important, chose how those operations would be accomplished.

The homemaker on the PGE line during the fifties was even more crucial to the company's success than were her sisters across the country to their utilities. The PGE homemaker continued to use about three times the electrical energy (5,966 kwh) of the national residential average in mid-decade.[91] This was attributable to the low cost of the region's electricity compared with other parts of the nation; because of these lower costs from 1949 through 1959, revenue from residential sales averaged about 55 percent of the total dollar sales of the company's power. Commercial sales were at an average of 27 percent and industrial sales at 11 percent.[92] A category of miscellaneous transactions made up the remainder.

The introduction of natural gas as a cheap and efficient form of energy for residential consumption in PGE's service area in 1956 heightened the utility's sensitivity to the homemaker still more. Clearly, with this energy at her disposal, she would be the focus of company marketing efforts, as her use of electricity continued to drive the utility's growth. More than ever, her acquisition of such relatively new appliances as the clothes dryer, the electric dishwasher, and others (mangle irons, for instance, a kind of clothes presser of the type usually found in commercial laundries, enjoyed a brief vogue during the fifties) increased the consumption of electricity.

263

The *Annual Report* of 1952 depicted electric power as the family's unobtrusive, well-mannered butler, a docile servant in the home, making possible a style of gracious and easeful living that most Americans had previously only dreamed of. The way for even more customers to use more electricity was cleared in 1954, when the company introduced a plan that would allow the purchase of new and more extensive wiring for existing homes. Modeled on a plan developed by Cincinnati Gas and Electric, the plan allowed customers to contract for a maximum of three hundred fifty dollars in residential rewiring, the payments to be combined with monthly electric bills over a period ranging from six months to three years. By the end of 1954, the company had 608 such wiring contracts, and the average electrical consumption of those customers had increased by half.[93]

By 1956, the company's tools for growth included the ultimate residential-marketing device, the "all-electric home." As cosponsor of Portland's all-electric display home, PGE received an award for the concept from the magazine *Living for Young Homemakers*. The dwelling featured an all-electric push-button kitchen, a "sunshine room" with built-in sun lamps, rheostatic lighting, a master panel in the bedroom that controlled electrical circuits throughout the house, and what was described as an "electrically operated weather control system which heats or cools the house as conditions dictate," later to be known as a heat pump.[94] At the end of the decade, PGE's all-electric home had become the Bronze or Gold Medallion Home, "a tangible concept of electrical excellence." In the PGE service area, where electricity was so cheap and where by 1959 the average residential consumption of electricity had reached an average of 9,186 kwh per year —about triple the national average—the Medallion homes were loaded with electrical appurtenances. In other parts of the country, an electric range and water heater might be the only requirements for the Medallion program. Builders were attracted to the concept because all-electric homes sold faster than conventional houses, and the program's marketing campaign had impressed upon the public that a Medallion home was "their assurance of Living Better Electrically."[95]

Americans since the war had discovered that living better was their birthright. With greater control over their own time than previously, Oregonians, like other Americans, spent more time on such things as picnicking, hiking, and fishing. An alien observing the rite for the first time might have been unable to discern whether Little League baseball was a pastime of children or their parents, but its growth and popularity in the summers of the decade were undeniable.

PGE adapted to this reality in the fifties and capitalized on it. The Pelton Dam controversy notwithstanding, the company recognized Oregonians' love of the outdoors. In 1955, the PGE *Annual Report* carried the following statement under the title "the wise use of our natural resources":

> In utilizing natural resources for the production of electric energy, Portland General Electric will, in the interests of sound conservation, endeavor to apply to its generation developments those policies which will preserve and make available for general public use and benefit, to the maximum extent that it is technologically and economically feasible, all of the multiple values other than power which may be associated with such a development.[96]

A 1956 display showing the virtues of electric water heaters. (PGE collections)

THE NATIONAL MEDALLION HOME PROGRAM was launched in 1958 by the Edison Electric Institute as a way of introducing customers to the advantages and luxuries of electric power and appliances and of promoting the use of electric power by home builders. The program used two designations, "Bronze" and "Gold," to indicate the extent to which a home was electrified. Gold Medallion homes were all-electric; Bronze homes may have had fewer appliances or some that were not powered by electricity. Utilities used the program to emphasize the advantages of proper lighting, major appliances, and other uses of electric power.

Standards in the PGE service area were higher than those nationwide because Oregon residents already used more electric power than people elsewhere in the country. In the PGE area, a Gold Medallion home was required to feature an electric water heater and range, additional appliances, proper outlets, improved lighting, and a minimum service capability of 200 amps. Builders responded favorably to the program, convinced that all-electric homes would sell faster; consumers further confirmed that belief as they eagerly bought Medallion houses. Oregonians were ready to "live better electrically."

A sketch of the scale model of Pelton Dam, complete with simulated rain. (OHS neg. OrHi 85013)

IN 1958, PGE BEGAN PREPARING for Oregon's state centennial celebration to be held the following year. The company hired an architect to design a modernistic building which included a tower lit by neon tubing that resembled lightning. Inside the building was a scale model of a dam resembling Pelton, complete with simulated rainfall to fill the reservoir, a cutaway waterwheel, a generator, model transmission facilities, and a miniature recreation area; presentations of industrial, commercial, agricultural, and residential uses of electricity; and displays of state-of-the-art electric appliances, including sonic dishwashers, "walls of light," and electronic ovens. An electronic system provided taped commentaries on the exhibits as visitors moved through the building.

AFTER WORLD WAR II, public pressure mounted for PGE to include parkland and recreation facilities around some of its operations, particularly at the sites of its hydroelectric plants. The company's first venture into the recreation business had begun in 1950, when accommodations for campers and fishers (picnic tables, rest rooms, boat facilities, fireplaces) were provided to the increasing numbers of visitors to the Austin Hot Springs area in the Mt. Hood National Forest.

The Austin Hot Springs project focused attention for the first time on the idea of recreational facilities on company property. The public, particularly sport fishers, felt strongly that company land that contained some of Oregon's best camping, hiking, and fishing sites should be available to the public, since the land was for the most part unspoiled except for the small areas occupied by the buildings and facilities. Many concerned Oregonians even opposed the construction of dams on the Deschutes River, believing that the harm to fish and fishing areas would be insupportable. PGE's plans to apply for construction permits for Pelton Dam on the Deschutes engendered much controversy, and the company went through a difficult period in its relations with the public. However, its right to build dams on the river was upheld by the Su-

preme Court, and the company proceeded with construction. It also proceeded with a program designed to repair its relations with the public, which focused on promoting conservation and developing parks and recreation facilities at many of its project sites. This undertaking came at a time when PGE was expanding its role and image as a public-service corporation. Board Chairman Thomas Delzell summed up the company's goals by saying that "Man does not live by bread alone. Neither can a corporation endure if it continues to be a producer only of material things."

By 1959, PGE owned and operated campgrounds at Hood View Forest Camp, Meditation Point, and Gone Creek Forest Camp at Timothy Meadows (before it became Timothy Lakes); camping and boating facilities at Pelton and Promontory Park at North Fork; and parks at River Mill Dam, Roslyn Lake, and Lake Harriet.

In 1963 the Federal Power Commission required that all utilities applying for licenses for hydroelectric projects file plans for the public recreational use of the land and water at the site. PGE had already established an admirable reputation for providing such accommodations (the year before, Gov. Mark Hatfield had praised the utility's efforts as outstanding), and the company had little trouble conforming to the new regulations.

267

The company promised, as a matter of policy, to design, build, and run its facilities consonant with the husbanding of such natural resources as were affected by its projects. The statement promised to avoid the alteration of resources or, if this proved necessary, to restore or replace "in equivalent form" such resources as would be "necessarily affected" by its work. Finally, it pledged that:

> Particularly, the company will, independently or in cooperation with cognizant public agencies, take adequate and practical means for making its project lands accessible to the public for recreational use and for providing facilities to enhance the enjoyment thereof; for avoiding the pollution of water courses and the atmosphere; for representation and revegetation of areas denuded by project construction, and for the control of erosion thereon; and for preserving fish and wildlife resources.[97]

By 1958, PGE was maintaining nine picnic parks and campgrounds, all of which were within a reasonable driving distance of Portland.[98] "Good citizenship is a corporate responsibility" became the catchphrase repeated in the company's annual reports and in other literature and official statements, with which the utility attempted to meet the recreating public.

Besides pursuing its conservation ethic, PGE sponsored four Little League teams and energetically boosted the annual Rose Festival by granting release time to employees who worked with the festival's committee, by publicizing the event in company newsletters, and by entering floats in the parade. In 1959, the company was an exhibitor, with its own pavilion, at the state's centennial celebration at Delta Park in north Portland.[99]

Delzell, from the vantage of the postwar Pacific Northwest, wrote in 1957 that "for all its complexities, the 20th century is fun to live in. It demands more, but it offers more than any period in our history."[100] The ingenuousness of such a statement (though hardly unusual for *Annual Report* rhetoric), startling in its amnesia on the subject of recently past tragedies, nevertheless comments powerfully on the state of Oregon's society at the time. If elsewhere people struggled, in the American garden of Oregon, life moved at a stately pace, and the glow of progress and prosperity was on the land. Delzell was not a foolish man. Times were good, but the oncoming years leading to the company's centennial were to prove that, for American society and American business, progress and prosperity were not enough. In Oregon, distant as the state was from the world's centers of political and economic struggle, harsh realities would once again intrude. The challenge would be to preserve the advantages of the past, while adapting to the new realities presented by the still metamorphosing society and economy. In a real sense, the fifties had been merely a dress rehearsal in the drama of change.

8 LINKAGES, TREATIES, DISASTER, & TRANSITIONS

F OR ALL ITS VAUNTED VOLATILITY, the first years of the sixties were, in many ways, little more than an extension of the fifties. To be sure, the administration of the fatherly, easygoing Ike and his staid coterie gave way to that of the youthful, vigorous, and seemingly icono-clastic John F. Kennedy and the "New Frontier," but this was mostly a cosmetic difference, and little, particularly in the realm of the economy, changed. The decade got under way in 1960 with a recession that was in many respects characteristic of the sluggishness of Eisenhower's second term, but this was only a temporary impediment to the general growth of the postwar years.[1]

For PGE, the sixties began as a carryover from the previous decade. The regional, state, and local economies continued to grow without serious pause. Population in Portland and the rest of the state grew as in the earlier years of the postwar expansion. By mid-decade, Oregon was the fastest growing state in the Pacific Northwest.[2]

A sense of the meaning and the apparent permanence of those statistics for the company is imparted by the fact that in 1961 PGE served some thirty thousand residential-heating customers. This was more than any other utility in the United States.[3]

As a result of this growth, the company continued its postwar policy of achieving greater generating capacity. The pursuit of more kilowatts and a better, more efficient system entailed new construction and continued improvement of the PGE transmission and distribution systems.

On 17 February 1961, the Oregon Hydroelectric Commission granted a license to build Round Butte Dam, which was eventually completed in 1964. This was the company's biggest cost item for construction during the decade, other than PGE's share of the Pacific Northwest-Pacific Southwest Intertie.

A full slate of construction and system improvements was undertaken in the sixties. In 1962, the Round Butte transmission line was begun. It was to run to the Bethel Substation in Salem. Between 1962 and 1964, the company budgeted $98 million for new construction, with the 1964 construction program alone at $24.4 million; nearly half that figure was for the completion of Round Butte. The heaviest concentration of expenditures in that year, however, was on improvements to distribution facilities.[4] The company also began the reconstruction of Cazadero Dam, washed out by flood in January 1965. Two other important projects were begun that year. PGE allocated $11.2 million for its part of the Pacific Northwest-Pacific Southwest Intertie. In 1967—the next year of significant construction activity—the company spent another $12 million on the intertie. It also built a new substation in Sherwood in southwestern Washington County. This was to accommodate load growth in the area, largely because of a new Publishers Paper plant in nearby Newberg.[5]

Although the growth of the sixties appears consistent with that of the earlier postwar years, almost from the opening of the decade there was a subtle change in the company's affairs. The postwar prosperity had marked Americans, to use historian David M. Potter's phrase, as a "people of plenty." The American way with nature was, if not profligate, certainly extravagant. The figures for the growth of electricity consumption bear this out. There seemed to be an unlimited supply of nature and its bounty. But there came a point when this was patently not the case. It came at the peak of American economic prepotency in the sixties. At that time it began to occur to some people that with continued population growth, increasing urbanization, quickening industrialization, ever-rising per-capita real incomes, and even greater consumer demand, there was only so much of nature to go around.[6]

In the Pacific Northwest's utility circles, this awareness dawned early. A comprehensive assessment of power needs undertaken by the Federal Power Commission indicated that long-term growth in regional and national energy demand would continue unabated.[7] The need for more generation would similarly continue. Meanwhile, the political and legal struggles of the postwar years over hydroelectric development had left many of the region's best dam sites undeveloped, but the truth was that most such sites had been identified and spoken for. In PGE's 1961 *Annual Report*, Delzell wrote that, while "falling water is still the base for electrical generation in the Pacific Northwest," while it remained an important advantage for the region's economy and should "be developed to the fullest, consistent with sound business principles," the company was nevertheless researching an alternative to hydropower, "looking forward to the day when the last economical hydroelectric site has been developed."[8]

It was a statement that must have slipped by even the more alert and informed stockholders, because the idea that the Northwest could run out of any of its more prominent natural resources would have seemed absurd on its face. In a land of enormous forests, huge salmon runs, and seemingly endless waters, a nature with limits was almost impossible to conceive. Still, that was

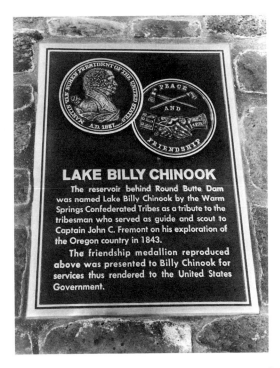

LAKE BILLY CHINOOK

The reservoir behind Round Butte Dam was named Lake Billy Chinook by the Warm Springs Confederated Tribes as a tribute to the tribesman who served as guide and scout to Captain John C. Fremont on his exploration of the Oregon country in 1843.

The friendship medallion reproduced above was presented to Billy Chinook for services thus rendered to the United States Government.

Lake Billy Chinook plaque was commemorated during the opening festivities for Round Butte Dam. Allan J. de Lay, photographer. (PGE collections)

FIVE HUNDRED GUESTS, braving a torrential rainstorm, attended the dedication ceremonies of Round Butte Dam on 17 June 1965. Governor Mark O. Hatfield gave the dedicatory address on a 1,000-foot cliff overlooking Lake Billy Chinook. He praised PGE's record of service in the public interest and spoke of the importance of water to Oregon's agriculture, industry, recreation, and tourism. The same afternoon, Charles Jackson, past president of the Warm Springs Tribal Council, dedicated a monument in memory of Wasco Indian Scout Billy Chinook, for whom the Round Butte reservoir was named. Tours of the powerhouse followed the dedications.

271

the subtext of Delzell's remark, whether or not he quite realized it himself. Because of its reality to the company and the region, PGE was to play a key role in two political developments slowly unfolding around it. They were to involve the company still more deeply in the local and regional economies while driving forward resolution of the problem of hydroelectric abundance, not just for the PGE service area but for the Northwest and almost the entire North American Pacific slope.

POWERING THE FUTURE

The story begins with the negotiation of the Columbia River Treaty of 17 January 1961.[9] The treaty resulted from efforts made by the United States and Canada to determine the mutual benefits of cooperative development of the Columbia River basin. The Boundary Waters Treaty of 1909 between the two nations had established the International Joint Commission to make this determination. In 1944, engineering studies were undertaken of potential water-storage sites in Canada for streamflow regulation. In 1959, the commission announced principles for the calculation and allocation of benefits from joint development of the sites. This initiative eventuated in the treaty itself.

The instrument signed by Prime Minister John Diefenbaker of Canada and President Eisenhower provided that Canada would build three water-storage projects—Arrow Lakes and Duncan and Mica dams—in its portion of the Columbia watershed. The treaty outlined the way these reservoirs would be operated over its sixty-year life. The United States was given a five-year option to build a fourth project with a reservoir that would extend into Canada. This was Libby Dam, on the Kootenai River in Montana, which eventually opened in 1975. The three Canadian projects promised to add a total of 15.5 million acre-feet of usable storage for flood control and hydropower production. Estimates in 1964 were that the Canadian dams would increase the dependable peaking capacity of the plants on the United States Columbia River Basin System to a maximum of 2.7 million kwh for 1974 and 1975, assuming the installation of new generating units in downstream plants in time to use the additional storage releases.

Ratification of the treaty dragged on for forty-four months because of political differences in the Canadian Parliament. When it was finally completed on 22 September 1964, the heads of state were President Lyndon B. Johnson and Prime Minister Lester B. Pearson. The agreement was a landmark in U.S.-Canadian relations, and it was pivotal in the expansion of the power supply in the Pacific Northwest and, as subsequent events proved, the entire Pacific slope.

From the first, PGE policy planners recognized the treaty's significance to the company and the region. The 1960 *Annual Report* spoke of a possible power shortage in 1964-66 which the facilities mandated by the treaty would partially address.[10] In 1964, Canada agreed to sell its power entitlement to Northwest public agencies and private utilities. These included BPA; Chelan, Douglas, and Grant counties; other Washington PUDs buying through a nonprofit corporation they had established for the purpose; Columbia Storage Power Exchange; and some Northwest private utilities, including PGE, which purchased 17.5 percent of the power.[11] In addition, the participating Northwest utilities entered into an agreement to ensure the optimum use of downstream benefits arising from the construction and operation of the Canadian dams.[12] These developments greatly brightened the long-range power picture.

A second development at the time was also significant in enhancing the Northwest's power supply. In 1963, Congress approved an agreement for the purchase by regional utilities of power produced at the Hanford nuclear reservation in Washington State.[13] In 1958, Congress had authorized construction of the "New Production Reactor" at Hanford, which was designed to convert its own waste heat from the production of plutonium into steam for generating electricity. The Washington Public Power Supply System eventually financed, built, and operated this facility. The plant came out of an arrangement made among Washington Public Power Supply System, BPA, and the Atomic Energy Commission, forerunner of the Nuclear Regulatory Commission. The authorizing legislation required that up to half of Hanford's steam plant output be available to the region's private utilities and industries. BPA and the Washington Public Power Supply System urged private utilities to partake to the maximum in the Hanford output, since prepayment for the energy they bought would help fund the plant's construction. Seventy-six electric utilities asked for allocations. PGE took 10 percent of Hanford's output.

The net effect of these two developments was to create a sense of stability and abundance for the Northwest's long-term energy outlook. This was not necessarily an accurate picture. Predictions of a power shortage as early as 1964, and of loads doubling in the region over the ensuing ten years, were given credence within the Northwest utility industry. Nevertheless, among outsiders the treaty and the Hanford plant created the impression of a region awash in a surplus of cheap electricity. Such a view was particularly alluring to power planners and politicians concerned with the needs of California, a state that depended on expensive oil and thermal generation for the greater part of its electrical loads. Moreover, California's peak demand was on a different cycle from the Northwest's—summer for the former, winter for the latter. The Northwest's summer reserves of electricity seemed to be an untapped source of nourishment for the power-starved state to its south.

A third development made it still more likely that California would get a share of this power. Since 1958 BPA had run annual deficits, owing mostly to the increase in nonfederal dams on the Northwest's secondary streams and the Columbia. Even with rural Washington PUDs, initially its most ardent defenders (and in the generation business themselves by the end of the fifties), the agency's power sales had eroded badly. The slump was compounded by stagnation in the aluminum industry. There were to be six straight years of steep deficits at the agency. A solution had to be found. In 1961, the Kennedy administration's choice to head the agency, Charles F. Luce, took office. Solving the agency's deficits was among his priorities.

For the dynamic Luce, as well as the increasingly hard-pressed utility executives in California (which was then growing at a phenomenal pace), a neat solution presented itself: an intertie between California utility and BPA transmission and distribution lines. On its face, the intertie concept seemed simple. Although it would entail a monumental construction project, the linkage would allow surpluses from the two large pools of power to be drawn upon reciprocally on their different peaking load schedules, thus leaving unthreatened the total pool of each region's own power.

The concept of a West Coast intertie had been gestating for many years. It had been broached in 1919 by a University of Washington engineering professor named Carl Edward Magnusson. He had proposed a 220,000-V interconnection stretching from Vancouver, B.C., to Los Angeles. In 1955, Charles F. Carey, an engineer with the Pacific Northwest Regional Planning Commission, had proposed what eventually became the BPA regional grid system. His blueprint had lines reaching to Montana, Idaho, Salt Lake City, Vancouver, B.C., and California.[14]

The idea of a California intertie received serious consideration only in the period from 1947 to 1951. In late 1947, the Federal Power Commission presented a small map illustrating the potential for interconnecting across the country, including the Northwest-California linkage. The BPA's advance programs of January 1948 also showed a line into California.[15] At the same time, a severe drought in central California prompted a large reduction in power production. In April, California Rep. Claire Engel introduced HR 6367, authorizing construction of an intertie for the purpose of selling or exchanging dump power.[16] Slowly, through a series of endorsements by prominent individuals and federal agencies, as well as through such circumstances as the power shortages in both the Northwest and California and the pressing power needs dictated by the Korean War, the intertie gained credence. On 17 January 1951, the concept's momentum was such that the secretary of Interior, Oscar L. Chapman, authorized an intertie between BPA and California's Central Valley Project, an irrigation enterprise of the Bureau of Reclamation.

It was not quite so easy. A far more volatile issue had emerged in the background. During the drought of 1948, Assistant Secretary of the Interior William Warne sent a letter to Norris Paulson, a California representative, stating that one solution to such problems in the future would be to divert Columbia River water to his state. The letter was inserted in the *Congressional Record*. Its publication provoked outrage in the Northwest, especially among electioneering politicians, that the region's water was to be stolen. Each politician intimated that he or she was the only person capable of preventing such a hijacking of the region's main asset. Opponents of the Truman administration's power program, including Oregon's Senator Cordon, used the issue to leverage resistance to the intertie in the Congress. As a result, in March 1952, the House Appropriations Committee blocked the intertie, stating in its report that construction by either the government or private interests should await a full examination of the issue. This effectively crippled it for the remainder of the decade.

The concept was not destined simply to die. In 1958 the idea was revived by one of the largest private utilities in the nation, the Pacific Gas and Electric Company of northern California. By that year the company's generating system was largely an oil-fired thermal one. With the cost of fuel more than doubled, from $1.00 to $2.50 per barrel, it required a cheaper source of power. Access to the Northwest's inexpensive hydropower seemed to be the answer. A mutuality of interests had been achieved with BPA simply by virtue of the agency's looming deficits. Pacific Gas and Electric proposed that in partnership with a southern Oregon utility known as California-Oregon Power Company, it be granted the right to build the intertie. (California-Oregon Power, it should be noted, merged with PP&L in June 1961.) Arthur Pearl, head of the BPA at the time, assented.

In early 1959 a hearing on the proposal was held by the U.S. Senate. Contracts between BPA and Pacific Gas and Electric were already drafted, but the hearing revealed opposition to them from the West Coast's three governors—Edmund Brown of California, Albert Rosellini of Washington, and Mark Hatfield of Oregon. They asked for a joint feasibility study on the issue and legislation guaranteeing each region's preference rights to power generated from its own resources. The heads of three of California's larger utilities—Southern California Edison, San Diego Gas and Electric Company, and California Electric Power Company—also objected to the proposed intertie on technical grounds.[17]

There matters stood as Luce took office. In the interim, a number of conferences had been held, a major consulting report had been issued, and in a speech on natural resources of 21 February 1961, President Kennedy pushed the idea of accelerating the interconnection and pooling of power resources.[18] Nevertheless, the political atmosphere surrounding the intertie remained charged.

There were three reasons for the continuing tensions. Luce, Northwest politicians, portions of the region's general public, and almost all its editorialists were deeply concerned that an intertie agreement might jeopardize the regional-power supply by inserting into the equation California public-power bodies that would be entitled to preference according to BPA's statutory mandate. The Los Angeles municipal utility district was the largest public utility in the world. By demanding its preferential position as a public body, the Los Angeles system alone could easily disrupt the Northwest's power, not to mention its economic-development plans. Northwesterners' worst nightmares were confirmed when an *Oregonian* headline on 5 November 1963 screamed that the Los Angeles municipal-power authority was studying the feasibility of constructing its own line direct to The Dalles.[19] (The intent, if such it was, eventually evaporated.)

As a consequence of these developments, there was a long battle over protective legislation drafted by the BPA to protect Northwest industry by giving the region's users first call on its own power. The bill also permitted the sale of surplus power only, mandated the right of withdrawal if the power were needed in the Northwest, and required the return of the surplus peaking capacity at off-peak to ensure that there would be no diminution of the pool of usable power.[20] A hue and cry went up from congressional opponents of federal power and from California representatives such as Craig Hosmer and Charles Gubser, opponents of public power whose districts were hungriest for the energy. They assiduously fought the two bills in which those principles were embodied. The debate was further complicated by an amendment to the House bill offered by Rep. Jack Westland, a Washington State Republican. This was an attempt to force the Kennedy administration to deal seriously with private utilities that wanted to build interties by requiring congressional approval of any proposed intertie.

That was also the second problem. Should the intertie be a private or public project? Wrangling over the issue produced a running philosophical battle in Congress between advocates and opponents of public power, with BPA in the middle. The agency, in the throes of its continuing budget crisis, had concluded that an intertie to the immense California market was the answer to its sagging power sales. It had long since reconciled itself to private participation if it would speed construction.[21] Meanwhile, significant in the administration's considerations, especially for Secretary of Interior Stewart Udall and Luce, was the perception among public-power advocates that not enough had been done to further public power while private interests had been too easily accommodated. One liberal Federal Power Commission member, Howard Morgan, an Orego-

275

nian, went so far as to inform President Kennedy that he did not desire reappointment because, he implied, the commission was a pawn of the private utilities. The administration's posture was to try to placate both sides in the intertie project. This opened the door for PGE.

In November 1962, following a request of Udall, Luce sent a letter to twenty-one public and private power agencies soliciting proposals on the intertie. He and Udall hoped they could stitch together a grand plan of participation in a regional interconnection that would appease both public- and private-power advocates—in other words, co-opt both politicians and utility representatives into support of the intertie and, at the same time, produce a program of construction acceptable to all sides in the issue. In his invitation, Udall had urged utility executives to "think big" in crafting their proposals.[22]

For PGE, the opportunity represented another chance to participate in what had become, since the beginning of the fifties, the company's favorite kind of large-scale-construction effort—one founded in public-private partnership. At the highest levels of the utility, the belief clearly persisted that participation in joint-power enterprises was the best way to realize PGE's objectives. Partnership—or perhaps more properly, joint participation—guaranteed a higher level of public regard by avoiding the stigma of a private monopoly controlling free resources; it gave access, if only indirectly, to public financing and lower interest rates; it meant larger, more nearly comprehensive kinds of projects based on the spending power of the federal government; and it would keep PGE rates low so as to avoid ratepayer revolts.[23]

Company President Frank Warren, in testimony before the House Interior Subcommittee on 13 June 1963, outlined PGE's argument for private participation on intertie construction. He stated the company's belief that extra-high-voltage connections between the Northwest and California would be beneficial.[24] He also stated firmly that PGE thought the federal government "should take the fullest possible advantage of nonfederal offers to provide a portion of the funds and physical facilities necessary to complete the interconnection."[25]

As a sidelight, it is interesting to note the continuing tension that still existed between the two organizations apparent in Warren's remarks. Appearing in support of BPA's budget request of $21.5 million for the initial stages of the intertie, Warren could not resist questioning whether "federal expenditures of the extent proposed are necessary to improve the Bonneville financial picture."[26] At the same time, he had to defend PGE's proposal from attacks by BPA spokespersons. They had suggested that the 500,000-v line envisioned by PGE was not adequate for the agency's needs, whereas he said they had already endorsed a similar proposal from PP&L. "If one-half of the capacity of the segment of the 500,000-v line between Round Mountain in California and Klamath Falls in Oregon is adequate for BPA purposes, one-half of the capacity of a 500,000-v line from Round Butte to Klamath Falls should also be adequate," Warren asserted.[27]

By January 1965, the intertie was under way. It was the biggest single electrical transmission program ever undertaken in the United States. Five private companies—Pacific Gas and Electric, PP&L, San Diego Gas and Electric, Southern California Edison, and PGE—in addition to BPA, the Bureau of Reclamation, and the City of Los Angeles Department of Water and Power participated in the construction. PGE's part of the four extra-high-voltage lines connecting the Northwest with California and Arizona (added later) was a 179-mile section of one of the 500-kv

AC circuits extending from the Grizzly substation in north central Oregon to Malin substation at the Oregon-California border. It included, in addition, fifteen miles of 500-kv line interconnecting the PGE system at Round Butte with the Grizzly substation. A contract was signed with BPA giving the company a priority in the sale of surplus power to California to the extent of 1.1 billion kwh per year. Under average water conditions, this would represent about 80 percent of the utility's expected available surplus. It was further anticipated that additional revenue would be realized from the lease of half the capacity of the company's line to the agency, and from the use of the PGE capacity by others when the company did not need it.

By the end of the sixties, the Columbia River Treaty and the intertie—and for that matter Hanford—had worked synergistically to create a sense of well-being with respect to the regional energy supply. The Hanford nuclear reactor had begun operation in September 1944, producing plutonium for atomic weaponry. In the late 1950s, the president of General Electric, the contractor then operating the plant for the U.S. Government, proposed the production and sale of electricity from waste heat generated by the reservation's reactors. Private utilities successfully blocked the initiative, but by 1961, with the addition of a new reactor, 13 million tons of steam per hour were being produced at Hanford, and President Kennedy proposed a federal generating plant to make use of it. Congress rejected the idea under pressure from the private utilities. However, with Luce's cooperation, the Washington Public Power Supply System offered to finance generating facilities.

Although the private utilities (including PGE) still opposed it, the Washington Public Power Supply System plan created a nonfederal basis for generation. Luce agreed to an exchange arrangement—BPA power for Hanford energy, with BPA rates offsetting the buyer's share of the costs of Hanford energy—and in September 1962 Kennedy made it law in the Atomic Energy Appropriations Act of 1963. In late 1966, the Washington Public Power Supply System generator at Hanford was activated and began producing power. In its best year, 1973, it produced 4.5 billion kwh.[28] But in the PGE executive suite there was a sense that the electricity provided by two essentially political creations would not be enough for long-term stability for either the Pacific Northwest or the company. PGE planners were, therefore, busily working to provide for the future through new techniques of power generation. In the next decade, these techniques would come to fruition in a process even more arduous than the combined political pitfalls of the treaty and the intertie. During the planning stage, that would not have been believed.

NATURAL AND CORPORATE TEMPESTS

Apart from weathering political storms, during the sixties the company endured several natural disasters. On 12 October 1962, the first of these occurred. On that day, winds of hurricane force —a "mid-latitude cyclonic storm" in meteorological terminology, but neither a hurricane nor a typhoon as local lore would have it—swept along the Northwest coastline, leaving in their wake a band of destruction approximately 125 miles wide. Covering the most heavily settled regions of Oregon and southwestern Washington State, the so-called Columbus Day Storm inflicted property damage estimated at approximately $200 million. Nearly a quarter of that figure was later paid out in insurance claims in Oregon alone.[29] Agricultural losses were estimated at $61 million. Eleven million board feet of timber were felled by the storm, not to mention the shade and fruit trees that were blown down. They caused most of the damage sustained by the region's utilities. The storm was the worst U.S. natural disaster of 1962. Its aftermath severely tested every aspect of PGE's capabilities. Organization, communication channels, manpower, equipment, public relations—all were tested.[30] The company met the challenge.

During the peak hours of the storm, between 4 and 6 P.M. PGE was operating at 15 to 20 percent of normal. Fewer than 5 percent of the company's customers had uninterrupted power.[31] Oregon's utilities, including telephone systems and BPA, suffered total damage of $13.8 million.[32] PGE's damage reached $4 million.[33] Of the utility's 270,000 customers within its 3,300-square-mile service area, some 81 percent relied on electric service for both cooking and heating water. The devastation meant they were without the essentials.[34] (By comparison, PP&L had 45,000 on its Portland lines.) Only the mild weather prevented greater hardships for them, meanwhile increasing the pressure on the utilities to restore service.

After the storm, PGE's load was reduced to 34 percent of normal. By Wednesday of the next week, the load was up to 88 percent. Thirty-eight megawatt-months of load had been lost.[35] But by 23 October, load was estimated to be 98 percent restored. Customers in densely wooded areas were virtually the only ones without service for two weeks. The devastation had divided the PGE system into six generation areas by knocking out major portions of the transmission network. By 14 October, these areas were restored to synchronism, and by the next day, power was available at all substations. Of PGE's 225,000 line and transmission poles, only 1,200 were damaged in the storm, a modest break for the company.[36] Of 75,000 pole-mounted transformers, a mere 1,200 had to be changed out. Only 231 had been burned out, some of them failing only on the overloads generated by the restoration of service to fully electrified homes.[37]

The PGE staff performed heroically. The *Oregonian* of 26 October carried a picture of a lineman, Bud Lepper, napping by a nest of equipment, on whom was hung a sign warning "Do Not Disturb." Lepper had worked 200 hours in two weeks.[38] During the evening of 12 October, regular employees had reported to the service center, and temporary headquarters were set up for outside divisions. Approximately 586 temporary employees of all kinds were hired, including those from other utilities and workers from electrical contractors. The company spent $500,000 on line materials and supplies, including 30,000 line splicers. Administrative staff processed the employment of 45 electrical contracting firms and handled thousands of expenses to be included in insurance claims. Under the circumstances, eighteen-hour workdays were not unusual for office employees; 500 of them were diverted to the operating departments, where they performed tasks utterly alien to them. PGE retirees were called in to fill gaps in a staff stretched to breaking point. Like their younger colleagues, they, too, worked on into the night.

Meanwhile, work crews and line-construction equipment were brought in from as far away as southern California and Colorado. Eleven other utilities provided 243 workers and 21 line trucks and pickups for PGE assistance. A total of 149,220 hours were eventually given to service restoration.[39] While about 41 percent of this total was accomplished by other utilities and contractors,

PGE workers did the rest. It was a real achievement from a company with only 1,600 regular employees, including only 333 regular line-crew members.[40]

Three operators were on the PGE switchboard when the storm hit; six more joined them in the days of reconstruction. They may have felt they had heard from each of the company's 269,000 Portland customers by the time normal operations were restored. The *Oregonian* reported that in the early hours of the storm the PGE operators averaged ten calls a minute.[41] By the following Thursday, the average had dropped to four calls a minute.[42] The earliest callers simply wished to report that they had lost their power. Six days later, the neglected wanted to know why they still had none.

The public responded with tolerance to the efforts of all the utilities to return the city to normal. They had to. Their own eyes told them that the havoc wreaked by the 116-mph winds would require superhuman efforts to be restored to normal. A public-opinion survey commissioned by PGE after calm had returned revealed that the company had done well in the public's view. The average customer had suffered an outage of less than two and a half days.[43] Only after the fifth day of service outage did those without electricity lose patience. Approximately 90 percent of those surveyed were highly complimentary of PGE's efforts.[44]

The *Oregonian* expressed the view of many Portlanders in an editorial on 17 October stating that "three or four days of cooking over an open fire, of going without hot water and baths, of stumbling to our cold beds by the dim light of flickering candles have made us respect our [pioneer] forebears more but their way of life less."[45] Relief at a return to life of furnaces, stoves, refrigerators, and water heaters that sent hot water rushing into the bathtub inspired the thought that the utility had worked diligently to inculcate: "Electricity, it's wonderful."[46]

Aside from the public's recognition of the importance of electrical energy to everyday life, the storm brought another positive advance for the company. Pressure became greater on building contractors to go to underground service. This was already one of PGE's foremost crusades of the decade, and the experience of the storm encouraged more residential and tract developers to participate in the company's liberal policy of financial assistance for underground distribution systems and services.[47]

However, other natural disasters were to come, though fortunately none reached the dimensions of the Columbus Day storm. Two more windstorms hit the region during the decade. On 27 March 1963, winds gusting to 68 mph in the Salem area and accelerating to 96 mph by the time they reached Portland caused considerable damage in the company's service area. Some 40,000 PGE customers lost their power for up to eleven hours.[48] The *Oregonian* reported the lament of a PGE spokesperson who said, "We were just getting things completely cleaned up from the Columbus Day Storm and now, here we go again."[49] A third windstorm which reached a peak velocity of 90 mph in Portland swept up the Willamette Valley on 2 October 1967. This time there was adequate warning of the impending disaster, and the company was able fully to implement its emergency plan. Twenty-six outside crews for line- and tree-clearing work were hired from among Portland-area contractors, as well as four from Washington utilities and yet others from nearby utilities.[50] Approximately seven hundred employees working systemwide—some for forty

279

ALICE CROCKWELL, secretary to Board Chairman T.W. Delzell, was going home during the height of the storm Friday night and passed the corner where a highly vocal zealot usually passes out religious tracts—at the top of his voice. The night of the storm he was exhorting the Lord to "Give it to 'em Lord; Show 'em who's boss; they-'ve had it too good for too long!"

Bullseye, 26 October 1962. Special storm edition

Load dispatchers Bob Summers (left) and Chuck Whittlesey during the Columbus Day Storm. (PGE collections)

PGE employees staffing phones after the Columbus Day Storm. (OHS neg. 84806)

Cleaning up after the storm. (OHS neg. 65382)

Part of a utility pole taken for a ride by the storm. Allan J. de Lay, photographer. (PGE collections)

An argument for covered parking. (OHS neg. 65299)

Help with the repairs came from out of state. C.R. "Bob" Thompson (left) of Utah Power & Light and Tom Bessler of PGE work south of Aurora in the aftermath of the storm. (OHS neg. OrHi 84809)

282

This Port Orford cedar was planted at the turn of the century in front of Portland City Hall. The tree was uprooted by the storm. It was replanted and survived. (OHS neg. 76579)

The novelty of living without electricity quickly wore off and many residents rejoiced when the power came on again. (PGE collections)

Bud Lepper worked two hundred hours in two weeks bringing power back to PGE's customers. (OHS neg. OrHi 84808)

straight hours—spent some eighteen thousand hours to restore full functioning of the PGE system. They were hindered by thunder, lightning, and rain.[51]

In the winter of 1968-69, snow, ice, freezing rain, sub-zero temperatures, and high winds caused further problems for PGE. From 27 December through 12 January, the company was affected by these conditions at Gresham, Mt. Hood and vicinity, Lake Oswego, Oregon City, Hillsboro, Newberg, St. Helens, and Salem.[52]

Earlier, during Christmas week in 1964, severe flooding—the worst in Oregon's history—had affected the Pacific Northwest, northern California, and parts of western Nevada. Twenty-one Oregonians lost their lives. Elsewhere, twenty-six persons died because of the high waters. Total damage in the region reached about $500 million.[53] Unusually large snowfalls had recently covered the ground in the Willamette and Deschutes rivers' drainage basins, terrain already saturated by heavy rainfalls. The moisture was locked in the frozen ground but was rapidly released by sudden, unseasonably high temperatures and warm rains on 21 and 22 December. The U.S. Geological Survey reported the flow in the Andiamos River to be 50 percent greater than at any time since 1907, as it peaked at 86,900 cubic feet per second.[54]

PGE suffered severe losses in the flood, totaling $2.2 million.[55] They included damage to the company's hydro generating facilities and to transmission and distribution lines and substations. At its most serious point, the flood left some three thousand of the company's customers out of service. The greatest damage to PGE facilities was at the Faraday project, where the original powerhouse was inundated with rock and silt, although Cazadero, the old timber-crib diversion dam, ran a close second. It was badly damaged, but never stopped supplying water to the Faraday forebay for the No. 6 generating unit.[56] A month later, on 29 January 1965, another flood on the Clackamas wiped out the Cazadero facility completely. It was replaced by the Faraday Dam, which was concrete.

Other PGE facilities affected by the flood included Oak Grove, where a mud slide and washout of the powerhouse road isolated the twenty families at the site. Supplies from Portland were flown in to them. The road was not fully repaired until 9 March. Downriver, a slide cut the double-circuit 115-kv transmission line.[57] At the North Fork forebay, a large accumulation of silt carried in by the floodwaters dramatically reduced the pondage and damaged the recreation grounds at the site.[58] Trees and logs filled the reservoir for about half a mile up. Fish-ladder transport over the Clackamas River dams was halted by the flood. Fish trapping took place temporarily, at River Mill, where a makeshift facility was installed so that fish could be taken there and trucked to North Fork Lake until the Faraday cofferdam was cleared and the North Fork-Faraday ladder was operable.[59]

The Bull Run project and the Sandy River diversion dam also suffered during the flooding. Perhaps the only positive note in all the travail was that the last thirty feet of the new Round Butte reservoir, known as Lake Billy Chinook, was filled in a matter of hours by the raging waters. Round Butte had not been expected to fill until the following year. This actually reduced the Deschutes flooding by 13,700 cubic feet per second and significantly controlled flood problems on the Lower Columbia River.[60] It also meant that high water flows were available at the Pelton-Round Butte site to offset the losses of Faraday and Bull Run.

Water gushes down the cliffs at the Faraday Dam.
Allan J. de Lay, photographer. (PGE collections)

Floodwaters at North Fork, 21 and 22 December
1964. (PGE collections)

Exterior photo of Lents substation during December 1964 flood. Allan J. de Lay, photographer. (PGE collections)

Forest trash in the North Fork Lake from December 1964 flood. This photo was taken on 30 December 1964. Allan J. de Lay, photographer. (PGE collections)

North Fork fish ladder viewing gallery. (PGE collections)

Interior of Lents substation during December 1964 flood. Allan J. de Lay, photographer. (PGE collections)

287

CORPORATE CITIZENSHIP

PGE's difficulties brought on by the weather caused Delzell to reflect in the 1962 *Annual Report* on the company's ability to adapt to changing circumstances and to carry on, in an enhanced fashion, its relationship with the public. He wrote that PGE's adaptability enabled it to survive both a public-utility-district election and the Columbus Day Storm with its reputation intact.[61] He noted the forces arrayed against the utility: sociological, political, ideological. PGE met the challenges arising from those forces by doing two things in its relations with the general public. The first was to maintain an awareness of the changing pattern of corporate ownership. By this Delzell meant "the wide spread of equity capital," as he called it, which had led to the rise of a management class in business as a separate and distinct entity from ownership.

This was not exactly breaking news (Adolphe Berle, Jr., and Gardiner Means had reported the prevalence of the phenomenon thirty years earlier in their classic study, *The Modern Corporation and Private Property*.) But Delzell's acknowledgment of it was still an indication of the self-awareness PGE had come to as a result of its toils since the thirties. It signified the realization that the company could not be run by management for itself or for a small group of controlling stockholders because, by that time, no investor owned more than 2 percent of the PGE common stock.[62] Rather, company policy had to address a wide range of constituencies among customers, the general public, various interest groups, PGE investors, and even government agencies. By the sixties, the utility employed farm-service experts, home economists, fish biologists, area-development coordinators, and government-relations specialists. In its early years, it had operated recreational facilities as an inducement to the public to use its trolley lines, but in the sixties it maintained them as a corporate responsibility to the public. In the summer of 1962 alone, some 336,000 campers, fishers, and picnickers used PGE parks.[63] The earnestness of its commitment to the recreating public was indicated by the fact that in 1962 the U.S. Department of the Interior recognized the company's park program with a special award recognizing its outstanding quality.

But corporate responsibility did not end with well-kept playgrounds, as Delzell recognized. The second response of PGE to its public concerned what he termed the loss of the great personal fortunes that had been built in the late-nineteenth century. As a result, he noted, the philanthropic ethic that had formerly motivated the wealthy individual to give copiously to charitable causes had atrophied. This meant that corporations had to fill the vacuum.[64] Although it was not strictly true that individuals no longer controlled large amounts of money, the thrust of Delzell's argument was well taken. Noblesse oblige, the "gospel of wealth," as espoused by Andrew Carnegie in the late-nineteenth century, was no longer a way of life for the rich. In the late-twentieth-century United States, large-scale personal philanthropy seemed vaguely disreputable and certainly ostentatious to a middle-class society. The burden of public-spiritedness had shifted since the Depression from the individual to large foundations and corporations. For the former, philanthropy was a raison d'etre; for the latter, a way of humanizing and personalizing an otherwise faceless entity. The corporation became not just a local business but a neighbor, in public-relations parlance. When rate raises were required, it was easier for a utility to deal with ratepayers whose children's Little League uniforms were subsidized by the company's largesse. The transaction then appeared more equitable, especially in the case of a utility that extracted a price for an invisible but essential commodity. We take, but we also give back, was the message.

Although Delzell's point was that PGE had responded positively to the recent ethic of corporate philanthropy, ironically, by the latter half of the decade, corporate civic-mindedness was to change drastically and create a dilemma for PGE as well as the other utilities, whose public-spiritedness redounded, strangely, to their detriment then and later.

Since World War II, the utilities had chiseled a niche for themselves in the civic landscape with a policy of relative openhandedness where community activities were concerned. Hillman Lueddemann, Jr., PGE vice president and assistant to the chairman of the board, who over the course of the decade gradually took charge of PGE's charitable activities, was to recall that most large community projects needed the utilities' participation to give them "a certain stamp of approval."[65]

One effect of the company's attempts to permeate the local consciousness with good deeds and neighborliness was seen clearly in the Keizer public-utility-district fight. The decade had barely begun when PGE experienced its first such vote in fifteen years. The election occurred during January 1962 in Keizer, an unincorporated, semirural area on the northern outskirts of Salem. For public-power advocates, Keizer was a test of a recent opinion of the Oregon attorney general that an existing special-service district could distribute electricity. Theoretically, this would simplify the electoral process for partisans of public power, who had always suffered in gaining public approval for PUDs in the state. Keizer's fire district was to be the basis of the PUD. Of the 3,600 electrical customers in the area, some 800 were served by Salem Electric Co-op, 2,800 by PGE. The manager of Salem Electric supported the measure by offering to manage the PUD and provide it with other services under contract. PGE's most potent argument was its century-long record of service to the area. The previous election turnout record was 380, but on 8 January, 842 showed up to vote against the PUD, while 443 voted for it.[66]

The Keizer victory was not an absolute test of the public-relations principle, but given the favorable record of the nearby co-op, it must have seemed to local residents that in retaining PGE they were voting on something other than simple electric service.

Another test of the company's standing within its service area also occurred during the decade. The old competitive relationship between PGE and Northwestern Electric made itself apparent once again. Its solution made for more efficient operations for both PGE and PP&L. At the same time, it integrated PGE's service area in a more coherent fashion.

Through the fifties and into the sixties an expansive PP&L, which, as noted had bought out Northwestern in 1947, engaged in a friendly but fierce turf battle with PGE. The postwar growth of Portland and its eastern suburbs brought the overlapping of territories, since PP&L was on the outskirts while PGE was inside Portland. There arose clashes between representatives of the two companies over new customers in areas of the expanded city that were essentially virgin territory.

Lueddemann was originally hired in 1964 as manager of commercial development, a new position, solely to lead the fight for new residential and especially for new business customers.

289

This occurred when PP&L was found to have signed up the developers of the Lloyd Center. A shopping mall, Lloyd Center was at one time reported to be the largest in the world, but PGE heard about it only when it was announced in the newspapers. Lueddemann, a man with many connections around Portland, was brought in to prevent future embarrassments of that kind and, of course, to bring in new business.

Although in the fifties the contest for customers had been spirited, the better organization and drive Lueddemann brought to the fray heated the race considerably. Lueddemann, whose acquaintances included bankers who gave construction loans, engineers, contractors, suppliers—all kinds of people involved in the construction process—used every resource at his command to develop new business. If a PGE salesperson called from the field with news of activity that might be construed as construction preparation, Lueddemann would work the phone even to the extent of tracking down the owner of the property from the car license number. When he had identified the potential customer, he relayed the intelligence to the salesperson, who would then pay a visit to the individual. As the project might only have been in the planning stage at the time, the customer was frequently taken by surprise. According to Lueddemann, the ensuing conversation usually took the following form, with the PGE employee beginning:

> "I understand that maybe you are interested in some property out on Sandy [for example]."
> "Yeah, we are looking at it. How did you know that?"
> "Well, somebody mentioned it, I can't remember." And so "We like to serve."
> "Well sure, gosh, you are on the ball. If I can do something there, you bet."
> We would sign them up. They [the salespersons] had more fun.[67]

Meanwhile, on the residential front, the competition was literally house to house. "They [PP&L] went down the same [streets] . . . that we did," Lueddemann recalled. "So, your house was on PGE and your next door neighbor was on PP&L, and there was a ferocious fight for every new connect. I mean, we laid awake at night trying to figure out how to sign people up."[68]

Eventually the utilities recognized that a "separation of services" had to be arranged, a view shared by the Portland City Council.[69] Duplication of services, poles, and lines, the creation of safety hazards, and "visual clutter" resulting from the forest of competing lines that went up in certain neighborhoods where both utilities had a presence made further competition absurd. Although ORS 758.400, the so-called "Allocation Law" of 1961, was an attempt by the state legislature to deal with duplication of services by utilities in general, exchanges of territory between the two Portland firms had proceeded only slowly. Not until 1969 did the city council generate a total-exchange resolution. The final transaction, approved by the public utility commissioner on 15 December 1972, gave PP&L essentially the east side of the city and PGE the west side. PGE also got PP&L's district office and territory in Rainier, in Columbia County, and sixteen miles of Columbia River frontage in the county, including the site of PGE's Trojan nuclear plant, which was built in the next decade.[70] At the time of the transaction, some sixteen hundred residential accounts and three hundred commercial and industrial customers were included.[71]

THE CURRENTS OF CHANGE

In a way that Americans began to understand only some years after the fact, society in the United States began to change in about the middle of the sixties. This was partly because of the sense of disillusionment after President Kennedy's assassination in November 1963, partly from growing political, economic, and social complications accompanying the Johnson administration prosecution of the widening war in Vietnam. It also partly resulted from the inevitable exhaustion of postwar American optimism and idealism in the face of such apparently intractable realities as poverty and racism. The change affected the way people regarded government, business, institutions such as universities and churches and their authority, and, for that matter, each other.

PGE was not exempt from this transformation of the national psyche. Ironically, Delzell's retirement in 1965 from the chairmanship and Warren's promotion to chief executive officer would come to reflect the changes in the company and the rest of society. Warren remained president and CEO for twelve years, never bothering, until 1977, to assume chairmanship. He wielded all the power he required from the president's office.

Delzell's own regime was marked by great corporate transformations and growth. But they had come in a vastly different context from the one in which Warren would find himself, and different too from the one in which Griffith had operated. Delzell's experience was, in essence, one of a transitional figure. He had completed much of the important work begun by Griffith. In particular, he solidified the reorganized utility after the bankruptcy of the thirties, regularized relations with BPA, undertook the overhaul of the antiquated transmission and distribution systems, and expanded the company's power supply by negotiation and, whenever possible, construction. In these enterprises, his technical background became less significant than his administrative and financial acumen. Avuncular and unprepossessing, he had nevertheless exerted a strong influence in the utility industry nationally and in the state. He had been president of the Northwest Electric Light and Power Association and a director of the National Association of Manufacturers, and he had served on the board of the Edison Electric Institute, as well as a host of civic organizations. One of the hallmarks of his stewardship of the company came in 1962, when PGE was given the Edison Institute's Edison Award, the utility industry's highest honor. The citation was based on the company's record of preservation of the environment, the creation of attractive recreational areas, and the conservation of fishing interests and water use at its hydroelectric development sites.[72]

Delzell, who died a few years after his retirement, on 20 January 1969, left only a faint personal mark on the utility. This was not because he was a lesser man than Griffith, but because, under him, PGE had become a different company. That fact was a measure of the company's evolution during the middle years of the century. Under Griffith, PGE had been a company. Under Delzell, it became a corporation. In Griffith's day, a few key people and a handful of their subordinates made all major policy decisions. The company's traditional mildly nepotistic hiring policy had made PGE an intimate organization.[73] By the time Warren became president in 1955, that, of necessity, had begun to change. On the business side, finance—particularly in light of the reorganization forced by the difficulties of the thirties and forties, as well as the heavy capital

291

IMAGINE THAT WE COULD COMPRESS the world's population of more than two and a half billion into one town of 1,000 persons in the exact proportions in which the world population is actually divided. In such a town of 1,000 there would be only 60 Americans! And these 60 Americans would receive half the income of the entire town. Only about 330 of the remaining 940 townsfolk would be classified as Christians. Fewer than 100 would be Protestants; some 230 Roman Catholics. At least 80 townspeople would be practicing Communists and 370 others under Communist domination.

The 60 Americans would have an average life expectancy of 70 years; the other 940 less than 40 years. The 60 Americans would have 15 times as many possessions per person as all the rest of their neighbors. The Americans would produce 16 percent of the town's food supply and, although they'd eat 72 percent above the maximum food requirements, they would either eat most of what they grew, or store it for their own further use, at enormous cost. (With most of the 940 non-Americans hungry, the food supply disparity might understandably lead to some ill-feeling.) There would be 53 telephones in this one-town world . . . Americans would have 28 of them. The Americans would also enjoy a disproportionate share of electric power, coal, fuel, steel, and general equipment.

The lowest income group among the Americans would be better off by far than the average of the other townsmen. The 60 Americans and about 200 others representing Western Europe and a few classes in South America, South Africa, Australia, and Japan would be relatively well off, by comparison.

Half of the inhabitants of our one-town world would be ignorant of Jesus Christ, but more than half would have heard, and would continue to hear of Karl Marx, Lenin, Stalin, and Krushchev.

Could this one-town world survive? If you were one of the 60 American townsfolk, what would you do to preserve this tiny world? Chances are you'd be plenty worried about the problem. Chances are you'd do *something*. What do you think it would be?"

Bullseye, March 1963

requirements of postwar construction—had evolved into a large-scale operation requiring higher and higher levels of different expertise. Marketing and sales developed into complex and intensive problems requiring specialized skills, especially with the rise of Northwest Natural Gas Company. Technically, an army of variously skilled engineers and technicians were required to deal with the refinement and expansion of the PGE systems and hydropower installations in the new era.

Elsewhere in the utility's daily existence, ratemaking and economic forecasting took on greater significance than under Griffith, requiring larger staffs. By the sixties, it was no longer possible to get an adequate reading of the economy's direction by consulting the Chamber of Commerce and the *Wall Street Journal*. The advice of trained economists was necessary in order to calibrate the company's response to economic trends and population growth. Government relations and public affairs had, in the postwar period, taken on almost primary importance in PGE's affairs. The company's relationships with BPA, the state agencies and the legislature, the general public, other utilities, and the Congress became preoccupations requiring attention from lobbyists. A full-time presence was maintained by the company in Washington, D.C., beginning with Bob Short (who would eventually rise to the company's chairmanship) in 1955. A growing army of lawyers also became necessary as a plethora of federal, regional, state, and local agencies gained a measure of oversight in the company's activities.

There could be no mistake. In Griffith's day, things were simpler, if nonetheless difficult. Delzell could no more "be" the company in the way that Griffith had "been" PGE, than Dwight Eisenhower, John Kennedy, or Lyndon Johnson could "be" the U.S. Government in the way that even Franklin Roosevelt, who started the trend toward a larger federal establishment, had "been" the government. It was the result of a phenomenon known as modern life. It was a development that overtook many institutions of the postwar world, and it engendered in them—whether they were corporations, government agencies, universities, or churches—a growing impersonality from which many Americans gradually became alienated.

This was Delzell's legacy to Frank Warren. Doing his skillful best, the chairman had brought the small, relatively uncomplicated entity of the early forties into modern corporate maturity. For Warren, this would mean dealing with a public and regulators suspicious of large-scale business, especially those in whose care was a portion of the environment or the public domain. It would prove to be a perilous challenge. Delzell's own bequest was a great accomplishment if an ambivalent inheritance.

NOTES

Chapter 1
Context and Commencement

1. Villard's life and his connections with Oregon are covered in Henry Villard, *Memoirs of Henry Villard*, vol. 2 (Boston: Houghton Mifflin, 1904), *see especially* chs. 39-43. *See also* E. Kimbark MacColl, *Merchants, Money, and Power: The Portland Establishment, 1843-1913* (Portland: The Georgian Press, 1988), 207-213, 220-26, and Gordon B. Dodds, *Oregon: A History* (New York: W.W. Norton, 1977), 136-38, for context.

2. *Oregonian*, 4 September 1880.

3. *Oregonian*, 4 September 1880.

4. Villard, *Memoirs*, 2: 325.

5. Villard, *Memoirs*, 2: 325.

6. Allan Nevins, *John D. Rockefeller*, abridged edition (New York: Charles Scribners Sons, 1959).

7. Howard Mumford Jones, *The Age of Energy, Varieties of American Experience, 1865-1915* (New York: Viking Press, 1970). The author extends his analysis into the twentieth century, seeing the American experience from the end of the Civil War to World War I as of a piece.

8. Vernon L. Parrington, *The Beginnings of Critical Realism in America: 1860-1920* (New York: Harcourt Brace, 1930), 23.

9. Parrington, *Critical Realism*, 26.

10. William Withers, *The Corporations and Social Change* (Woodbury, N.Y.: Barron's Educational Series, 1972), 10-11. For additional background on pre-Civil War American Industry, consult Douglass C. North, *The Economic Growth of the United States, 1790-1860* (New York: W.W. Norton, 1966), 10-11. *See also* chs. 7, 12, and 15.

11. *See* J.B. James, *The Framing of the Fourteenth Amendment* (Urbana: University of Illinois, 1956), and Kenneth M. Stampp, *The Era of Reconstruction, 1865-1877* (New York: Vintage

Books, 1965).

12.　Alexis de Tocqueville, *Democracy in America* (New York: Random House, 1981), 338. *See also* Irving H. Bartlett, *The American Mind in the Mid-Nineteenth Century* (Northbrook, Ill.: AHM Publishers, 1967), 25-29, for a discussion of the sociocultural context in which nineteenth-century scientific investigation was conducted.

13.　Harold G. Vatter, *The Drive to Industrial Maturity: The U.S. Economy, 1860-1914* (Westport, Conn.: Greenwood Press, 1975), 73-74.

14.　*See* Vatter, *Industrial Maturity*, 71-73, for a discussion on linkages in the post-Civil War American economy.

15.　My discussion of electricity and the pioneers of its technology is summarized from Stephen S. Hall, "The Age of Electricity," in *Inventors and Discoverers*, ed. Elizabeth L. Newhouse (Washington, D.C.: National Geographic Society, 1988), 44-79; Margaret Cheney, *Tesla: Man Out of Time* (New York: Laurel Books, 1981), chs. 3-5; and Thomas P. Hughes, *Networks of Power: Electrification in Western Society, 1880-1930* (Baltimore: John Hopkins University Press, 1983), chs. 1-6.

16.　Hughes, *Networks of Power*. 16.

17.　*See* Samuel Gompers, *Seventy Years of Life and Labor*, Nick Salvatore, ed. (New York: ILR Press, 1984), 95-99, for a discussion of the eight-hour movement by a participant; and Harry Braverman, *Labor and Monopoly Capital: The Degradation of Work in the Twentieth Century* (New York: Monthly Review Press, 1974), Parts 1 and 2 for a brilliant discussion of the impact of technological advancement on workers.

18.　Hall, "Age of Electricity," 76.

19.　Henry Adams, *The Education of Henry Adams* (Boston: Houghton Mifflin, 1961), 342.

20.　Richard B. DuBoff, "The Introduction of Electric Power in American Manufacturing," *Economic History Review*, 20 (1967): 515.

21.　Edward Chase Kirkland, *Industry Comes of Age: Business, Labor, and Public Policy, 1860-1897* (Chicago: Quadrangle Books, 1961), 169.

22.　Gordon B. Dodds, *Oregon: A Bicentennial History* (New York: W.W. Norton, 1977), *see* 131-39; *see also* the same author's *The American Northwest: A History of Oregon and Washington* (Arlington Heights, Ill.: The Forum Press, 1986), ch. 8, for a discussion of the regional context of Oregon's economic history in this period; *see also*

Samuel N. Dicken and Emily F. Dicken, *The Making of Oregon: A Study in Historical Geography* (Portland: Oregon Historical Society Press, 1979), ch. 7.

23.　Dodds, *Oregon*, 138.

24.　E. Kimbark MacColl, *The Shaping of a City: Business and Politics in Portland, Oregon, 1885-1915* (Portland: The Georgian Press, 1976), 1.

25.　A projection based on information from MacColl, *Shaping of a City*, 492.

26.　*See* Craig Wollner, "The Willamette River," *Rolling Rivers: An Encyclopedia of America's Rivers*, Richard A. Bartlett, ed. (New York: McGraw-Hill, 1984), 383-86, for a discussion of economic development along the Willamette from earliest white settlement to the late twentieth century.

27.　Wollner, "Willamette River," 384; Orin B. Coldwell, "Early Days of Electricity in Portland," *Oregon Historical Quarterly*, 42 (Winter 1941): 281.

28.　Coldwell, "Early Days," 282.

29.　Coldwell, "Early Days," 282.

30.　Coldwell, "Early Days," 284.

31.　P. Meischer, "Use of Water Power of Willamette Falls, Oregon City" (2 May 1884), 2, unaccessioned files of Portland General Electric Company, hereafter cited as (PGE). Proprietary documents unavailable to the public are labeled (P).

32.　*Oregonian*, 8 July 1907.

33.　Coldwell, "Early Days," 287.

34.　*Oregonian*, 9 April 1885.

35.　Coldwell, "Early Days," 284.

36.　Water rights at Willamette Falls are traced to their earliest sources in white settlement, R.R. Robley, ed. *Compilation of Water Power Rights at Willamette River Falls*, Oregon City, Oregon, vol. 1, Priority Rights 1-14 (Portland: Portland General Electric, 1930). (PGE).

37.　*Oregonian*, 8 July 1907.

38.　See Coldwell, "Early Days," 289-90; and R.R. Robley, *Portland Electric Power Company With Its Predecessor and Subsidiary Companies, 1860-1935* (Portland: Portland General Electric, 1935), 20 (hereafter cited as Robley's *PEPCO*) (PGE).

39.　Coldwell, "Early Days," 289.

40.　Robley, *PEPCO*, 20.

41.　Coldwell, "Early Days," 291.

42. Coldwell, "Early Days," 291; Robley, PEP-CO, 20.

43. Coldwell, "Early Days," 291; Robley, PEP-CO, 20.

44. *Oregonian*, 4 June 1889.

45. *Oregonian*, 4 June 1889.

46. MacColl, *Shaping of a City*, 80.

47. *West Shore* (March 1889), 153.

48. Robley, *PEPCO*, 60.

49. Robley, *PEPCO*, 28.

50. MacColl, *Shaping of a City*. 21. The figures profiled here receive extensive treatment also in MacColl, *Merchants, Money, and Power: The Portland Establishment, 1843-1913* (Portland: The Georgian Press, 1988). This is essentially a revision of *Shaping of a City*, but contains new information and perspectives on the city's business life.

51. MacColl, *Shaping of a City*, 23.

52. *See* John T. Labbe, *Fares, Please! Those Portland Trolley Years* (Caldwell, Idaho: Caxton Printers, Ltd., 1982), for a complete history of the Portland street railways and interurbans. Mac-Coll, *Shaping of a City*, chs. 3 and 5, and Robley, *PEPCO*, ch. 3, also contain extensive discussions of Portland's railway industry, while Robley includes an extensive chart of early mergers and acquisitions in the Portland railway industry.

53. Coldwell, "Early Days," 292; Robley, PEP-CO, 28.

54. Robley, *PEPCO*, 31.

55. George Rogers Taylor, "Building an Interurban Transportation System," *The Urbanization of America: An Historical Anthology*, ed. Allen W. Wakstein, (Boston: Houghton Mifflin, 1970), 149.

56. Robley, *PEPCO*, 29.

57. Kirkland, *Industry Comes of Age*, 239.

58. Kirkland, *Industry Comes of Age*, 239.

59. Kirkland, *Industry Comes of Age*, 242.

60. See MacColl, *Shaping of a City*, appendices N, O, and P, 492-97, for a listing of the city's chief enterprises, associations, and law firms and their participants.

61. *Oregonian*, 4 October 1903.

Chapter 2
The Making of a Monopoly

1. *Bulletin of the Portland General Electric Company* (November 1905) 3.

2. *Bulletin* (November 1905) 12.

3. *See* Samuel Hays, *Conservation and the Gospel of Efficiency*, (New York: Atheneum, 1975), 123-24, for a discussion of the importance of this concept for business of the day.

4. *Oregonian*, 10 March 1895.

5. Arthur H. Greisser, *PGE: History of Portland General Electric Company, 1889-1981* (Portland: Portland General Electric, 1982), 6-7. (PGE).

6. Robley, *PEPCO*, 36.

7. Robley, *PEPCO*, 36; Greisser, *History of Portland General Electric*, 51.

8. Robley, *PEPCO*, 36; Greisser, *History of Portland General Electric*, 51.

9. *Oregonian*, 8 July 1904.

10. *Oregonian*, 8 July 1904.

11. Henry Reed, in an article that was essentially a memoir of Goode, "H.W. Goode: He Made Northwest Lights Shine Brighter," *Oregonian*, 28 April 1935.

12. Thomas Hughes, *Networks of Power: Electrification in Western Society, 1880-1930* (Baltimore, Johns Hopkins University Press, 1983), 77, 163.

13. *Oregonian*, 28 April 1935, Reed article.

14. *Oregonian*, 28 April 1935, Reed article.

15. *Oregonian*, 28 April 1935, Reed article.

16. *Bulletin* (April 1906), 2.

17. *Oregonian*, 28 April 1935, Reed article.

18. *Bulletin* (July 1906), 9-12.

19. *Bulletin* (September 1906), 2.

20. *Bulletin* (September 1906), 3.

21. *Oregonian*, 28 April 1935, Reed article.

22. *Oregonian*, 18 April 1935, Reed article.

23. Carl Abbott, *The Great Extravaganza: Portland and the Lewis and Clark Exposition* (Portland: Oregon Historical Society Press, 1981) 15, and throughout for a complete discussion of the event. MacColl, *Shaping of a City*, 261-70 and passim is also good on the fair.

24. Howard Mumford Jones, *The Age of Energy: Varieties of American Experience 1865-1915* (New York: Viking Press, 1970), 279-80 is good, if brief, on the cultural significance of the major fairs of the age; Gilman Ostrander, *American Civilization in the First Machine Age, 1890-1940* (New York: Harper & Row, 1970), 3-4, gives some insight into the American fascination with technological advancement as a motivation for staging such events. The ambivalence of much of nine-

teenth-century America toward technology as viewed at these occasions is classically exposed in Henry Adams, *The Education of Henry Adams* (Boston: Houghton Mifflin, 1961), chs. 22 and 25.

25. Abbott, *Great Extravaganza*, 14.

26. MacColl, *Shaping of a City*, 264, 266; Abbott, *Great Extravaganza*, 20; Gaston, Joseph, *Portland, Oregon, Its History and Builders* (Portland, S.J. Clarke, 1911) 1:583.

27. Lewis and Clark Exposition Collection, Board of Directors' correspondence file, Box 6, Oregon Historical Society.

28. Lewis and Clark Exposition Collection, Board of Directors' correspondence file, Box 6, Oregon Historical Society.

29. Lewis and Clark Exposition Collection, Board of Directors' correspondence file, Box 6, Oregon Historical Society.

30. *Bulletin* (September 1905), 2.

31. *Bulletin* (September 1905), 2.

32. Fred Lockley, *History of the Columbia River Valley from The Dalles to the Sea* (Portland: S.J. Clarke, 1928), 2: 7.

33. Abbott, *Great Extravaganza*, 69.

34. Harold G. Vatter, *The Drive to Industrial Mautrity: U.S. Economy 1860-1914* (Westport, Conn.: Greenwood Press, 1975) 186-87. *See also* Thomas Cochrane, *Basic History of American Business* (Princeton: Van Nostrand, 1959), 46, for an overview of the evolution of the American businessman. Abbott also offers comments in *Great Extravaganza*, 74, on this phenomenon as it bears on the exposition.

35. *Oregonian*, 28 April 1935.

36. Portland General Electric Bylaws and Minutes of Stockholders' and Directors' Meetings of Portland Consolidated Railway Company, 1904. Quoted from meeting on 13 October 1904. Minutes of the Board of Directors' Meetings (December 1904), 79 (PGE)(P).

37. *St. Johns Review*, 26 February 1981, 6.

38. "Report of Audits," 31 December 1906, (PGE)(P).

39. "Report of Audits," 31 December 1907, PGE Files, PGE History Collections. (PGE)(P).

40. Lockley, *Columbia River Valley*, 2:7.

41. Greisser, *History of Portland General Electric*, 12.

42. *Oregonian*, 4 May 1906.

43. Richard Hofstadter, *The Age of Reform*

(New York: Vintage books, 1955), 164. *See also* Vatter, *Industrial Maturity*, 188-89.

44. Vatter, *Industrial Maturity*, 175-76.

45. Portland General Electric Company, "Generation, Receipts, Deliveries, and Net System Load," 18 February 1978: 1, a document compiled specifically for this project by the PGE engineering staff. (PGE).

46. Portland Railway Light and Power (hereafter used as PRL&P) Prospectus, "A Traction Stock with a Future," (1911), 10.

47. Robley, *PEPCO*, 117.

48. Vatter, *Industrial Maturity*, 186.

49. *Oregonian*, 4 May 1906.

50. James Weinstein, *The Corporate Ideal in the Liberal State 1900-1918* (Boston: Beacon Press, 1968), 71.

51. Weinstein, *Corporate Ideal*, 71. *See also* Hofstadter, *Age of Reform*, 237-38, and John Morton Blum, *The Republican Roosevelt* (New York: Atheneum, 1974), 108-10 and 115-23 for insight into the conservative-Progressive fear of big business.

52. John T. Labbe, *Fares, Please!*, 108.

53. Robley, *PEPCO*, 81.

54. Robley, *PEPCO*, 84.

55. Labbe, *Fares, Please!*, 26.

56. Labbe, *Fares, Please!*, 68.

Chapter 3
The Annals of Bigness

1. MacColl, *Shaping of a City: Business and Politics in Portland, Oregon, 1885-1915* (Portland: The Georgian Press, 1976), 10.

2. MacColl, *Shaping of a City*, 368.

3. MacColl, *Shaping of a City*, 1.

4. *Oregon Journal*, 15 September 1908.

5. *Oregon Journal*, 15 September 1908.

6. *Oregon Journal*, 26 March 1908.

7. *Oregon Journal*, 26 March 1908, 2, 27 March 1908.

8. *Oregon Journal*, 5 April 1908.

9. *Oregon Journal*, 5 April 1908.

10. *Oregon Journal*, 5 April 1908.

11. *Oregon Journal*, 7 April 1908.

12. *Oregon Journal*, 8 April 1908.

13. *Oregon Journal*, 8 April 1908.

14. *Oregon Journal*, 8 April 1908.

15. *Oregon Journal*, 24 November 1908.

16. *Oregon Journal*, 22 December 1908.

17. *Oregon Journal*, 30 December 1908.
18. *Oregon Journal*, 30 December 1908.
19. *Oregon Journal*, 30 December 1908.
20. *Oregon Journal*, 24 December 1908.
21. *Oregon Journal*, 31 December 1908.
22. *Oregon Journal*, 15 January 1909.
23. Labbe, *Fares, Please!*, 21.
24. *Public Service*, PRL&P, April 1907, 9.
25. *PRL&P Bulletin* 2(February 1906); *Oregon Journal*, 2 May 1908.
26. *PRL&P Bulletin* 3(March 1906); *Oregon Journal*, 10 May 1908.
27. *PRL&P Bulletin*, 4(April 1906); *Oregon Journal*, 18 May 1908.
28. *PRL&P Bulletin*, 6(June 1906); *Oregon Journal*, 21 June 1908.
29. *Oregonian*, 29 March 1913.
30. *Oregon Journal*, 29 March 1913.
31. *Evening Telegram*, 29 March 1913.
32. See PRL&P's annual reports, 1915-20. The handful of owners and the number of their shares are listed.
33. Charles M. Clark to Benage S. Josselyn, 21 October 1911, (PGE) (P).
34. Franklin T. Griffith "Biography" (PGE); *Oregonian*, 7 September 1916.
35. E. Kimbark MacColl, *The Growth of a City: Power and Politics in Portland, Oregon, 1915-1950* (Portland: The Georgian Press, 1979), 119, and Franklin T. Griffith, Papers, Scrapbook No. 1, 1913-17 (Portland: Oregon Historical Society), 6-7.
36. Herbert Croly, *The Promise of American Life* (New York: Capricorn Books, 1964), 374.
37. Labbe, *Fares, Please!*, 22.
38. *Portland City Club Bulletin*, 1, (1 July 1921): 3.
39. *Portland Carman*, 5 (February 1912): 5-10.
40. Robley, *PEPCO*, 154.
41. Robley, *PEPCO*, 154.
42. *PRL&P Annual Report*, 1915, 7.
43. Robley, *PEPCO*, 164-65; *PRL&P Annual Report*, 31 December 1915, 7.
44. *PRL&P Annual Report*, 1920, 7.
45. Carlos Schwantes, "The West Adapts the Automobile: Technology, Unemployment and the Jitney Phenomenon of 1914-17," *Western Historical Quarterly*, 16 (July 1985): 313.
46. *PRL&P Annual Report*, 31 December 1915, 7.
47. The problem of "bigness" in business as a panacea had been hotly debated in the United States since at least the turn of the century. It was a live issue in public discourse in such works as Croly's *Promise of American Life*, in the work of such social refomers as Louis Brandeis, and in the presidential election of 1912. While bigness had many advocates in the business community, some thoughtful individuals like Griffith had come to realize that it was a flawed technique of development and, indeed, a double-edged sword. *See* Harold G. Vatter, *The Drive to Industrial Maturity: U.S. Economy, 1860-1914* (Westport, Conn.: Greenwood Press, 1975), 170-80, for a discussion of the economics and mechanics of bigness at the time. Arthur S. Link's *Woodrow Wilson and the Progressive Era, 1900-1917*, (New York: Harper & Brothers, 1954), esp. chs. 1-3 and Blum, *The Republican Roosevelt*, are excellent for an overview of the two main protagonists in the debate.
48. *PRL&P Annual Report*, 1914, 5.
49. *PRL&P Annual Report*, 1915, 4.
50. *PRL&P Annual Report*, 1914, 5.
51. *PRL&P Annual Report*, 1915, 5.
52. *PRL&P Annual Report*, 1916, 4.
53. *PRL&P Annual Report*, 1916, 5-6.
54. Schwantes, "The West Adapts the Automobile," 313.
55. *PRL&P Annual Report*, 1915, 6, on the Supreme Court decision as interpreted by Griffith; *PRL&P Annual Report*, 1916, 6.
56. *PRL&P Annual Report*, 1917, 7.
57. *PRL&P Annual Report*, 1917, 8.
58. *PRL&P Annual Report*, 1917, 8.
59. *PRL&P Annual Report*, 1916, 5.
60. *PRL&P Annual Report*, 1917, 8.
61. *See* Claude R. Lester Papers, "Investigations of Public Utilities" (Eugene: University of Oregon Special Collections Library Boxes; 1-3). *See* MacColl, *Growth of a City*, 119-30.
62. MacColl, *Growth of a City*, 123.
63. *PRL&P Annual Report*, 1917, 8.
64. MacColl, *Growth of a City*, 130.
65. *PRL&P Annual Report*, 1919, 7.
66. *PRL&P Annual Report*, 1919, 6.
67. *PRL&P Annual Report*, 1918, 10.
68. *PRL&P Annual Report*, 1918, 9.
69. *PRL&P Annual Report*, 1919, 8.
70. *PRL&P Annual Report*, 1919, 8.
71. *PRL&P Annual Report*, 1919, erratum following p. 8.
72. *PRL&P Annual Report*, 1919, 12.

Chapter 4
The Hard Lessons of Prosperity

1.   George E. Mowry and Blaine A. Brownell, *The Urban Nation: 1920-1980* (New York: Hill & Wang, 1981), 3.

2.   William Leuchtenburg, *Perils of Prosperity: 1914-1932* (Chicago: University of Chicago Press, 1958) 130, 190-191.

3.   Portland General Electric Company "History of PGE Rates, Residential Service, 1908-1987," prepared by the PGE rates staff specifically for this project, 1988, (PGE).

4.   Frederick Bracher, "How It Was Then: The Pacific Northwest in the Twenties," Part 2, *Oregon Historical Quarterly*, 85 (Spring 1984):51-52.

5.   Bracher, "How It Was Then," 51-52.

6.   Bracher, "How It Was Then," 51-52.

7.   Bracher, "How It Was Then," 39.

8.   Bracher, "How It Was Then," 39.

9.   Bracher, "How It Was Then," 39.

10. Bracher, "How It Was Then," 39.

11. *PRL&P Annual Report*, 1928, 4-5.

12. Robley, *PEPCO*, 207.

13. *PRL&P Annual Report*, 1920, 9; *PRL&P Annual Report*, 1921, 8; *PRL&P Annual Report*, 1922, 10

14. *PRL&P Annual Report*, 1923, 9.

15. *PRL&P Annual Report*, 1926, 7.

16. *PRL&P Annual Report*, 1921, 8.

17. *PRL&P Annual Report*, 1922, 9-10.

18. *PRL&P Annual Report*, 1926, 7.

19. *PRL&P Annual Report*, 1925, 11-13.

20. *PRL&P Annual Report*, 1925, 13.

21. *PRL&P Annual Report*, 1925, 13.

22. *PRL&P Annual Report*, 1925, 13.

23. *PRL&P Annual Report*, 1926, 8.

24. *PRL&P Annual Report*, 1927, 7.

25. *PRL&P Annual Report*, 1925, 13.

26. *PRL&P Annual Report*, 1925, 13.

27. Robley, *PEPCO*, 183-84.

28. Robley, *PEPCO*, 190.

29. Robley, *PEPCO*, 187.

30. *PRL&P Annual Report*, 1919, 9.

31. *PRL&P Annual Report*, 1920, 7.

32. *PRL&P Annual Report*, 1920, 7.

33. *PRL&P Annual Report*, 1920, 8.

34. *PRL&P Annual Report*, 1921, 6-7.

35. *PRL&P Annual Report*, 1921, 7.

36. *PRL&P Annual Report*, 1922, 8.

37. *PRL&P Annual Report*, 1922, 7-8.

38. *PRL&P Annual Report*, 1922, 8.

39. *PRL&P Annual Report*, 1923, 10.

40. *PRL&P Annual Report*, 1923, 10.

41. *PRL&P Annual Report*, 1924, 13.

42. *PRL&P Annual Report*, 1924, 15.

43. *PRL&P Annual Report*, 1924, 15.

44. *PRL&P Annual Report*, 1924, 15.

45. *PRL&P Annual Report*, 1925, 17.

46. *PRL&P Annual Report*, 1925, 17.

47. *PRL&P Annual Report*, 1925, 19.

48. *PRL&P Annual Report*, 1926, 9.

49. *PRL&P Annual Report*, 1927, 7.

50. *PRL&P Annual Report*, 1928, 5.

51. *See* William Leuchtenburg, *Perils of Prosperity*, 245-271.

52. *PRL&P Annual Report*, 1929, 4.

53. *PEPCO Synchronizer* 1 (January 1926): 10.

54. *PEPCO Synchronizer* 1 (May 1926): 23.

55. *PEPCO Synchronizer* 1 (April 1926):14. Other *Synchronizer* notes relevant to this section are 1 (May 1926):23; 2 (February 1927):15; 1 (December 1926):9; 4 (December 1928):3-5, 8; and 1 (May 1926): 23.

56. *Portland Carman* 2 (11 July 1910): 17.

57. *PEPCO Synchronizer* 1 (June 1926): 2.

58. *PEPCO Synchronizer* 1 (November 1925): 3.

59. *PEPCO Synchronizer* 1 (November 1925): 4.

60. Arthur H. Bone, ed., *Oregon Cattleman/Governor/Congressman: The Memoirs and Times of Walter M. Pierce* (Portland: Oregon Historical Society Press, 1981), 252-53 and passim, for the views of a leading Oregon Progressive of the day on the power companies. Pierce's anti-utility bias was ferocious. When he won the position of Democratic national committeeman in 1930 against another former governor and fellow Progressive, Oswald West, who had at one time lobbied for PEPCO, he suggested that West "resign from the Democratic party and join the Republicans and that he be branded GOP on one buttock and PEP on the other, 'so that he may be recognized and properly classified from either direction.'" *See also* Gordon B. Dodds, *The American Northwest: A History of Oregon and Washington* (Arlington Heights: Forum Press, 1986).

61. Robert Heilbroner, *The Making of Economic Society* (Englewood Cliffs, NJ: Prentice-Hall, 1962), 117.

62. Dodds, *American Northwest*, 211; Dorothy

O. Johansen and Charles M. Gates, *Empire of the Columbia: A History of the Pacific Northwest,* (New York: Harper & Row, 1967), 520.

63. Dodds, *American Northwest,* 228.

64. Johansen, *Empire of the Columbia,* 520.

65. "History of of PGE Rates."

66. Johansen, *Empire of the Columbia,* 520.

67. R.R. Robley, "Memorandum to Team Captains Division C" (2 February 1927) (PGE).

68. *Portland Electric Power Company, Annual Report,* 1929, 13.

69. Puget Sound Power and Light Company, "The Truth about Rural Electric Rates in Ontario: Photographic Facts from Official Records. . . .," (1930) (PGE).

70. Proposed Amendment for the Oregon Constitution: Water and Power Development," (PGE).

71. "The Czarists of Oregon," Water and Power Board Measure File, (1926), (PGE).

72. "The Czarists of Oregon." (PGE).

73. *PEPCO Synchronizer* 3 (March 1928): 3.

74. *PEPCO Synchronizer* 3 (March 1928): 4.

75. *PEPCO Synchronizer* 2 (December 1926): 13.

76. *PEPCO Synchronizer* 3 (March 1928): 5.

77. *PEPCO Synchronizer* 2 (March 1928): 2.

78. *Oregon Journal,* 11 March 1928.

79. *Oregon Journal,* 11 March 1928.

80. Portland *Telegram,* 27 March 1928.

81. *PEPCO Synchronizer* 3 (April 1928): 2.

Chapter 5
The Perilous Years

1. John Kenneth Galbraith, *The Great Crash* (New York: Avon Books, 1980), is an excellent synopsis and analysis of the collapse of the financial markets. I have referred to it extensively for the overview presented here.

2. Dorothy O. Johansen, *Empire of the Columbia: A History of the Pacific Northwest* (New York: Harper & Row, 1967), 501.

3. E. Kimbark MacColl, *Growth of a City* (Portland: The Georgian Press, 1979), 453.

4. Craig Wollner, *The City Builders: One Hundred Years of Union Carpentry in Portland, Oregon, 1883-1983* (Portland: Oregon Historical Society Press, forthcoming), 100.

5. MacColl, *Growth of a City,* 401-2.

6. Portland General Electric Company, "Generation, Receipts, Deliveries and Net System Load," 18 February 1978 (PGE).

7. PGE "Generation Receipts" *To The Stockholders For The Year Ended December 31, 1933,* Portland, 1934.

8. *Portland Electric Power Company Annual Report* (14 March 1934): 2.

9. Franklin Griffith, "Memorandum to All Employees [on pay cuts]" (30 April 1933) (PGE).

10. Griffith, "Memorandum."

11. Griffith, "Memorandum."

12. Thomas P. Hughes, *Networks of Power* (Baltimore: John Hopkins University Press, 1983), 393 and ch. 12; and Forest McDonald, *Insull* (Chicago: University of Chicago Press, 1962), especially chs. 9-12 for an understanding of the rationale of the holding company in the utility industry.

13. Galbraith, *Great Crash,* 39.

14. Robert Heilbroner, *The Making of Economic Society* (Englewood Cliffs, NJ: Prentice-Hall, 1962), 144.

15. Franklin T. Griffith, "Ten Year Story on PEPCO Finances With Respect to Public Utility Holding Company, Central Public Service System, Chase National Banks, Harris Forbes and Company, and the Shareholders, 1929-1939" (July 1939), Portland General Electric Company files, Transfer File 3, Miscellaneous correspondence relating to reorganization folder, University of Oregon, Eugene. I have taken the liberty of entitling this document because of its importance in understanding PGE' finances in this period. It appears to be an extensive recapitulation of Griffith's knowledge of the events surrounding the merger of PEPCO and Central Public Service and the subsequent bankruptcy. A loose note in the folder in Griffith's hand, addressed to "Mr. D.," refers to the "Ten Year Story," apparently the report cited, hence my title. In connection with the bankruptcy and subsequent reorganization, *see also* "Memorandum to File" by W. Stevens Tucker, attorney for the Securities and Exchange Commission, 3 October 1934. This document summarizes Stevens' findings for the SEC regarding the PEPCO reorganization plan. It differs somewhat from Griffith's account, especially regarding the PEPCO management's motivations in constructing their plan and their representations of its efficacy to stockholders. *See* Transfer File 4, "SEC Report on Committees and Conflicts of Interest" folder, PGE files, University of Oregon. "Testimony of

Franklin T. Griffith, May 21, 1942," in U.S. District Court in PEPCO's petition (No. B-23986), reiterates Griffith's view of events in the thirties. *See* Transfer File 3, "Petitions and Court Orders Relating to PEPCO," PGE files, University of Oregon. *See also* Griffith's letter to J.S. Clark of 23 December 1933 on Central Gas in Transfer File 3. I have relied substantially on Griffith's version of events because although doubt was from time to time cast on his motives and on the outcome, no court or administrative body ever disciplined him or PEPCO officers who acted with him in the bankruptcy and reorganization periods, while his account of the time remains the most complete.

16. Griffith, "Ten Year Story," 1.
17. Griffith, "Ten Year Story," 1-2.
18. Griffith, "Ten Year Story," 2.
19. Griffith, "Ten Year Story," 4-5.
20. Griffith, "Ten Year Story," 5.
21. Griffith, "Ten Year Story," 12.
22. Griffith, "Ten Year Story," 7.
23. Griffith, "Ten Year Story," 6.
24. Griffith, "Ten Year Story," 8.
25. Griffith, "Ten Year Story," 12.
26. Griffith, "Ten Year Story," 7.
27. Griffith, "Ten Year Story," 9-10.
28. Griffith, "Ten Year Story," 13.
29. Griffith, "Ten Year Story," 14.
30. Griffith, "Ten Year Story," 15.
31. MacColl, *Growth of a City*, 431-32.; Griffith, "Ten Year Story," 15.
32. Griffith, "Ten Year Story," 16.
33. Griffith, "Ten Year Story," 19.
34. Griffith, "Ten Year Story," 20.
35. Griffith, "Ten Year Story," 21.
36. Griffith, "Ten Year Story," 22-3.
37. Griffith, "Ten Year Story," 23.
38. Griffith, "Ten Year Story," 24.
39. "Franklin T. Griffith is on the Spot," *Oregon Voter* 70(27 August 1932):9, 24-25.
40. MacColl, *Growth of a City*, 434.
41. Griffith, "Ten Year Story," 24. *See also Pacific Northwest Public Service Company Annual Report to the Stockholders for the Year Ended December 31, 1932* (hereafter referred to as PNPS), 15 March 1933, 4-5.
42. Griffith, "Ten Year Story," 24.
43. MacColl, *Growth of a City*, 435.
44. MacColl, *Growth of a City*, 435.
45. *Oregonian*, 19 December 1932.
46. Griffith, "Ten Year Story," 31; *see also Oregonian*, 27 March 1935; and "PEPCO Crisis," *Oregon Voter*, 76 (17 February 1934), 16-20.
47. Griffith, "Ten Year Story," 33.
48. *PNPS Annual Report to the Stockholders for the Year Ended December 31, 1931* (1 April 1931), 3.
49. *PNPS Annual Report, 1931*, 3.
50. *Portland Electric Power Company Annual Report to the Stockholders for the Year Ended December 31, 1934* (15 July 1935), 3.
51. *Portland Electric Power Company Annual Report to the Stockholders for the Year Ended December 31, 1935* (29 April 1936), 2.
52. *PEPCO Annual Report, 1935*, 2; *PNPS Annual Report, 1931*, 3.
53. Portland General Electric Company "History of PGE Rates, Residential Service, 1908-1987." 1988 (PGE).
54. PGE, "Generation, Receipts."
55. *PNPS Annual Report, 1930*, 4-5.
56. *PNPS Annual Report, 1932*, 4-5.
57. Refer to PNPS and PEPCO annual reports, 1930-39, for yearly figures. The number presented here is the total for all the years of the decade.
58. *PEPCO Annual Report, 1935*, 2.
59. *Portland Electric Power Company Annual Report for the Year Ended December 31, 1937* (27 April 1938, 3.
60. Gus Norwood, *Columbia River Power for the People* (Washington, D.C.: U.S. Government Printing Office, 1981), 26.
61. *Oregon Journal*, 22 September 1932; Norwood, *Columbia River Power*, 26.
62. *See* Stewart Holbrook, *The Columbia* (New York: Holt, Rinehart & Winston, 1965), ch. 16, for a discussion of the origins of the first scheme to control the Columbia; Norwood, *Columbia River Power*, ch. 2; Gene Tollefson, *BPA and the Struggle for Power at Cost* (Portland: Bonneville Power Administration, 1987), ch. 13; and Daniel M. Ogden, Jr., "The Development of Federal Power Policy in the Pacific Northwest" (Ph.D. diss., University of Chicago, 1949), chs. 1-5, offers information on the federal role in securing dams on the Columbia. Ogden may provide the single most detailed description of the process to be found anywhere).
63. *See* Norwood, *Columbia River Power*, 43-44, for a good synopsis of the issue; Ogden, "Federal Power Policy," ch. 5, especially 145-55; and Philip Funigiello, *Toward A National Power Poli-*

cy, *The New Deal and the Electric Utility Industry, 1933-1941* (Pittsburgh: University of Pittsburgh Press, 1973), ch. 7, for detailed discussions of the role of the u.s. Army Corps of Engineers in Columbia River power planning, esp. the legislative phase.

64. Funigiello, *National Power Policy*, 174. Funigiello and Ogden provide the basis for the information given in this section. Norwood and Tollefson are less detailed, but can give the interested reader some insight into the development of regional power policy in the Pacific Northwest in the New Deal era. MacColl, *Growth of a City*, 436-48 offers a perspective specific to Portland. Other works of note are Roy Bessey, *Pacific Northwest Regional Planning: A Review* (Olympia: State of Washington, 1963), 30-35; Charles McKinley, *Uncle Sam in the Pacific Northwest* (Berkeley and Los Angeles: University of California Press, 1952), 157-68; Herman Voeltz, "Genesis and Development of a Regional Power Agency," *Pacific Northwest Quarterly*, 53 (April 1962), 65-78; u.s. Cong. House. *Hearings on HR 7642.* 75th Cong., 1st sess., 1937; and articles from the Portland newspapers of the period 1933-39. William Leuchtenburg, *Franklin D. Roosevelt and the New Deal, 1932-1940* (New York: Harper & Row, 1963) provides a standard overview of the Roosevelt presidency in the thirties.

65. Gordon B. Dodds, *American Northwest: A History of Oregon and Washington* (Arlington Heights, IL: Forum Press, 1986), 229.

66. Dodds, *American Northwest,* 229; Funigiello, *National Power Policy*, 175.

67. Funigiello, *National Power Policy*, 177.

68. Funigiello, *National Power Policy*, 179-80.

69. Funigiello, *National Power Policy*, 181.

70. *PEPCO Annual Report, 1933,* 4. Ironically, PEPCO had made borings and preliminary plans as early as 1929 for a dam of its own near the eventual site of Bonneville. The project was dropped because of the prohibitive cost. For a discussion of this episode, *see* William F. Willingham, *Waterpower in the "Wilderness": The History of the Bonneville Lock and Dam* (Portland: u.s. Army Corps of Engineers, 1987), 1.

71. *PEPCO Annual Report, 1933,* 5.

72. *PEPCO Annual Report, 1933,* 5.

73. "We'll Build Our Own Prosperity," *PEPCO Synchronizer,* 1 (6 January 1934).

74. *Portland Electric Power Company Annual Report to the Stockholders for the Year Ended December 31, 1936* (21 April 1937), 3.

75. Funigiello, *National Power Policy,* 184.

76. Funigiello, *National Power Policy,* 193-94.

77. Funigiello, *National Power Policy,* 194.

78. Funigiello, *National Power Policy,* 195.

79. *PEPCO Annual Report, 1937,* 4.

80. Franklin T. Griffith, "Address by Mr. Franklin T. Griffith Before the Chamber of Commerce of Oregon City, Oregon, Tuesday, March 29, 1938," 9-10 (PGE).

81. Wesley Arden Dick, "Visions of Abundance: The Public Power Crusade in the Pacific Northwest in the Era of J. D. Ross and the New Deal" (Ph.D. diss., University of Washington, 1973), 304.

82. *PEPCO Annual Report, 1937,* 5.

83. *Oregonian,* 1 December 1938. The intensive public relations offensive PEPCO undertook in the 1938 campaign yielded a blizzard of flyers, broadsides, advertisements, and editorials. "Facts on the PUD Scheme: Compare Your Present Bonneville Bargain With the 8 PUD Risks" for example, charged that "Risk No. 1" was the "Creation of a New Tax-Levying Body," "Risk No. 2" promised "$79,380 New Taxes Every Year for Five Years," and so forth. (PGE).

84. *Oregonian,* 1 October 1937.

85. Quoted in Dick, "Visions of Abundance," 305.

86. *PEPCO Annual Report, 1937,* 5.

87. Griffith, "Address," 34-5.

88. Griffith, "Address," 35.

89. J.E. Hedges in Griffith, "Address," 2.

90. Funigiello, *National Power Policy* is particularly clear on this point. *See* 186-88, 193-94, and 259. *See also* Leuchtenberg, *FDR and the New Deal,* 336, for a succinct summary of the New Deal's general approach to private enterprise.

91. Leuchtenburg, *FDR and the New Deal,* 336, forcefully makes this point.

92. Arthur H. Greisser, *History of Portland General Electric,* 89.

93. Greisser, *History of Portland General Electric,* 89.

94. *PEPCO Annual Report, 1933,* 6.

95. *PEPCO Annual Report, 1933,* 6.

96. George E. Mowry and Blaine A. Brownell, *The Urban Nation: 1920-1980,* 85-86.

97. *PEPCO Annual Report, 1933,* 6.

98. *PEPCO Annual Report, 1934,* 4.

99. *PEPCO Annual Report, 1934*, 4.

100. Carey and Harlan, "Traction Plan," 20 January 1930, 5 (PGE).

101. Carey and Harlan, "Traction Plan" and "Report to Mayor and Council," 1930, 89 (PGE).

102. Carey and Harlan, "Traction Plan," 8-9. *See also* Labbe, *Fares, Please!*, ch. 11, for a narrative and pictorial overview of the PEPCO trolley years.

103. "Rejection of Carey and Harlan Traction Plan Recommended by Committee, *City Club Bulletin*, 11 (30 January 1931): 1.

104. City Club, "Rejection of Carey and Harlan Plan," 13.

105. Portland *Telegram*, 23 January 1930.

106. Portland *Telegram*, 19 February 1930.

107. Portland *Telegram*, 3 March 1930.

108. *Oregonian*, 9 March 1930.

109. Portland *Telegram*, 6 March 1930.

110. *PEPCO Annual Report, 1934*, 4.

111. *PEPCO Annual Report, 1934*, 4.

112. *PEPCO Annual Report, 1935*, 3.

113. *PEPCO Annual Report, 1937*, 3-4.

114. *PEPCO Annual Report, 1937*, 4.

115. *Portland General Electric Company Annual Report to the Stockholders for the Year Ended December 31, 1939*, 1.

116. *See Oregonian* and *Oregon Journal*, 5 January 1939.

Chapter 6
A Hazard of Old Fortunes

1. Arthur H. Greisser, *History of Portland General Electric Company*, 102. *See also* Portland General Electric Company *Synchronizer*.

2. Greisser, *PGE: History of Portland General Electric Company*, 102.

3. Court order, 19 March 1939.

4. Greisser, *PGE: History of Portland General Electric Company*, 103.

5. *Oregon Journal*, 16 February 1940.

6. *Oregon Journal*, 10 February 1940.

7. Jonathan Daniels, "Pearl Harbor Sunday: The End of an Era, 1919-1941," in *The Aspirin Age*, ed. Isabel Leighton, (New York: Simon and Schuster, 1949), 48.

8. *Portland General Electric Company Annual Report to the Stockholders for the Year Ended December 31, 1941* (2 March 1942), 10.

9. *PGE Annual Report, 1941*, 10.

10. *Portland General Electric Company Annual Report, 1942*, (10 March 1943), 1.

11. *PGE Annual Report, 1942*, 13.

12. *PGE Annual Report, 1944*, 1.

13. Richard Polenberg, *War and Society* (New York: J.B. Lippincott, 1972), 30.

14. "91% of Portland General Electric Company Employees Sign for War Bonds," *Bullseye* (November 1942): 3.

15. "Employees Sign for War Bonds," *Bullseye*, 4.

16. "Getting Along Without," *Bullseye* (June 1944): 9.

17. *See* Frederic C. Lane, Blanche D. Coll, et al., *Ships for Victory: A History of Shipbuilding Under the U.S. Maritime Commission in World War II* (Baltimore: Johns Hopkins University Press, 1951), 204, for comments on spread of production in the Kaiser yards, and 154 and passim for comments on the importance of electrical power to the wartime shipbuilding enterprise.

18. "Armada Built with Portland General Electric Company War Power," *Bullseye* (June 1944): 1.

19. "To The Wars: Enough Copper for a Line from Portland to Juneau," *Bullseye* (November 1942): 3.

20. Portland General Electric Company, "Generation, Receipts, Deliveries, and Net System Load," 18 February 1978.

21. *Portland General Electric Company 1945 Annual Report*, (1 June 1946). The 1944 *Annual Report* listed 215 employees in military service.

22. Stone and Webster Service Corporation "Report on Portland General Electric Company" (5 June 1941), 26-27 (PGE).

23. Stone and Webster, "Report on Portland General Electric" 26.

24. James H. Polhemus "Modern Trolley Coach Operation," paper delivered to the American Transit Association in Los Angeles, 1937 (PGE).

25. Polhemus, "Modern Trolley Coach Operation," *see* 1-4.

26. John T. Labbe, *Fares, Please!*, 148.

27. Greisser, *History of Portland General Electric*, 106.

28. Bob Lee, interview with the author, 26 January 1988, Oregon Historical Society Sound Recording Archive, hereafter cited as OHS/SRA.

29. *Portland General Electric Company 1940*

Annual Report (31 March 1941), 11.
30. *PGE Annual Report,* 1940, 10-11.
31. *PGE Annual Report,* 1940, 5.
32. *PGE Annual Report,* 1940, 5-6.
33. Portland General Electric Company, "Residential Service, 1908-1987" (PGE).
34. Frank Warren, interview with the author, 23 December 1987 OHS/SRA.
35. Portland General Electric Company, "History of PGE Rates, Residential Service, 1908-83" (PGE).
36. *PGE Annual Report,* 1940, 4.
37. *PGE Annual Report,* 1940, 9.
38. *PGE Annual Report,* 1941, 4.
39. "Residential Service, 1908-87."
40. *PGE Annual Report,* 1941, 10.
41. *PGE Annual Report,* 1941, 13.
42. *PGE Annual Report,* 1945, 4.
43. *PGE Annual Report,* 1946, (1 June 1947), 2.
44. *Portland General Electric Company 1947 Annual Report* (1 June 1948), 13.
45. *Portland General Electric Company 1948 Annual Report* (11 February 1949), 9.
46. Stone and Webster, "Report," 6.
47. Stone and Webster, "Report," 6.
48. Funigiello, *National Power Policy,* 211-17. *See also* Funigiello "Kilowatts for Defense—The New Deal and the Coming of the Second World War," *Journal of American History* 56 (December 1969), 614 ff. Funigiello's work on the issue of Banks transition period and the early days of Raver's administration is the most complete and objective account. I have based my description on his research.
49. Funigiello, *National Power Policy,* 217-18, and "Kilowatts for Defense," 214.
50. Dick, "Visions of Abundance," 304.
51. See PGE annual reports for 1940, 1941, 1942, and 1944 Annual Reports for an overview of rate reductions.
52. Stone and Webster, "Report," 6-7.
53. Alan Hart interview with Jim Strassmaier, 20 May 1986 (OHS/SRA).
54. *PGE Annual Report,* 1940, 14.
55. *Refer to* Funigiello *National Power Policy,* Dick, "Visions of Abundance," and Herman C. Voeltz, "Proposals for a Columbia Valley Authority: A History of Political Controversy" (Ph.D. diss., University of Oregon, 1960).
56. *Portland General Electric Company 1949 Annual Report,* (15 February 1950), 14.
57. Dick, "Visions of Abundance," 384.
58. Funigiello *National Power Policy,* 220. *See also* Voeltz "Proposals for a Columbia Valley Authority," and Dick "Visions of Abundance."
59. Funigiello, *National Power Policy,* 215-16.
60. Franklin T. "Address Before the Progressive Business Man's Club of Portland, Cooperation Not Antagonism," 11 March 1943, 2.
61. Griffith, "Cooperation Not Antagonism," 3.
62. Griffith, "Cooperation Not Antagonism," 3-4.
63. Griffith, "Cooperation Not Antagonism," 4.
64. Griffith, "Cooperation Not Antagonism," 4.
65. Griffith, "Cooperation Not Antagonism," 4. *See also* letter to Board of Directors from Thomas W. Delzell and R.L. Clark, 28 September 1942 (PGE Board of Directors' Minutes, 30 September 1942).
66. Griffith, "Cooperation Not Antagonism," 5.
67. Funigiello, *National Power Policy,* 224. For corroboration of this point, refer to Herman C. Voeltz, "Genesis and Development of a Regional Power Agency in the Pacific Northwest, 1933-1943," *Pacific Northwest Quarterly,* 53 (April 1962), 71-74.
68. Ed Wildfong interview with the author, 5 March 1987; Glen Bredemeier interview with the author, 19 May 1987; Frank Warren interview with the author, 23 December 1987 OHS/SRA.
69. Paul J. Raver to James H. Polhemus, 2 April 1948, (PGE Board of Directors' Minutes, 6 May 1948) (PGE).
70. Raver to Polhemus, et al.
71. James H. Polhemus and other Pacific Northwest Utility Presidents to Paul J. Raver, 21 April 1948 (PGE Board of Directors' minutes, 6 May 1948) (PGE).
72. Lee interview.
73. *PGE Annual Report,* 1945, 24.
74. *PGE Annual Report,* 1947, 2. The Stone and Webster report makes reference to the differences over policy between the independent trustees and the PGE Board. *See* 5.
75. *PGE Annual Report,* 1947, 2.
76. *PGE Annual Report,* 1947, 2.
77. Greisser, *History of Portland General Elec-*

tric, 106.

78. *PGE Annual Report, 1947*, 2.

79. *PGE Annual Report, 1949*, 14.

Chapter 7
The Quest for Kilowatts

1. U.S. Bureau of the Census, *Historical Statistics of the United States, Colonial Times to 1970, Part 1*, (Washington, D.C.: U.S. Government Printing Office, 1973), 51-52 and 224.

2. *Historical Statistics of the United States, Part 2*, 716.

3. See McKinley, *Uncle Sam*, ch. 1.

4. Walter W.R. May, "Memorandum for H.B. Beckett, Attorney for Preferred Stockholders Committee, Portland General Electric Company," (1 February 1943), 1. (PGE).

5. *Oregonian*, 6 September 1947.

6. *Oregonian*, 19 September 1947.

7. *Oregonian*, 13 February 1948.

8. *Historical Statistics, Part 1*, 36.

9. *Historical Statistics, Part 1*, 33.

10. *Historical Statistics, Part 1*, 33, 36.

11. *Oregonian*, 24 September 1947.

12. Norwood, *Columbia River Power*, 159.

13. *See* Manly Maben, *Vanport* (Portland: Oregon Historical Society Press, 1987), for a complete account of the flood and its impact.

14. Norwood, *Columbia River Power*, 160.

15. *Portland General Electric Company Annual Report, 1950* (2 April 1951), 6.

16. *Portland General Electric Company Annual Report, 1952* (7 March 1952), 6.

17. *Portland General Electric Company Annual Report, 1953* (26 March 1954), 5.

18. *Portland General Electric Company Annual Report, 1954* (21 March 1955), 7.

19. *PGE Annual Report, 1953*, 3-4.

20. *Portland General Electric Company Annual Report, 1956* (20 March 1957), 7-8.

21. *Portland General Electric Company Annual Report, 1959* (25 March 1959), 2.

22. William G. Meyer and John E. Barkle, Jr., "General System Planning Study Made for The Portland General Electric Company by Westinghouse Electric Corporation" (January 1948), 2. (PGE).

23. Meyer and Barkle, "General System Planning Study," 3.

24. "Excerpt from Minutes of the Meeting of the Fish Commission of the State of Oregon of Tuesday, August 22, 1950," in PGE Board of Directors' Minutes, 13 February 1951, 2 (PGE).

25. *Oregonian*, 8 November 1954.

26. *Supreme Court Reports*, U.S. 349, 437: 122t.

27. *See Thirty-Second Annual Report of the Federal Power Commission, Fiscal Year Ended June 30, 1952* (Washington, D.C.: U.S. Government Printing Office, 1953).

28. Dwight D. Eisenhower, *Mandate for Change: The White House Years* (New York: Signet, 1965), 456.

29. *Public Papers of the Presidents, Dwight D. Eisenhower, 1953* (Washington, D.C.: U.S. Government Printing Office, 1956), 12-34.

30. *Oregonian*, 5 April 1953.

31. *PGE Annual Report, 1952* (1 May 1953), back of front cover.

32. *See* Franklin D. Mahar, "Douglas McKay and the Issues of Power Development in Oregon, 1953-1956" (Ph.D. diss., University of Oregon, 1968), 181, for corroboration of this assertion.

33. *Portland General Electric Company Annual Report, 1949* (15 February 1950), 3.

34. Thomas W. Delzell, "Recommendations for Federal Power Policy Submitted by Portland General Electric Company to the Water Resources Policy Commission, June 1950," 6 (PGE).

35. Delzell, "Recommendations to the Water Policy Commission, 1950," 8, and "Statement by Pacific Power and Light Company, Portland General Electric Company, and the Washington Water Power Company Before Task Force on Water Resources and Power of the Commission on Organization of the Executive Board of the Government at Portland, Oregon, 28 June 1954," 8 (PGE).

36. *Oregonian*, 8 February 1953. *See also Oregonian*, 8 June 1953, which reported that Delzell testified at a hearing of the Oregon Public Utilities Commission that the generation of the more expensive steam-produced electricity averted a power curtailment three to five times greater than the 10 percent curtailment ordered by the Defense Electric Power Administration.

37. *Oregonian*, 8 February 1953.

38. *Oregonian*, 17 January 1953.

39. *Oregonian*, 6 February 1953. *See also Ore-*

gonian, 8 June 1953.

40. *Oregonian*, 23 January 1953.

41. *Oregonian*, 3 May 1956.

42. *PGE Annual Report, 1952*, 2.

43. *Oregonian*, 17 January 1953.

44. Mahar, "Douglas McKay," 185-86.

45. Norwood, *Columbia River Power*, 195, and Mahar, "Douglas McKay," 158-59.

46. Mahar, "Douglas McKay," 158.

47. Mahar, "Douglas McKay," 160.

48. Mahar, "Douglas McKay," 159-60.

49. *Oregonian*, 3 September 1953.

50. *PGE Annual Report, 1953*, 9.

51. *PGE Annual Report, 1953*, 9.

52. Portland General Electric Company Board of Directors' Minutes for 7 February 1954, 8. (PGE).

53. Ralph A. Tudor, "I'm Glad I Went to Washington," *Saturday Evening Post*, 227 (27 November 1954): 30 and 137-40.

54. Norwood, *Columbia River Power*, 196.

55. "Ideas of Mr. Polhemus on the John Day Project" (10 February 1954), in PGE Board of Directors' Minutes for 9 February 1954, 1 (PGE).

56. "Ideas of Mr. Polhemus," 1.

57. "Ideas of Mr. Polhemus," 1.

58. "Ideas of Mr. Polhemus," 2.

59. Mahar, "Douglas McKay," 168.

60. *Oregon Grange Bulletin*, 5 April 1954.

61. *Congress. Record*, 83rd Cong., 2nd Sess., 1954, Vol. 100, 7041, 7119.

62. Mahar, "Douglas McKay," 170.

63. Mahar, "Douglas McKay," 171.

64. *See* Mahar, "Douglas McKay," 166. *See also* A. Robert Smith, *Tiger in the Senate: The Biography of Wayne Morse*, (Garden City, NY: Doubleday, 1982), 302, esp. ch. 15.

65. *Oregonian*, 9 June 1954, 12 June 1954, 31 January 1956.

66. *Oregonian*, 22 April 1955.

67. *See PGE Annual Report, 1955*, 7.

68. Mahar, "Douglas McKay," 182. Thomas Delzell, "Testimony to Subcommittee on Public Works," 17 May 1957. (PGE).

69. Mahar, "Douglas McKay," 182.

70. *Oregon Journal*, 22 January 1956; *Oregonian*, 26 January 1956.

71. *Oregonian*, 26 January 1956.

72. "Area, System, and Financial Facts About Sandy Co-Op," (25 February 1956), 1 (PGE).

73. "Area, System, and Financial Facts About Sandy Co-Op," 4.

74. Mahar, "Douglas McKay," 123; *Oregon Grange Bulletin*, 20 December 1955.

75. *Oregonian*, 26 January 1956.

76. *Oregonian*, 26 April 1956.

77. *See* Dodds, *Oregon: A Bicentennial History*, 230.

78. Greisser, *History of Portland General Electric*, 173.

79. Greisser, *History of Portland General Electric*, 173.

80. *PGE Annual Report, 1959*, 6; Greisser, *History of Portland General Electric*, 174.

81. Art Porter interview with the author, 1 April 1988, (OHS/SRA).

82. *PGE Annual Report, 1959*, 7.

83. *PGE Annual Report, 1954*, 14.

84. *PGE Annual Report, 1959*, 14.

85. *PGE Annual Report, 1953*, 5-6.

86. *PGE Annual Report, 1951*, 2.

87. Portland General Electric, "Generation Receipts, Deliveries, and Net System Load," 18 February 1978. (PGE).

88. *PGE Annual Report, 1952*, 12.

89. *See* William Leuchtenburg, *A Troubled Feast: American Society Since 1945* (Boston: Little, Brown, 1973), 63.

90. Leuchtenburg, *Troubled Feast*, 65-67. See also Mowry and Brownell, *The Urban Nation*, 176-177.

91. *PGE Annual Report, 1952*, 10; *PGE Annual Report, 1955*, 8.

92. *PGE Annual Report, 1959*, 13.

93. *PGE Annual Report, 1954*, 13.

94. *PGE Annual Report, 1956*, 11.

95. *PGE Annual Report, 1959*, 10.

96. *PGE Annual Report, 1955*, back of front cover.

97. *PGE Annual Report, 1955*, back of front cover.

98. *PGE Annual Report, 1957*, 10.

99. *See* PGE annual reports, 1950-1959.

100. *PGE Annual Report, 1957*, 3.

Chapter 8
Linkages, Treaties, Disasters, and Transitions

1. *See* Lester C. Thurow, *The Zero Sum Society: Distribution and the Possibilities for Change*

(New York: Basic Books, 1980), 42-43, for a discussion of the mechanics of the inflation of the sixties and seventies. Jim F. Heath, *Decade of Disillusionment: The Kennedy-Johnson Years* (Bloomington: Indiana University Press, 1975), esp. 261-262, gives the political and policy history of the phenomenon.

2. *Portland General Electric Annual Report, 1965* (3 March 1966), 7.

3. PGE, "Portland General Electric, Generation Receipts, Deliveries, and Net System Load," 18 February 1978. (PGE).

4. *Portland General Electric Annual Report, 1964* (8 March 1965), 6.

5. *Portland General Electric Annual Report, 1967* (23 February 1968), 5.

6. *Portland General Electric Annual Report, 1961* (19 March 1962), 2.

7. *PGE Annual Report, 1961*, 2.

8. *PGE Annual Report, 1961*, 2.

9. For discussions of the Columbia River Treaty of 1961 and its impact on regional politics, economics, and the hydro power situation, *see* Norwood, *Columbia River Power*, 181, 242-243 and Tollefson, *Struggle for Power at Cost*, 333-336, 339-340. For the PGE perspective, *see* overviews in Greisser, *PGE: History of Portland General Electric*, 83-84 and *Portland General Electric Annual Report, 1960* (23 March 1961), 6, and *PGE Annual Report, 1964*, 8.

10. *PGE Annual Report, 1960*, 6.

11. *PGE Annual Report, 1964*, 8.

12. *PGE Annual Report, 1964*, 8.

13. Greisser, *History of Portland General Electric*, 84.

14. Norwood, *Columbia River Power*, 237.

15. Norwood, *Columbia River Power*, 237; "BPA Advance Program," 1948 (PGE).

16. Norwood, *Columbia River Power*, 238.

17. Norwood, *Columbia River Power*, 241-42.

18. *New York Times*, 22 February 1961.

19. *Oregonian*, 5 November 1963. *See also Oregon Statesman*, 5 November 1963.

20. *Capital Journal*, 1 June 1962 for Luce's view of the benefits of the intertie to the region. A more technical and comprehensive statement of the BPA position on the intertie is found in Charles F. Luce and J. Kenneth Kaseberg, "The Bonneville Power Marketing Area Legislation: Is Regionalism in Electric Power Planning Old Fashioned?" *Oregon Law Review*, 45 (June 1966), 251-277.

21. *Oregonian*, 19 May 1962; *Oregon Statesman*, 26 June 1962; *Capital Journal*, 1 June 1962, and *Portland Reporter*, 12 April 1962, for reports and opinion of the Oregon press on this issue.

22. *Oregonian*, 15 January 1963. Frank Warren testimony before House Interior Subcommittee, 13 June 1963, Bob Short interview with the author, 7 July 1988 and 20 September 1988. (OHS/SRA).

23. *Oregonian* 14 June 1963. Warren testimony, Short interview. (OHS/SRA).

24. *Oregonian* 14 June 1963. Warren testimony, Short interview. (OHS/SRA).

25. *Oregonian* 14 June 1963. Warren testimony, Short interview. (OHS/SRA).

26. *Oregonian* 14 June 1963. Warren testimony, Short interview. (OHS/SRA).

27. *Oregonian* 14 June 1963. Warren testimony, Short interview. (OHS/SRA).

28. Norwood, *Columbia River Power*, 226.

29. Arthur H. Greisser, "Windstorm damage problems," paper presented to the Edison Electric Institute Hydraulic Power Committee Meeting, San Francisco, May 7-8, 1963-1; (PGE). *See also* Ellis Lucia, *The Big Blow: The Story of the Pacific Northwest's Columbus Day Storm* and *PGE Bullseye*, 26 October 1962, Special Storm Edition.

30. Greisser, "Windstorm damage problems," 1.

31. Greisser, "Windstorm damage problems," 1.

32. Greisser, "Windstorm damage problems," 2.

33. Greisser, "Windstorm damage problems," 2.

34. Greisser, "Windstorm damage problems," 2.

35. Greisser, "Windstorm damage problems," 2.

36. Greisser, "Windstorm damage problems," 2.

37. Greisser, "Windstorm damage problems," 2.

38. *Oregonian*, 26 October 1962.

39. Greisser, "Windstorm damage problems," 4.

40. Greisser, "Windstorm damage problems," 4.

41. *Oregonian*, 19 October 1962.

42. *Oregonian*, 19 October 1962.

43. Greisser, "Windstorm damage problems," 4.

44. Greisser, "Windstorm damage problems," 4.

45. *Oregonian*, 17 October 1962.

46. *Oregonian*, 17 October 1962.

47. Greisser, "Windstorm damage problems," 5.

48. Greisser, *History of Portland General Electric*, 155.

49. *Oregonian*, 28 March 1963.

50. *PGE Bullseye*, "Another October Storm Damages System" (October 1967), 6-7.

51. *PGE Bullseye*, "Another October Storm," 6.

52. Greisser, *History of Portland General Electric*, 156.

53. Greisser, *History of Portland General Electric*, 157.

54. Greisser, *History of Portland General Electric*, 157.

55. Greisser, *History of Portland General Electric*, 157.

56. Greisser, *History of Portland General Electric*, 157.

57. Greisser, *History of Portland General Electric*, 158.

58. Greisser, *History of Portland General Electric*, 158.

59. Greisser, *History of Portland General Electric*, 158.

60. Greisser, *History of Portland General Electric*, 159.

61. *Portland General Electric Annual Report, 1962* (15 March 1963), 3-4.

62. *PGE Annual Report, 1962*, 4.

63. *PGE Annual Report, 1962*, 4.

64. *PGE Annual Report, 1962*, 4.

65. Hillman Lueddemann interview with the author, 25 November 1987, (OHS/SRA).

66. *Oregon Statesman*, 9 January 1962. *See also PGE Annual Report, 1962*, 9, and *PGE Bullseye*, "Citizens Veto PUD," (January 1962), 2.

67. Lueddemann interview.

68. Lueddemann interview.

69. Portland City Council Ordinance No. B4416, 14 April 1972.

70. Portland City Council Ordinance No. B4416.

71. *Portland General Electric Annual Report, 1972*, (26 February 1973), 11.

72. *PGE Bullseye*, (January 1969), 3

73. Glen Bredemeier interview with the author, 19 May 1987, and Ed Wildfong interview with the author, 5 March 1987.

SOURCES

PUBLIC DOCUMENTS

Congressional Record. 83rd Cong. 1954. Vol. 100, 7041, 7119.

Energy in Transition 1985-2010: Final report of the Committee on Nuclear and Alternative Energy Systems. San Francisco: National Research Council of the National Academy of Sciences. W.H. Freeman, 1980.

Historical Statistics of the U.S., Colonial Times to 1970. Bureau of the Census, 1960. Washington, D.C., 1973

Public Papers of the Presidents, Dwight D. Eisenhower, 1953. Washington, D.C.: U.S. Government Printing Offfice, 1956

Thirty-Second Annual Report of the Federal Power Commission, Fiscal Year Ended June 30, 1952. Washington, D.C.: U.S. Government Printing Office, 1953.

U.S. Congress. House. *Hearings on HR 7642: Columbia River (Bonneville Dam), Oregon, and Washington.* 75th Cong., 1st Sess., 1937.

United States Supreme Court Reports. New York: Bank and Brothers, Law Publishers, 1884.

PORTLAND GENERAL ELECTRIC COMPANY PAPERS

"Area, System, and Financial Facts About Sandy Co-Op," 1956. Unaccessioned Files.

"Bonneville Power Administration Advance Program," 1948. Unaccessioned Files.

Bulletin of the Portland General Electric Company, 1901-1906.

Carey and Harlan, "Report to the Mayor and Council," 1930. Unaccessioned Files.

———. "Traction Plan," 1930. Unaccessioned Files.

Clark, Charles M. Letter to Benage Josselyn, 21 October 1911. Unaccessioned Files.

"The Czarists of Oregon." Water and Power Board Measure File, 1926. Unaccessioned Files.

Delzell, Thomas. "Recommendations for

Federal Power Policy submitted by Portland General Electric Company to the Water Resources Policy Commission," June 1950. Unaccessioned Files.

———. "Statement by Pacific Power and Light Company, Portland General Electric Company, and the Washington Water Power Company Before Task Force on Water Resources and Power of the Commission on Organization of the Executive Board of the Government at Portland, Oregon," June 1954. Unaccessioned Files.

———. "Testimony to Subcommittee on Public Works." 17 May 1957. Unaccessioned Files.

"Generation Receipts, Deliveries, and Net System Load," 18 February 1978. Unaccessioned Files.

Griffith, Franklin T. "Address before the Chamber of Commerce of Oregon City, Oregon," 29 March 1938. Unaccessioned Files.

———. "Address Before the Progressive Business Man's Club of Portland, 'Cooperation Not Antagonism,'" 11 March 1943. Unaccessioned Files.

———. "Memorandum to All Employees [on pay cuts]." 30 April 1933. Unaccessioned Files.

———. "Ten Year Story on PEPCO Finances With Respect to Public Utility Holding Company, Central Public Service System, Chase National Banks, Harris Forbes and Company, and the Shareholders, 1929-1939." Miscellaneous correspondence relating to reorganization folder, Transfer File 3, University of Oregon, Eugene.

"History of PGE Rates, Residential Service, 1908-1987. 1988.

May, Walter W.R. "Memorandum for H.B. Beckett, Attorney for Preferred Stockholders Committee, Portland General Electric Company," 1 February, 1943.

Meischer, P. "Use of Water Power of Willamette Falls, Oregon City," 2 May 1884. Unaccessioned Files.

Meyer, William G. and John E. Barkle, Jr. "General System Planning Study Made for *The Portland General Electric Company* by *Westinghouse Electric Corporation*." January 1948.

Pacific Northwest Public Service Company.

Annual reports, 1930-39.

———. *Bulletin*.

———. Prospectus, "A Traction Stock with a Future," 1911. Unaccessioned Files.

Portland Electric Power Company. Annual reports, 1929-39.

Portland General Electric Company. Annual reports, 1939-72.

———. Minutes of Board of Director's Meetings, 1902-65.

Portland Railway Light and Power. Annual reports.

"Proposed Amendment for the Oregon Constitution: Water and Power and Development." Unaccessioned Files.

Puget Sound Power and Light Company. "The Truth About Rural Electric Rates in Ontario: Photographic Facts From Official Records . . . ," 1930. Unaccessioned Files.

"Report on Audits," 1906. Unaccessioned Files.

Robley, R.R. "Memorandum to Team Captains Division C," 2 Febraury 1927. Unaccessioned Files.

Stone and Webster Service Corporation. "Report on Portland General Electric," 1941. Unaccessioned Files.

"Utilities and the City of Portland." City of Portland Archives and Record Center, Portland.

"Utilities and the Pacific Northwest." National Archives and Records Administration, Seattle.

UNPUBLISHED WORKS

Bredemeier, Glen. Interview with the author, 19 May 1987. Oregon Historical Society, Sound Recording Archive.

E.W. Clark Papers. Historical Society of Pennsylvania. Philadelphia, Pennsylvania.

Thomas Delzell Papers. Special Collections Library, University of Oregon, Eugene.

Dick, Wesley Arden. "Visions of Abundance: The Public Power Crusade in the Pacific Northwest in the Era of J.D. Ross and the New Deal." Ph.D. diss., University of Washington, 1973.

Franklin, Griffith T. Papers, Scrapbook No. 1, 1913-17. Oregon Historical Society.

Greisser, Arthur. "Windstorm Damage Problems." Paper presented to the Edison Electric Institute Hydraulic Power Committee Meeting, San Francisco, 7-8 May 1963.

History of Pacific Northwest Industries Collection. Oregon Institute of Technology, Klamath Falls.

Lee, Bob. Interview with author, 26 January 1988. Oregon Historical Society, Sound Recording Archive.

Lester, Claude R. "Investigations of Public Utilities." Special Collections Library, Boxes 1-3. University of Oregon.

Lewis and Clark Exposition Collection. Board of Directors' Correspondence File, Box 6. Oregon Historical Society.

Lueddemann, Hillman. Interview with author, 2 November 1987. Oregon Historical S ciety, Sound Recording Archive.

Mahar, Franklin D. "Douglas McKay and the Issues of Power Development in Oregon, 1953-1956." Ph.D. diss., University of Oregon, 1968.

Mitchell, Thomas. "Know Nukes: A Model for Teaching Controversial Issues." Ed.D. diss., University of Massachusetts, 1986.

Ogden, Daniel M. Jr. "The Development of Federal Power Policy in the Pacific Northwest." Ph.D. diss., University of Chicago, 1949.

Polhemus, James H. "Modern Trolley Coach Operation." Paper presented to the American Transit Association, Los Angeles, 1937.

Porter, Art. Interview with the author, 1 April 1988. Oregon Historical Society, Sound Recording Archive.

Portland City Council Ordinance No. B4416, 14 April 1972.

Short, Robert. Interview with the author, 7 July and 20 September 1988. Oregon Historical Society, Sound Recording Archive.

Voeltz, Herman C. "Proposals for a Columbia Valley Authority: A History of Political Controversy." Ph. D. diss., University of Oregon, 1960.

Warren, Frank. Interview with the author, 23 December 1987. Oregon Historical Society, Sound Recording Archive.

Warren, Frank. Interview with Judy Hartman, 2 November 1988. Oregon Historical Society, Sound Recording Archive.

Wildfong, Ed. Interview with the author, 23 December 1987. Oregon Historical Society, Sound Recording Archive.

PERIODICALS AND NEWSPAPERS

Bullseye (PGE publication)
Capital Journal (Salem)
Economic History Review
Electric Perspectives
Electrical World
EPRI (Edison Power Research Institute) *Journal*
Evening Telegram (Portland)
Journal of Economic History
National Electric Light Association Bulletin
New York Times
New Yorker
Nuclear Industry
Nuclear News
Oregon Grange Bulletin
Oregon Historical Quarterly
Oregon Journal
Oregon Law Review
Oregon Statesman (Salem)
Oregon Voter
Oregonian
PEPCO Synchronizer (PGE publication)
Portland Carman (PGE publication)
Portland City Club Bulletin
Portland Rail Light and Power Bulletin
Portland Reporter
Public Service (PGE publication)
Public Utility Fortnightly
St. Johns Review (Portland)
Saturday Evening Post
Watt's Watt (PGE publications)
West Shore (Portland)

SECONDARY SOURCES

Abbott, Carl. *The Great Extravaganza: Portland and the Lewis and Clark Exposition.* Portland: Oregon Historical Society Press, 1981.

Adams, Henry. *The Education of Henry Adams.* Century ed. Boston: Houghton Mifflin Company, 1961.

Bartlett, Irving H. *The American Mind in the Mid-Nineteenth Century.* Northbrook, Ill.: AHM Publishers, 1967.

Berle, Adolphe, Jr., and Gardiner Means. *The Modern Corporation and Private Property.* New York: Harcourt, Brace & World, 1968.

Bessey, Roy. *Pacific Northwest Regional Planning: A Review.* Olympia: State of Washington, 1963.

Blum, John Morton. *The Republican Roosevelt.* New York: Atheneum, 1974.

Bonbright, James C., Albert L. Danielsen, and David R. Kamerschen. *Principles of Public Utility Rates*. Arlington: Public Utility Reports, 1988.

Bone, Arthur H., ed. *Oregon Cattleman/Governor/Congressman: The Memoirs and Times of Walter M. Pierce*. Portland: Oregon Historical Society Press, 1981.

Braverman, Harry. *Labor and Monopoly Capital: The Degradation of Work in the Twentieth Century*. New York: Monthly Review Press, 1974.

Cheney, Margaret. *Tesla: Man Out of Time*. New York: Laurel Books, 1981.

Cochrane, Thomas. *Basic History of American Business*. Princeton: Van Nostrand, 1959

Croly, Herbert. *The Promise of American Life*. New York: Capricorn Books, 1964.

Danforth, Sandra C. *Nuclear Energy as a Political and Social Issue: A Bibliography*. Monticello: Vance Bibliographies, 1982.

Daniels, Jonathan. "Pearl Harbor Sunday: The End of an Era, 1919-1941." In *The Aspirin Age*, edited by Isabel Leighton, New York: Simon and Schuster, 1949.

Dicken, Samuel N. and Emily F. *The Making of Oregon: A Study in Historical Geography*. Portland: Oregon Historical Society Press, 1979.

Dodds, Gordon B. *Oregon: A Bicentennial History*. New York: W.W. Norton, 1977.

————. *The American Northwest: A History of Oregon and Washington*. Arlington Heights, Ill.: The Forum Press, 1986.

Eisenhower, Dwight D. *Mandate for Change: The White House Years*. New York: Signet, 1965.

Funigiello, Philip. *Toward a National Power Policy, The New Deal and the Electric Utility Industry, 1933-1941*. Pittsburgh: University of Pittsburgh Press, 1973.

Galbraith, John Kenneth. *The Great Crash*. New York: Avon Books, 1980.

Gaston, William. *Portland, Oregon, its History and Builders in Connection with the Antecedent Explorations, Discoveries and Movements of the Pioneers That Selected the Site for the Great City of the Pacific*. Vol 1. Portland: S.J. Clarke, 1911.

Gompers, Samuel. *Seventy Years of Life and Labor*. Edited by Nick Salvatore, New York: ILR Press, 1984.

Gunther, John. *Inside U.S.A.* New York: Harper & Brothers, 1947.

Hall, Stephen S. "The Age of Electricity," in *Inventors and Discoverers*, edited by Elizabeth L. Newhouse. Washington, D.C.: National Geographic Society, 1988.

Hays, Samuel. *Conservation and the Gospel of Efficiency*. New York: Atheneum, 1975.

Heath, Jim F. *Decade of Disillusionment: The Kennedy-Johnson Years*. Bloomington: Indiana University Press, 1975.

Heilbroner, Robert. *The Making of Economic Society*. Englewood Cliffs, N.J.: Prentice-Hall, 1962.

Hofstadter, Richard. *The Age of Reform*. New York: Vintage Books, 1955.

Holbrook, Stewart. *The Columbia*. New York: Rinehart, 1956

Hughes, Thomas P. *Networks of Power: Electrification in Western Society, 1880-1930*. Baltimore: The John Hopkins University Press, 1983.

Hyman, Barry, and Charles R. Peterson. *Electric Power Systems Planning: A Pacific Northwest Perspective*. Seattle: University of Washington Press, 1988.

James, J.B. *The Framing of the Fourteenth Amendment*. Urbana: University of Illinois, 1956.

Johansen, Dorothy O. and Charles M. Gates. *Empire of the Columbia: A History of the Pacific Northwest*. New York: Harper & Row, 1967.

Jones, Howard Mumford. *The Age of Energy, Varieties of American Experience, 1865-1915*. New York: Viking Press, 1970.

Josephson, Matthew. *The Robber Barons: The Great American Capitalists*. New York: Harcourt Brace, 1934.

Kirkland, Edward Chase. *Industry Comes of Age: Business, Labor, and Public Policy, 1860-1897*. Chicago: Quadrangle Books, 1961.

Krutilla, John. *The Columbia River Treaty*. Published for Resources for the Future. Baltimore: Johns Hopkins University Press, 1967.

Labbe, John T. *Fares, Please! Those Portland Trolley Years*. Caldwell, Idaho: The Caxton Printers, 1982.

Lane, Frederic C., Blanche D. Con, et al. *Ships*

for Victory: A History of Shipbuilding Under the U.S. Maritime Commission in World War II. Baltimore: Johns Hopkins University Press, 1951.

Leuchtenburg, William. *Perils of Prosperity: 1914-1932*. Chicago: University of Chicago Press, 1958.

———. *Franklin D. Roosevelt and the New Deal 1932-1940*. New York: Harper & Row, 1963.

———. *A Troubled Feast: American Society Since 1945*. Boston: Little, Brown and Company, 1973.

Link, Arthur S. *Woodrow Wilson and the Progressive Era, 1900-1917*. New York: Harper and Brothers, 1954.

Lockley, Fred. *History of the Columbia River Valley from The Dalles to the Sea*. Portland: S.J. Clarke, 1928.

Lucia, Ellis. *The Big Blow: The Story of the Pacific Northwest's Columbus Day Storm*. Portland: News-Times, 1963.

Maben, Manly. *Vanport*. Portland: Oregon Historical Society Press, 1987.

MacColl, E. Kimbark. *The Shaping of a City: Business and Politics in Portland, Oregon, 1885-1915*. Portland: The Georgian Press, 1976.

———. *The Growth of A City: Power and Politics in Portland, Oregon, 1915-1950*. Portland: The Georgian Press, 1979.

———. *Merchants, Money, & Power: The Portland Establishment*. Portland: The Georgian Press, 1988.

McDonald, Forest. *Insull*. Chicago: University of Chicago Press, 1962.

McKinley, Charles. *Uncle Sam in the Pacific Northwest*. Berkeley and Los Angeles: University of California Press, 1952.

Mowry, George E., and Blaine, Brownell A. *The Urban Nation: 1920-1980*. New York: Hill & Wang, 1981.

Myhra, David. *WHOOPS!/WPPSS: Washington Public Power Supply System Nuclear Plants*. Jefferson, N.C.: McFarland, 1984.

Netboy, Anthony. *The Bonneville Power Administration and the Northwest Power Pool*. Portland: Bonneville Power Administration, 1954.

Nevins, Allan. *John D. Rockefeller*. Abr. Ed. New York: Charles Scribner's Sons, 1959.

Newcomer, Mabel. *The Big Business Executive: The Factors That Made Him, 1900-1950*. New York: Columbia University Press, 1955.

North, Douglas C. *The Economic Growth of the United States, 1790-1860*. New York: W.W. Norton, 1966.

Norwood, Gus. *Columbia River Power for the People*. Washington, D.C.: U.S. Government Printing Office, 1981.

The Nuclear Waste Primer: A Handbook for Citizens. New York: League of Women Voters Fund, 1985.

Ostrander, Gilman. *American Civilization in the First Machine Age, 1890-1940*. New York: Harper & Row, 1970.

Panati, Charles. *The Extraordinary Origins of Everyday Things*. New York: Harper & Row, 1987.

Parrington, Vernon L. *The Beginnings of Critical Realism in America: 1860-1920*. New York: Harcourt, Brace, 1930.

Passer, Harold C. *The Electrical Manufacturers, 1875-1900: A Study in Competition, Entrepreneurship, Technical Change, and Economic Growth*. Cambridge: Harvard University Press, 1953.

Polenberg, Richard. *War and Society*. Philadelphia: J.B. Lippincott, 1972.

Ramsay, M.L. *Pyramids of Power: The Story of Roosevelt, Insull and the Utility Wars*. New York: Bobbs-Merrill, 1937.

Robley R.R., ed. *Compilation of Water Power Rights at Willamette River Falls*. Vol. 1, *Priority Rights*. Portland: Portland General Electric, 1930.

———. *Portland Electric Power Company With Its Predecessor and Subsidiary Companies, 1860-1935*. Portland: Portland General Electric, 1935.

Rybczynski, Witold. *Home: A Short History of an Idea*. New York: Penguin, 1986.

Schwantes, Carlos A. and G. Thomas Edwards. *Experiences in a Promised Land: Essays in Pacific Northwest History*. Seattle: University of Washington Press, 1986.

Smith, A. Robert. *The Tiger in the Senate: The Biography of Wayne Morse*. Garden City, N.Y.: Doubleday, 1962.

Stampp, Kenneth M. *The Era of Reconstruction, 1865-1877*. New York: Vintage Books, 1965.

Starr, Philip, and William Pearman. *Three Mile Island Sourcebook: Annotations of a Disaster.* New York: Garland Publishing, 1983.

Taylor, George Rogers. "Building an Interurban Transportation System," in *The Urbanization of America: An Historical Anthology.* Edited by Allen W. Wakstein. Boston: Houghton Mifflin, 1970.

Thurow, Lester C. *The Zero Sum Society: Distribution and the Possibilities for Change.* New York: Basic Books, 1980.

Tocqueville, Alexis de. *Democracy in America.* New York: Random House, 1981.

Tollefson, Gene. *BPA and the Struggle for Power at Cost.* Portland: Bonnneville Power Administration, 1987.

Twain, Mark, and Charles Dudley Warner. *The Gilded Age: A Tale of Today.* New York: Harper & Brothers, 1915.

Udall, Stewart. *The Quiet Crisis.* New York: Holt, Rinehart & Winston, 1963.

Vatter, Harold G. *The Drive to Industrial Maturity: The U.S. Economy, 1860-1914.* Westport, Conn.: Greenwood Press, 1975.

———. *The U.S. Economy in the 1950s.* Chicago: University of Chicago Press, 1963.

Villard, Henry. *Memoirs of Henry Villard.* Vol. 2. Boston: Houghton, Mifflin, 1904.

Weart, Spencer R. *Nuclear Fear: A History of Images.* Cambridge: Harvard University Press, 1988.

Weinstein, James. *The Corporate Ideal in the Liberal State, 1900-1918.* Boston: Beacon Press, 1968.

Willingham, William. *Waterpower in the "Wilderness": The History of the Bonneville Lock and Dam.* Portland: U.S. Army Corps of Engineers, 1987.

Withers, William. *The Corporations and Social Change.* Woodbury, N.Y.: Barron's Educational Series, 1972.

Wollner, Craig. *The City Builders: One Hundred Years of Union Carpentry in Portland.* Portland: Oregon Historical Society Press, forthcoming.

———. "The Willamette River." In *Rolling Rivers: An Encyclopedia of America's Rivers.* Edited by Richard A. Bartlett. New York: McGraw-Hill, 1984: 383-386.

JOURNAL ARTICLES

Bracher, Frederick. "How It Was Then: The Pacific Northwest in the Twenties." Parts 1, 2 *Oregon Historical Quarterly* 85 (Winter 1983, Spring 1984): 39-52, 341-64.

Coldwell, O.B. "Early Days of Electricity in Portland." *Oregon Historical Quarterly* 42 (Winter 1941): 281-92.

DuBoff, Richard B. "The Introduction of Electric Power in American Manufacturing." *Economic History Review* 20 (1967): 509-518.

Funigiello, Philip. "Kilowatts for Defense—The New Deal and the Coming of the Second World War." *Journal of American History* 56 (December 1969): 604-620.

Luce, Charles F., and J. Kenneth Kaseberg. "The Bonneville Power Marketing Area Legislation: Is Regionalism in Electric Power Planning Old Fashioned?" *Oregon Law Review* 45 (June 1966): 251-77.

Schwantes, Carlos. "The West Adapts the Automobile: Technology, Employment and the Jitney Phenomenon of 1914-17." *Western Historical Quarterly* 6 (July 1985): 307-26.

Tudor, Ralph A. "I'm Glad I Went to Washington." *Saturday Evening Post* (27 November 1954):30, 137-140.

Voeltz, Herman C. "Genesis and Development of a Regional Power Agency." *Pacific Northwest Quarterly* 53 (April 1962): 65-76.

INDEX

317

319

321

COLOPHON

The typeface used for both text and display in *Electrifying Eden* is a photographic version of Electra. Electra was designed by W. A. Dwiggins (1880-1956) as a Linotype face and was issued to the public in 1948. Dwiggins was a distinguished American calligrapher, designer of books (he did nearly three hundred for Alfred Knopf, eminent publisher of the Borzoi titles), type, and decoration whose work did much to revive interest in good trade book design. In American book production, Electra ranks as a modern classic.

Electrifying Eden is printed on 70 lb. Halopaque cream white vellum, which is 50 percent recycled and conforms to all significant criteria for archival quality. It is bound in Holliston Crown Linen, holly (13737) with green/white headbands. The endpapers are Rainbow Colonial white.

The production of *Electrifying Eden* was accomplished through the cooperation and professional skills of the follow persons and firms:

TYPESETTING: Irish Setter, Portland

PRINTING: Artline Printing, Beaverton

PAPER: Fraser Paper, Portland

BINDING: Lincoln & Allen, Portland

ILLUSTRATIONS (pages 8-13): Evelyn Hicks

MAPS (pages 28, 223): Christine Rains

PAGE MAKEUP: Christi Payne

This book was designed and produced by the Oregon Historical Society Press.